CREOLIZATION AND CON‗ ‗ ‗ ‗ ‗ ‗ ‗

CREOLIZATION AND CONTRABAND

Curaçao in the Early Modern Atlantic World

LINDA M. RUPERT

The University of Georgia Press

ATHENS AND LONDON

LIBRARY OF CONGRESS CATALOGING-IN-PUBLICATION DATA

Rupert, Linda Marguerite.
 Creolization and contraband : Curaçao in the early modern Atlantic world /
by Linda M. Rupert.
   p. cm.—(Early American places)
 Includes bibliographical references and index.
 ISBN 978-0-8203-4305-1 (cloth : alk. paper)
 ISBN 0-8203-4305-6 (cloth : alk. paper)
 ISBN 978-0-8203-4306-8 (paper : alk. paper)
 ISBN 0-8203-4306-4 (paper : alk. paper)
  1. Curaçao—History—17th century. 2. Curaçao—History—18th century. 3. Curaçao—
Commerce—History. 4. Curaçao—Social conditions. 5. Creoles—Curaçao—History.
6. Slaves—Curaçao—History. 7. Sephardim—Curaçao—History. 8. Intercultural
communication—Curaçao—History. 9. Papiamentu—Curaçao—History.
10. Smuggling—Curaçao—History. I. Title.
F2049.R87 2012
972.986—dc23

                                                              2011050386

    British Library Cataloging-in-Publication Data available

Na pueblo di Kòrsou

Contents

Acknowledgments   xi

Introduction   1

PART I Emergence of an Entrepôt

1 Converging Currents   17
2 Atlantic Diasporas   43
3 "Cruising to the Most Advantageous Places"   67

PART II Sociocultural Interactions in a Maritime
      Trade Economy

4 A Caribbean Port City   103
5 Curaçao and Tierra Firme   163
6 Language and Creolization   212

Conclusions   245

Notes   253
Bibliography   311
Index   339

Acknowledgments

Substantial funding for this project was provided by the American Association of University Women, the American Council of Learned Societies, the Coordinating Council for Women in History, the J. William Fulbright Foundation, the National Endowment for the Humanities, the Social Science Research Council, and the University of North Carolina Greensboro (UNCG). I also received assistance from the American Historical Association, the Center for Jewish Studies (University of California Los Angeles), Harvard University's International Seminar on the History of the Atlantic World, and the Scaliger Institute at Leiden University (the Netherlands). A variety of entities at Duke University provided research support for the earliest stages. At different times I found a congenial intellectual home as a fellow at the KITLV Institute (Leiden University, the Netherlands), the Scaliger Institute (Leiden University) and at Duke University's John Hope Franklin Institute for Interdisciplinary Studies. My analysis has been honed by discussion with colleagues affiliated with the Forum on European Expansion and Global Interaction (FEEGI), the Triangle Early American History Seminar, the Dutch Atlantic Connections working group in the Netherlands, my mentors at Duke, and my colleagues in the History Department at UNCG. The many people who have shaped my intellectual development and provided personal support over the years are too numerous to list. I am most grateful to them all. I deeply appreciate the professionalism and patience of Derek Krissoff and the entire team at the University of Georgia Press. Many thanks to Phil

Morgan and Wim Klooster for their incisive comments on the manuscript. I regret that I have not been able to incorporate all their suggestions. Research would not have been possible without the tireless efforts of the archivists and librarians at all the collections listed in the bibliography. Several graduate research assistants did yeomen's duty with a slew of tasks to prepare the manuscript for publication. Richenel Ansano deserves special mention for his support over many years. My daughters, Naomi and Aisha, grew up with this project as an unwanted third sibling. It is a pleasure and a relief to see them and the book reach maturity.

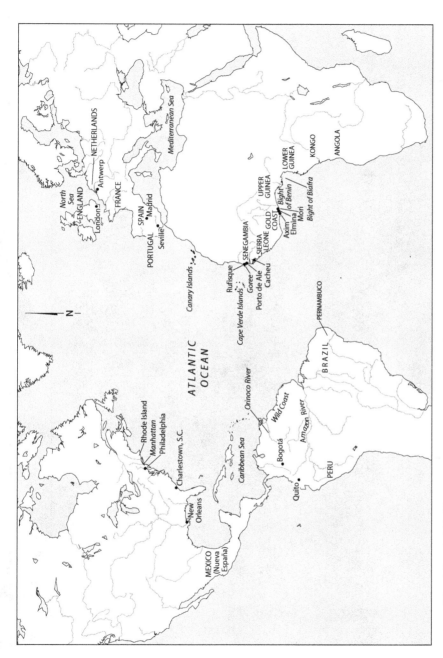

MAP 1. The Atlantic World.

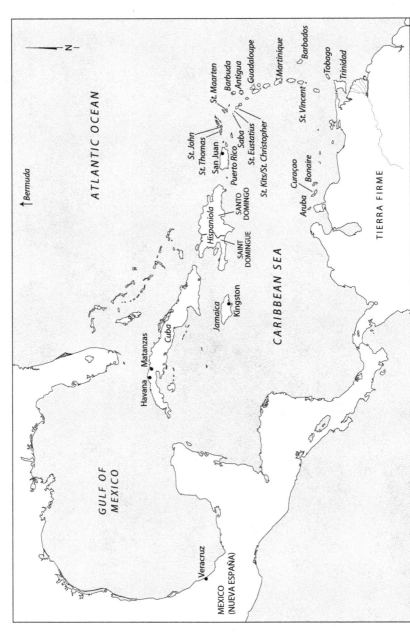

MAP 2. The Caribbean.

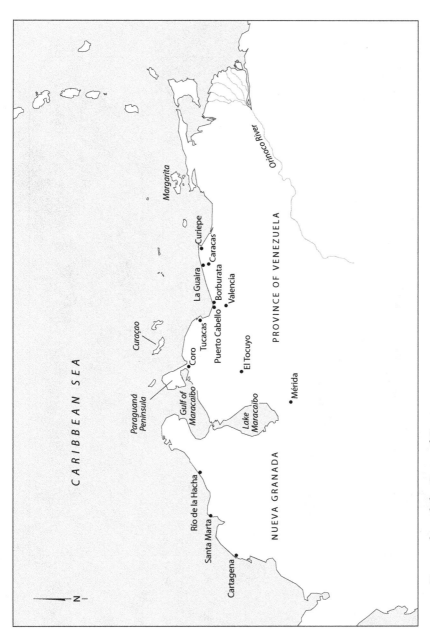

MAP 3. Venezuela and the Coast of Caracas.

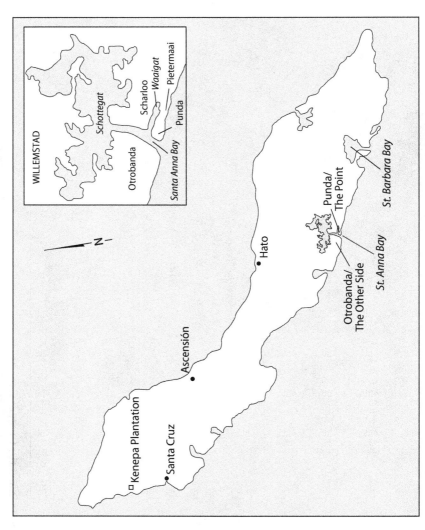

MAP 4. Curaçao.

CREOLIZATION AND CONTRABAND

Introduction

A 1786 townscape shows the bustling port of Willemstad, located on the small island of Curaçao in the southern Caribbean.[1] Several full-masted ocean-going ships stand in and just outside the harbor. A dozen Dutch flags fly from these vessels and from official buildings. In the center of the drawing, securely ensconced behind the walls and protected by an imposing row of cannon, is Fort Amsterdam, seat of the Dutch West India Company. Surrounding the fort is the town, which, over the previous hundred years, had grown from a tiny outpost to become a thriving regional trade center. The West India Company (WIC), which governed the island and also dominated its trade, had been founded 165 years before, in 1621. At that time, the Caribbean was still largely a Spanish sea, but emerging European powers were beginning to gain sufficient power to challenge Spain's territorial dominance of the region. The company's first charter, issued by the Dutch States General on 3 June 1621, is one of the earliest articulations of the Atlantic world as a cohesive entity, centered on networks of trade that stretched from Europe to Africa to the Americas. The charter granted exclusive trading rights to the company for an initial period of twenty-four years, "to sail to, navigate, or frequent" an area that encompassed "the coast and countries of Africa from the Tropic of Cancer to the Cape of Good Hope," and America and the West Indies, "beginning at the fourth end of Terra Nova, by the straits and passages situated thereabouts to the strait of Anien, as well on the north sea as the south sea."[2]

FIGURE 1. This 1786 townscape portrays Willemstad as a bustling Caribbean port, powered by both the Dutch empire and the working majority of African descent. (© National Maritime Museum, Greenwich, UK)

Thirteen years after founding the WIC, in 1634, the Dutch seized Curaçao, a small, arid island located just off the northern coast of South America. Although initially the island served as a naval base, over the decades it became a regional trade center. After the first WIC went bankrupt and was replaced by a second incarnation in 1675, the Dutch opened the island to free trade. This move was highly unusual for the times. Thenceforth Curaçao, once a backwater in the Spanish empire, was transformed into a major Caribbean commercial center, and a hub in the Dutch Atlantic system. Although the intercolonial trade conducted from Curaçao was perfectly legal under the Dutch system, much of it contravened the laws of the other European powers that had established colonies in the region. Thus, it is usually described in the non-Dutch sources as smuggling, illicit trade, or contraband.[3] This vigorous maritime commerce dominated the island's economy. It was conducted via the port of Willemstad, which was transformed from a small naval base into a cosmopolitan maritime center.

Behind the Dutch flags, the transoceanic ships, and the imposing fort, Willemstad was much more than the regional seat of a European power. The town was also a dynamic Caribbean port city. Close examination of the 1786 townscape reveals dozens of workers on the docks, lightermen rowing small boats in the harbor between the larger vessels, and fishermen. The majority of these harbor workers were of African descent. On the left side of the townscape, west across the bay, stretches another part of the port. The legend identifies it as Oversijde, literally the "other side" of town. By the end of the eighteenth century locals were calling the area Otrobanda, using the island's developing creole language, Papiamentu.[4] No Dutch flags fly over Otrobanda, nor are its impressive buildings confined behind a wall. Here, the population was more varied and multiethnic. By the eighteenth century, Otrobanda was home to a vibrant enclave of free blacks and urban slaves who lived apart from their masters and earned wages in the maritime economy.

This book traces the changing configurations of Curaçao—or Kòrsou, as it is known in Papiamentu—during the time the island was governed by the West India Company (1634–1791). Throughout this period, intercolonial commerce was not only the bedrock of the island economy, it also shaped local society. This trade provided especially rich opportunities for sociocultural interactions across established lines of race/ethnicity, social class, and even empire. Along with the well-established European merchants who were affiliated with the WIC, Curaçao's non-Dutch inhabitants, who constituted the majority of the population, also participated in the extensive regional trade that made the island a prosperous Caribbean hub. Women and men from two Atlantic diaspora groups in particular, Sephardic Jews and people of African descent, sustained the port city of Willemstad. They also forged close ties with communities around the Caribbean, especially with the nearby Spanish America mainland, known then as Tierra Firme (an area encompassing present-day Venezuela and parts of Colombia), and particularly with the province of Venezuela. (Contemporaries also called the Caribbean coastline of this area the Coast of Caracas.)

Creolization and contraband are the two themes that unify this book. The interplay of these two processes molded Curaçao's emerging colonial society, I argue. These extra-official exchanges were not unique to Curaçao. Nor were they marginal. Each was prevalent in colonial societies throughout the early modern world, wherever expanding European empires thrust different peoples together and sought to control commercial exchanges. Each represented a form of transgression of the established imperial order and thus was an expression of colonial agency. Both contraband and creolization were dynamic processes that were born of unequal power relations and became the very building blocks of colonial societies. Both were anything but subsidiary to the development of colonies such as Curaçao. They intersected, interacted with, and were influenced by, but were also somewhat independent of, official economic and sociocultural power structures. Both contraband trade and processes of creolization can be seen as ways in which subordinate classes sought to carve out their own spaces within the wider imperial project. Analyzing their centrality, as well as their intersection, in a specific colony gives us a nuanced understanding of the complex connections between imperial structures and colonial agency.

Smuggling often has been portrayed as the illegitimate stepchild of officially sanctioned commerce. It was, as one observer noted in 1715, "a capital contradiction against all the laws of the Indies."[5] This was its very essence. Smuggling, in all its forms, was simply any trade that had been outlawed by the powers that be. Such illicit commerce occupied a central role in many colonial economies. Contraband was widespread across the early modern world, wherever political powers tried to stake an exclusive economic claim.[6] It often flourished in the shadows of legitimate trade, and was "elusive, secretive, and subtle," in the words of one historian.[7] But the relationship between official and extra-official trade was complicated and multifaceted. Smuggling often complemented rather than replaced officially sanctioned commerce. Both types of trade often involved the same participants.[8] Intercolonial commerce was especially prevalent across the Americas, where the needs and wants of colonial denizens often conflicted with the restrictive mercantilist policies of imperial powers.[9] Whereas officials saw smuggling as a crime—albeit one in which many of them were complicit—participants saw it as an opportunity, even a "form of self-help."[10] As Alan Karras has noted, smuggling was a "perfect compromise" for all parties involved, because it allowed goods to be distributed according to the demands and logic of the free market while preserving, at least nominally, the integrity of imperial legal, economic, and political systems.[11]

Illicit commerce simultaneously served and violated empire. As Michael Jarvis has noted in the case of Bermuda, local traders "served larger imperial goals as they pursued profit for their own ends."[12] In their pursuit of profit, however, they often went beyond the economic realm and violated the very terms on which empires were constructed. Apart from the legal distinction, there often was a fundamental market difference between officially sanctioned trade and contraband commerce in the early modern world. Smugglers aggressively sought out markets and provisioned them with the commodities they needed (or desired). .In contrast, imperial authorities seemingly were less responsive to the market, bound, as they were, by mercantilist restrictions.[13] Contraband's relationship with legal trade was far more complex than simply being in opposition to it. In fact, the two complemented each other, with smugglers filling in gaps in the regular market cycles of supply, demand, and pricing.[14] But extralegal trade filled more than an economic role. Smugglers and their far-flung networks provided structure and coherence—often an entire quasi-infrastructure—in entire areas that were outside the effective control of the imperial state apparatus.[15] Contraband goods and their traders frequently traveled along routes that were more direct or more efficient than the often cumbersome official trade channels. Smuggling also helped develop colonial consumerism, by providing colonists across the socioeconomic spectrum with access to coveted commodities that otherwise would have been too expensive or difficult to obtain through official means.[16] Thus, it had a major impact on the development of colonial material culture and on culture generally.

The rich and varied forms of sociocultural intermixing which constituted creolization similarly have been portrayed erroneously as confined to the peripheries of colonial society. Like contraband, creolization allowed nonelites to express themselves more fully within the parameters of colonial societies, by breaking through established norms to interact with and borrow from a wide variety of people. At its most basic, creolization refers to processes of sociocultural exchange and adaptation that occurred among all the diverse peoples of the early modern world who were thrust together with the rise of European overseas empires.[17] That is the definition I use here. (It bears remembering that, in much of the Latin American historiography, the term creole refers more narrowly to Europeans who were born in the Americas.) Such cultural intermixing shaped every colonial society in the Americas, although it varied according to the specific ethnic, racial, and imperial configurations of each settlement.

Much of the recent historiography on creolization has focused on the population of African descent, especially plantation slaves, and it has framed the analysis in terms of the decades-old debate about African retentions versus new cultural creations in American slave societies.[18] Without discounting the importance of this approach for understanding American and especially Caribbean slave societies, this book takes a broader approach. I understand creolization to include cultural interactions across social class and ethnicity, and I focus on the particular configurations of this process as it played out in an urban, maritime setting. As to the question of African retentions versus new cultural creations, I am most persuaded by interpretations that present both as occurring along a continuum, as well as being time and place specific, dichotomies rather than absolutes.[19] In many places, cultural practices from across the Atlantic (European as well as African) were retained as well adapted, even while new ones were being created. A broad definition of creolization allows for all these possibilities.

As Nigel Boland has argued, a full understanding of the multifaceted processes of creolization allows us to reconceptualize the development of colonial societies in the Caribbean, moving away from a narrow focus on the plantation paradigm to appreciate the larger processes and contradictions that were at work as new hybrid societies were being created.[20] Some historians have noted that creolization often was more vigorously expressed, or at least more apparent, among the lower classes, because they did not have access to the material abundance and resources from Europe and instead had to adopt local resources creatively.[21] On the one hand, creolization implied the deployment of raw power and the development of overarching structures that were part and parcel of European overseas expansion. On the other hand, it witnessed the exercise of human agency to resist and adapt creatively to these very structures. Thus, in spite of the dynamic cultural creativity that it embodied, creolization ultimately was also an expression of and a response to the "brutal realities of power" that existed in colonial slave societies.[22]

Contraband and creolization were widespread and closely linked in the early modern Atlantic world. From the earliest moments of European expansion along the western coast of Africa and into the Americas, processes of creolization went hand in hand with the development of an incipient global trade, much of which was conducted in the shadows of officially sanctioned commerce.[23] Together, these two processes were foundational in shaping colonial societies in the circum-Atlantic.[24] Although historians have noted the impact of contraband trade on sociocultural interactions in the Caribbean, these connections have not been explored sufficiently.[25] Creolization largely has been studied as a cultural phenomenon, contraband as an economic system. But, as the history of Curaçao demonstrates, creolization and contraband were intertwined. Contraband trade had an impact far beyond the economic sphere. It opened channels of communication and opportunities for interactions among a variety of participants from different social classes, ethnicities, and imperial affiliations. Likewise, creolization was not confined to the cultural sphere. Economic interactions required and facilitated social interactions, which, in turn, were deeply influenced by specific economic configurations. Creolization and contraband thus were symbiotically and dialectically related. Such connections were not confined to the early modern Caribbean or Atlantic. Trade has been a catalyst for cultural and social interactions throughout human history. Markets "are socially constructed and socially embedded," as Kenneth Pomerantz and Steven Topik have noted, and trade "involves the interlinking of politics and economics, social organization, and culture."[26] Cultures have intermingled whenever diverse groups of people come together to trade. David Hancock has imagined the multiple economic interactions that took place in the early modern Atlantic world as conversations, conjuring up the image of social and cultural exchanges interwoven with economic ones.[27]

The Caribbean was the epicenter of smuggling and perhaps the most dynamic site of creolization in the early modern world—a veritable crush of competing cultures, peoples, empires, and economies. Throughout the Caribbean, the explicitly interimperial character of smuggling set up alternate links and routes to the official ones that European powers developed. In the process it created vibrant creole identities that sometimes were only tangentially linked to the metropole.[28] People of African descent, in particular, took advantage of the intercolonial connections that both legal and illicit trade opened up, and they used these connections to develop their own broad communications and exchange networks throughout the circum-Caribbean.[29] The symbiotic relationship between contraband trade and creolization unfolded around the early modern Caribbean with a raw intensity, as European powers played out their economic and political rivalries. The forced migration of millions of enslaved people from Africa through the transatlantic slave trade, along with the consolidation of an export-oriented plantation system, geared much of the region's economy to maritime commerce, and pushed unprecedented numbers of people from disparate cultures, language groups, and ethnicities into contact with each other. Maritime trade, both legitimate and illicit, was an integral part of the Caribbean plantation complex. By necessity pan-Caribbean and transatlantic, the plantation system depended on regional and Atlantic trade circuits. Plantations required seaborne commerce, much of it illicit, for the import of enslaved laborers, livestock, and manufactured goods, and of a variety of goods that sustained the entire way of life of the planter class, as well as for the export of their agricultural products. Caribbean ports were vital nexuses within the wider Atlantic commercial system.[30]

With its cosmopolitan, polyglot, and ethnically diverse port population, extensive regional and global commercial ties, and rich merchant archives, Curaçao is an excellent crucible in which to analyze the interplay between extra-official economic and sociocultural exchanges in the early modern Caribbean and Atlantic. As the commercial and administrative seat of the West India Company in the Americas (1675–1791), Curaçao was a major Caribbean smuggling center and a vital hub in the Atlantic commercial system. The port of Willemstad was home to half the island's population by the mid-eighteenth century, and a major Caribbean trade center. The town's inhabitants included a small Dutch merchant elite and a motley crew of sailors, as well as skilled slaves, a large free colored population, and the largest and most prosperous Jewish community in the Americas. All of these people depended on interimperial maritime trade for their livelihood. The Dutch depended on them to turn the wheels of the island's commercial economy. Although this semiclandestine commerce broke no Dutch laws, it was strictly prohibited by Spanish, English/British, and French authorities, whose colonial subjects nevertheless participated enthusiastically. .

From the docks of Willemstad, to the decks of schooners, to the shores of Tierra Firme, illicit commerce provided rich opportunities for social and cultural exchange across surprisingly porous boundaries of geography, empire, race/ethnicity, social class, and gender. Whereas well-established Dutch merchants coordinated Curaçao's transatlantic commerce, members of two diaspora groups—people of African descent and Sephardic Jews—traded around the Caribbean and the Americas.[31] Curaçao's diasporic denizens were thrown together via the maritime economy, both at sea and in their shoreside dealings. Curaçao provides an opportunity to examine how creolization played out in a maritime economy, among the inhabitants of a port city, across geopolitical boundaries, and between diaspora groups, in a system where transimperial and intercolonial trade, much of it contraband, was the economic bedrock. This book documents the multifaceted human interactions that developed around the smuggling economy, and their wider impact on colonial society. It chronicles connections that extended across political, geographic, legal, socioeconomic, and ethnic boundaries, beyond a single colony or empire.

* * *

Creolization and Contraband is organized chronologically and thematically. Part I traces processes that set the stage for Curaçao to become a major Caribbean and Atlantic trade center by the end of the seventeenth century. Chapter 1 situates the island in Caribbean exchange circuits from pre-Columbian times, sketches the emergence of the Dutch as an Atlantic power, and documents Curaçao's early role as a naval base following the Dutch takeover of the island from the Spanish in 1634. Although Curaçao's role in Caribbean commercial networks expanded greatly under the administration of the West India Company, I argue that this built on the island's existing role in the Caribbean before the arrival of Europeans and during the 135 years of Spanish rule. Island inhabitants had especially close ties with neighboring Tierra Firme. Dutch expertise in maritime trade, and the unusual degree of commercial freedom that the Dutch allowed their merchants, positioned them to fashion an enhanced role for the island and its inhabitants in the Dutch imperial project and in emerging regional and Atlantic economic systems.

Curaçao's success as a trade center depended on the Dutch commercial system and on the economic and political administration provided by the West India Company. At the same time, two Atlantic diaspora groups played a vital role in shaping and sustaining the local society and economy. Chapter 2 follows the paths of enslaved Africans and Sephardic Jews, from their roots in the eastern Atlantic to their dispersal and eventual arrival in Curaçao. I examine similarities and differences in their transatlantic trajectories. The development of imperial spheres and far-flung Atlantic trade networks provided the context for both diaspora groups to arrive in Curaçao, where they took up different but complementary and equally pivotal roles in the colonial economy and society. Despite dissimilarities and inequalities in their respective roles in the Dutch empire and in local slave society, people of African descent and Sephardic Jews shared certain common characteristics in their diasporic experiences and in their local dealings that defined their integration into the emerging island society.

Chapter 3 documents Curaçao's transition from a small Dutch naval outpost into a major Caribbean entrepôt in the period between the 1648 Treaty of Westphalia (which ended the Eighty Years War between the Netherlands and Spain and formally recognized the Dutch Republic and the legitimacy of its colonial possessions) and the War of the Spanish Succession (1702–1713). Intercolonial trade was the economic impetus that transformed Willemstad from a small settlement overshadowed by the fort into a full-fledged Caribbean port. Curaçao's regional rise paralleled the relative decline of the Dutch as a global and Atlantic power. The Dutch decision to open Curaçao to free trade in 1675, and the island's brief but central role as a slave transshipment center in the 1670s and '80s, had sociocultural as well as economic dimensions. Although the island remained firmly within the Dutch realm, religious and economic geographies did not correspond to neat political demarcations. This was especially clear in Curaçao's developing relations with neighboring Venezuela, and extended well beyond illicit trade. Sociocultural networks were shaped by the fact that Curaçao's Roman Catholic Church remained under the jurisdiction of the Bishop of Venezuela. This resulted in the creation of a black Catholic majority in a Dutch Protestant colony.

Ast the first three chapters document, by the end of the seventeenth century, the major elements were in place that would define the very character of Curaçao over the next hundred years. The political and economic administration of the island and the port was centrally coordinated by the Dutch WIC, from its base at Fort Amsterdam. Under the WIC umbrella, Sephardic Jews and people of African descent were the motor of the island economy and society, and were instrumental in positioning Curaçao as a Caribbean exchange center. They developed especially vibrant intercolonial networks with Tierra Firme, especially in the economic and religious realms. These would continue to expand throughout the eighteenth century.

Part II considers sites of interconnected economic, social, and cultural exchange throughout the eighteenth century. Chapter 4 focuses on Willemstad. I examine the growth of a colonial port that served both as the political and economic seat of Dutch power and as a nodal point for Caribbean and Atlantic exchange circuits. From demographic diversity to physical expansion to legal codes, Willemstad's development was textured by its role as the Caribbean's only free trade center. Processes of creolization were evident in the development of new neighborhoods beyond the confines of the town's original walls, the adaptation of traditional Dutch architecture to the tropics, and in the overlap between social class, ethnicity, and religion among the port's inhabitants. As the town expanded and grew in complexity, authorities faced the challenge of governing a society based on enslavement in an economy based on freedom of movement and trade. The developing colonial legal regime reflected and responded to this inherent contradiction.

The panorama widens in Chapter 5, which analyzes the interface between illicit interimperial trade and concomitant sociocultural interactions across neatly conceived political jurisdictions. Tierra Firme, especially the province of Venezuela, served as Willemstad's economic hinterland. I argue that inhabitants treated the two areas as a single, well-integrated region, even when authorities mapped them in separate imperial spheres. Religious geographies also were transcolonial, as the organization and reach of the Roman Catholic Church transcended political borders. This had a particular impact on Curaçao's black majority. Colonists took advantage of opportunities that were created when European powers rather arbitrarily superimposed demarcations that ignored centuries-old exchange circuits. Diasporic groups dominated economic, cultural, and social intercolonial exchanges. Paradoxically, for Afro-Curaçaoans, participation in interimperial exchanges could be both a continuation of enslavement and a path to freedom. Once again, the contraband economy shaped opportunities for exchange and interaction that were available to colonial denizens.

Chapter 6 focuses on cultural space. It analyzes the development and consolidation of Curaçao's creole vernacular, Papiamentu, which was based not on Dutch but rather on Iberian tongues. I document Papiamentu's emergence as the island's lingua franca during the eighteenth century; review linguistic theories of its likely origins in the context of the development of creole languages; consider how the port of Willemstad promoted its acceptance across the socioeconomic spectrum; and then briefly follow its diffusion beyond Curaçao along contraband trade paths. I argue that the smuggling economy facilitated Papiamentu's development and also its widespread acceptance across lines of social class and ethnicity, especially among the island's two diaspora groups. Papiamentu's relative success compared to most other Caribbean creole languages is yet another example of how contraband facilitated creolization. It is evidence of the porous boundaries and the opportunities for human interaction that illicit economic exchanges created.

Studying processes such as contraband trade and creolization in the early modern world invariably raises problems of evidence and sources. As many historians have noted, it is impossible to quantify contraband.[32] Statistics from the transatlantic trade between Curaçao and Amsterdam give us some approximations, but they are limited. Numbers are often incomplete. Even contemporaries noted that it was hard to document the amount and value of smuggling, let alone the participants or the transport of goods in remote areas of Tierra Firme.[33] Similarly, processes of creolization can be difficult to document using traditional archival sources. Documentation about the island's earliest inhabitants, the Caquetios, is similarly sparse. A full study of the creolization of Curaçao's material culture remains to be written. The extensive Dutch archives have much more material to yield about Curaçao's slaves and free blacks, about the tenor and texture of religious life among the island's Catholics (and religious syncretism between Catholicism and Judaism), about the life of Curaçao's rural slaves in the seventeenth and eighteenth centuries, and about the island's European population, especially the Dutch elite.[34]

* * *

Historians are rethinking the complex interaction between European powers and their overseas holdings in the early modern world. Many have moved from a rigid, top-down approach of center/metropole versus periphery/colony to recognizing that colonial events and processes played a major role in shaping overall imperial formations.[35] In grappling with how best to describe empire in a less hierarchical way, some historians have spoken of a "web of empire."[36] Others have envisioned a process of negotiation between the seat of power and colonial actors.[37] As Lauren Benton has noted, the demarcations of early modern European empires themselves often were more imagined than real. They "composed a fabric that was full of holes" in their actual occupation of colonial space, according to Benton.[38] Such a shift in perspective allows one to reformulate the debate about the relative importance of institutional structure and human agency in historical processes. Rather than conceiving these as absolutes, an either/or proposition, it is more fruitful to recognize that structure and agency were dialectically related and that most often there was a spectrum of possibilities, a "balance point" between the two.[39]

Often there was a tension between emerging states and processes that transcended imperial boundaries. This is most clearly seen in the development of Atlantic and global trade. The structures of empires, and the outlines of the mercantile systems that drove them, did not correspond neatly to the developing Atlantic economic system, which was decentralized and linked by networks.[40] The intersection between static state structures and more fluid networks has increasingly interested historians in recent years.[41] Commercial networks criss-crossed imperial demarcations. Historians have variously noted the "unbounded behavior" of those who participated in Atlantic exchanges, the "flux and reflux" of systems, and the "multitude of fractal whorls spinning at every edge" of colonial centers.[42] In conceptualizing early modern Atlantic commercial interactions as ongoing conversations among various actors, David Hancock envisions "intricate webs of cooperation and conflict" that were born out of economic necessity and market opportunities rather than intentionally created.[43] By definition, his largely decentralized world of overlapping networks cut around and through imperial spheres.

This book studies some of the transimperial, intercolonial, and maritime forces that molded the early modern Caribbean. It traces the multifaceted relationship between trade and culture, reformulates the study of empires by examining processes that played out in colonial societies, and documents the role of Atlantic diasporas in shaping the contours of the early modern world. During the period when Curaçao was ruled by the West India Company, the island's role as a Dutch free trade center and as a site for vigorous intercolonial commerce influenced the emerging colonial society. Smuggling contributed to dynamic processes of social and cultural exchange, both within the port of Willemstad and in inhabitants' interactions farther afield, most especially in their multiple dealings with Tierra Firme. The intersection of these nonhegemonic processes of economic and sociocultural exchange had a lasting impact on people both on the island and across imperial boundaries. It left its mark on the very character of empire.

PART I

EMERGENCE OF AN ENTREPÔT

1 / Converging Currents

In May 1565 the English privateer John Hawkins spent ten days on the small Caribbean island of Curaçao, then a minor outpost of the vast Spanish American empire. Hawkins sought to procure hides in exchange for cloth and ten slaves he had brought from Senegambia and Sierra Leone.[1] Although his visit to Curaçao often has been portrayed as piracy, an extant receipt for the transaction and a letter to Hawkins from the island governor, Lázaro Bejarano, indicate that this commercial exchange was cordial and voluntary on both sides.[2] In two separate transactions with the governor and another local resident Hawkins traded his wares for over a thousand hides.[3] Thus, seventy years before the Dutch seized Curaçao from the Spanish, and over a century before the island officially became a free trade center, local inhabitants already were trading clandestinely across imperial divides for their own benefit, in clear violation of the restrictive mercantile policies of Spanish authorities. To do so, they took advantage of both the regional geography and the market realities of this relatively neglected corner of the Caribbean.

Such dealings were not limited to Curaçao. As they traveled around the Caribbean, Hawkins and his crew found eager trade partners in many neglected Spanish possessions, whose inhabitants were strictly forbidden from commercial intercourse with foreigners. Hawkins successfully negotiated agreements with governors throughout the region, to the consternation of Spanish authorities.[4] In May 1565, for example, authorities in the small town of Río de la Hacha, on the northwestern coast of South America (in present-day Colombia), granted Hawkins a license to trade freely with all the townspeople, and a certificate stating that he had displayed good conduct, "maintaining the peace" and "working no harm to any person" during his twelve-day stay.[5] Aware that such open agreements sparked the ire of higher-ups, Hawkins had tried another tactic the previous month in the mainland town of Borburata. Pleading that he had been inadvertently "by contrary weather driven to these coasts," where he sought refuge to repair his damaged vessels, he requested permission to sell his cargo of goods and slaves "at acceptable prices" so he could pay for his ships and crew and obtain needed supplies. The request included a thinly veiled threat to "seek my own solution" if his petition was not granted, and noted that he could not be responsible for any ensuing "harm and damage."[6] Traders of different ethnicities and affiliations would continue to use the same excuse of bad weather to justify their own illicit interimperial trade for centuries to come, even though the narrow channel of water separating Curaçao from the mainland is remarkably calm, outside the hurricane belt, and generally well protected from high winds and contrary currents. From Curaçao, Hawkins proceeded southwest along the Caribbean littoral of the Spanish American mainland, following the prevailing currents and trade winds along a route that had been used by indigenous peoples for thousands of years.

Curaçao in the Caribbean

Close contact between Curaçao's inhabitants and those of the nearby mainland predated the arrival of Hawkins and other Europeans. The island's native inhabitants, the Caquetios, were a group of Arawaks who were members of the same linguistic and ethnic group as the people of the northern coast of South America. They likely migrated to the islands of the southern Caribbean from the Maracaibo Basin area of the mainland around 600 CE.[7] Archaeological data and early Spanish accounts indicate that there were close economic and cultural ties between the peoples of Tierra Firme and those of neighboring Caribbean islands during pre-Columbian times.[8] But the record is also somewhat contradictory. Although the Spanish reported that Curaçao's Caquetios were under the jurisdiction of a mainland leader named Manaure (sometimes called Anaure) on the Paraguaná Peninsula, archaeological evidence seems to indicate that the island peoples likely had a relatively self-sufficient society and were not part of a broader political structure.[9]

Organizational autonomy would not have precluded close contact or economic exchanges between people in the two areas. The inhabitants of both places cultivated similar food crops (maize, manioc, beans, sweet potatoes, cactus fruits, and agave); traded tobacco and other products with each other; and showed signs of mutual cultural influence.[10] Ceramic styles, burial patterns, tools, and other artifacts indicate regular contact between the island and several mainland coastal communities, especially those around Lake Maracaibo and also ones near present-day Puerto Cabello, by 800–1000 CE.[11]

The ties between Curaçao's inhabitants and those of neighboring South America were facilitated by the area's physical geography. Prevailing winds and ocean currents have encouraged contact between people in the two areas from prehistoric times to the present.[12] Curaçao is the second largest in a string of over a dozen islands and atolls in the southern Caribbean, stretching from Margarita (the largest) in the east, westward to Aruba. The entire island string is roughly parallel to the Caribbean coast of South America. Most of these islands are small and uninhabited. The entire island group is just south of the so-called hurricane belt, and receives steady east-northeast and east trade winds the entire year. Together, the islands and the northwestern coast of the mainland form part of a single larger environmental zone, the semidesert southern Caribbean region, which is characterized by a scarcity of fresh water, sparse rainfall, intense sun, rapid evaporation, and limited flora and fauna.[13] Some geographers have suggested that such island strings in the Caribbean should be conceptualized as a continuum connected by the sea, and that, together, they have functioned more as a unified continental space than as small, autonomous units.[14]

Curaçao, near the westernmost end of the island string, is located just 70 kilometers off the South American coast at 12 degrees north and 69 degrees west. It has a total area of 440 square kilometers and is approximately 60 kilometers long by 12 kilometers at its widest, 2 kilometers at its narrowest.[15] The island's northern coast, on the open Caribbean, is a series of steep, rocky limestone terraces, pounded by rough seas. In contrast, the southern coast has over a dozen wide, deepwater bays that open onto relatively calm seas facing the nearby mainland. These bays were formed by fluctuating sea levels alternating with periods of increased precipitation, which resulted in major erosion several thousand years ago.[16] The total shoreline perimeter of these natural harbors, not all of which are accessible to easy landings, is 79 kilometers, and represents 53 percent of the island's total coastline of 148 kilometers. Most of the remaining shore is steep, rocky cliffs, especially along the northern coast.[17]

To the north of the island strong surface ocean currents course due west at an average speed of over 32 km/day; slightly less powerful ones flow from the southern coast westward toward the mainland.[18] These currents complement the ever-present trade winds that blow in the same direction. The strength and direction of these winds and currents often make contact between the islands much more difficult than direct transit to and from the mainland.[19] Unlike the islands of the eastern Caribbean, Curaçao is not within visibility range of its neighbors. Occasionally, however, when the sky is clear, hills on the mainland are faintly visible on the horizon from elevated points on the island's southern coast.[20]

The proximity of the southern region islands both to each other and to the continent, and the resulting regular trade and communication that developed between area inhabitants, facilitated the development of indigenous seafaring that was primarily coastal in style, even when it occurred between islands and around a relatively large physical maritime space. This characterized pre-Columbian seafaring throughout the Caribbean.[21] Islanders traveled deftly around the region in dugout canoes known as piraguas. The Spanish repeatedly noted natives' maritime skills in the early sixteenth century.[22] Contact between the indigenous inhabitants of Curaçao and the mainland continued long after Europeans arrived and began superimposing imaginary imperial boundaries on the region. By continuing their centuries-old trade patterns, and ignoring the seemingly arbitrary new political demarcations, the Caquetios thus pioneered the transcolonial exchanges that became the hallmark of the Caribbean under European rule. In subsequent centuries, immigrants from Europe and Africa used the same sailing routes that indigenous people had developed, taking advantage of regional geography, winds, and currents.

Curaçao's first documented contact with Europeans occurred with the arrival of Amerigo Vespucci's second expedition in May 1499. At the time, approximately two thousand people lived on the island in four settlements. Three of these settlements were located on sheltered southern bays, further suggesting regular contact with the mainland.[23] On this same voyage Vespucci and his entourage, including Alonso de Ojeda and the pilot and cartographer Juan de la Cosa, made the first known European reconnaissance along the northern coast of South America, stopping at the numerous southern Caribbean islands along the way. From Curaçao, they continued westward along the coastline, past the Paraguaná Peninsula and the Gulf of Maracaibo, then turned north toward Hispaniola. The information obtained in this reconnaissance made its way into de la Cosa's *Mapamundi*, the first known world map to depict the Americas, which was first published in 1500. Early Spanish maps variously referred to the island as Curaçote, Curasote, and Curasaure; by the 1550s the name appears as Quracao, and by 1634 the spelling had become Curaçao (and not, interestingly, the present-day hispanicized version, Curazao), although variations recur in documents at least through the eighteenth century.[24] There is some controversy as to origin of the name. One possibility is that it is a derivation of the Portuguese word for heart, which the earliest European sketches of the island erroneously resembled.[25]

Early European explorers followed the basic routes between Curaçao, the mainland, and the Greater Antilles that thousands of merchants and seafarers would travel in subsequent years. Although Vespucci claimed the island and its neighbors for the Crown, Spanish attention to Curaçao was erratic. They largely neglected Curaçao, along with neighboring Aruba and Bonaire (the so-called ABC islands), until 1513, when the viceroy of Hispaniola, Diego Colón, officially declared all three to be among the "useless islands" of the Caribbean, that is, devoid of marketable natural resources, especially gold. This allowed the enslavement and deportation of natives to provide labor for the developing gold mines and the small sugar plantations of Hispaniola, then the largest Spanish settlement in the Americas. That same year a Spanish expedition headed by Diego Salazar rounded up the entire population of Curaçao, taking twelve hundred people to Hispaniola and the rest to Tierra Firme.[26] Thus, Curaçao's first export under European rule was slaves. Many of the exiles perished shortly after arriving in Hispaniola.[27] Following this mass deportation, the Spanish once again neglected the island for over a decade. In November 1526, the Spanish Crown granted Juan de Ampíes the right to hold and populate Curaçao, Aruba, and Bonaire, as well as exclusive commercial rights to the three islands. Ampíes (whose name is sometimes rendered as Ampués and sometimes without an accent) soon repopulated Curaçao, bringing twenty-five Indians from Hispaniola in two groups, along with clothing, knives, "and things that the Indians need."[28] From his account it is not clear if the people he brought back were returning Caquetios or members of another ethnic group. Thereafter, the three so-called ABC islands were part of a single political jurisdiction, first under the Spanish and later under the Dutch. Shortly thereafter (the report is not dated), Ampíes reported that Curaçao's population had grown to two hundred, including "people of all ages," and indigenous emigrants from the mainland. He did not specify the number of Spaniards. Ampíes also noted the ongoing close contact with Caquetios from other islands and Tierra Firme.

Ampíes played up the supposedly close political ties between the natives of Curaçao and the nearby Paraguaná Peninsula to bolster his own unsuccessful efforts to gain jurisdiction over northern Tierra Firme. He sent a boat to the peninsula with five Spaniards and several Indians to investigate reports of "a great *cacique* [chief], who is ten leagues inland in the Province of Coro, whose name is Anaure," said to be revered by the islanders, as he wrote to the Spanish Crown.[29] During his stay in Tierra Firme in late 1528 and early 1529, Ampíes developed close ties with Manaure and other mainland indigenous leaders and encouraged Caquetios to return to Curaçao. Ampíes may well have exaggerated, if not downright fabricated, the political ties between indigenous groups in the two areas. He and others clearly recognized that alliances with natives on both the island and the mainland were key factors in the emerging struggles for political control of the area, as the Spanish Crown sought to claim and administer vast tracts of the Americas. Documenting a supposedly close link between Caquetios on the island and the mainland would strengthen his own claims against those of rivals.

Ampíes was unable to gain political jurisdiction over Tierra Firme. He lost out to the German commercial house of Welser, to whom the Spanish Crown granted political and economic control of the northern littoral of Tierra Firme in 1528.[30] The ABC islands were not included in the Welser grant, however. Although this may have been due in part to Ampíes's successful political maneuverings, apparently the Welsers were not interested in acquiring territory for its own sake. Rather they were in search of the elusive "El Dorado," an imaginary kingdom deep within South America that was rumored to have large amounts of gold. Ampíes gained administrative and economic jurisdiction over the three islands in 1526. Almost exactly a year later, a Spanish royal decree of November 1527 gave Ampíes and a Seville merchant, Juan Fernández de Castro, exclusive right to cut brazilwood on Curaçao and export it to Spain for a period of thirty years. They proved unable to meet the rather ambitious terms of the contract, however, which required the export of sixty tons of wood annually.[31] Brazilwood and salt, harvested from several shallow bays on the sheltered southern coast, were the island's only exports during Ampíes's tenure.[32] These would be the very same resources that attracted the Dutch to the island one hundred years later.

Ampíes's negotiations with Manaure spurred the continued emigration of mainland Caquetios to Curaçao, where they lived under the political jurisdiction of the Spanish administrator and a local island chief appointed by the Spanish.[33] Regardless of Manaure's actual political or economic power over Curaçao's natives, then, Ampíes successfully used the Caquetio leader's supposed jurisdiction over the island as a pawn in his own political maneuverings with the Spanish Crown and the Welsers. Some Venezuelan historians have seen Curaçao as the "jumping off point" for Spanish colonization of the mainland.[34] Ampíes also changed the overall political organization of Curaçao's natives, brought in many newcomers, modified the form of their local organization, and grouped them all together under Spanish supervision. The Caquetío settlements on Curaçao retained some degree of autonomy.

When Ampíes died in 1533, administration of the ABC islands passed to his daughter, María Ampiés, and her husband, Lázaro Bejarano, a satirical poet who had a brush with the Inquisition. Bejarano administered the three islands for thirty-five years, mostly in absentia from the nearby mainland and from Hispaniola, leaving them without effective authority for much of the time. Bejarano traveled regularly between Curaçao and Coro for the first decade of his governorship and apparently resided on the island briefly. Transit between the two areas was relatively easy. By canoe, the crossing took less than a day; a sailing vessel could make the journey in about six hours.[35] Occasional stormy weather, however, could make the voyage lengthy and treacherous, or even deadly. After Bejarano's death in the 1560s, records of the Spanish political administrators of the three islands are incomplete, perhaps indicating their relative lack of importance in the emerging Spanish imperial project. With the termination of the Welser grant in 1556 the ABC islands came under the same political administration as the mainland and became part of the province of Venezuela. The province encompassed a section of the northern littoral of mainland South America between the Caribbean Sea in the north and the Orinoco River in the south. This political jurisdiction held for the remaining years of Spanish tenure.[36]

Although political administration of the ABC islands was separated from that of the mainland during the Welser grant (1528–56), both areas came under the same religious jurisdiction. Initially, both were administered from the first Spanish seat of religious and political power in Santo Domingo. In 1531 the islands passed to the newly created Bishopric of Venezuela in Coro, under whose control they remained for the next 106 years.[37] Already by the 1530s, the Spanish Crown was concerned about the lack of spiritual and material attention to the islands' native inhabitants. In 1538 the Crown charged the bishop of Coro, Rodrigo de Bastidas, to visit Curaçao and take responsibility for its neglected indigenous population.[38] A year later, the Crown again expressed concern about the spiritual and physical neglect of Curaçao's natives.[39] Governor Bejarano built a simple stone church on Curaçao in 1542, in the small settlement just northeast of St. Barbara Bay. (The chapel's ruins appear on several seventeenth- and eighteenth-century Dutch maps of the island.)[40] Apparently this lacked official support, and the absence of a permanent priest there during most of Bejarano's thirty-five year tenure of the island created tensions between him and the bishop of Venezuela. This seems to have been a factor in Bejarano's trial for heresy by the Inquisition in 1558, along with the irreverent nature of his satirical poems.[41] Bejarano continued to administer the ABC islands even after his conviction in 1559, which did not carry a death sentence. With the establishment of an official Spanish evangelization policy for Venezuela in 1561, the islands of Curaçao, Aruba, and Bonaire officially became part of the Diocese of Coro.[42] The Crown's justification for this was that the island Caquetios were "of the same language and nation as those of the city of Coro."[43] Thus, although the ABC islands were part of a political jurisdiction separate from the mainland, authorities recognized that the close ties between the indigenous people of the two areas justified their inclusion under a single ecclesiastical umbrella. This religious affiliation with the Spanish American mainland would continue long after the Dutch takeover of the island, and it was crucial in facilitating and strengthening ties between inhabitants of the two areas across separate imperial spheres. The Crown ordered the first official report about evangelization on Curaçao in 1564. In 1571 colonial authorities expressed concern that the spiritual life of the island's small indigenous population was being neglected.[44] This religious domain also had a political dimension: reports in the 1560s and again in 1571 forcefully denounced the incursions of "Lutheran" English and French corsairs who destroyed statues of saints and other relics in their visits to the mainland coast, even as they brought contraband slaves and other forbidden merchandise.[45]

The Spanish did not establish any major urban centers or ports on Curaçao. The only two Spanish settlements, Santa Ana in the east and Ascensión in the west, were located well inland. Demographic data from the Spanish era is sketchy. According to a 1620 report commissioned by the bishop of Coro, a total of just 160 people lived in the two villages, with another forty in Bonaire and twenty in Aruba.[46] It is not clear if this refs to the total number of inhabitants, including indigenous people, or just to Spaniards. The Spanish concentrated the indigenous population of Curaçao in the two settlements at Ascensión and Santa Ana, close to freshwater wells and to Spanish supervision.[47] Later Dutch maps from the seventeenth and eighteenth centuries clearly depict the location of these wells, an indication of the ongoing importance of sources of fresh water for the inhabitants of this arid island.[48]

The Spanish conquest of wealthy indigenous kingdoms in Mexico and Peru in the 1520s and '30s, and their discovery of major silver mines in both places, shifted imperial focus away from the Caribbean and toward the interiors of northern Central America and the Andes. Thereafter, both Tierra Firme and the adjacent islands, including Curaçao, played a minor role in the empire's wider geopolitical aims. Nevertheless, South America's Caribbean coast remained important for strategic reasons, as a buffer to protect the mainland against the ever-increasing incursions of pirates and privateers from rival European powers. John TePaske suggests that Tierra Firme was a "vital periphery" in Spanish America, one of several colonial frontiers that were "integral parts of an organic whole" within the Spanish enterprise, although they were not central to the Spanish imperial project.[49] This peripheral role to the central economic and political projects of the emerging Spanish American empire may explain the relative lack of documentation about the island, including the names of its political administrators after Bejarano, in the extensive Spanish archives. Throughout their tenure the Spanish continued to take advantage of and build on the existing ties between native peoples of Curaçao and the mainland. They also relied on indigenous people and their networks for sailing from the mainland to the islands. There also was some racial mixing, not surprising given that the Spanish settlers were almost entirely men. A 1640 report mentions Juan Mestiço (mestizo) who was over ninety years old and had been born and raised on the island.[50]

If Bejarano showed little interest in administering the ABC islands, he did develop their commercial potential. His most important legacy was the introduction of large numbers of livestock, which successfully bred to the point that they almost overran the island. By the mid-1500s, the Spanish had transformed Curaçao into a large, self-contained ranch. They raised cattle and other livestock primarily for their hides, which they shipped in large quantities back to Europe.[51] Writing in the late 1570s, Father Pedro de Aguado noted that, under Bejarano, the island "has done well with all types of livestock that are raised there, and in other husbandry aided by the Indians."[52] Ranching yielded enormous amounts of fresh meat that far outstripped the needs of the small local population and could not be exported across the Atlantic without spoiling. Word of this resource soon spread among the many seafarers who were sailing the Caribbean in increasing numbers by the second half of the 1500s. In 1565, John Hawkins saw over one hundred skinned animals lying in a field, their unused flesh rotting in the tropical sun. He was delighted to find "great refreshing both of beefe, mutton and lambes, whereof there was such plenty, that saving the skinnes, we had the flesh given us for nothing."[53] Hawkins stockpiled the meat to feed his crew on his ventures around the Caribbean. He claimed that there were at least 100,000 head of cattle roaming the island.[54] Hawkins's estimates may have been somewhat exaggerated. Sixty years later a report by a Spanish priest estimated over 10,000 head of cattle, 14,000 sheep, 2,000 goats, and 6,000 horses and mules.[55] Even this more conservative estimate, however, indicated that livestock then outnumbered humans on Curaçao by a ratio of two hundred to one.

Spanish authorities were concerned about the political implications of the meat glut. In 1567, following an attack by French corsairs on the mainland, Bishop Pedro de Agreda wrote that Curaçao was a threat to Spanish interests because the plentiful meat could provision pirates who regularly attacked settlements along the coast of Tierra Firme. Noting that the island governor freely trafficked with foreigners—probably a reference to Bejarano's exchanges with Hawkins two years before—the bishop recommended depopulating Curaçao as a security measure.[56] A Spanish royal decree of 1569 echoed these concerns, noting that the island's large number of cattle, sheep, and goats made it an attractive stopping point for French corsairs en route to Coro, on the mainland.[57] These corsairs and many others no doubt did as the English privateer James Langton and his crew had done: Upon arriving at Curaçao, they "landed and refreshed themselves with Fresh water and victualls" before proceeding to the mainland.[58]

The concerns of Spanish officials were no match for market demands, however. John Hawkins returned to Curaçao in 1568, where he took on provisions, presumably meat, before continuing to Tierra Firme.[59] Official collaboration was rather more muted during Hawkins's second visit to the island, perhaps due to interim visits by several groups of English and French privateers and corsairs, which had polarized the situation. Another factor was, perhaps, the Spanish Crown's clear displeasure over the previous commercial pacts Hawkins had signed with

Governor Bejarano. Although colonial authorities forcefully condemned the acts of pillage and violence that the foreigners supposedly committed, they openly acknowledged that itinerant traders filled an important economic niche. "These corsairs come fully supplied with all lines of merchandise, oils and wines and everything else which is lacking in the country," lamented one mainland authority to the Spanish king in 1568. He further noted that locals were so anxious to trade that "neither penalties nor punishments suffice to prevent them from buying secretly what they want."[60] Other officials wrote similar reports.[61] By the 1560s, the shift in Spanish imperial focus to Mexico and Peru had resulted in the glaring neglect of the colonial inhabitants of the circum-Caribbean and its littorals. This forced them to look beyond the empire to meet their basic needs and to fulfill their commercial aspirations. Colonial authorities faced an intense conflict of interest as they simultaneously tried both to serve the needs of locals and to represent the interests of the Crown.

This conflict of interest called for creative record-keeping. In January 1568, officials in Rio de la Hacha reported that, after terrorizing the local population for days (who, they claimed, heroically resisted all pressure to trade), the Englishman John Lovell had "set ashore ninety-six of the oldest, thinnest slaves that he had, *because they were dying in his hands.*" They requested that the supposedly worthless slaves become the property of the townspeople who, incidentally, desperately needed labor to work their fields.[62] Eight months later, the same authorities, with no apparent sense of irony, reported in almost identical language that John Hawkins, in a fit of remorse, had "landed in this city as many as seventy-five head of slaves *who were dying in his hands* . . . not a slave worth anything at all . . . in recompense for the damage he had done." The locals later auctioned them for a good price.[63] Local whites no doubt gave thanks for the miraculous delivery of 161 enslaved Africans in less than a year, at absolutely no cost to them, and the subsequent profits they reaped from the use and/or sale of these supposedly worthless chattel, whom they had acquired for free. Authorities, meanwhile, reported to the Crown that, by exchanging enslaved labor for European merchandise, Hawkins and others carried out "a business of some importance."[64] Both the basic market problem and the inventive solutions would be long-standing ones for authorities on the mainland and the island alike.

Challenging Iberian Hegemony: The Dutch in the Atlantic

In the summer of 1568, while John Hawkins traded brazenly around the southern Caribbean, events that would have an enormous impact on Curaçao were unfolding rapidly across the Atlantic. In a prosperous corner of northwestern Europe hugging the North Sea, Prince William of Orange joined an incipient rebellion against Spanish Hapsburg rule. As King Philip II's lieutenant in the northern Low Countries' provinces of Holland, Zeeland, and Utrecht, William "the Silent" was an important ally for the rebels, giving them a much-needed legitimacy and ending any hope for a peaceful settlement of the uprising. The long and bloody Dutch struggle against the Spanish Crown, known as the Eighty Years' War (1568–1648), culminated in the emergence of the independent Republic of the United Provinces of the Netherlands in the seven northernmost provinces of the Low Countries. (The southern provinces became the Spanish Netherlands and, ultimately, after several French occupations in the eighteenth and nineteenth centuries, the modern country of Belgium.) The House of Hapsburg had acquired the seventeen provinces of the Netherlands (including present-day Luxemburg, Belgium, and part of northern France) between 1506 and 1543. Holy Roman Emperor Charles V (ruled 1519–56, and as Charles I of Spain from 1516), united the seventeen provinces into a single federation in 1548. Having been born and raised in the Low Countries, Charles allowed them much local autonomy. When Charles abdicated in 1556, he partitioned his unwieldy empire between his son and his brother, leaving Spain, its overseas possessions, and the Netherlands to the former, who ruled as Philip II (1556–98). Philip's heavy-handed political and economic control of the Dutch provinces, coupled with the Protestant Reformation, which swept northern Europe, fueled anti-Spanish resentment, which burst into outright revolt by the 1560s.

The Eighty Years' War fused nascent, proto-nationalist resentment against Spain and the intense religious fervor of early Calvinism. The Dutch rebels developed a strong, focused hatred of both the Spanish and the Portuguese (whose crowns were united during much the same period, 1580–1640).[65] Thus, the rebellion shaped the character of early Dutch overseas expansion into Spanish strongholds in the Americas, especially in the Caribbean. In 1585, the Spanish occupied Antwerp in the southern Netherlands, then the largest, busiest, and most prosperous port in northwestern Europe. The Spanish required all who lived there to embrace Catholicism and to swear an oath to the Spanish Crown.

When the rebellious Dutch maritime force (the so-called Sea Beggars) successfully blockaded the port, strangling its commerce, thousands of merchants, financiers, artisans, and tradesmen fled to the north. Many of them were Calvinists, or at least sympathizers. More than 100,000 people left between 1585 and 1587. Jonathan Israel has called this exodus "one of the four great west European migrations of early modern times."[66] This emigration drained Antwerp and completely transformed the northern Low Countries. Towns located in the western maritime provinces of Holland and Zeeland successfully absorbed the newcomers, and converted the confiscated Catholic monasteries and convents into workshops, warehouses, and family dwellings.[67] These towns already had been vibrant centers of population, wealth, and commerce before the rebellion broke out. With between thirty and thirty-five people per square mile, they had the highest population density in Europe. By the sixteenth century, half the Dutch population lived in towns and cities. Literacy was exceptionally widespread throughout the Low Countries.[68]

The port city of Amsterdam received the greatest number of immigrants from the south, some 30,000 people. By 1600 these immigrants constituted fully one third of the city's total population.[69] Sitting on an inlet of the relatively protected Zuider Zee, with access to trade in both the North Sea and the Baltic, Amsterdam was particularly well situated to serve as a European entrepôt. It already was an established manufacturing and shipping center, a hub of the prosperous maritime province of Holland, the richest part of Europe north of the Alps.[70] As the seven northernmost provinces successfully held their own against Spanish attempts to quash the rebellion, Amsterdam soon became the economic, political, and cultural center of the emerging United Provinces. Amsterdam quickly replaced Antwerp as the most dynamic Atlantic port city of northern Europe. The port's population reached 115,000 by 1630.[71] This success, in turn, attracted more merchants, including refugees from Antwerp who initially had migrated to German cities.[72] In some city neighborhoods French and Flemish were more widely spoken than Dutch. As late as 1664 a German visitor noted that Amsterdam was a place "where the whole world trades," and was home to almost a dozen different national groups.[73] This influx of prosperous and well-trained immigrants ushered in the so-called Golden Age of the Dutch Republic, known not only for its affluence based on trade, but also for advanced craftsmanship, map making, and fine painting, skills which eagerly were sought out and paid for by rising merchants.[74] By the seventeenth century, powerful merchants dominated urban politics.[75] In the seventeenth

and eighteenth centuries, Amsterdam would serve as a model for Curaçao's port city of Willemstad.

Amsterdam also became a haven for religious refugees who were fleeing persecution from around war-torn Europe. The Union of Utrecht
in 1579, which established the terms of coordination between the seven
rebellious provinces (and is widely regarded as the founding document
of the Dutch Republic), explicitly guaranteed freedom of conscience to
all inhabitants of the rebellious provinces (Article XIII). Along with the
Act of Abjuration of 1581, the Union of Utrecht established the terms
for a confederation of political power in the emerging republic, distributed among three different bodies: the overarching States General, the
state assemblies of each province, and the city magistrates. Provinces
and cities alike retained relative autonomy in this system.[76] Among the
new immigrants were Sephardic Jews who previously had found refuge
in Antwerp after being expelled from Spain and Portugal in the 1490s.
Sephardim soon become one of Amsterdam's most important merchant
groups.

The rebellion against Spain shaped the initial period of Dutch overseas expansion in the 1580s and 1590s. It played out particularly intensely in the Atlantic and the Caribbean.[77] From 1585 to 1590, Spain's
Philip II closed all Iberian ports to Dutch vessels and cut off the supply
of salt, which was indispensable to the profitable Dutch fish-curing industry. Dutch vessels tentatively began to explore beyond Europe for new
sources of the vital mineral. They crossed the Atlantic to the Americas
and reconnoitered the Caribbean and the coast of Brazil in search of
unguarded salt pans. The Dutch also established a presence in the Mediterranean, ventured along the western coast of Africa, and penetrated
into the Indian Ocean and beyond, to Indonesia and Japan.[78] The prolonged independence war against Hapsburg rule shaped the character of
early Dutch expansion in the Atlantic and allowed the Dutch to envision
themselves as victims of Spanish tyranny rather than as an emerging
power.[79]

After Philip II lifted the embargo in 1590, Dutch merchants, particularly those in Amsterdam, developed a thriving inter-European trade
in luxury goods (spices, sugar, silks, dyestuff, fruit, and wine from the
Mediterranean, and American silver) in addition to the basic bulk commodities from the Baltic and North Seas (grain, timber, salt, herring,
and wine) that traditionally had been the mainstay of Dutch shipping
and commerce. Merchants from the maritime provinces of Holland and
Zeeland already had been major players in inter-European trade long

before the revolt broke out.[80] The Dutch soon dominated this trade, linking markets throughout all the major European sea basins and coasts from the Baltic to the Mediterranean. When Philip III, newly ascended to the throne, closed the Spanish ports again in 1598, Dutch merchants redoubled their commercial ventures throughout the Atlantic and Indian Oceans. They also began to invest extensively in the burgeoning trade with the East and West Indies.[81]

Dutch merchants soon sought more formal organizational structures to better coordinate their trade, reduce risks, and increase profits. As early as 1594, nine elite Amsterdam merchants formed the private Long-Distance Company (Compagnie van Verre). The company reaped modest profits on its first trade venture to the Indian Ocean the following year; it did rather better on a second voyage in 1598. By 1599, eight different companies from the provinces of Holland and Zeeland were organizing trade ventures to the Indian Ocean and successfully encroaching on Portuguese domains there.[82] Dutch merchants and investors risked undercutting each other as they rushed to capitalize on the opportunities for commerce. To promote cooperation rather than rivalry, and to better compete against the Portuguese, a group of Dutch merchants founded an entirely new kind of company in 1602 to trade with the East. The Dutch East India Company (or VOC, an acronym for its Dutch name, Verenigde Oost-Indische Compagnie) was a chartered, joint-stock monopoly that, while backed by the state and operated by a federated board of governors, was divided into several distinct chambers, each of which maintained its own separate capital and commercial operations. Thereafter, the East Indies trade, largely in luxury goods, was highly lucrative for the Dutch. The VOC became the world's first truly multinational corporation. It was both an extremely profitable economic enterprise and a major political actor in the Indian Ocean.[83]

The Dutch began regular forays into the circum-Caribbean in the 1590s, thirty years before they established any permanent settlements in the Americas. Throughout the last decade of the sixteenth century, at least one hundred Dutch vessels visited the Caribbean annually. They dramatically increased their presence in the region after Philip III reimposed the trade embargo in 1598.[84] Dutch vessels regularly visited the salt pans of Margarita, an island in the eastern part of the southern Caribbean chain, until a Spanish fleet routed them in 1605. Some of the captured crew members were hanged; the rest were taken as slaves to Cartagena.[85] Independent merchants and adventurers attacked Spanish settlements, where they acquired pearls, hides, tobacco, salt, dyewood, sugar, and silver from the inhabitants; they also reconnoitered the sparsely inhabited islands of the Lesser Antilles.[86] Commercial aims fused with geopolitical motives as Dutch merchant vessels attacked Spanish settlements. Some of this commerce was consensual on both sides. As early as 1606 Dutch trade with the inhabitants of Tierra Firme was so extensive and blatant that the Spanish Crown issued a royal decree imposing the death penalty on locals who traded with foreigners.[87] It is unclear how many—if any—people were executed as a result of defying this decree, which, in any case, was largely ignored. There was never the same intense rivalry between Dutch merchants and trading companies in the Americas and the Caribbean that there was in the Indian Ocean.

Willem Usselincx, an Antwerp-born merchant who emigrated to Amsterdam, first proposed the creation of a West India Company in 1592, even before the East India Company was formed. The Dutch States General approved plans for such a company fourteen years later, but they shelved them as serious peace negotiations with Spain unfolded that same year. By the time Spain and the Netherlands signed a twelve-year truce in 1609, the United Provinces were de facto an independent country, and Dutch merchants were trading regularly with settlements throughout the Americas, along the western coast of Africa, and throughout the Indian Ocean.[88] Dutch trade in the Atlantic expanded greatly during the truce years of 1609–21. Interest in establishing a West India Company revived as the truce drew to an end. When the peace expired in 1621, the States General chartered the first West India Company (WIC) for an initial twenty-four year period. Like the larger and highly successful Dutch East India Company after which it was modeled, the WIC was a joint-stock company whose investors were drawn from the merchant community. Its ten directors represented the five major provinces of the Netherlands, with the chamber of Amsterdam holding the most shares. The company allowed shareholders of any nationality, ethnicity, or religion. The States General extended the company's charter periodically until 1674, when they disbanded and completely reorganized it, halved the number of directors, and streamlined its operations. The second West India Company existed from 1675 until it was disbanded in 1791.[89]

The WIC charter reads like a detailed description of the geographic parameters of the emerging Atlantic world. The company had a complete monopoly on Dutch shipping and trade throughout much of the Atlantic, including all of the Americas, Africa south of the Tropic of Cancer, and all the islands in the Atlantic and Pacific between the Cape of Good Hope and eastern New Guinea—in short, all of the world that was not already covered by the charter of the VOC. Unlike the VOC in the Indian Ocean, the WIC had a military as well as a trade mission, and it served to continue the war against Iberia, especially in the period between 1580 and 1640, when the Crowns of Spain and Portugal were united.[90] Most Dutch commercial activity in the Atlantic soon was coordinated under the WIC umbrella. Privateering, which conveniently linked the two mandates of trade and warfare, was a central activity of the WIC from the beginning. The most dramatic success was Pieter Heijn's seizure of the Spanish silver fleet at Matanzas, Cuba, in 1628, which netted the company gold, silver, and merchandise worth between 11.5 and 15 million guilders.[91] The psychological impact of this lucrative haul was almost as powerful as the economic boost to Dutch coffers; it extended beyond the United Provinces to Spain and throughout Europe.[92] Such a windfall was rare, however. Overall, the West India Company was substantially less profitable than the VOC.

During the twelve-year truce, the Dutch established small outposts around the Atlantic basin to coordinate the burgeoning trade. Several of these became full-scale colonies by the 1620s and '30s. By the 1610s Dutchmen from the province of Zeeland had several small bases on the so-called Wild Coast. This no-man's-land between the mouths of the Orinoco and Amazon Rivers on the northeastern coast of South America has been described rather poetically by one Venezuelan historian as "a great geographic secret between two gigantic rivers."[93] Here, dense jungle and inaccurate cartography confused the boundaries of Iberian jurisdiction, while numerous rivers such as the Essequibo, Demerara, Berbice, Suriname, and Wiapoco provided natural harbors and access to the interior from the coast. The Zeeland chamber of the WIC administered several of these settlements beginning in the 1620s. Information about the founding and early years of many of these outposts is sketchy and incomplete.[94] On the Atlantic littoral of North America, the WIC founded a colony on the island of Manhattan at the mouth of the Hudson River in 1624. It was based on a trading post that fur traders had started in 1614 under the auspices of the New Netherland Company. New Netherland briefly became the most prosperous Dutch commercial center in the Americas after the company declared it a free trade center in 1640.[95] In the southeastern Atlantic, the Dutch established their first outpost in Africa, Fort Nassau (Mori) on the Gold Coast (modern-day Ghana) in 1612.[96]

Early Dutch settlements in the Caribbean were somewhat tentative. They established a foothold on the island of Tobago, east of the southern

Caribbean island chain and just north of Trinidad, in 1628, and abandoned it two years later because of attacks by Caribs from nearby St. Vincent; then they returned in 1633. Although they nominally held Tobago until 1678, the Dutch never had a permanent settlement there. They also had a brief presence on the northern coast of Trinidad in 1636, but soon were ousted by the Spanish governor.[97] More lasting and important were the Dutch settlements on St. Martin and St. Eustatius. In 1635, the Zeeland chamber of the WIC granted permission to a mariner from Flushing, Jan Snouck, to set up a colony on St. Eustatius, although the chamber retained governing rights.[98] Early colonists cultivated tobacco, using indigenous labor, which they sometimes procured in raids on nearby islands. By 1630, the Dutch settlement on St. Martin was under the control of the Amsterdam chamber of the West India Company. It was anchored in a bustling port that exported salt, which was extracted from several broad, shallow bays. Although the Dutch briefly were ousted in 1633, they soon returned. The French had a small settlement on the other end of the island.[99]

Company officials soon set their sights on Portuguese Brazil, whose prosperous sugar plantations were then the most productive in the Atlantic world, and whose defenses were relatively more permeable than those of the Spanish American possessions.[100] Dutch merchants and shippers, who had carried a large proportion of Brazilian sugar to Europe since the 1590s, resented Spain's decision to exclude them from this trade after 1605. Throughout the 1620s, after the twelve-year truce expired, the Dutch regularly attacked hundreds of Portuguese ships that traded with Brazil. After unsuccessful attempts on Brazil at Bahia and Salvador in 1623 and 1624, and armed with the wealth from Piet Heijn's successful venture of 1628, the Dutch seized Pernambuco in northeastern Brazil and the surrounding captaincies in 1630. They maintained a foothold in the area until 1654, when they were ousted by a revolt by local Portuguese Catholic planters that had began in 1645.[101]

Some historians have argued that, for the WIC directors, territorial conquest was always subordinate to commercial and military aims. In this view, forts and trading posts, rather than settlement colonies or plantations, were always the preferred form of incursion.[102] In taking a longer historical view of the Dutch project, however, one clearly can trace changes through the seventeenth century. As early as 1609, Hugo Grotius argued that territorial possession was compatible with a mercantile project.[103] From the beginning of their overseas expansion the Dutch established towns even as they focused on commerce and military might.[104] For a brief period in the mid-seventeenth century, the Dutch had control over a significant swath of territory which cut across all the major geographic and geopolitical areas of the Atlantic world, with strategically located nodal points on every continent. A land-based Dutch empire certainly was not out of the question in those years. The impressive, if brief, Dutch territorial expansion in the two decades following the establishment of the WIC was a "textbook case" of Atlantic history, according to Benjamin Schmidt, even while it exhibited its own peculiarities.[105] The Dutch emphasis on maritime trade was not incompatible with empire building even if, in the long haul, the development of mercantile networks apparently trumped territorial occupation. But the Dutch were not unique here. As Lauren Benton has noted, imperial sovereignty in the early modern era often was exercised in ways other than via the strict claiming of territory.[106]

From Spanish Cattle Ranch to Dutch Naval Base

Curaçao was among the first Caribbean islands that emerging European powers seized as they successfully began to challenge Iberian hegemony in the Americas. Throughout the 1620s, the English, French, and Dutch occupied a handful of the smaller islands in the eastern Caribbean that the Spanish largely had neglected. By the end of the decade northern Europeans had footholds on St. Kitts, Barbados, St. Croix, Nevis, Barbuda, Antigua, Montserrat, St. Eustatius, and St. Martin. It is often difficult, if not impossible, to ascertain the exact date of the first permanent European settlements on specific islands of the Lesser Antilles, given the presence of so many itinerant vessels sailing the region. Similarly, the varied nationalities of most of the crews sometimes make it difficult to ascribe any precise single European domination to these earliest settlements. Blurry demarcations and changing imperial jurisdictions further complicate the political history of the seventeenth-century Caribbean.[107] After the Dutch temporarily lost St. Martin and its crucial salt pans in 1633, WIC officials set their sights on the southern Caribbean. Curaçao's numerous natural deepwater harbors, and its strategic proximity to Tierra Firme, made it particularly attractive as the potential site for a naval base. The salt pans on its sheltered southern bays had commercial potential. The Dutch had begun visiting the ABC islands regularly in the 1620s, to gather salt and to cut brazilwood trees. These resources seem to have been the main attraction for the Dutch vessels, although Johannes de Laet's description of the West Indies in 1624 hardly mentioned them and instead focuses on Curaçao's abundance of livestock and hides.[108] However, this might indicate that de Laet's principal sources were Spanish, rather than firsthand Dutch reports. In August 1632 the mayor of Coro, in Tierra Firme, reported that eighteen foreign vessels, several of which were Dutch, had visited Bonaire already that year to take on wood.[109] The following year, Francisco Nuñez Melián, governor of Venezuela, complained that "every year many vessels of enemy corsairs arrive at our ports," noting that "especially I know that different people on the islands of Curasao and Boynare regularly help many Dutch vessels load wood." Fifteen vessels had come in June alone, according to the governor.[110]

In April 1634, the Amsterdam chamber of the WIC unanimously approved a plan to seize Curaçao from the Spanish. The company provided detailed instructions, provisioned and armed six vessels for a nine-month stay, and ordered that the invasion take place on a Sunday or other holy day, when Spanish ships in the harbor likely would be unmanned.[111] The chamber commissioned Joannes van Walbeeck to direct a conquering force of four hundred men, a mixed group that included Englishmen, Frenchmen, Scots, Walloons, and Germans, as well as Dutchmen, and at least one professional Caribbean privateer named Diego de los Reyes (who may have been at least partly of African descent).[112] Van Walbeeck's extensive previous experience included serving in the Nassau fleet, which had circumnavigated the globe in the mid-1620s; presiding over the Council of Dutch Brazil; and leading several (unsuccessful) missions to establish a Dutch foothold in southern South America. His commander of forces, Pierre le Grand, had led a large militia the Dutch sent to Brazil in 1633, and he had also overpowered a Spanish fleet.[113] The entourage, which significantly outnumbered the Spanish on the island, took Curaçao almost without struggle on July 28, the feast day of St. Anne. The Dutch promptly named the long, narrow channel on which they founded their main settlement in her honor.[114] They christened the capacious natural harbor at the end of St. Anna Bay, Schottegat ("sheltered inlet").

The Dutch found Curaçao to be sparsely populated. The Spanish inhabitants numbered less than three dozen, including a priest, the governor, and the latter's twelve children.[115] There were some five hundred Caquetios, most of whom were quickly deported to Coro. Fourteen indigenous families (about seventy-five people) remained on the island.[116] What Curaçao lacked in people, it made up for in livestock. Van Walbeeck reported that the island had 750 horses, numerous cattle, and thousands of goats and sheep.[117] A Dutch map published in 1640 brings this home more graphically. It shows livestock dotting the entire countryside, with certain areas devoted to specific species. The eastern end of the island, for example, is overrun by amorphous creatures that resemble a hybrid sheep/goat, with the notation, "here can be found many thousands of sheep," while wild horses prance on the northern coast (duly noted in both Dutch and French). In the middle of the island, which is curiously devoid of drawings, is the annotation, "there are a lot of cattle here."[118] Dutch rule apparently did not benefit the four-footed majority, however. Just twenty-three years after van Walbeeck landed, the island's vice-director, Matthias Beck, remarked that, although there had been 18,000 head of cattle at the time of the Dutch takeover, "such a quantity of meat that they could not profit by it," the Dutch had destroyed them all within two decades, and now had to import more from Tierra Firme.[119] There is no mention of how higher-up authorities felt about this early intercolonial trade. Mindful of the island's value as a strategic military base, van Walbeeck submitted to his superiors a list of the island's principal harbors and their characteristics, as well as the major natural resources, the scattered population centers where the Dutch and the few remaining Caquetios lived, and the scant freshwater wells and underground springs.[120] Sources of fresh water were especially critical because Curaçao had no rivers, lakes, or streams, and rainfall was sparse. The Dutch were especially attracted by the numerous natural deepwater harbors along the island's southern coast, which are clearly delineated in van Walbeeck's sketches.[121] However, while earlier Dutch reconnaissance had claimed that these were impervious to attack, le Grand's report stressed their vulnerability. Both men urgently requested that the WIC send adequate ammunition and provisions.[122]

The Spanish Crown and colonial authorities in Tierra Firme alike were greatly concerned about the Dutch takeover of Curaçao.[123] The Spanish tried three times to retake the island between 1636 and 1642, sending two expeditions from Spain and one from Tierra Firme.[124] They also conducted regular espionage missions to Curaçao. For this purpose they often used Caquetios, who easily crossed over from the mainland in their piraguas and could land surreptitiously on one of the many sheltered bays of the southern coast to gather information.[125] Even during their tenure of Curaçao, the Spanish regularly had sent out Caquetios from the mainland to spy on foreign vessels that arrived to trade clandestinely with the islanders.[126] After the Dutch captured Curaçao, Spanish spies themselves sometimes traveled to the island from Tierra Firme in piraguas. Another important source for updated information about the island were French and Dutch sailors whom the Spanish captured in nearby waters and sometimes took to Coro for questioning.

Following the change in jurisdiction, Curaçao's remaining Caquetios continued their centuries-old ties with native peoples in Tierra Firme, who retained virtually autonomous control of entire coastal areas of the mainland until well into the eighteenth century.[127] For the indigenous population, the new European political demarcations between Curaçao and the mainland were hardly an impenetrable barrier. There is no indication that native people felt any loyalty to the new, arbitrary borders that Europeans sought to impose.[128] Their comings and goings aroused suspicion and confusion among Dutch authorities, who were concerned about possible collusion with enslaved Africans on the island and also possible Spanish espionage.[129] Caquetios continued to travel back and forth between the island and the mainland at least until the final decades of the seventeenth century and probably well into the eighteenth.[130]

In spite of the new imperial boundaries, the Roman Catholic Church considered the ABC islands to remain under the religious jurisdiction of Tierra Firme. They continued to be administered by the bishop of Coro. This arrangement was accepted at least tacitly by the WIC, which was dominated by Protestant merchants who apparently had relatively little interest in converting people living in their domains. Although the WIC prohibited the open practice of Catholicism in its overseas possessions, it tolerated some dissent.[131] Dutch aversion to Roman Catholicism was colored not only by doctrinal differences but also by the eighty-year struggle against Hapsburg rule. The resident priest who had been living on Curaçao fled with the rest of the Spaniards. Thereafter there were no permanent Roman Catholic clergy on the island for several decades, although there were some reports of semiclandestine, temporary visits by itinerant priests.[132]

The Dutch established their base at the mouth of St. Anna Bay. This geographic positioning indicated the Dutch dual concern with trade and security. It was in marked contrast to the Spanish settlements, all of which had been inland. Defense was a central concern of the WIC, especially given that the island's numerous natural harbors on the southern coast all faced the nearby Spanish mainland, and thus posed a significant security risk. Whereas the Spanish had built no fortifications during their hundred-year possession of the island, van Walbeeck's forces immediately sought to protect the harbor entrance. They built the Waterfort, a simple, strong structure located on a point of land at the eastern mouth of St. Anna Bay. Van Walbeeck's 1634 sketches of the harbor included plans for a larger pentagonal fort, which was soon built on the point, and also indicated four places for ships to dock.[133] A year later, in 1635, the Dutch broke ground on the more elegant Fort Amsterdam at the harbor entrance. Financed by a major subsidy from the Dutch States General, Fort Amsterdam occupied the southwestern part of the peninsula at the entrance to St. Anna Bay.[134] It boasted walls that were eighteen feet high and eight feet thick. Fort Amsterdam accommodated the director of the West India Company and his entourage. It served both as company headquarters and as the seat of government for all the Dutch Caribbean islands until 1791. Its sturdy walls enclosed both residences and administrative offices. The Waterfort and Fort Amsterdam later became part of an island-wide system of fortifications that the Dutch constructed to protect Curaçao from attack by the Spanish, French, and English.[135]

Although van Walbeeck's drawings showed no plans for a town, a small, compact settlement soon developed just north of the forts. This became the nucleus for the island's developing port, which the Dutch eventually named Willemstad, in honor of William of Orange, who held the highest administrative position, *stadthouder*, in the Dutch Republic. There were several Williams of Orange and Dutch historians disagree about which one the town was named after.[136] This name did not come into widespread use until the eighteenth century, however. Until then, the entire area encompassing the fort and the adjacent settlement was referred to simply as "Fort Amsterdam and environs," and official written communiqués typically were issued "from Fort Amsterdam on the Island of Curaçao," a clear indication of the military character of the Dutch presence and the ancillary role of the town in these early years.[137]

Curaçao's conquest proved to be easier than either maintaining an effective occupation or addressing the questions of its viability and value as a colony. Initially, the Dutch were uncertain about the commercial prospects that the island offered, and they were ambivalent about their long-term tenancy. In December 1634, the majority of WIC directors voted to give up control of the island, a decision that the Zeeland chamber reversed six months later.[138] Some members of the WIC directive thought the island held promise as a strategic base from which to attack Spanish possessions and vessels and that it was well-positioned as a refueling station and refuge for Dutch privateers in the Caribbean.[139] Others pointed to the potential of its salt ponds and livestock herds.[140] But not everyone concurred. "We know that there is nothing profitable for the Company to be had here in the area," Governor Peter Stuyvesant wrote almost ten years later; "we are uncertain whether anything profitable can be accomplished."[141]

In 1635, the Amsterdam chamber of the company took over the administration of the ABC islands via Curaçao. Thereafter, for the next 156 years, the Amsterdam chamber controlled these islands politically and economically. and the chamber even appointed the governor.[142] For the first decades of Dutch rule the islands were administered from afar, reflecting their relatively low importance. They came under the jurisdiction of Pernambuco, Brazil, until 1645, when the outbreak of the Portuguese rebellion crippled the Dutch administrative structure there. Subsequently, the islands were administered by a company director based in New Netherland, the Dutch outpost in North America. A vice-director who lived in Fort Amsterdam on Curaçao oversaw the day-to-day business of the three islands. Curaçao was subordinate to New Netherland both commercially and administratively until the English seized the North American settlement in 1664 during the second Anglo-Dutch War. (They permanently acquired the settlement in 1674, and renamed it New York.) The company director then was relocated to Fort Amsterdam in Curaçao. From there he reported directly to the Amsterdam chamber of the WIC in the Netherlands. Thereafter, from 1664 until 1791, the West India Company director in Curaçao simultaneously ran the company and governed the ABC islands. He was assisted by a nine-man Island Council, which also included company representatives.

For the first fourteen years that the West India Company governed Curaçao, the Dutch were still embroiled in their independence struggle against Spain. Curaçao was well positioned to serve as a Caribbean naval base, as it was strategically located to attack the nearby Spanish American possessions and the vessels that cruised along the mainland coast and in the surrounding sea. For example, in 1642 Governor Stuyvesant sent an expedition to attack Puerto Cabello, the second largest port on the coast of Tierra Firme, in retaliation for a Spanish attack on Bonaire.[143] The sheltered, natural deepwater harbor of St. Anna Bay was a secure home port for Dutch vessels. Warships that ventured into Spanish American territory from Curaçao soon developed a trade component. They returned to port laden with wine, flour, hides, iron, and other valuable commodities that they had obtained from the Spanish colonies (sometimes seizing them from Spanish vessels, other times trading clandestinely with colonials). Local residents kept small amounts of provisions for local consumption; enslaved dock workers loaded the rest onto larger ocean-going vessels and shipped them to Amsterdam.

This transshipment trade soon became immensely profitable to the WIC. However, some company officials opposed Curaçao's trade on the grounds that it competed with New Netherland.

The early need to trade in order to meet inhabitants' most basic necessities helped lay the foundation for Curaçao's subsequent role as a regional commercial center. The island's lack of fresh water, frequent droughts, poor harvests, and famines were all evident from the beginning. Even the most basic foodstuffs had to be imported already in the first decades of Dutch rule.[144] Although in the early years of the Dutch occupation company officials promoted the development of agriculture for both local consumption and export, these efforts largely failed.[145] Agricultural output was poor on the arid island. In fact, both food and the commodities to exchange for it were so scarce that when WIC officials came across a small group of blacks and mulattos who were trying to flee the island in 1644 they commuted their death sentences and instead traded them to English islands for badly needed provisions.[146]

Under the forty-year tenure of the first West India Company (1634–74) Curaçao's population remained small, and it was concentrated around the fort at the mouth of St. Anna Bay. This early settlement was little more than a military outpost, dominated by the two forts. Local inhabitants were almost entirely male, primarily sailors, soldiers, and employees of the WIC. By one estimate there were 462 people in 1635, a year after van Walbeeck's invasion, including fifty Caquetios and 412 Europeans of several nationalities, of which 350 were soldiers, thirty-two sailors, twenty noncombatants, and ten civilian and military authorities. The only women were six Caquetios.[147] In April 1644, the sudden influx of 450 refugees from Dutch Brazil, in the wake of the Portuguese uprising there, temporarily doubled the local population and exacerbated a chronic food shortage. A month later WIC officials persuaded most of the new arrivals to emigrate to New Netherland.[148] Spanish intelligence calculated that between two hundred and five hundred people lived on the island during the first decade of Dutch possession, mostly men, primarily soldiers and mariners, including a variety of European nationalities.[149]

The Treaty of Westphalia in 1648 ended the Eighty Years' War and formally recognized both the independence of the Netherlands and the legitimacy of its colonial possessions around the world. This ushered in a new era for Curaçao. Over the next three decades, the island and its inhabitants went through a transition period. A series of factors came together that set the stage for Curaçao to become a major Caribbean and

Atlantic trade center, culminating in the Dutch decision to open the island to free trade in 1675. That same year, the WIC was reorganized under an entirely new charter. Thereafter, until the company was abolished in 1791, it played a dual role on Curaçao. On the one hand the WIC governed the island and thus fulfilled a quasi-state function. On the other hand, as a merchant federation, it served as the umbrella under which much of the island's trade was organized. A variety of people traded around the Caribbean, the Atlantic, and beyond, thanks to the structures that were put in place by the WIC. These political and economic roles were complementary but sometimes conflicting, and they left their imprint on local colonial society. Curaçao's subsequent success as a Caribbean entrepôt throughout the long eighteenth century owes much to the peculiarities of its status under the WIC, a position that influenced the opportunities available to island denizens across the socioeconomic spectrum. In positioning Curaçao as a trade hub, the Dutch both built on the island's established history in the region and took advantage of developing currents in the wider Atlantic world. These currents also brought to the island two diaspora groups which became the foundation of the local colonial society: Sephardic Jews and enslaved Africans.

On a Friday evening in early September 1688 a small boat left Curaçao bound for Coro, carrying a Sephardic Jewish woman, four black women, and three Spanish-speaking sailors. But the vessel did not complete what should have been a short, easy voyage lasting only a few hours. Instead it was caught in an off-season storm and dashed to bits along the southeastern desert shore of the Paraguaná Peninsula. Only one of the sailors, Miguel Francisco, survived to tell the tale of this unfortunate group of shipmates. Everyone else perished. Miguel Francisco testified that he had met the Sephardic woman in Curaçao, where she had begged him to help her flee the island undetected, and that she carried papers written by a Franciscan priest, introducing her to religious and secular authorities in Coro, where she intended to convert to Catholicism. Miguel Francisco was silent about the intentions of the four black women, and he gave no names for any of the five. Records of the shipwreck, assembled by officials in Coro and based on Miguel Francisco's testimony over several days, mention the women only in passing. Local authorities were much more concerned with the disputed ownership and distribution of the vessel's valuable cargo, several barrels of contraband alcohol that washed ashore intact alongside the mangled bodies.[1] No additional archival documents provide clues to the women's identities, their lives, or the fate of their corpses.

The tragic outcome of the women's short journey is somewhat ironic, considering that they belonged to two major Atlantic diaspora groups whose foremothers had weathered much longer and more traumatic dislocations and journeys to cross the ocean and arrive in Curaçao. People of African and Sephardic descent came to Curaçao by different routes and in markedly dissimilar circumstances. Yet women and men of both groups were propelled by some of the same currents that were coursing through the Atlantic world and that converged to bring members of both diasporas to the island in the second half of the seventeenth century. These same currents briefly thrust the United Provinces of the Netherlands onto the world stage as a major power at midcentury. The emerging primacy of the Netherlands, in turn, shaped the transatlantic migration of each group, albeit in markedly different ways. The development of imperial spheres and Atlantic trade networks provided the vehicle for both diaspora groups to arrive in Curaçao, where they took up different but complementary roles in the local economy and society.

The Sephardic Trade Diaspora

Like all early American Jewish communities, Curaçao's was founded by the descendants of refugee Sephardim, Jews who had fled the Iberian Peninsula at the end of the fifteenth century. (The Hebrew name for Iberia was Sefarad.) After being expelled from Aragon and Castile in 1492, and facing the choice between exile or forced conversion in Portugal in 1497, the Sephardim scattered widely. By the end of the sixteenth century, increasing numbers found their way to Amsterdam, which, by the second half of the seventeenth century, became the hub for an extensive overseas Sephardic trade network.[2] Most of the Iberian refugees were crypto-Jews, that is, Jews who had converted to Christianity at least nominally to avoid persecution but who often retained some degree of their previous ethnic or religious identities. They were known as *conversos* in the Spanish realm and as New Christians in Portugal and its possessions.

Terminology seems straightforward but is somewhat tricky here. Historians often use the term crypto-Jews to refer to people who only nominally converted under duress and secretly maintained some degree of Jewish identification and practice, and the term *conversos* for those whose conversion seems to have been bona fide. The terms Sephardic and Sephardim refer to people who openly practiced Judaism. (They are also known as normative Jews.) Often, however, these terms are used loosely and interchangeably. Moreover, it is often not clear which term is the most appropriate for a specific person in a given historical situation.

Among the challenges: Contemporaries often referred to all crypto-Jews, conversos, and Sephardim in Spanish America as "Portuguese" regardless of their open religious identification; in some cases historical records contain names that are clearly Sephardic although the self-identity of the people in question is not known; there was a continuum rather than a neat line between supposedly full converts and those who maintained some level of Jewish identity; the full spectrum often occurred within families; individuals often self-identified in different ways at different times in their lives according to changing historical and/or personal circumstances. There is also inconsistency in and disagreement over the use of these terms in the historiography. Some historians prefer to use the term *marranos* to refer to Jews who secretly maintained and practiced Judaism. Other eschew the word, noting its historically pejorative connotations.[3]

Ongoing repression by the Spanish and Portuguese Inquisitions led to subsequent waves of emigration from Iberia throughout the early modern period. Many exiles maintained contact with family and coreligionists in Iberia.[4] The refugees' identification with Judaism and with their Sephardic heritage varied. The issue of identity was complex and multifaceted in the various diasporic cycles over the centuries. It was shaped both by specific situations and by wider currents across time and place, and it was expressed along a continuum that included interconnected religious, ethnic, cultural, and historical dimensions. At one extreme were those who fully converted to Christianity and retained only nominal reference to or kinship ties with Judaism. At the other end were those whose conversion had been coerced and superficial, who secretly continued to practice Judaism, and who quickly and openly embraced their faith when they had the opportunity. There were many gradations in between. Succeeding generations of immigrants complicated the expressions of identity in areas where refugees settled over the decades.[5]

Unique among the various early modern European trade diasporas, only the Sephardim developed commercial networks that crossed all the major religious, imperial, and geographic divides.[6] Several historians have analyzed how their multiple layers of identity, among other factors, facilitated their role in interimperial and intercolonial trade.[7] I suggest that the generations-long tradition of negotiating clandestine religious/ethnic/cultural identities that often was based on the surreptitious exercise of forbidden Jewish practices (lighting Sabbath candles, saying Hebrew prayers, fasting, keeping kosher, etc.), made it relatively easier for Sephardim to engage in other forms of clandestine activity, including extralegal trade. Their extensive experience in operating skillfully outside of formal political structures, while simultaneously appearing to conform to these very structures, and maneuvering across established political boundaries, was useful in developing extralegal commercial networks within Europe, in the colonies, and in emerging transatlantic circuits. This ambivalent relationship to authority and power influenced the Sephardim's relationship to the state apparatus and legal codes more generally, as well as their abilities to negotiate these successfully to maximum benefit.

Conversos and New Christians played a role in the earliest Iberian explorations and colonization.[8] Their presence and importance has been largely ignored by historians until recently, however, due in part to the challenges of tracing them in the historical record.[9] Jonathan Israel argues that two separate and distinct Sephardic diasporas made their mark across the early modern Atlantic: an older one made up of crypto-Jews who spread out across the new Iberian empires from the earliest days of European expansion and a newer one of self-identified Sephardim who had an increasing and open presence in non-Iberian overseas colonies beginning in the mid-seventeenth century and who had especially close connections to Amsterdam.[10] Both played a vital role in developing and sustaining interimperial trade, much of it illicit. There were conversos in almost every Spanish American colony from the earliest days after the conquest, where they experienced varying degrees of repression.[11] The first legal codification of "race" in the New World, a 1521 Mexican law that required prospective emigrants to prove that they had at least four generations of Catholic ancestry, was aimed specifically at keeping conversos out of Spanish America.[12] Such strictures, however, were largely unsuccessful. From the 1580s through the 1640s, conversos settled throughout all the Spanish American colonies, including several parts of Tierra Firme, where they left their imprint on the configurations of the emerging Spanish empire.[13] By the mid-seventeenth century, there were conversos in Maracaibo (1640s), Santa Marta (1660s), and perhaps even Tucacas.[14] There was even a kosher butcher in Santa Marta at the end of the seventeenth century.[15]

Conversos actively participated in the earliest (illicit) intercolonial commerce between Spanish America and non-Iberian Europe, including importing enslaved Africans. They helped set the stage for the development of widespread contraband trade networks, as well as facilitating commercial inroads for merchants from rising European powers, especially the Dutch.[16] Conversos may have facilitated Dutch commerce with Spanish America as early as the 1590s.[17] By the 1630s, there was a "spreading web" of converso trade throughout Spanish America, according to Jonathan Israel.[18] Crackdowns by the Inquisition throughout Spanish America by the mid-seventeenth century dismantled their extensive trade networks, or at least drove them underground, although isolated groups and individuals continued to trade clandestinely.[19] Their decline coincides with the rise of openly Sephardic Atlantic trade networks, initially based in Amsterdam. Increasingly, by the second half of the seventeenth century, they were tied to Sephardic communities in the Americas.

There was not such a clear shift from covert to openly Jewish trade networks in Atlantic Africa. Sephardim apparently had an open presence much earlier in western Africa, although this largely has been overlooked in the historical record.[20] They probably were involved in early Portuguese explorations along the Atlantic coast throughout the fifteenth century, decades before their expulsion from Portugal in 1497. Thereafter, many New Christians fled to trading posts in western Africa, where they may very well have encountered coreligionists. There, they could take advantage of emerging economic opportunities and maintain ties to Iberia while being one step removed from the reach of the Inquisition.[21] There were New Christians in Kongo and Angola as early as the 1550s.[22] Apparently some New Christians found religious and cultural freedom as well as economic opportunities in Portuguese Africa. Several traders openly identified as Jews as early as the 1560s in Senegambia.[23] In 1606, there were enough openly practicing Jews among the merchants in Senegal to support at least two synagogues. In 1612 the majority of the white population of Porto de Ale was Sephardic.[24] (The presence of a synagogue required at least ten adult men who openly professed Judaism.) Seventeen years later, a Portuguese flotilla destroyed a synagogue in Rufisque.[25] There were also clandestine Jews in Portuguese settlements stretching hundreds of miles along the coast.[26]

Like the conversos in Spanish America, Sephardim in Atlantic Africa participated in a parallel commercial economy that was outside official control, and they played a significant role in opening up local trade beyond the Iberian realm. In Africa, they helped Dutch merchants in particular to challenge Portuguese dominance.[27] Sephardim also were involved in the nascent transatlantic slave trade from the Cape Verde Islands, along the Guinea coast, and in Angola and Kongo.[28] All of this trade was illegal from the perspective of the united Iberian Crowns, although it seems to have been tolerated by the few Portuguese officials on the ground. In 1617, a New Christian merchant held the *asiento de negros*, the contract to supply enslaved African labor to Spanish America.[29] Africa's Sephardim were also part of wider transatlantic networks. By the second decade of the seventeenth century, at least a dozen Jewish merchants in Angola had ties to Portugal, the Netherlands, and Brazil.[30]

Beyond the economic sphere, historians have documented the rich sociocultural exchanges that took place between Sephardim and locals in Atlantic Africa.[31] Like Portuguese immigrants, Sephardic men intermarried with local women and contributed to the development of vibrant creole communities along Africa's Atlantic littoral.[32] Locals sometimes converted to Judaism in the areas of western Africa where Sephardim lived and traded.[33] There is abundant evidence that the sociocultural impact of this spread well beyond the immediate confines of small coastal trading posts, back to Europe. By the 1620s, several Sephardic merchants who had been in western Africa returned to Amsterdam, along with children and household members, at least some of whom were of mixed race.[34] As Mark and da Silva note, the relatively small size of the Amsterdam congregation at that time means that they would have had a disproportionate sociocultural impact.[35] Amsterdam's Talmud Torah congregation had several black and mulatto members in 1644, just five years after it was founded.[36] The register book of Amsterdam's Beth Haim cemetery records the burial of one black woman and one mixed-race woman in 1647.[37] Sephardim who remained in Senegambia maintained close ties with the growing Jewish community in Amsterdam.[38] Many of those who returned to Amsterdam continued their commercial ties to western Africa.[39] By the 1630s, the openly Jewish enclaves in Senegambia and elsewhere in western African were disappearing, however, although the extent to which this was due to persecution, as was the case in the Americas, or simply to the lack of lucrative economic opportunities, is subject to debate.[40]

Between 1640 and 1668, a series of geopolitical changes set the stage for the relative decline of these initial groups of crypto-Jews and Sephardim in Iberian overseas colonies and gave rise to a new transatlantic Sephardic network. Within the Iberian realm, these changes included Portugal's successful breakaway from the Spanish Crown, the uprising of Portuguese planters in Brazil, and the ongoing war between the two Iberian powers. On the world stage, Dutch independence from Spain, the Peace of 1648, the rise of other European powers, and the establishment of thriving non-Iberian colonies in the Americas also had a major impact.[41] By the second half of the seventeenth century, commercial dynamism shifted to a second Sephardic diaspora, one that was openly Jewish and that had close ties to the growing Sephardic community in Amsterdam.[42]

The development of Amsterdam's vibrant Sephardic community had its roots in Article XIII of the Union of Utrecht (1579), which guaranteed freedom of conscience to all inhabitants of the seven rebellious provinces of the United Netherlands. Two years later, the States General of Holland signed an agreement with Sephardic merchants ensuring that they would have the same protections given to all merchants. This was a highly unusual move for the times. Thereafter, Sephardim actively supported the Dutch revolt. Jews did not enjoy full legal rights in the rebellious United Provinces, however. They were excluded from most of the guilds and were prohibited from holding civil or military office until the nineteenth century. Nevertheless, in general, they had more privileges than did most European Jews at the time.[43] Many Sephardim came to Amsterdam via Antwerp, as part of a larger emigration of merchants and others who fled increased Hapsburg repression following the Spanish occupation in 1585. By 1603, there was a small but recognizable converso community in Amsterdam.[44] Economics as well as the desire for religious freedom spurred this immigration. The Sephardic presence in Amsterdam grew significantly during the Twelve Years' Truce (1609–21), paralleling the growth in the port's maritime sector, and continued to increase throughout the seventeenth century.[45] Amsterdam's Sephardic population reached one thousand by the 1630s, and numbered between 2,500 and 5,000 by the 1670s, representing perhaps as much as 6 percent of the town's total population. (Historians disagree about the exact numbers.)[46] Early Sephardic immigrants to Amsterdam were not wealthy. Many had been forced to abandon their property and most of their possessions when they fled Iberia. Nevertheless, overall they seem to have been slightly better off than the average Dutch citizen.[47]

Miriam Bodian has suggested that Sephardim were "custom-made" for their role in Amsterdam's burgeoning global commerce: Their knowledge of and close personal ties to the Iberian peninsula enabled them to conduct profitable commerce, while their status as exiles and their presumed hostility to the Spanish Crown ensured that they would not be accused of political subversion within the United Provinces when they sought out contacts in Iberia.[48] Reflecting multiple, sometimes contradictory identities, Amsterdam's Sephardim were variously called, by themselves and by others, the "Portuguese nation," the "Jewish nation," or the "Hebrew nation."[49] They carried these names and identities abroad. Amsterdam's thriving Jewish community served as the hub for an openly Sephardic trade diaspora that spread around the Atlantic throughout the second half of the seventeenth century. Sephardim maintained close links to conversos throughout Iberia and beyond. They took advantage of these connections to engage in clandestine trade. The Twelve Years' Truce, in particular, expanded possibilities for clandestine trade between the United Provinces and the Iberian Peninsula. Sephardim were particularly well equipped for such clandestine commerce, given their ongoing close ties to converso communities in Iberia and their knowledge of Spanish and Portuguese. However, as Jews, they incurred personal risks by trading with Spain, Portugal, and the Iberian colonies. This included being captured, tortured, and imprisoned by the Inquisition. The Sephardic trade diaspora displayed several characteristics that were shared by other emerging merchant communities throughout the early modern Atlantic world. These included deploying extensive interpersonal networks and taking advantage of far-flung kinship ties.[50] Trust was an inherent element of successful long-distance trade networks.[51] One should not overestimate the cohesiveness of such ties, however, among Sephardim or any other ethnic/national merchant groups. Intragroup rivalries existed and could be intense.[52]

As they participated in the growing Dutch commerce, Amsterdam's Sephardim developed close ties with colonial possessions overseas, especially in the Americas. This eventually led to emigration. Concomitantly, there was a wave of migration by crypto-Jews from Iberian possessions to new American colonies, especially those in the growing Dutch and English spheres. Dating the exact year a Sephardic community appeared in a given colony is problematic for a number of reasons. Individual merchants often established trade ties or took up temporary residence in an area years before a group of families arrived and put down roots. Intended settlements could be unsuccessful in the long term, but even when some technically failed, some individuals often remained. Some Sephardic settlers were conversos who (at least initially) did not openly identify as Jews and so were not registered as such in the records, or members of a community might alter their public religious identification according to changing geopolitical circumstances (as happened, for example, across time in Iberia, Amsterdam, and Atlantic Africa, as well as in the Americas). This also raises the difficult question as to whether and in what circumstances historians should count groups of conversos as bona fide Sephardic communities. It is particularly difficult, for example, to document Sephardic enclaves in the French sphere, where authorities repeatedly extended and then revoked permission for Jews to settle throughout the seventeenth and eighteenth centuries. The situation was especially strained following Louis XIV's revocation of the Edict of Nantes in 1685, which resulted in greater religious repression in the French realm. In some French colonies, local officials, who were cognizant of the Sephardim's beneficial commercial ties, apparently underreported their numbers or even studiously ignored their presence.[53] Some of these issues are relatively less problematic for the Dutch realm.

Emigrants from the Netherlands established the first openly Jewish community in the Americas in Pernambuco, Brazil, in 1637, seven years after the Dutch seized the area from the Portuguese. The West India Company recognized the importance of religious freedom for the commercial success of its possessions. Article Ten of the sixty-nine administrative rules for governing the American colonies, which was approved by the WIC's executive council and by the States General of the Netherlands in 1629, guaranteed full religious freedom to all residents of eventual Dutch colonies, including Roman Catholics and Jews.[54]

Pernambuco's Sephardic community numbered 1,450 people at its height. This represented fully half the total white population.[55] Its members began to disperse when Portuguese Catholic planters revolted against Dutch rule in 1645. At least 600 Jews left en masse in 1654, when the Dutch formally ceded Pernambuco back to the Portuguese. Several hundred remained in Brazil, choosing to eschew at least the open profession of their religion and thus technically becoming conversos (further blurring the distinctions between the two groups).[56] Despite its relatively brief existence, the Dutch colony at Pernambuco was pivotal in developing Sephardic trade networks around the Atlantic.[57] Sephardic merchants were cultural as well as economic brokers, and they served as effective intermediaries between officials of the West India Company and Portuguese Catholic planters.[58] They also developed close ties with New Christians who already had been living there for several generations.[59] The Brazil trade also benefited Amsterdam's Sephardim, who controlled at least one half of the total WIC trade with Dutch Brazil.[60]

The first permanent Sephardic settlers in North America arrived in Dutch New Netherland directly from Pernambuco in September 1654. They were twenty-three desperate and penniless refugees—four couples, two widows, and thirteen children—who could not afford to pay their transatlantic passage to return to the Netherlands. Two Sephardic merchants had arrived from the Netherlands several months earlier, with full permission from the WIC to trade.[61] Most Sephardim who left Brazil returned to Amsterdam. Some then set out again across the Atlantic, traveling to London, New Netherland, and Dutch Essequibo on the Wild Coast. Many others chose the Caribbean. A 1655 letter from leaders of Amsterdam's Sephardic community to the directors of the West India Company indicates that there were then Jewish settlements in English Barbados and in the French colonies on Martinique and St. Christopher.[62] Apparently there was already a sizable Sephardic community in Martinique and Guadaloupe in 1658.[63] There were permanent, openly Sephardic communities in Dutch America (Curaçao, New Netherland, and the Wild Coast) by the second half of the seventeenth century, and in the English colonies of New York, Barbados, and Jamaica by the last quarter of the century.[64] (The English had seized Jamaica from the Spanish in 1655.)

The nascent Sephardic communities of the Americas maintained tight economic, social, and cultural ties with each other and with conversos who remained in the Iberian colonies. By the second half of the seventeenth century, Sephardim were part of an interconnected, highly mobile trade diaspora that linked commercial enclaves in port cities around the Atlantic world.[65] Many individuals traveled and traded freely across geopolitical boundaries. A typical example of a "wandering Jew" of the time is Abraham de Suosa Mendes. Registered as a "free denizen" of England in Jamaica in 1670, he shows up in synagogue records in London in 1677 and then in the tax list of Barbados in 1680; in 1683 he was granted a permit to "trade and traffique" in New York City, and subsequently he moved to Curaçao.[66] By the second half of the seventeenth century, the island had become a nodal point in the developing Sephardic diaspora.

"The Sharp Dealing and Selling of the Jewish Nation"

Sephardim played a central role in developing Curaçao's trade networks even before they established a visible, permanent community on the island in 1659. Individual Sephardim were in Curaçao from the earliest days of Dutch rule. An interpreter named Samuel Cohen, who had participated in the Dutch conquest of Brazil, accompanied the Dutch expedition that seized the island from the Spanish in 1634. Cohen remained in Curaçao for several years as a company employee; he may have been accompanied by others who stayed on after he left.[67] (Because of their fluency in multiple languages, Sephardim often were employed as interpreters in early modern Europe.) A converso named Juan de Araujo (also known as Julio) lived in Curaçao in the 1640s before resettling in Mexico, where he had a run-in with the Inquisition.[68] If others arrived in these early years, their activities have not made it into the historical record.

The first two organized attempts to establish a permanent Sephardic community in Curaçao were unsuccessful, although they paved the way for a later venture. In March 1651, responding to a general call by WIC officials inviting settlers to the island, João de Yllan received approval from the company to take fifty Sephardic colonists there.[69] De Yllan, who was born in Portugal in 1609, became a well-established merchant in Amsterdam. He had close commercial ties with his uncle in Pernambuco and had himself spent time in Dutch Brazil.[70] His small group of colonists apparently engaged in trade as well as planting. They also included a few independent businessmen who invested in the project, at least one of whom had spent time in Dutch Brazil. But the group did not meet the basic terms of the settlement contract. In 1654 the island's vice-director reported that de Yllan had recruited only ten to twelve settlers, far short of the requisite fifty he needed to bring within four years in order to retain the contract.[71] By 1655, de Yllan was back in the Netherlands, having relinquished everything he held in Curaçao to his brother-in-law, and focusing on more ambitious ventures.[72] At least some of the colonists he brought to Curaçao apparently stayed on the island. For example, Abraham Drago tried to recruit additional settlers and was involved in some small-scale trade ventures, including investing in a vessel to sail to Coro.[73] A year after granting approval to de Yllan, in February 1652, the Amsterdam directors similarly gave permission for Joseph Nunes de Fonseca, also known as David Nassi, to establish a colony of fifty people in Curaçao.[74] (In addition to the spelling variations that are common in names in the early modern period Sephardic merchants also frequently had two completely different names, a Hebrew one that they used within their communities and an Iberian one that they used for trade, especially in the Spanish and Portuguese realms.) Nassi also had spent time in Dutch Brazil and may well have known João de Yllan.[75] Company directors developed a twelve-point set of "Freedoms and Exemptions" to govern the terms of de Fonseca's settlement.[76] The primary occupation of the settlement was to be agriculture and cattle raising. For this, the company provided a stretch of land (two miles for every fifty colonists) that was tax exempt for a period of ten years, as long as cultivation and improvement took place within the first year and the requisite number of colonists was there within four years. The island's salt pans and dyewood groves were off limits, although settlers could petition for the right to sell these products. The colonization grant also gave the settlers the right "to seize and capture Portuguese ships," although the prizes had to be registered by the company, which would levy appropriate duties.[77] Apparently Nassi never took anyone to the island or ever went there himself.[78] By the late 1650s he was in Amsterdam, petitioning the West India Company to found colonies on the Wild Coast.[79] Thus, the first two organized attempts to establish a Jewish settlement on Curaçao were not successful. This was owing to a combination of factors, including the arid climate and poor soil, lack of labor, and the less than enthusiastic support from either the originators of the projects, the local Dutch, or company officials. Several individual Sephardic merchants and planters apparently remained on the island, however, and in the mid-1650s more people arrived from Dutch Brazil and from the French islands.[80]

Although João de Yllan had been unsuccessful in founding a settlement on Curaçao, he played a significant role in the island's commercial history. De Yllan conducted the earliest known independent trade between Curaçao and mainland North America (that is, trade that was not carried out via the WIC), when he began exporting horses and timber to New Netherland in 1652.[81] Four years later, in 1656, Jeosuah Henriquez imported merchandise into Curaçao from New Netherland.[82] Subsequently, other Sephardic families in Curaçao expanded these ties with New Netherland, which remained a valuable trading partner of Curaçao long after the English seized the North American settlement and renamed it New York.[83] De Yllan's independent ventures outraged Dutch merchants. "We have viewed with displeasure and dissatisfaction the extensive disruption caused there by the Jewish nation and Jan de Yllan in the sale of their produce and old trifles at such excessively high prices, which your honor is instructed and ordered to prevent by all means and not allow any longer," the Amsterdam directors wrote to Curaçao's vice-director, Lucas Rodenburch, in July 1654. They further noted that "the colonist Jan de Yllan accomplishes little there."[84] Such hostility had an impact. Rodenburch observed that the few Sephardim who remained on the island would leave happily if they could be relieved of their obligations.[85] In 1656 the island's new vice-director, Matthias Beck, reported that several Jews had petitioned to leave the island, a request that he had granted "because they are more of a liability than an asset in the countryside."[86]

Similarly, just a few weeks after the first Sephardim arrived in New Netherland in 1654, Governor Peter Stuyvesant, who jointly administered both the North American settlement and Curaçao for the WIC, asked company officials in Amsterdam to expel them. The settlers appealed to the Sephardic community in Amsterdam, which, in turn, asked company directors to guarantee that New Netherland would remain open to Jewish trade and settlement.[87] The company agreed, and instructed Stuyvesant to let the Jews remain, but it gave them a less than ringing endorsement. The directors concurred with Stuyvesant that the colony should not be "infected by people of the Jewish nation" but pointed out that they could not ignore "the large amount of capital which they still have invested in the shares of this company."[88] Stuyvesant replied that "to give liberty to the Jews will be very detrimental there, because the Christians there will not be able at the same time to do business."[89] The company's rejection of Stuyvesant's petition to expel the Sephardim clearly took into account the economic interests of Amsterdam's Sephardic merchant community, some of whom were company shareholders. Thus, they favored company interests over those of the independent Dutch merchants in the colonies, who felt threatened by the economic competition.[90]

In 1656, the same year that João de Yllan began trading from Curaçao, the Sephardic merchant Isaeck de Fonsekou (possibly a relative of Joseph Nunes de Fonseca) brought a shipment of much-needed foodstuffs to Curaçao from Barbados, including flour, oil, brandy, and assorted other goods. He requested permission to trade freely and directly with local inhabitants, without having to go through the West India Company. De Fonsekou's proposal prompted two emergency meetings of the Island Council in the governor's home, and intense negotiations. Local officials initially seemed disinclined to accept his terms. But after de Fonsekou threatened to take his business to Jamaica instead, they reluctantly agreed to allow him "to trade the remaining items, not needed by the company, to the freemen in the country."[91] These negotiations recall similar maneuvers between the English privateer, John Hawkins, and Spanish colonial administrators a century before. Curaçao's ever-dire food shortages no doubt factored into the company's decision. In the meeting, island administrators criticized "the sharp dealing and selling of the Jewish nation."[92] It is likely that WIC resistance to the commercial activities of Curaçao's Sephardim was due, in part, to the company's economic interests in New Netherland, then the preeminent Dutch trade center in the Americas.[93] It is clear that individual Sephardim had a pioneering role in opening Curaçao's trade beyond the control of the West India Company two decades before the island officially became a free port in 1675 and even before there was a permanent Sephardic community on the island.

The third attempt to establish a permanent Sephardic community on Curaçao was successful. In March 1659, the WIC granted Isaac da Costa the right to take a group of seventy men, women, and children to Curaçao from Amsterdam. Many of them, like da Costa, previously had lived in Dutch Brazil. Others had spent time in Dutch settlements on the Wild Coast, Tobago, and New Netherland.[94] Da Costa's contract was superior in several important ways to the terms that the WIC had granted to David Nassi's aborted settlement: The local government would support the Jewish community in disciplining its members; the colonists could buy enslaved Africans to labor for them and build their houses; and they were guaranteed certain religious freedoms.[95] Company officials in Amsterdam charged the island's vice-governor to supply the colonists with slaves, horses, land, and other material assistance.[96] This contract allowed Curaçao's Sephardim to purchase slaves locally from the WIC, although neither they nor any other private citizens were allowed to import slaves on their own until 1674.[97] Like the two previous groups, they were granted a two-mile-long strip of land along the northern edge of the inner Schottegat harbor, and many of the immigrants first tried their hand at agriculture.[98] They soon turned to regional trade, however. Drawing on commercial networks of coreligionists in port cities around the Atlantic littoral, Curaçao's Sephardim quickly made a niche for themselves.[99]

Dutch and West Africans in the Transatlantic Slave Trade

In contrast to Sephardim, few Africans arrived in Curaçao of their own free will. The overwhelming majority were forcibly captured and transported across the Atlantic. Once they set sail, their trajectory was apt to be more direct than that of the Sephardic immigrants, although their experience of capture and enslavement before the Middle Passage often followed more convoluted routes. The arrival of enslaved Africans to Curaçao depended on the actions and strategies of others, especially the West India Company and Dutch slavers. Nevertheless, diasporic Africans were propelled by some of the same economic, political, and sociocultural currents of the emerging Atlantic world that also brought Sephardic Jews to the island during the second half of the 1600s. Like Sephardim, people of African descent were involved integrally in the extralegal economic exchanges that shaped both the emerging Atlantic world and Curaçao. They, too, made their mark on the very culture and character of the emerging island society. Unlike the Sephardim, however, most Africans who arrived in Curaçao participated in these exchanges against their will, as commodities and forced laborers rather than as free traders. Regardless of how they arrived on the island, people of African descent, like Sephardim, also played a major role in developing Curaçao as a center of illicit interimperial trade. Their participation, if more constrained, was no less vital.

Although estimates vary, historians agree that the Dutch shipped more than half a million slaves from the western coast of African to the Americas over the centuries, virtually all of them in the 1600s and 1700s.[100] The estimates of Van Welie and also of Vos et al. put the number at 554,300.[101] Assuming a mortality rate of about 14 percent during the Middle Passage, over 476,000 enslaved Africans arrived in the Americas on Dutch vessels.[102] The Dutch were responsible for only 6.6 percent of the total transatlantic slave trade in the period 1601–1800. Their role was particularly important throughout the seventeenth century, when they carried almost 220,000 enslaved Africans, representing 11.7 percent of the entire trade.[103] (Although the Dutch shipped half again that many slaves during the eighteenth century, their relative role then was much less, due to the larger overall numbers.) In the peak period of their involvement, 1651–75, the Dutch carried 101,000 of the 500,000 Africans who were forcibly transported across the Atlantic, a full 20 percent of the total.[104] Half of these people were disembarked at least initially to the Dutch Caribbean islands, primarily Curaçao, from where the majority then were transshipped to Spanish America, as commodities in both legal and extralegal trade.[105]

Early Dutch participation in the slave trade had intertwined economic and geopolitical dimensions. Like other Dutch commercial enterprises of the same period, slaving clearly was influenced by the ongoing Dutch independence struggle against Spain. Spanish American markets were easy targets for smugglers. Portuguese vessels and possessions became fair game after the union of the Iberian Crowns in 1580. The earliest recorded Dutch slaving voyage was by a Rotterdam vessel, which delivered 130 captives to the port of Middelburg, Zeeland, in the southern United Provinces in 1596.[106] The captives, who were from Angola and probably seized from a Portuguese slaver, were freed when it was discovered that they were all Christian.[107] Ten years later, the first known Dutch slaving ship crossed the Atlantic, delivering 470 enslaved Angolans to Spanish planters on the island of Trinidad.[108]

Dutch scholars have stressed the ad hoc nature of early Dutch participation in the transatlantic slave trade. Johannes Postma has characterized their initial entry as "more by accident than by design" and "haphazard and incongruous." Pieter Emmer has referred to an "incidental slave trade" in the early period.[109] Dutch slaving initially took the form of privateering. In the early seventeenth century, Dutch privateers captured Portuguese vessels off the Atlantic coast of Africa, seized their cargo, which they regarded as contraband, and sold the slaves in the Americas. Before the 1630s, the Dutch often let go of the human captives they seized in these raids because they lacked the markets to make the trade profitable and the infrastructure to care for the human commodities.[110] As Linda Heywood and John Thornton have noted, this initial illicit trade opened the opportunity for the Dutch to establish a permanent presence in the Americas, and it also established a precedent for using enslaved Africans as labor in the new colonies.[111] Slaves captured from Portuguese vessels figured among the earliest colonists of the Dutch Americas.[112]

As with other forms of commerce in this period, privateering was the first, crucial step in developing a more coherent policy. The emergence of Atlantic empires initially fueled privateering and contraband slave trading to the Caribbean by the Dutch.[113] But capturing slave ships on the high seas was an uncertain and unreliable way to procure captives. Once privateers had opened the basic channels, more established merchants followed in their wake. The development of permanent Dutch and English colonies created new and legitimate markets for slaves, beyond the illicit trade to Spanish America. As demand for enslaved labor in the Americas expanded and became more predictable, more regular supply sources were needed. Individual Dutch privateers and merchants began trading regularly on the Atlantic coast of Africa as early as the 1590s. By 1600, Dutch merchants were a major force in the West African trade. They sent an average of twenty ships a year to the area between 1599 and 1608.[114] They traded in a variety of commodities, including gold and ivory. This trade soon was vigorous enough to raise the ire of the Portuguese.[115] In 1612, during the Twelve Years' Truce, the Dutch established their first outpost in Africa, Fort Nassau on the Gold Coast (modern-day Ghana).[116] As the Dutch established slaving forts on the western coast of Africa, they opened up direct supply markets. This diminished their need to attack Portuguese vessels and allowed them to set up a more regular, rationalized chain linking supply and demand markets.[117]

The founding of the West India Company at the conclusion of the Twelve Years' Truce in 1621 provided an umbrella under which to coordinate the burgeoning trade from western Africa and to begin to move to more rationalized forms of slave trading. The company was not involved in slaving in its earliest years, although by the late 1620s it was confiscating human cargo regularly from the slaving ships of other European powers, and purchasing small cargoes of its own on the Atlantic coast of Africa.[118] As early as 1623, at one of the first meetings of the WIC board of directors, some concern was raised about the legitimacy of the slave trade.[119] In the late 1630s, company directors regularly debated whether monopoly or free trade should predominate. These discussions continued for decades, until the company was reorganized in 1674.[120] Thereafter, the WIC held a monopoly of the Dutch slave trade until it was fully opened to independent merchants in the 1730s.[121]

Successful incursions into Portuguese-held territory on both sides of the Atlantic facilitated Dutch ascent in the emerging Atlantic commercial system. Within a little over a decade after seizing sugar-producing regions in northern Brazil, the WIC took over three major Portuguese slaving forts along the western coast of Africa: Mouree (1635), São Jorge de Elmina (1637), and Axim (1642). Once the Dutch had their own slaving forts in Africa and could import slaves directly to the Americas, privateering decreased in importance.[122] By the mid-seventeenth century, direct trade from Africa had surpassed privateering in supplying captives for the expanding Dutch slave trade. Both privateering and contraband trade continued throughout the seventeenth century, however.[123] With their holdings in Brazil and western Africa, the Dutch now had vested interests in both the supply and the demand sides of the emerging transatlantic slave trade and the plantation complex. The rebellion of Portuguese planters in Brazil beginning in 1645, which culminated in the expulsion of the Dutch in 1654, disrupted what otherwise might have developed into a long-standing and direct Dutch southern Atlantic slave trade similar to the one the Portuguese sustained between Brazil and Angola for several hundred years.

Although the West India Company played an important role in the transatlantic slave trade, especially in the second half of the seventeenth century, the company never formally held the *asiento de negros*, the official contract which allowed foreigners legally to supply enslaved African labor to Spanish American colonies. The asiento first was instituted by Spain's Charles I in 1518 because the 1494 Treaty of Tordesillas prohibited Spanish access to the western coast of Africa. The Spanish Crown granted the first slaving contract to the German financial family of the Welsers in 1528, in conjunction with their political jurisdiction over Tierra Firme.[124] For over one hundred years thereafter, the Portuguese held most of the asientos, by virtue of their monopoly of the Africa trade.

During the period when the Spanish and Portuguese crowns were united (1580–1640) there was no need for a formal asiento because the major source and demand markets were under a single imperial umbrella (although much of the colonial administration of each sphere remained separate). On several occasions individual merchants received smaller contracts and licenses. After the Portuguese broke away from the Spanish Crown in 1640, Spain resisted granting the asiento to a non-Iberian power, especially to a non-Catholic rival. Spain instead experimented with a system of multiple individual licenses between 1640 and 1662. Apparently these licenses, like the asiento, were a lucrative way for their holders to conduct illicit commerce with the Spanish colonies. In 1662, the Crown reinstituted the single asiento in an effort to recoup lost revenue and belatedly to assert control over the developing commerce of its American colonies and their continued demand for enslaved labor (although the Crown occasionally continued to issue individual contracts and licenses alongside the asiento).[125] By the 1660s, however, the geopolitics of the emerging Atlantic world had changed dramatically. As France, England, and the Netherlands challenged Iberian hegemony throughout the Americas, in western Africa, and on the sea lanes of the Atlantic and the Caribbean (as well as in the Indian Ocean basin), their own trading companies and independent merchants increasingly were able to procure and deliver the human commodities needed to sustain the emerging slave societies of the Americas. The establishment of successful, permanent colonies by these emerging powers, and the rise of the plantation complex in the Caribbean, meant that non-Iberian slavers could sell captives within their own sphere or to each other's colonies, rather than exclusively depending on Spanish American markets.

Between 1662 and 1713, the asiento was highly coveted and a major source of ongoing political and economic negotiation in the Atlantic world. It often figured prominently in international trade and diplomatic negotiations.[126] Even when one country or company clearly held the contract, there was intense maneuvering for subcontracting or otherwise providing the chattel from western Africa to Spain's labor-starved colonies. Although the WIC never formally held the asiento, for almost three decades beginning in the early 1660s it found itself in a privileged position in relation to the contract, with direct financial interests in the system. Throughout most of this period, the company was the chief supplier to those who held the contract. On several occasions independent merchants who held the asiento had direct ties to the West India Company, and to Curaçao.[127]

TABLE 2.1

Origins of Dutch slave exports from Africa, 1651–1700

Source area	Number	Percentage
Bight of Benin	71,300	38.25
West Central Africa	67,400	36.16
Bight of Biafra	20,300	10.89
Gold Coast	18,200	9.76
Senegambia	8,400	4.50
Sierra Leone	800	0.43
Total	*186,400*	*99.99*

SOURCE: Adapted from Rik van Welie, "Slave Trading and Slavery in the Dutch Colonial Empire: A Global Comparison," *New West Indian Guide 82*, no. 1/2 (2008): 55, table 2.

What do we know about the ethnicity and culture of the people who were forcibly carried across the Atlantic by the Dutch in this early period? Using data from the transatlantic slave trade database, Van Welie has found that, between 1651 and 1700, the Bight of Benin and West Central Africa together supplied almost 75 percent of all enslaved Africans who were transported by the Dutch, with the Bight of Biafra and the Gold Coast each making up about another 10 percent (see table 2.1). This provides limited information, as the database only indicates the centralized points of departure, not the wider areas of capture. However, from this one can extrapolate the probable larger catchment areas and so draw some tentative conclusions about the likely ethnic, cultural, and linguistic characteristics of the people who were captured.

West Central Africa stretched from present-day Republic of the Congo in the north approximately six hundred miles south to Benguela in modern Angola. This entire area developed regular, sustained contact with the Portuguese by the mid to late 1500s. People throughout this large region spoke dozens of closely related Bantu languages, including several mutually intelligible Kikongo and Kimbundu dialects. There were also religious similarities among the area's peoples. The area was divided into several different polities, including emerging larger states such as Kongo, Ndongo, Benguela, and Loango, as well as smaller groupings. Of these,

Kongo was the most centralized and had the most sustained impact on future developments. Linda Heywood and John Thornton have called West Central Africans "founders and creators" of African American culture, because of their predominance in the early Dutch and English slave trades.[128]

The early presence of Portuguese explorers and traders, including Sephardim, in the area means that the peoples of West Central Africa had experienced a high degree of early creolization already by the 1500s and already were well integrated into an emerging Atlantic world. West Central Africans had sustained contact and exchange with Europeans from the mid-1400s. By the 1500s, they were the foundations of what Ira Berlin has called Atlantic Creole culture. Before the consolidation of plantation agriculture and slave societies in the Americas in the seventeenth century, cosmopolitan, often mixed-race Atlantic Creoles from West Central Africa enjoyed a certain freedom of movement around the Atlantic world.[129] By the early seventeenth century, Christianity was already well established in West Central Africa, meaning that many—perhaps the majority—of the captives whom the Dutch carried to the Americas in this early period may already have been baptized Catholics.[130] Many people from Kongo likely had been exposed to Roman Catholicism or even converted before crossing the Atlantic.[131] In addition to Kikongo and Kimbundu, many also spoke an Afro-Portuguese creole language, the legacy of two hundred years of Portuguese presence in Atlantic Africa. West Central Africans predominated in the early Dutch slave trade through the 1660s. They likely were the first Africans to reach Curaçao in significant numbers in the early decades of Dutch rule.

Curaçao's entry into the slave trade mirrored that of the Dutch. Initially it was slow and took the form of privateering and smuggling. A request to transfer to St. Christopher some slaves who had arrived in Curaçao in 1639 may well have been the island's earliest participation in the Caribbean trade. These Africans likely were captured in a privateering raid on a Portuguese slaving vessel.[132] Around the same time, the slave trade regularly came up as a topic of discussion in the minutes of the directors of the WIC. By 1641, the Zeeland chamber of the company was claiming a monopoly on all blacks who were captured in the Caribbean by Dutch captains, requiring that they be delivered to Curaçao and sold exclusively to the governor. The next year, a memorial to the directors discussed "how and in what way the trade in Negroes from Luanda to Curaçao should be directed." A report by Arnout van Liebergen that same year noted Curaçao's geographic suitability.[133] Peter Stuyvesant was among those who heartily embraced the idea that Curaçao could become a regional slave trade center. But apparently not everyone associated with the company supported the idea. The Zeeland representative to the company directorship thought the island was "totally unsuitable" and favored Brazil instead, which could provide lucrative return cargoes of brazilwood and sugar. Others expressed concern that using Curaçao as a slaving station would provoke Spain to retake the island.[134] By 1641, the WIC was using Curaçao as a collection point for enslaved Africans who were captured from foreign vessels on the seas and then sold illicitly throughout the region.[135]

Black Majority

It is clear from the records of John Hawkins's ventures that enslaved Africans already lived in Curaçao and also were important commodities in Caribbean trade by the mid-sixteenth century, while the island was still under Spanish rule. In 1565 Hawkins left ten bondsmen from Sierra Leone and Senegambia on the island, along with several bolts of cloth, in exchange for hides.[136] The record is silent about the subsequent fate of the captives he delivered, although they likely remained enslaved. It is possible that eventually they may have found their way to the nearby mainland, either by force or of their own accord. Heywood and Thornton note that Hawkins's voyages marked a transition in the emerging transatlantic slave trade, by patently ignoring Portuguese claims to exclusivity on the western coast of Africa, and "establishing a new pattern of illegal trade in Spanish America."[137] It is historically fitting that Curaçao was one of Hawkins's destinations, given the island's subsequent major role in contraband commerce and the central role of people of African descent in all levels of this trade. Apparently there was an incipient slave trade from the island to Tierra Firme under the Spanish. In 1613 Venezuelan authorities reported that Portuguese slavers had arrived on the island the year before with a cargo of 208 slaves from Guinea and that subsequently two small piraguas had carried forty-four of them to Coro.[138]

Demographic information from the Spanish period is sketchy. A Spanish royal decree of 1569 mentions "a black man named Pedro" who apparently collaborated with French corsairs who attacked the island two years earlier, indicating that he had wider ties and alliances beyond the Spanish imperial sphere.[139] There is no hard evidence that any people of African descent remained on the island after the Dutch takeover in 1634.

The Spanish likely took their few slaves with them to the mainland. Accurate demographic data about the African presence in Curaçao during the early Dutch years is also incomplete. Diego de los Reyes, the professional Caribbean privateer who accompanied Johannes van Walbeeck's expedition in 1634, may well have been an Atlantic Creole, perhaps a mulatto. Seventeen years later, the group of Sephardic Jews who intended to settle on Curaçao included one African, Juan Pinto, who was described as a thirty-three year old native of Angola.[140] These individuals, and perhaps others for whom no documentation survives, arrived on the island outside the regular distribution channels of the emerging transatlantic slave trade, although they certainly were not immune to its influence.

Although the earliest transatlantic slaving voyages to Curaçao listed in the online slave trade database date from 1657, there is ample evidence that enslaved Africans lived in Dutch Curaçao well before then. They likely were brought by Dutch naval and/or merchant vessels that engaged in privateering against the Portuguese on the open seas. Company instructions issued to incoming Governor Tolck in 1638 repeatedly mention "black men and women belonging to the Company," "black women," and "black servants."[141] By the early 1640s, the company apparently owned approximately forty slaves in Curaçao.[142] In 1643 and 1644, Governor Peter Stuyvesant repeatedly reported that he had sent all the company's slaves from Curaçao to work the salt pans of neighboring Bonaire, "because for the present nothing more profitable and beneficial can be performed by them."[143] Salt was a vital commodity on the Atlantic market. The quest for salt to preserve fish was what first had drawn the Dutch to the region in the late sixteenth century. Harvesting it from shallow coastal pans that reflected the blazing tropical sun was a brutal, back-breaking task, which in later years would serve as punishment for rebellious slaves. Stuyvesant was concerned about feeding these laborers. Noting the importance "that those working in the salt pans have proper nourishment," he dispatched soldiers to some of the smaller, uninhabited atolls nearby to hunt turtles.[144] Stuyvesant also worried that some of the slaves might try to escape, and perhaps form an alliance with the few indigenous people who lived on Bonaire.[145] In 1644 he suggested transporting "as many Negroes and as much equipment as can suitably be carried" to Hispaniola (echoing Spanish transport of indigenous people between the two islands over one hundred years before).[146] We do not know if there were any free blacks or Atlantic Creoles on the island in these early years.

WIC authorities demonstrated an early interest in creating a slave society on Curaçao. The island's first governor, Johannes van Walbeeck, was well acquainted with the benefits of employing the labor of enslaved Africans, having had previous experience in Dutch Brazil. Shortly after taking the island, van Walbeeck requested that the WIC directors send "a good prize with Negroes, to use them for all kinds of labor on the land."[147] Governor Tolck, who succeeded van Walbeek in 1638, also requested the delivery of slaves to work on Curaçao.[148] In spite of Tolck's request, apparently the Dutch did not immediately begin shipping enslaved Africans to Curaçao after they seized the western African slaving station of Elmina from the Portuguese in 1637, even though the mechanisms for transatlantic shipment were already well established and they soon began transporting chattel directly to other destinations in the Americas.

WIC directors understood that the availability of enslaved labor would be an important enticement for potential settlers. In 1659, the terms of the contract that Curaçao's vice-governor offered to the group of Sephardic Jewish settlers brought by Isaac da Costa included a guarantee that they would be allowed to purchase slaves directly from the *asiento de negros*.[149] White settlers clearly expected to find at least some of the amenities of a slave society. Authorities were able to meet those expectations, despite the fact that Curaçao had no large-scale plantations that produced cash crops for export. The 1659 contract also indicates that the Sephardic settlers, many of whom previously had worked in the sugar economy of Dutch Brazil, did not bring large numbers of enslaved Africans with them when they fled Brazil after the Portuguese takeover. One explanation for this may be that, while these Jews had traded in African slaves when they lived in Brazil, few of them had owned plantations.

From the beginning, the Dutch had to decide how to incorporate people of African descent into the legal framework they were developing for the island. Lacking their own legal traditions to legislate slavery, the Dutch drew on Roman law to formulate their colonial slave codes.[150] In 1638, just four years after the Dutch took the island, the Amsterdam directors of the WIC issued instructions regarding the governance of Curaçao that included protective measures for and also restrictions on the island's black population. These included punishments for men who treated black women "dishonestly" or associated with them "lasciviously, whether voluntarily or by force," and sanctions against black men or women who ran away. Unbaptized Indians and blacks were not allowed to marry. There were also guidelines for supervising "Black servants," including an encouragement that they be employed in agriculture.[151] Three years later, the company decisively moved to protect the provisioning grounds owned by blacks and indigenous people. WIC officials declared that any company employees who plundered these plots would be punished with the death penalty, and that ex-company employees who sought to cultivate their own lands must not infringe on "any gardens presently cultivated by the Indians or the Company's employed Blacks."[152] Many of these points were echoed fifteen years later in the twenty-eight point list of instructions that Director Peter Stuyvesant left for Vice-Director Matthias Beck in 1655 when Stuyvesant departed for New Amsterdam. Stuyvesant repeated the admonition that no one "should treat the women or female blacks dishonestly, much less have unchristian-like intercourse with them," and reiterated protection for all gardens.[153] The strict legislation protecting slaves' small agricultural plots and the surprisingly harsh penalties for infractions reflect the ever-present threat of famine that haunted the arid island throughout the first decades of the West India Company's tenure, before well-established trade networks guaranteed a steady influx of foodstuffs from more fertile areas.[154] It also may have indicated an appreciation for the documented agricultural skills of the West Central Africans who were arriving on the island in these early years.[155] Similarly, the seemingly surprising regard for enslaved women may have been, in part, acknowledgment of the agricultural knowledge they brought from West Central Africa.[156] The extent to which these laws were followed, however, is unclear.

Curaçao's residents of African descent, like the Sephardim, arrived on the winds and currents of the emerging Atlantic commercial system, both literally and figuratively. Unlike Sephardim, the overwhelming majority of Africans came to Curaçao forcibly as commodities. They were unable to maintain their transatlantic contacts, and had limited ability to define the terms or conditions of their stay. Sephardim clearly had a more privileged position. They participated fully in Curaçao's emerging slave society from the beginning, regularly purchased enslaved Africans, and relied on captive labor in both the domestic sphere and in their commercial enterprises. Yet, in spite of their different origins, experiences, and opportunities, there were also similarities between the two groups. The diasporic experience left an indelible mark on the communities each group would fashion in Curaçao. Within the confines of their particular situations, members of both diaspora groups seized opportunities in Curaçao's emerging commercial economy. The five anonymous women who died leaving the island in 1688 represent thousands of such people who traveled across the Atlantic, made new homes in the emerging American colonies, and struggled to take advantage of new possibilities that opened to them.

In 1638, just four years after the Dutch seized Curaçao from the Spanish and ten years before the Treaty of Westphalia formally recognized the Dutch Republic and its colonies, the West India Company issued detailed instructions to its director on the island, Jacob Pietersz Tolck, regarding the management of island affairs and company interests. "Especially he shall not allow that the ships and yachts . . . waste their time unprofitably in the harbors," Company officials urged, but rather should "keep them always at sea, cruising to the most advantageous places." Upon the vessels' return, company officials instructed Tolck to "provide them as quickly as possible with all appropriate necessities and send them back to sea as soon as possible."[1] By insisting that vessels be kept at sea rather than staying in port, company officials encouraged their local representatives to become familiar with the region and to develop contacts that would prove useful in increasing Dutch commerce, in addition to fulfilling their mission to patrol and protect area waters. Thus, from the earliest days of Dutch tenure, defense and commerce were intertwined in Curaçao. Naval patrols often captured prizes that netted cargoes that could be sold profitably around the region or across the Atlantic.[2] Other vessels were sent out to cruise the Caribbean "so that they do not lie idle in the harbor," according to a communiqué by island officials in 1644, "in order to help promote the Company's profit and gain at the expense of our common enemy."[3] Perhaps unwittingly, the WIC instructions also encouraged individual merchants and seafarers who manned these vessels to develop their own contacts across imperial and geographic divides. By the end of the century, these independent traders, including many people of African and Sephardic descent, would emerge as key players in Curaçao's commerce, even as they operated under the umbrella of a political and economic system that was controlled by the WIC. This system increasingly assumed a commercial character, with trade eventually replacing strategic considerations. The creative tensions between the official power structures that were developed by the WIC and the regional networks that were forged by local traders shaped the very character of the island's society and economy throughout the second half of the seventeenth century, as Curaçao made the transition from a small Dutch naval outpost to a thriving Caribbean trade center. Intercolonial commerce was the primary grid onto which all other types of networks were superimposed.

From Naval Base to Free Trade Center

By midcentury, new geopolitical configurations began to transform the island. The 1648 Treaty of Westphalia between the United Provinces and Spain was a watershed. It set the terms both for the role of the Dutch in the emerging Atlantic world and for the position Curaçao would assume in it. The treaty officially ended the Eighty Years' War and formally recognized both the independence of the Dutch Republic and the legitimacy of its colonial possessions in the East and West Indies, including Curaçao. The treaty and a short addendum, the "Articulo Particular tocante a la Navegacion y Comercio," which was signed just a few months later, set the basic guidelines that regulated commerce between the Dutch and Spanish spheres. A subsequent treaty that was written in 1650 (and signed and ratified in 1651), fleshed out many of the general strictures which had been laid out in the 1648 accord. Together, these three documents provide insight into the processes at work as these two powers began to regulate the terms and conditions under which they would conduct their diplomatic dance around intercolonial trade, well into the eighteenth century.[4]

Most of the seventy-nine articles of the Treaty of Westphalia addressed the complicated logistics related to ending a prolonged war that had lasted over two generations, mopping up the various messes that were left, and getting everything back on track. Only six articles (V, VI, VII, XI, XX, and XXIII) dealt specifically with issues related to intercolonial trade. Together, these articles give a glimpse of the difficult balancing act the treaty's authors faced as they simultaneously acknowledged the Dutch right to trade freely outside the sphere of Spanish influence, while at the same time fully respecting the Spanish Crown's control of its possessions.[5] Article V acknowledged the right of the Dutch to trade freely. Article VI prohibited the Dutch from "sailing and trafficking" in any Spanish areas of West Indies, including areas where the latter had any ports or forts. It likewise prohibited Spanish subjects from "sailing or trafficking" in Dutch-held areas. Article VII recognized the logistical limitations of enforcing European treaties overseas and provided a six-month grace period for peace to take effect in the West Indies, and a full year in the East Indies. Somewhat confusingly, the short text of Article XI guaranteed the rights of subjects of both powers to be in contact and trade with each other.[6] Article XX prohibited the arbitrary confiscation of traders, sailors, pilots, vessels, and merchandise.[7] Finally, Article XXIII, while prohibiting unauthorized vessels from entering ports without the necessary paperwork, allowed an important exception for those that were caught in bad weather or otherwise incapacitated by unforeseen circumstances, allowing them to find safe haven in any port of call, even without the required documentation.[8] Traders took full advantage of this provision in subsequent decades, often claiming that bad weather or other dire circumstances had forced them to seek haven in unauthorized ports such as Curaçao, where they then had to offload their cargo before it spoiled. This, despite the fact that Curaçao lies outside the hurricane belt, and severe storms rarely touched the island. Such claims echoed those made by the English privateer, John Hawkins, in the 1560s (see Chapter 1). A short addendum to the Treaty, the Specific Article related to Navigation and Commerce, set forth specific terms governing these vital activities. It acknowledged the Dutch right to sail and traffic anywhere they had friendly or neutral relations and noted that the Spanish could not limit or impede such activity due to past conflicts. At the same time, it prohibited the Dutch from trading in banned merchandise or contraband with Spain's enemies; required Dutch vessels that entered Spanish ports to show passports with detailed lading lists, appropriately approved, before proceeding to enemy ports; and stipulated that any illicit items would be confiscated. Subjects of the Spanish Crown were given the same reciprocal rights.[9]

But the 1648 accords left some loose ends. The language regarding responsibility for trade and sanctions for related violations was imprecise, at best. Diplomacy thus required another go-round. Noting that there had been "several disputes and differences regarding the real meaning of the Article," as it concerned navigation, trade, and related issues, in 1651 the two powers signed an eighteen-point treaty that fleshed out in much more detail the general points and guarantees of the 1648 Specific Article.[10] The language of the 1651 treaty was much more precise, even when it covered many of the same general points, and it specified lines of responsibility in greater detail rather than just issuing vague pronouncements. It also included numerous small adjustments in language that no doubt reflected important concessions on both sides, which were made after extensive debates and diplomatic negotiations. Article VI enumerated the variety of arms, munitions, ammunition, and related paraphernalia which were considered to be contraband merchandise. Article VII listed the various foodstuffs that, because they contributed to "sustaining and nourishing life," were allowed to be transported almost anywhere, even to the territory of Spain's enemies, although not to areas under Spanish siege or blockade.[11] Subsequent articles spelled out in much more detail the mechanisms for registering and inspecting Dutch vessels and their cargoes, for checking up on what they actually carried, and for handling infractions. To what extent these carefully crafted specifications actually were followed was an entirely different matter.

The formal establishment of peace in 1648 occurred in the midst of several decades of unprecedented Dutch expansion around the Atlantic world. It was followed by a similarly precipitous decline. By mid-century, the Dutch had anchored themselves at key maritime points throughout the Americas, from New Netherland in the north, to a half dozen Caribbean islands grouped in two clusters, to the Wild Coast of northeastern South America, and south to Brazil. They also had ousted the Portuguese to establish themselves at several valuable trading forts along the Atlantic coast of Africa. During these decades at midcentury, no other European power had an equivalent geographic range of strategically placed settlements around the Atlantic rim that tapped into so many different potential markets and were so well located along the paths of winds and currents. Together, these bases gave the Dutch access to the developing trades of every other European power and to every major Atlantic commodity then being traded.[12] In spite of such promising beginnings, these territorial gains proved ephemeral. By 1667, at the conclusion of the second Anglo-Dutch War, the Dutch had lost important footholds in both North and South America. They retained only the Wild Coast settlements in northeastern South America and a few small Caribbean islands—Aruba, Bonaire, Curaçao, Tobago (which they lost in 1678), Saba, St. Eustatius (commonly known as Statia), and the southern half of St. Maarten. (The northern half was

French.) Of these, Curaçao was the largest and most important. Thereafter, the Dutch abandoned further efforts at territorial conquest and instead turned their full attention to commerce. Curaçao played a key role in this new configuration. In just a few decades, the island was transformed from a minor naval outpost into a Dutch linchpin in the emerging Atlantic commercial system.

The decades following the peace of 1648 were a time of transition for Curaçao. If the island's rise was not as meteoric as that of the Netherlands, neither was its fall. The relative Dutch decline provided new opportunities for the island, especially in regional commerce. The changeover from naval base to entrepôt was not entirely smooth, however. Although the basic mechanisms of interimperial trade were in place already by the 1650s and 1660s, less than a generation after the Dutch took Curaçao, the port still lacked much of the infrastructure that it needed to become a major regional trade hub. In 1659, Vice-director Matthias Beck complained to company officials in Amsterdam that he needed "provisions, necessary equipment, and other repair materials for the Spanish ships" that called to trade, and that he lacked basic dock facilities and an adequate garrison to defend the island against pirates and privateers.[13] Beck reiterated this concern five years later.[14] He also repeatedly remarked on the lack of vessels to carry out trade and the sailors to man them, and complained that boats were in such short supply that they were frequently stolen.[15] According to Beck's missives, there also were chronic shortages of suitable commodities to offer in exchange either for provisions to be consumed locally or for slaves to be resold in Spanish America.[16] Although one must always employ a healthy dose of skepticism in evaluating the pleas of subordinates for more assistance from their superiors, there was a certain urgency in Beck's repeated entreaties that suggests authenticity.

Local officials in Curaçao often assembled an array of wares as best they could. They bartered with visiting crews for goods salvaged from shipwrecks, or purchased small amounts of merchandise from a variety of sources.[17] The WIC, still smarting from the loss of its thriving sugar plantations in Brazil, was focusing its attention on New Netherland. Beck discreetly sought out appropriate contacts in Tierra Firme. He was well aware of the attractive and eager markets there, and their easy accessibility for Curaçaoan traders. He took care, however, to report his activities and intentions to his superiors in the Netherlands. Curaçao was not yet open to free trade, and all of the island's commerce still had to be authorized by high-level company officials in the Netherlands.

Beck's attempts to establish clandestine yet quasi-official commercial channels with his counterparts in Spanish America provides a window into the complex connections that were needed for successful intercolonial trade. "I dispatched the freight-boat to the Biscayan at the appointed and designated place," Beck wrote to the Amsterdam directors, explaining his attempts to gain the confidence of a trade partner in Tierra Firme. "The aforesaid Biscayan, now here, has given me such explanations and further information on that point," he explained, "that we can come to no other conclusion than that a good and favorable result is to be expected from it." Beck trusted his new associate to provide accurate intelligence about how the trade might be carried out on the mainland: "He has communicated to me the most direct and shortest route, how and in what manner not only one shipload of negroes, but gradually more, with good salable merchandise besides, could be traded off," he explained. But Beck required assistance and approval from company authorities to comply with his end of the deal, given the scant resources he then commanded on the island: "Were a ship with necessaries in the harbor here he would be willing, on receiving notice thereof at the appointed place, to come here and enter into such agreement with the Company, from which, as he firmly believes, he and the Company would derive great advantage."[18]

Reliable and trustworthy intermediaries such as the nameless Biscayan were vital to the success of any interimperial trade venture. No high level company functionary, no matter how experienced in administrative affairs, could pull off such a rendezvous successfully while seated in the comfortable confines of the West India Company offices, be they in the city of Amsterdam or in Curaçao's more modest and self-contained Fort Amsterdam. WIC officials soon realized that it was to their advantage to leave the logistics to traders who were on the front lines, rather than attempt to micromanage from afar. Curaçao's Sephardim were especially well positioned to serve as intermediaries. Already in the 1650s, even before there was a permanent Jewish community on the island, Jewish traders such as João de Yllan, Jeosuah Henriquez, and Isaeck de Fonsekou were trading with New Netherland and the English Caribbean islands.[19]

As Matthias Beck's 1657 missives to the Amsterdam directors clearly show, enslaved Africans also participated in Curaçao's developing regional trade from the earliest years, albeit primarily as commodities. The traffic in human beings also facilitated other commerce with Spanish America. Beck outlined a detailed plan explaining how supplying slaves surreptitiously to contacts on the mainland would open up much more lucrative markets for both the extraction of agricultural goods and the delivery of European manufactures.[20] Throughout 1657, Beck noted his ongoing communication with a variety of people in Tierra Firme, including the governor of Caracas, a Spanish merchant, and a Roman Catholic priest, to exchange slaves for hides and tobacco.[21] By engaging in this small-scale commerce, "a trail would thereby be blazed," Beck explained, "establishing a trade of importance" between the two areas in the future.[22] "I have witnessed with pleasure your honors' diligence in providing us here from time to time with negroes," Beck wrote to the company directors in Amsterdam three years later. "That will be the only bait to allure hither the Spanish nation, as well from the Main as from other parts, to carry on trade of any importance. But the more subtly and quietly the trade to and on this island can be carried on, the better will it be for this place and yours."[23] Using the slave trade as an entry for other merchandise built on a strong historical precedent. So-called Portuguese merchants, most of them probably conversos, had used their role in the *asiento de negros* earlier in the seventeenth century as an entry point to trade nonhuman merchandise with Spanish America. Tierra Firme was one of their main markets.[24] Locals in Venezuela who colluded with the Dutch in the illegal import of enslaved Africans faced imprisonment and the confiscation of their vessels and human cargo if they were caught, but even the imposition of such strict sanctions did not stem this unofficial trade.[25] Curaçao's role in the nascent Dutch slave trade to Spanish America did not go unnoticed by colonial officials elsewhere in the Caribbean. "Were ye Dutch driven from thence, their trade in Guinny should not bee halfe so considerable as it is, and the Spanyards would soone court the Royall Company with pieces of Eight," an English official in New York wrote wishfully to his superiors in 1666.[26]

By the 1650s and '60s, WIC representatives in Curaçao actively were pursuing trade ties throughout the Americas and the Caribbean.[27] Throughout the second half of the seventeenth century, the clear delineation of European colonial spheres in the Americas and the rise of the plantation complex opened new regional markets, concomitantly spurring Curaçao's development as a trade center. Merchants in Curaçao traded actively with French and English colonies throughout the Caribbean and North America. They also increased their trade with Spanish America.[28] This trade violated the restrictive commercial policies of the other emerging European powers and caused great consternation among authorities, who regarded Dutch and Curaçaoan merchants as smugglers and even pirates.[29] The governor of Jamaica's characterization of Curaçao in 1664 as a "cursed little barren island" is typical.[30] It was a sentiment that the island's early directors no doubt could relate to, albeit for markedly different reasons, as they lamented the lack of agricultural fertility that made trade in all its iterations the only viable economic option. The alternative was starvation. Indeed, famine was never far from the minds of locals. Company officials repeatedly found themselves having to ration foodstuffs and other basic commodities. "Our food supply dwindles daily and we believe that the pottage and bread cannot last more than 4 to 5 weeks," Peter Stuyvesant complained in 1643.[31] Subsequent governors repeatedly voiced similar concerns. Such very real fears of privation spurred authorities' interest in promoting regional trade.

Changing geopolitics further bolstered the island's emerging commercial role. The decline of the Dutch and the rise of rival European empires opened new opportunities for Curaçao. The English Navigation Acts of the 1650s, protective tariffs launched by the French under Colbert in 1664, and the three Anglo-Dutch Wars during the 1650s, 1660s, and 1670s, all were aimed, at least in part, at stemming Dutch trade with the American colonies of rival empires, much of it via Curaçao.[32] After the Dutch lost Pernambuco in Brazil and New Netherland in North America, Curaçao became the most important Dutch port in the Americas.

The mid 1670s were a watershed for Curaçao. After the charter of the WIC expired in 1674, the company was reorganized and streamlined.[33] In 1675 the WIC opened Curaçao to free trade, a move that was highly unusual in the prevailing mercantile climate. Curaçao now became the only open trade center in the Americas. (The English had abolished New Netherland's free trade status when they seized it from the Dutch, bringing the port of New York tightly into the folds of their mercantilist policies, at least in theory). Vessels of all flags freely entered St. Anna Bay and traded their wares along the wharves adjacent to Fort Amsterdam. They paid a fee on the value of their cargoes for the privilege, originally 5 percent and later raised to 8 percent.[34] Intercolonial trade broke no laws of the Dutch Republic, the West India Company, or the island of Curaçao, and it was fully sanctioned by WIC officials both in Curaçao and in the Netherlands.[35] Curaçao's regional traders violated the mercantile laws of rival European powers, however. Their activities did not escape the notice of the respective colonial authorities. Noting how a vessel from Curaçao brazenly had entered Philadelphia's harbor in 1698 to unload contraband wares and reload local products, Robert Quarry wrote to the English Council of Trade and Plantations that, "there is no checking this illegal trade without a small man-of-war . . . for if they forcibly take seized goods from the custody of the law, what can I do but complain to you?"[36] Many others made similar observations.[37]

By the last quarter of the seventeenth century, the Dutch had consolidated their presence on six Caribbean islands: the three ABCs, also known as the Dutch Windward Islands, just off the coast of Venezuela, and, hundreds of miles to the north, the three so-called Leeward Islands (St. Eustatius, also known as Statia; Saba; and the southern half of St. Maarten). Curaçao was the most important economically, and the most populated, of the six. In the southern Caribbean, flanking Curaçao, Aruba was valued mainly as a cattle ranch, and Bonaire was prized for its salt pans, which were worked by exiled slaves from Curaçao as early as the 1640s.[38] To the north, on Statia, sugar was replacing tobacco as the primary crop by the 1650s, with enslaved Africans the new labor force of choice. Cotton and indigo were also cultivated in smaller quantities. Statia also was beginning to develop as a regional trade center in the northeastern Caribbean, although its shipping would not overtake that of Curaçao for another hundred years.[39] By the 1670s, Dutch vessels were carrying tobacco from Montserrat and Antigua to Statia; by the 1680s its merchants were supplying slaves, sugar, and a variety of European products to the French islands.[40] The 1648 Treaty of Westphalia had granted the Dutch possession of St. Maarten's salt pans, which remained lucrative. The border between French St. Martin and Dutch St. Maarten remained unclear and contested until well into the eighteenth century. Tiny, volcanic Saba, within sight of Statia, was colonized from the latter island in 1640, and soon began producing small quantities of cotton, coffee, indigo, and tobacco. Saba also served as a shoe warehouse, and many inhabitants supported themselves by fishing.[41] All three Dutch Leeward Islands remained demographically small. Statia's population was just under 800 at the turn of the century, almost equally divided between whites and blacks; that of Saba was 453, and St. Maarten just 300.[42] Slavery already was an integral part of local economies and societies. By 1665 there were at least 840 slaves on Statia and 70 slaves on tiny Saba.[43] By 1715, Statia's population had increased to 1274, with a black majority of 59 percent. Saba and St. Maarten had just 512 and 605 inhabitants, respectively, and both had white majorities. Saba's white population had actually declined, with many people moving to Statia.[44]

That the Leeward Islands were relatively less important for the Dutch than the ABCs is clear from the WIC account books. In the period 1681–83, for example, the so-called Curaçao islands accounted for the lion's share of expenses for the nine overseas possessions listed, totaling over

62,000 guilders, followed by the Wild Coast colony of Essequibo with 41,500. St. Eustatius and Saba were a distant third at 12,500, followed by Angola at 8,800. Suriname received only 2,800 guilders.[45] The early governing structure of the Dutch Leeward Islands was somewhat different from that of the settlements on the ABCs and the Wild Coast. As a result, wealthy private citizens who had no ties to the WIC were able to attain relatively high positions, something that was much more difficult, if not impossible, in the Dutch Windwards. The Dutch governed their Leeward Islands as proprietary colonies until 1683, when they were fully incorporated into the WIC structure.[46] Unlike the ABCs, which remained under uninterrupted Dutch control, the Dutch Leewards changed hands frequently throughout the seventeenth century, most especially during the Anglo-Dutch wars, and into the early eighteenth century.[47]

As Curaçao's merchants followed commercial opportunities around the Caribbean, they sometimes put down more permanent roots. By the end of the seventeenth century, there was a significant group of Dutch planters and merchants living on the small Danish islands of St. Thomas and St. John. St. Thomas served as a regional trade center in the northeastern Caribbean, similar to Curaçao in the south. In 1691, twenty years after the Danish took the island, there were 145 Dutch people out of a total white population of 383, of which 109 had relocated from Curaçao or Statia. Dutch merchants remained a major presence throughout the eighteenth century.[48]

Curaçao's emerging role as the administrative seat of the West India Company in the Americas gave the island a privileged economic status within Caribbean and Atlantic trade systems, even as the overall Dutch role declined. By the end of the seventeenth century, the balance of economic power in the Atlantic world had tipped away from the Dutch, even as Curaçao's relative importance in the Dutch Atlantic commercial system burgeoned. During the last quarter of the seventeenth century and the first half of the eighteenth, the transit trade via Curaçao totaled half the value of all Dutch Atlantic commerce.[49] One central part of this commerce was the slave trade.

Curaçao as a Slave Transshipment Center

For a few brief decades at the end of the seventeenth century, Curaçao was a central Caribbean distribution point in the transatlantic slave trade. Dutch participation in the slave trade reached its height, 20 percent of the total, in the period 1650–75, the very years when Curaçao was consolidating its role as a Caribbean and Atlantic commercial hub, culminating in its establishment as a free trade center.[50] During these decades, the slave trade shaped the contours of Curaçao's economy and society, and helped consolidate links with the island's most important market, Tierra Firme. Curaçao received over half of the 156,800 enslaved Africans that the Dutch transported across the Atlantic between 1651 and 1700.[51] In the period 1674–89, Curaçao was the destination for 59 percent of all Dutch slave exports from Africa.[52] The vast majority of the human commodities were soon reexported to Tierra Firme.

Curaçao's short-lived but vital role as a major American slave depot completely transformed the island in the last decades of the seventeenth century, and helped insert it into broader regional commercial networks, especially extra-official ones. Changing geopolitics propelled the island into a prominent role as a major Caribbean slave transshipment center for several decades, a role it would retain until the War of the Spanish Succession once again altered imperial and regional dynamics. Curaçao's consolidation as a major Caribbean trade hub was symbiotically linked to its role in the Dutch Atlantic slave trade. The trade in enslaved human beings fed and, in turn, was fed by, commerce in nonhuman commodities. In both cases, contraband figured prominently, and in both cases ties were particularly strong with Tierra Firme. People of African descent, enslaved and free, played a pivotal role in Curaçao's society and economy, first as both commodities and laborers in the emerging maritime economy, and later sometimes also as independent traders themselves. In all three roles they were central actors not only in the contraband economy but also in parallel sociocultural exchanges.

A WIC report considered using Curaçao as a slave depot as early as 1642. Because the company's focus was then on Brazil, no plan was developed.[53] By 1641, the WIC was using the island as a transshipment point for slaves who were captured at sea from Portuguese and other vessels.[54] The first contract to deliver slaves in the Americas via Curaçao was signed in Amsterdam in 1657, not with the WIC but rather with a competitor, the Swedish-African Company, although it is not clear if any actual slaves were transported as a result.[55] Company officials approved a proposal to use Curaçao as a slave depot in 1654.[56] By this time, Dutch slavers already had penetrated the market in Tierra Firme. In 1656, the Spanish Crown sent a missive to the governor of Mérida expressing concern that locals had colluded with Dutch merchants for the illicit transport of more than eight hundred African slaves to the Spanish colonies.[57]

For most of three decades, from the early 1660s through the end of the 1680s, the West India Company and its affiliated merchants were the primary suppliers to those who held the *asiento de negros*. The company thus played a central but unofficial role in supplying slaves to Spanish America. Authorities in Tierra Firme were well aware of the chronic labor shortage there and eager to receive slaves, especially to work the growing cacao haciendas.[58] Curaçao served as an important station for Dutch subcontractors and was the major transshipment center to Spanish America, regardless of who held the actual contract. Throughout the second half of the seventeenth century, complex intrigues were woven around the asiento, as assorted players jockeyed for a piece of this highly lucrative contract. Although the ultimate prize might seem to have been the contract itself, duly signed and conferred by the Spanish Crown, the role of the subcontractor, who actually furnished the human commodities to the official asiento holder, was at least as important. If he played his cards well, the subcontractor could enjoy the maximum economic benefits of the slave trade to Spanish America, without having to become entangled in the tedious legalities and restrictions of the contract. Savvy asiento holders, in turn, often depended on the freedom of their subcontractors to circumvent the numerous restrictions that the Spanish imposed.

When the Spanish Crown signed an asiento agreement with the Genoese commercial house of Domingo Grillo and Ambrosio Lomelino in 1662, the merchants immediately made it clear that they would purchase captives from English and Dutch middlemen, rather than procuring them directly from Africa, much to the consternation of Spanish authorities.[59] Grillo and Lomelino soon set up an agent on Curaçao to coordinate purchases and deliveries and generally manage transactions. Similarly, when the Portuguese Antonio García won the asiento in 1670, he arranged to purchase all the slaves from the WIC in Curaçao, rather than using established Portuguese supply chains. Grillo and Lomelino briefly held the asiento again after Garcia, during which time they contracted the services of two Amsterdam merchants who had close ties to the WIC, Balthasar and Joseph Coymans. When Garcia's contract was renewed in 1674 (the year the first WIC was abolished), he contracted the services of the Coymans brothers to act as bankers and as official asiento representatives. Once again, they used Curaçao as their primary transshipment center. After Garcia's contract expired in 1678, the House of Coymans continued to serve as the representative for the new contract holder, the commercial house of Barroso and Porcio, and to use

Curaçao as the primary transshipment center. Balthasar Coymans was director of the asiento from 1684 until his death in 1686; his firm continued its involvement through 1689.[60] Dutch influence on the asiento likely peaked during the second Garcia contract, with such a heavy investment of Dutch capital via Coymans that Garcia was for all practical purposes merely a concessionaire to WIC interests.

By the 1690s, after the Coymans House lost the asiento, many WIC vessels began bypassing the island to deliver their human cargo directly to Spanish America.[61] Thereafter, the relative role of the Dutch in the transatlantic slave trade declined dramatically, whereas that of the English and French rose proportionally, although the WIC continued to have an important role in provisioning the asiento through the end of the century. Within the Dutch commercial system, the WIC technically held a monopoly on slave trading until 1730, although already by the early eighteenth century independent Dutch merchants increasingly dominated the slave trade. Cornelius Goslinga suggests that the end of the Coymans asiento was a watershed for Curaçao's participation in the slave trade, with smuggling eclipsing legal trade thereafter. By the time the Dutch lost their primary role in the asiento it had served a function that went well beyond provisioning slaves to Tierra Firme, strengthening ties between a wide variety of people in the two areas.

The slave trade shaped the human geography of the emerging island society. It was especially influential in developing the infrastructure and society of the port adjacent to Fort Amsterdam. Curaçao's role as a slave depot for the asiento trade transformed the island in the 1660s–80s. The WIC built large warehouses on the inner shores of the capacious Schottegat harbor to house the thousands of captives temporarily as they recovered from the transatlantic voyage.[62] The vast majority of them were then shipped, often clandestinely, to Tierra Firme.[63] Exactly how long they were held depended, in part, on fluctuating demand on the mainland, as well as on their relative health, and on the stability and efficacy of intercolonial merchant networks. The vicissitudes of the markets, and the imprecision of balancing the number of arrivals from Africa with corresponding demand in Tierra Firme, resulted in greatly fluctuating numbers of these transient migrants on Curaçao. For example, at one point in 1668 the island's holding pens were packed with over three thousand people awaiting shipment to Tierra Firme. This resulted in a near crisis, as locals struggled to provide adequate food and water to the captives.[64] Twenty years later, in 1688, the WIC once again held a surplus of five thousand Africans on Curaçao, with no guaranteed buyers on the mainland.[65] Holding such large numbers of human beings in a state of limbo stretched the port's facilities and infrastructure to the breaking point, to say nothing of the suffering of the Africans themselves. The company established small plantations in the countryside, worked by enslaved laborers, to provide food for the new arrivals. In times of drought, water and food were scarcely enough to meet the needs of locals. The threat of famine often loomed large.

The regular arrival of large numbers of human commodities strained the resources of the town. It required the development of new infrastructure and helped convert the small Dutch military outpost into a full-fledged Caribbean port. Operation of the entire slave distribution system required the full resources of the developing entrepôt, spurred the rise of small-scale ancillary industries, and transformed the very face and character of the small settlement. All the temporary residents—sailors, ships' officers, merchants, as well as slaves—had to be fed, clothed, tended to medically, entertained, and have their bodily waste disposed of. Slave trading vessels needed to be serviced, provisioned, and repaired, as well as laded and unladed. The influx of transatlantic ships and smaller regional craft alike required a steady supply of able-bodied men to sail them. Itinerant sailors flocked to the pubs, brothels, shops, and inns that sprang up near the wharves; captains, officers, and asiento representatives sought more upscale entertainment venues. "Ports and prostitution go together and Curaçao is no exception," the Dutch clergyman Philippus Speght wrote to his superiors in Amsterdam in 1673.[66]

Curaçaoan merchants received, catalogued, and dispatched the human cargo, drawing on their extensive commercial contacts in Tierra Firme to plan and execute timely delivery. The streets adjacent to the wharves soon were lined with their multistory dwellings. Patterned after the Dutch style, these contained offices, counting houses, and depots on the lower floor and the family residence on the upper levels. Outside the narrow confines of the walled town enclave, which was largely inhabited by whites, Curaçao's black majority began to establish small settlements.[67] The arrival of increasing numbers of slaving vessels greatly expanded opportunities for company officials and merchants to correspond with their colleagues and superiors across the Atlantic and beyond. Similarly, the regular departure and arrival of smaller regional sailing vessels strengthened communication between merchants and sailors in the circum-Caribbean.[68]

Alongside the official trade that took place via the *asiento de negros*, Curaçao also developed a thriving clandestine commerce in human cargo with Tierra Firme. The contraband trade in enslaved Africans predated Curaçao's role as an official slaving depot for the West India Company. It continued unabated throughout the WIC dominance of the Atlantic slave trade, and persisted well into the eighteenth century, long after the Dutch lost their primacy in the asiento trade and Curaçao was no longer an official transshipment center. In years when supply from Africa greatly outstripped the abilities of the official trade channels to distribute the chattel legally, this illicit commerce was an important safety valve for the entire system, allowing it, in practice, to operate along the lines of a free market. Like nonhuman commodities, slaves were best smuggled ashore at night, under cover of darkness.[69] Besides the economic impact, the constant movement of human beings across the imperial divide also had a major social and cultural impact.

WIC officials were well aware of the demand for enslaved labor in Tierra Firme. In the early years, however, erratic supply hampered their efforts to develop a reliable provisioning system. The emerging Atlantic system soon remedied this irregular supply problem, bringing to bear the full resources of the emerging colonial administrative structure of the WIC. In 1657, WIC officials signed a contract that promised to deliver five hundred to six hundred enslaved Africans to Curaçao.[70] Although the exact outcome of this commitment is unclear, researchers have documented the arrival of ten slaving voyages from Africa to Curaçao between 1657 and 1659, two each during the years 1657 and 1658 and six in 1659. Half of these voyages were in vessels owned by the WIC. One of these, *Koning Salomon* (King Solomon), made three separate journeys. The vessel's name strongly suggests Sephardic ownership. Together, these vessels disembarked a total of 2,371 enslaved Africans on the island.[71]

Three of the Dutch vessels that sailed to Curaçao in 1659 listed Spanish America as a destination.[72] When the *Koning Salomon* arrived in Curaçao in July 1659 with 331 enslaved Africans from Ardra in West Africa, Governor Beck immediately sold 300 of them to a Spanish merchant from Tierra Firme, at a price of 150 pieces of eight each.[73] A decade later, the WIC promised to deliver four thousand enslaved laborers annually to Spanish America via Curaçao, making the island then the busiest slave depot in the Caribbean.[74] It is not clear how many actually were delivered for this contract, however. In spite of strict prohibitions by the Spanish Crown, demand in Tierra Firme for enslaved labor fueled a growing clandestine commerce in human cargo via Curaçao. This increased in the second half of the seventeenth century.[75] Between 1659 and 1700, only thirteen vessels that landed at Curaçao listed Spanish America as a destination. All but one of these arrived before 1675. Together, these vessels carried a total of just 4,643 slaves.[76] Actual Dutch deliveries of slaves to Spanish America via Curaçao were much higher, however. The majority of Dutch slave exports to Tierra Firme were in the form of contraband trade, which would not appear in the registers. A high percentage of enslaved Africans whose final destination was listed as Curaçao were subsequently transshipped to Tierra Firme, after first spending several weeks recovering from the transatlantic voyage in holding pens on the northern shore of the Schottegat harbor. The slave trade also provided an easy conduit for the entry of contraband goods into the Spanish colonies, and so helped Curaçaoan traders develop contacts with merchants and markets on the mainland.[77]

Although Spanish America was by far the largest market for slaves who arrived in Curaçao, it was not the only one. In August 1659, Governor Matthias Beck reported that he was prepared to deliver fifteen or sixteen enslaved Africans to New Netherland via Curaçao, "but because we lack heavy cloth here with which to clothe them, we were afraid that they would not be able to survive there during the winter." He postponed their delivery until the following spring.[78] At least eighty-four enslaved Africans were shipped from Curaçao to New Netherland between 1659 and 1661.[79] New Netherland might have continued to be a major market for Dutch slavers had the English not captured it. In July 1659, the slaving vessel *Gideon* delivered 291 enslaved Loangos to the North American settlement, where they were sold at public auction. The *Gideon* had first stopped in Curaçao to leave 57 captives.[80]

The coexistence of a contraband slave trade alongside the official asiento trade influenced the demography of both Curaçao and Tierra Firme. Asiento buyers often were in the best position to negotiate for the highest quality human merchandise, followed by buyers on the intercolonial smuggling circuit. Thus, the strongest and fittest-appearing slaves often were shipped off the island, while local buyers had to be satisfied with those who could not be sold on the international market. Throughout the transatlantic slave trade, the human commodities were measured not as individuals, but according to their value as labor. Although exact accounting practices varied, typically a healthy man or woman between the ages of eighteen and thirty-five counted as one full *pieza de India* (literally, "piece of the Indies"); children, the elderly, and the sick, injured, or handicapped were various fractions thereof.[81] Many asiento contracts specifically stipulated that all slaves delivered must be full *piezas de*

India, leaving the less-than-ideal ones (called *macquerons* by the Dutch) for the contraband and local trades.[82] The percentage of such damaged human merchandise arriving in Curaçao via transatlantic shipment varied, but apparently was somewhere between 10 and 20 percent.[83] Local slave owners thus ended up with a disproportionally high percentage of *macquerons*, although they also listed *piezas de India* among their holdings. For example, on the ten rural estates that the WIC owned in 1707, only 33 percent of the enslaved labor was listed as *piezas de India* (both male and female) while 52 percent were *macquerons*. (The remaining 15 percent were children.) The value of these *macquerons* varied between 46 and 79 percent of the value of a full *pieza de India*.[84]

The illicit import of enslaved Africans into Tierra Firme from Curaçao, alongside the official asiento trade, continued—and may even have intensified—after the island became a free trade center. This commerce was so prevalent that it caused the Spanish Crown a legal headache: what to do with the existence of large numbers of enslaved workers whose labor was welcome in the underpopulated areas of Tierra Firme but whose very presence testified to the brazenly successful contraband trade that was conducted by the Dutch? The Crown's solution was innovative: It proposed to free such slaves. Between 1685 and 1692, Spain's ailing Charles II issued three strongly worded decrees aimed at these "blacks of bad entry"(*negros de mala entrada*), which threatened to grant freedom to any slave on the mainland whose owner could not produce a legitimate bill of purchase via the asiento.[85] In 1685, just three weeks after the Crown authorized Balthazar Coymans to complete the remaining two years of Barrozo and Porcio's asiento contract, it issued a royal decree that granted freedom to all slaves in Tierra Firme whose owners could not produce a valid bill of purchase via the asiento. The decree further required the owner to pay the asiento for the full value of the slave. Five years later, the Crown issued a similar decree that specifically mentioned "the fraud which was committed" by the Coymans asiento, which, it claimed, had "introduced over 400 heads of bad entry, of which no more than sixteen have been captured." The Crown further noted "that the Governor of the island of Curaçao has opened trade from there with the Ports of the Indies and daily there arrive boats of Spaniards to trade, exchanging black slaves for cacao, hides and other goods."[86] The Spanish Crown was well aware of the extent of the illicit trade in slaves and that it was used as a cover for the broader contraband trade in other commodities.

Colonial officials in Tierra Firme were also aware of the extent of the illicit trade in slaves and of its importance for the local economy. In early

1689, the governor of Mérida (west of Coro) petitioned the Crown to allow local slaveholders to keep without reprisals the many bondsmen they had purchased illegally via Curaçao, citing the ease with which foreigners trafficked on the vast, open coast. (His request is reminiscent of that of the residents of Rio de la Hacha to the Crown in 1568.)[87] But the king's reply was clear. Citing the full text of the previous two royal decrees of 1685 and 1690, Charles again ordered all such slaves freed.[88] A royal decree in 1705 once again echoed the Crown's earlier concern, fined owners in Tierra Firme two hundred pesos for each illicitly obtained slave, and granted the slaves their freedom.[89] It is unclear to what extent these decrees or the fines were enforced, and how many enslaved Africans, if any, actually obtained their freedom in this way. The very fact that the Crown issued at least four such similar decrees in less than twenty years is powerful evidence not only of the trade itself, but of the Crown's ineffectiveness in combating it. Similarly, the failure of these and other official efforts to curb the clandestine trade indicates its appeal, not only for Curaçaoan traders, but also for merchants and plantation owners in Tierra Firme. The opinion of the slaves in question is not recorded, although one can assume that they would have welcomed any opportunities to obtain freedom.

The slave trade was not only an important trade in its own right; it also was the entry point for commerce in a wide variety of other, nonhuman goods between Curaçao and Tierra Firme. It was clear to the Spanish Crown, and to everyone else involved, that the asiento was often used as a front for a far more extensive, far more lucrative trade in a wide variety of contraband goods to Spain's neglected American colonies. The license that the Spanish Crown issued to Juan Barroso del Pozo in February 1680 noted how the Dutch "furtively introduce" a variety of products, including "clothing, fruit, and, merchandise, which results in grave damages," and it specifically prohibited the introduction of any such goods alongside the human commodities.[90] This prohibition was blatantly ignored. This clandestine trade also opened multiple opportunities for cultural and economic exchanges between Curaçao and Tierra Firme. Curaçao was not unique in this respect. Commerce in enslaved human beings was an entry point to intercolonial trade in a variety of other goods with the restricted markets of Iberian colonies throughout the Americas.[91]

Dutch primacy in the slave trade, and Curaçao's pivotal role as a major transshipment center for human commodities, proved to be brief. By the end of the seventeenth century, the Dutch had lost both their advantageous connections with the asiento and their privileged position in the Atlantic commercial system. This had a corresponding major impact on Curaçao. With the outbreak of the War of the Spanish Succession (when the asiento temporarily passed to the French and then, at war's end, to the English), the WIC dismantled much of the infrastructure it had built on the island to accommodate the captives, dismissed the medical personnel, rented out or sold most of the company's rural estates to private merchants, and significantly reduced the company workforce on the island. The WIC kept the Hato plantation, on the north-central coast, to be able to accommodate any future slave arrivals, and a few other holdings.[92] The company sold many of the other estates to individual merchants, many of whom had acquired sufficient wealth so that they welcomed obtaining such a clear Caribbean marker of prestige. Dutch merchants continued to transport enslaved Africans across the Atlantic to Curaçao throughout the eighteenth century, but on a smaller scale. Independent Curaçaoan merchants also continued to deliver enslaved African laborers clandestinely to Tierra Firme.

Religious Matters

Whereas diplomatic treaties clearly consigned Curaçao to the Dutch political sphere, the religious realm was carved up differently. The ABC islands had been administered continuously by the diocese of the Roman Catholic Church in Coro since 1531. The Dutch tacitly allowed this situation to continue even after they seized Curaçao in 1634, although WIC regulations clearly prohibited the open practice of Roman Catholicism in the Dutch colonies.[93] In 1637, because of internal reorganization within the colonial Roman Catholic Church, the islands were transferred to the Bishopric of Caracas. Curaçao retained close religious connections with Coro.[94] Apparently the Roman Catholic Church did not officially authorize any priests to visit the island for over four decades after the Dutch takeover. There is, however, evidence of unofficial visits by individual clergy.[95] Several historians have speculated that priests regularly arrived from Venezuela from the beginning of the Dutch tenure and that they frequently participated in the contraband trade, as well as ministering to the island's Roman Catholic population, which included a handful of Europeans and Caquetios, in addition to the captives who were brought via the slave trade.[96] Although apparently turning a blind eye to these occasional visits, the Dutch made some effort to limit formal clerical contact and to exercise some level of at least nominal jurisdiction, however. In 1661, the Dutch States General required that any Catholic priest who wished to settle on the island obtain a permit from the West India Company.[97] Apparently they reissued this requirement in 1705, indicating that perhaps it had been ignored in the interim.[98] This had the result of encouraging the visits of itinerant priests, many of whom found Curaçao to be a convenient way station in their transatlantic voyages, since the island had reliable transportation connections to points around the region and beyond. Other clergy visited to purchase basic necessities or slaves.[99]

Curaçao's ties to the Roman Catholic Church in Tierra Firme became closer around the same time that the island became a free trade center. In 1677, the bishop of Caracas issued an extensive pastoral letter encouraging evangelization in Curaçao. He authorized Juan Gomez Manzo, a pastor in Coro, to travel immediately and clandestinely to the island with a portable altar to perform baptisms, marriages, and other sacraments in secret, and even to wear secular clothing, if necessary, to escape detection. (Thus he would comply with the Dutch prohibition of open evangelization on the part of Roman Catholics.)[100] The bishop's letter further included a broad authorization for any traveling priest who found himself on the islands and who was "not affiliated with an enemy of the church" to celebrate mass, perform sacraments, and generally attend to the spiritual needs of local Catholics, without needing prior or formal approval from the church hierarchy.[101] The bishop's general authorization would be invoked repeatedly over the coming decades by both individual priests and the Roman Catholic hierarchy in Tierra Firme. It proved to be a highly effective way for the church to maintain an ongoing presence among the island's population (especially slaves) and to minister to their spiritual needs without having to engage in any political entanglements, and without having to obtain authorization from the States General. Priests and their superiors thus could easily circumvent the States General's requirement that they obtain a permit from the company in order to settle on the island. Most were highly discreet in their behavior and dress.

In 1677, Gómez Manzo arrived on the island with D. Nicolás Caldera de Quiñones, on the first officially sanctioned visit by Roman Catholic clergy since the Dutch takeover. In addition to the bishop's directive, their visit may also have been in response to a request by island Caquetios to the bishop of Caracas. (This attested to the continued presence and ongoing importance of indigenous people on the island.)[102] The priests spent almost two months on Curaçao, during which time they traveled around the island to baptize people in several small rural settlements, including Ascención (where the Spanish had made their primary settlement), San Juan, and two landholdings owned by Balthazar Beck (Santa Cruz and Sabonet). Gómez Manzo and Caldera baptized 320 people, of whom over two-thirds were of African descent, including 209 slaves and 15 free blacks and mulattos. Most of the rest (approximately 100) were Caquetios; there were also a few whites, perhaps including some Spaniards who had remained on the island. Apparently only adult Caquetios were baptized, no children. Among the people of African descent, only 20 of the mothers—less than 10 percent—were not themselves already baptized. Either clandestine, unregistered visits by clergy over the previous decades had been highly successful in baptizing newly arrived slaves, or, more likely, these women already had been Christian before they left West Central Africa. The priests also performed six marriages, including those of two indigenous couples.[103] Thereafter, as Curaçaoan traders regularly went to Tierra Firme to conduct clandestine commerce, clergy traveled in the opposite direction to evangelize surreptitiously. Between 1680 and 1707, more than 50 priests visited from Tierra Firme to convert and baptize the small population of Caquetios and the growing number of inhabitants of African descent, as well as to minister to a handful of European Catholics.[104] They included Dominicans, Franciscans, Capuchins, Augustinians, and Fathers of Mercy, who stayed on the island anywhere from one to eleven months at a time. Most were in transit to or from Europe and arrived on the island due to its excellent transportation connections.[105]

Because of the regular visits of Catholic priests and the apparent lack of interest in prosletyzing on the part of the Dutch, virtually the entire black and mulatto population of the island was Catholic by the second half of the seventeenth century, a situation that continued in subsequent centuries.[106] Henceforth, Roman Catholicism was the predominant religion among the island's majority of African descent. Between the visits of the itinerant priests the island's Roman Catholics largely were left to fend for themselves. Such neglect was not limited to Curaçao. Entire areas of Venezuela often went years without clerical attention. As one report lamented, "Many of the faithful die without receiving the sacrament."[107] Perhaps ironically, it was relatively easier for visiting priests from Venezuela to keep up with baptisms in Dutch Curaçao, given the small size of both the island and its population, which also was concentrated in just a few places.

The burgeoning slave trade also had an impact on the island's religious configuration. In order to reap the economic benefits of the trade, the

WIC had to make certain sociocultural and religious concessions to the Spanish Crown. Baltazar Coymans's asiento specifically required that he attend to the spiritual needs of the captives by providing ten priests to minister to them during their transatlantic transport, although it is not at all clear how rigorously he met these guidelines. The contract further authorized two Capuchin priests to stay on the island to attend to the arrivals. In a marked break with established Dutch policy, they were allowed to dress in full habit and to move freely around the island to reach all the slaves. Although, at the time, Roman Catholic priests were not allowed to wear habits or to preach openly anywhere in the Dutch Republic, on Curaçao the commercial needs of the asiento apparently took precedent over Dutch religious sensibilities.[108] In 1685, the priests installed a small chapel in a merchant house on the Handelskade, the main street along the waterfront of St. Anna Bay, with sleeping quarters for the priests upstairs, and the altar next to the sink.[109] There, they openly ministered to local Catholics under the guidelines that the bishop of Caracas had set forth in 1677 and according to the terms of the asiento.[110] The Roman Catholic Church had no permanent building on the island until the eighteenth century. Until then, priests performed religious services either in their own homes or in makeshift chapels they fashioned in houses they bought or rented in the walled town. Some carried portable altars like the one Gómez Manzo and Caldera de Quiñones had used.[111]

During their visit to the island in 1677, at the behest of the bishop of Caracas, Gómez Manzo and Caldera de Quiñones were based in the home of the asiento factor, Captain Galesio. This indicates the close relations between the church and the slave trade.[112] Some Roman Catholic clergy who arrived as chaplains on slaving vessels subsequently stayed on the island for several weeks or months.[113] Visiting priests took advantage of the orders issued by the bishop of Caracas in 1677, which authorized them to perform sacraments and tend to the spiritual needs of locals .[114] Apparently the WIC accepted this situation. In the weeks and months that saw shiploads of enslaved Africans biding their time on the island awaiting transit to the Spanish mainland, itinerant Roman Catholic priests literally would have found a captive audience for their ministry.

Some priests also dabbled in illicit intercolonial trade to supplement their meager incomes. Freely allowed to cross political borders due to the ongoing Spanish religious administration of the island, with their loose, flowing vestments, and toting cases ostensibly fulfilled with religious accoutrements, clergy were well-positioned to smuggle. As early as 1657, Vice-director Matthias Beck mentioned one Fray Francisco, a

priest from the mainland, who came to Curaçao to trade "for some par-
cels of goods and one or two small Negro girls."[115] Clergy also engaged
in smuggling in Tierra Firme. In 1664, residents of Coro denounced two
priests for selling clothing in exchange for slaves from Curaçao.[116] Father
José Pimentel was widely accused by Venezuelan authorities of smuggling both commodities and slaves. He was imprisoned in Caracas when
he was found with a suitcase full of precious stones, expensive textiles,
clothing, gold, silver, and books.[117] In the first decade of the eighteenth
century, Father Alexius Schabel, who served on the island from 1704
until 1713, wrote of his own commercial dealings between the two areas and also of those of other priests.[118] Schabel had particularly harsh
words for his rival and successor, Father Augustín Caicedo, whom he
accused of being a "contrabandist and heretic," and who regularly traded
in Venezuelan tobacco.[119] Lacking state support, and with their superiors
in Venezuela focused on closer members of the flock, Curaçao's Roman
Catholic clergy often lived perilously close to poverty. Many depended
on the extra earnings they could glean through contraband trade.[120]

Smuggling and religion were closely linked in the major imperial
conflict that opened the eighteenth century, the War of the Spanish Succession. Here, Curaçao's close, illicit ties with neighboring Venezuela
took a particularly interesting turn, one in which both contraband and
creolization figured prominently. When Spain's ailing Charles II died
with no clear heir, simmering rivalries between European empires broke
out into full-fledged warfare. Many foreign priests in Spanish America,
notably the Jesuits, openly supported the Austrian claimant to the Spanish throne, who was backed by the Dutch and the British. The (ultimately
successful) Bourbon candidate was favored by the Spanish and French
crowns, as well as by high level authorities of the Roman Catholic Church,
including the bishop of Caracas. In 1703, the Crown ordered restrictions
on the movements of foreign clergy, noting with concern that priests un-
obtrusively could hide letters and important documents in their robes.[121]
Many of the clergy who supported the Austrian claimant held respected
positions within local American societies and so were well positioned
and eager to serve as allies in trade with Spain's enemies.[122] Clergy and
other supporters of the Austrian contender saw their sympathies as reflecting local realities and needs, over policies that were being imposed
from across the ocean.

A temporary blockade of Venezuela by supporters of the French
Bourbon contender for the Spanish throne completely suspended all
legitimate commerce to the area, and forced even more people to turn

to contraband. As tensions escalated, intercolonial smuggling circuits became the networks along which information was transmitted. The same vessels which laded contraband goods also carried ideas and news. Both were flagrant violations of the established norms that Spain was trying to enforce. Curaçaoan merchants and sailors who traveled along the coast passed on relevant information between different local groups. Slaving vessels that sailed legitimately to the mainland via the *asiento de negros* proved to be another effective conduit for information. When the situation polarized in Venezuela, Curaçao provided a haven for those who supported the Austrian contender and feared persecution, a refuge from which they could regroup and strategize. The island was the site of organization of several attempted Anglo-Dutch attacks on Venezuela in support of the Austrian claim. Contraband trade with Curaçao thus opened ties with foreigners, served as a conduit for reliable information from Europe, provided asylum to sympathizers from Venezuela, and created an atmosphere for supporting the non-Bourbon contender to the Spanish throne.

Caribbean Entrepôt

In 1680, the editors of a Dutch naval atlas published the second edition of a simple copperplate engraving of Curaçao which included an insert showing Fort Amsterdam and the adjacent settlement. Drawn by Johannes Leupenius in 1676, just a year after the island became a free port, this is the earliest known depiction of the town and the only one from the seventeenth century.[123] The engraving shows a small, dense settlement of approximately twenty-six blocks, tightly clustered just northeast of Fort Amsterdam.[124] Ensconced on the interior shores of St. Anna Bay, the town was well protected. Between it and the sea lay first the sturdy fort complex and then a flat, undeveloped tract of land, which served as a buffer zone and gave garrison soldiers unencumbered sight across the waters toward Tierra Firme. On a clear day, men stationed on the lookout might even see the faint outlines of Coro's hills on the distant horizon. It was almost impossible for a ship to arrive at the port undetected. Vessels were in view of gunners for hours as they approached, then had to sail right past the ramparts, within easy shooting distance, as they navigated the narrow harbor entrance before reaching the docks and wharves along the bay's interior. (Today it is rumored that the hotel which now occupies part of the old fort complex is the only such property in the world to carry marine collision insurance.)

The compact geography of the fort and port facilitated Curaçao's development as a regional trade center. The small town lay immediately adjacent to the wharves. It was surrounded by walls on two sides, one that separated it from Fort Amsterdam to the south and the other on the east. On the north and west it was bounded by water—St. Anna Bay and the Waaigat inlet—providing town residents with easy access to the docks and seacraft. The town's roots as a naval base are patently obvious from the engraving; not only does it abut the garrison, but small fortified towers mark each corner of the walls. Nestled behind the walls and along the inlet, the port and its population were well protected from external threats. At the same time, they also were easily accessible to ships that had been allowed into the protected harbor. Because of the barriers made by the walls and the water, the town was closely confined, with no easy room for expansion. Until the early eighteenth century, the town remained completely contained in this small area. As Leupenius's map also clearly shows, the settlement was well positioned to serve as a trade center. Arriving ships, once they cleared the narrow, well-protected harbor entrance, found ample space to unload their wares on the spacious wharves that lined St. Anna Bay. The harbor's geography was highly conducive to shipping. The level land along both sides was easily turned into mooring sites, with minimal infrastructural requirements. Beyond the bay's long, narrow channel, there opened up the vast, protected Schottegat, which was virtually unaffected by sea currents and shielded from the trade winds. The Schottegat's shores and the small islands that dotted its interior provided additional docking sites. Curaçao soon became known for the quality of its natural harbor. The northern shores of the Schottegat, well past the fort and town, were also the site of some of the island's first rural landholdings, several of them held by Sephardim, as well as the Jewish cemetery.[125] Throughout the last quarter of the seventeenth century, Curaçao's burgeoning role in regional and transatlantic trade boosted the stature of the settlement adjacent to Fort Amsterdam.

The reorganization of the WIC and the decision to open the island to free trade presaged a new era for the emerging town.[126] Perhaps not coincidentally, it is in the years immediately following the island's declaration as a free trade center that the port began to be identified with a specific name, Willemstad, rather than simply as an appendage to the fort.[127] A petition signed by several merchants "of the Jewish nation," in 1680 mentioned "Willemstadt on Curaçao" in the dateline. It is the earliest known reference to the town by name in an official document.[128] The choice of terms probably was not coincidental. Given that the document related to an ongoing dispute the Sephardic traders were having with local government officials, it made sense to distinguish the merchant town from the administrative seat of the WIC. The name Willemstad did not begin appearing regularly in official WIC correspondence out of Curaçao until the early 1700s, however. Datelines on communiqués and laws from the late seventeenth century usually indicate that they were issued from Fort Amsterdam, or simply Curaçao, or sometimes both ("Ft. Amsterdam on Curaçao"), but make no mention of the town.[129] That was legally accurate, since the fort was the seat of government and clearly set off geographically from the town. The earliest known law that specifically mentioned that it originated in Willemstad was signed "in Ft. Amsterdam and Willemstad on Curaçao" on 17 August 1705.[130] The phrase, *in deze haven* ("in this harbor"), also appears frequently in the text of missives as does the term, *de stadt* ("the town").[131] The name Willemstad appeared in the 1715 census but was inconsistently used to refer to the town in written documents until well into the eighteenth century.[132] Island maps from the late seventeenth and early eighteenth centuries clearly depict the town but do not name it.[133]

Increasing use of the name Willemstad by the turn of the century reveals that the town was taking on its own identity separate from the adjacent fort, in whose shadow it had remained for over half a century. But colonial identities are never simple. In a typical colonial irony, the choice of name clearly marked the town's ties to the wider Dutch imperial project, at the very time that it was gaining its own regional stature within the Caribbean. There was a certain geographic literalism in the naming process of the wider harbor area. The Dutch called the area housing Fort Amsterdam and the town *de punt* (literally, "the point"), a clear reference to the fact that they were located on a small peninsula that jutted out into St. Anna Bay. Similarly, the Dutch referred to the land across the bay as *de overzijde*, "the other side" of the harbor. This designation may also have had a colonial character: A district of Amsterdam called *de Overzijde* is located across a wide canal/inlet of the sea from the city center. The area bears enough geographic similarity to the two sides at the entrance to St. Anna Bay that it may have evoked nostalgia among the early Dutch inhabitants. Such references to European places with similar geography were frequent in colonial settlements throughout the Americas.

Demographic data from these transition years are sketchy. In the 1660s and 1670s colonial administrators in the English Caribbean reported that Curaçao's small population totaled between 500 and 800 inhabitants, already with a majority of African descent.[134] From the baptismal records of Manzo and Caldera, we know that there were at least 209 slaves and 15 free blacks and mulattos on the island in 1677, and close to 100 Caquetios. Among the slave owners listed in these baptismal records were 3 free blacks, one of whom was a woman.[135] Additional demographic information for this period is hard to come by.

By the turn of the century, Willemstad had become a thriving entrepôt, linking markets throughout the Caribbean and the Americas to those in Europe, Africa, and beyond. Frigates, brigantines, and other large ships departed regularly from the port for Europe, carrying tobacco, cacao, hides, coffee, indigo, sugar, precious metals, and dyewood from source markets around the region and returned with European manufactures.[136] Smaller vessels connected Willemstad to ports throughout the Caribbean. Owned by island merchants and manned by local sailors, these vessels sustained the island's successful intercolonial trade. The emerging trade boosted the importance of the settlement adjacent to Fort Amsterdam. By the end of the seventeenth century, illicit interimperial trade permeated all levels of Curaçao's economy and society. Besides the prosperous merchants and high-level administrators who were affiliated with the WIC, and the independent Dutch merchants, the majority of Curaçao's inhabitants across the socioeconomic spectrum also worked in maritime-related activities. They continued to trade extensively with the ports of mainland North America. In 1698, a peak year according to colonial authorities, fifteen vessels officially cleared the port of New York for Curaçao.[137] Many more slipped through unofficially.[138] The trade included building materials, provisions, foodstuffs, and merchandise from the north, which were exchanged for horses, slaves, and salt from the Caribbean.

Although the WIC headquarters and the center of its economic activities were located at Fort Amsterdam, the company also owned scattered rural landholdings around the island. Curaçao's so-called plantations did not produce cash crops for export, but rather small amounts of food to be consumed locally by inhabitants and by the enslaved Africans who were in transit to Spanish American markets. The WIC tried, briefly and unsuccessfully, to cultivate cash crops such as cotton and indigo for export.[139] Through the end of the seventeenth century, some rural landholdings also were used to house temporarily the newly arrived human cargo. In 1702, the WIC owned eight rural plantations, which together had a total of 493 slaves, 60 percent of whom were men. These represented 59 percent of the total number of slaves owned by the company; the rest were employed in urban and domestic activities.[140] Originally the WIC held a monopoly on these rural estates. After its role in the transatlantic slave trade peaked, the company began selling some of these holdings to private owners, a process that intensified in the first decades of the eighteenth century. The decline of the company corresponded to a rising prosperity among local merchants who engaged in regional trade. By the eighteenth century, owning a rural estate was a sign of wealth and prestige among Curaçao's merchants, even if the holding itself did not produce significant income.[141] They were also places for families to retreat from the heat and the hustle and bustle of the port. Curaçao's emergence as a Caribbean trade center provided expanded opportunities for its diasporic denizens. Sephardim played a vital role in developing the island's commercial circuits across emerging imperial boundaries. They quickly tapped into developing regional trade networks that some of their itinerant predecessors had helped establish, making a niche for themselves in the island's growing intercolonial commerce. In 1660, Ysaac Pereyra was trading horses between Curaçao and Aruba and selling sugar between several islands, and the Pereira brothers were conducting commerce between Curaçao, Amsterdam, and Honduras. Sephardic men traded extensively with friends and family throughout the Atlantic basin from their earliest years on the island, taking advantage of far-flung contacts throughout the diaspora. Many traveled in their own vessels around the Caribbean for weeks at a time, leaving the community in Willemstad dominated by women.[142]

Sephardim also tried their hand at local agriculture. At least a dozen Sephardim were recorded as owning country estates between 1660 and 1700 in the so-called Joode Quartier (Jewish Quarter), a two-mile area along the inner rim of the Schottegat inlet, well beyond the walled-in town but still protected by the island's defenses that guarded the harbor entrance.[143] In 1682, Jewish planters sold goats and sheep to the island governor to feed slaves owned by the WIC. Gabriel Levy and Aron Levy Maduro each purchased a plantation from the company that included unlimited rights to pasture livestock in spite of the fact that the company held a monopoly on this activity.[144] Others tried their hand at cash crops such as sugarcane, tobacco, and cotton, as well as produce for local consumption. But droughts were an ongoing problem, occurring several times a decade.[145] This, combined with the overall poor quality of the soil, greatly limited the productivity of agricultural holdings, and thus their economic viability. Curaçao's Sephardic community thrived in the open trade economy. The group drew up its earliest internal regulations in 1671, and received its first full-time rabbi in 1674.[146] By the last quarter of the seventeenth century, the island was home to the largest and most prosperous Jewish settlement in the Americas, a distinction it would retain through the first quarter of the nineteenth century.[147] Steady immigration was fueled by the island's reputation for tolerance, as part of the Dutch realm. Contact among friends, associates, and relatives in the emerging Sephardic Atlantic networks provided another incentive. In 1685, a group of Jews arrived from Martinique, fleeing increased religious repression in the French orbit following Louis XIV's revocation of the Edict of Nantes. Immigrants also continued to arrive regularly from Amsterdam.[148] Although there are no precise demographic figures for these early years, a new synagogue that was constructed on the island in 1696 held enough seats for 200 men and boys and 80 women.[149] The fact that it was the island's fifth synagogue in less than half a century testifies to the steady growth and solvency of the Jewish community from its earliest days. Curaçao's tax list of 1702 included 101 Jewish families.[150] Isaac and Suzanne Emmanuel calculated that another 25 Sephardic families were too poor to pay taxes, raising the total to 126 families.[151]

Curaçao's black majority also developed their own regional networks in this period, shaped by their own particular circumstances. If Sephardim found a certain economic freedom by participating in the regional contraband economy, people of African descent sometimes found a more basic and literal human freedom by smuggling themselves. Enslaved people regularly fled Curaçao to Tierra Firme from the earliest years of Dutch tenure, following routes that had been well established by the area's indigenous peoples long before the arrival of Europeans. Company documents mention fugitive slaves as a problem as early as 1638.[152] Apparently already by then local authorities in Venezuela were dealing with extraterritorial fugitives.[153] In May 1644, just ten years after the Dutch took the island, Governor Stuyvesant happened upon several "Negroes and Mulattoes who had begun to build a raft near the east point while we were on a cruise, and had almost completed it in order to go to the mainland."[154] Ten years later, Governor Rodenburch complained that a black who was sent to repair the town's fort instead had "run away from here to the mainland with a canoe."[155] In 1657 Governor Beck noted that a plan for "a good quantity of Negroes" to steal a boat and escape from one of the island's sheltered southern bays had been narrowly avoided. "Every evening we have to secure our boat and other small vessels with a chain, no matter how poor their condition," Governor Beck complained, "in order to prevent Negroes or whites from being able to make off with them."[156] Women as well as men occasionally fled the island by sea. The four anonymous black women who perished in the waters between Curaçao and Tierra Firme in 1688 may well have been slaves who were seeking their freedom on the mainland.[157] Fugitive slaves took full advantage of and further developed the contacts between the island and the nearby mainland, which dated from pre-Columbian times, and which were expanded by the contraband trade in human beings and other commodities. They were not oblivious to the wider geopolitical context in which they moved. Sometimes they were able to seize the opportunity to capitalize on political and economic rivalries between the Dutch and Spanish. The group of would-be runaways that authorities captured in 1644 intended "to go to the mainland to reveal our departure and the weakness of the fort," according to Governor Stuyvesant.[158]

If they had come to the island by force, and remained there under duress, then those who left voluntarily (as opposed to those who were forcibly exported as commodities) did so in an effort to obtain their freedom. Marronage (slaves' flight to freedom) from Curaçao increased in the final decades of the seventeenth century, facilitated by the consolidation of illicit interimperial trade routes, with nearby Tierra Firme the most accessible destination. Increased shipping expanded opportunities to flee, as dozens of seacraft began sailing regularly between Curaçao and the mainland. Many ship captains were not inclined to inquire too closely as to the credentials of all their passengers, and might be paid to accept a few stowaways. The regular flow of human beings strengthened ties between the two areas, despite the fact that they officially belonged to separate and rival imperial spheres. The area around Coro, at the base of the Paraguaná Peninsula, was a particularly favorite destination for Afro-Curaçaoans who sought to escape enslavement, just as it was a magnet for illicit intercolonial commerce. This was not a coincidence. Traders and fugitives alike took advantage of the favorable geography, which facilitated contact. Ocean currents and trade winds alike flowed toward the southwest, pushing vessels that departed from Curaçao's shores directly to the base of the Paraguaná Peninsula. Perhaps unknowingly, fugitive Afro-Curaçaoans were following the paths of indigenous peoples who had traveled freely between the two areas since pre-Columbian times. As a smuggling center already by the 1650s, frequented by small-scale merchants and seafarers, Coro offered rich and varied opportunities for runaways. New arrivals found ample opportunities to work in contraband and to become part of local networks.[159] Already by the 1680s, local authorities were complaining that slaves in Tierra Firme were actively involved in contraband trade with the Dutch island.[160] Authorities in Coro caught fourteen runaway Curaçaoan slaves in 1690, and thirty more in 1702.[161] Twenty-three more arrived in Coro in 1703.[162] By 1704, there were so many fugitive Afro-Curaçaoans living in the area around Coro that the local government considered rounding them up and centralizing them in a special, newly created town.[163] Such marronage would skyrocket throughout the eighteenth century.

Sephardim and people of African descent found different options open before them in the emerging Dutch colonial slave society and in the developing Caribbean contraband economy. During the years that the West India Company ruled Curaçao, members of both Atlantic diaspora groups played a pivotal role in sustaining Curaçao's maritime economy and ensuring Curaçao's success as a regional trade hub. As they encountered each other at home in the port of Willemstad, on board seacraft, and in their forays to markets around the Caribbean, they interacted with each other in dynamic processes of creolization, which shaped the very character of local society. By the late seventeenth century, both diasporic groups were poised to become an integral part of Curaçao's maritime economy and society, as the island shifted from a naval base to a full-fledged trade center. Both groups played vital and overlapping, if different, roles in this process, which played out with particular intensity in the port city of Willemstad and in contacts with Tierra Firme.

The War of the Spanish Succession ushered in a new era in European, imperial, and Atlantic dynamics. The war was a watershed for imperial relations in the Atlantic and Caribbean. By its conclusion, the English and French had consolidated their positions as the premier imperial powers. The Dutch were well past their prime as a dominant power, relegated to a decidedly secondary position, although they continued to play a major role in global and intercolonial trade. England's success ultimately in wrestling control of the *asiento de negros* from France was a major victory, consolidated in the Treaty of Utrecht. The asiento opened possibilities for expanding British commerce with Spanish American colonies, both legitimate and illicit, well beyond the trade in enslaved human beings.[164] By the end of the war, the British had consolidated important political and economic victories in the development of their overseas empire. During the war, their vessels had an increased presence around the Caribbean, well beyond areas in which they exercised political jurisdiction. This included the waters between Curaçao and Tierra Firme, which the Dutch had treated as their own for decades.[165] In early 1702, the governor of Jamaica reprimanded the Dutch for having a warship off the Venezuelan coast near Puerto Cabello, and trading with the enemy in wartime.[166] A year later, in 1703, the English seized several Dutch sloops that were trading with Tierra Firme, and again chastised the Dutch for trading with the Spanish.[167] French privateers also plied these waters.[168] Traders in Curaçao and Tierra Firme continued to develop their own close ties with each other, but increasingly they also had to take into account the presence of English and French vessels in regional waters, which sometimes complicated matters. The new actors added new elements to the traditional rivalry between the Dutch and the Spanish for control of the area.

The war, and the concomitant shifting imperial dynamics, had a major impact on Curaçao in the first decade of the eighteenth century. Smuggling thrived during the war, providing expanded opportunities for everyone who worked in the island's maritime trade economy.[169] French control of the *asiento de negros* during most of the war created distribution problems for slave traders in Curaçao, who sometimes found themselves with a surplus of hundreds of human commodities waiting on the island for weeks or months at a time, and the related challenges of meeting their basic needs.[170] Dealing first with the French representatives of the asiento, and later with the British, added another layer of negotiations in trade with Tierra Firme. Geopolitical alliances that were brokered and held fast in Europe often played out very differently in the waters of the Caribbean. For example, even while the Dutch States General officially was at war with the French and Spanish in Europe, the West India Company and affiliated merchants traded openly with these same powers in the Caribbean via its base in Curaçao.[171] Such a disjuncture between official imperial policy and on-the-ground colonial reality would become standard during the wars of the eighteenth century. It signaled a maturation of colonial identities and interests independent of those of the distant motherlands, based partly on simple and pragmatic economics.

By the turn of the century, the Dutch were well past their peak on the world and Atlantic stages, even as Curaçao was assuming an increasingly important role in regional commerce. Historians debate the extent to which the Dutch overseas project in the eighteenth century fits the classic imperial model.[172] Clearly, by the last quarter of the seventeenth century, the Dutch increasingly focused on maritime commercial networks rather than on territorial control. Whether this in itself is sufficient grounds for questioning their status as an imperial power is debatable, however. As Lauren Benton has argued, territorial control often was an "incidental aim of imperial expansion" in the age of European overseas expansion.[173] There is no doubt that, in the few areas where the Dutch maintained political jurisdiction, their role and manner of governance closely resembled that of other European powers, even if they exercised control via a centralized merchant federation rather than through a hegemonic, monarchical state. How much different this made on the ground is arguable. At the same time, the company's commercial structure, networks, and manner of operating provided specific opportunities for those who lived within its orbit, especially via intercolonial trade.

Curaçao is the leading example of how this played out. By the end of the seventeenth century, the island had proved its value as a Caribbean and Atlantic commercial center at multiple levels. Over several decades, the small settlement adjacent to Fort Amsterdam was transformed from a small military outpost into a vibrant regional port, one that depended on its dynamic diasporic denizens as well as on the continuing commercial connections of its European administrators and elites. The port's inhabitants further developed their regional ties, especially to the nearby Spanish America mainland. In many ways these were stronger than the links they had with the Netherlands across the Atlantic. Even with the relative decline of the Dutch as a major world power, Curaçao's heterogeneous population was well positioned to take advantage of new opportunities that developed in the emerging Atlantic commercial system. Throughout the eighteenth century, the island's very character would be formed by its multiple, overlapping, and sometimes conflicting roles in Caribbean, Dutch, and Atlantic exchange circuits. Within the port of Willemstad and also in the networks its inhabitants developed with Tierra Firme and beyond, Curaçao's role in illicit intercolonial commerce opened up opportunities for sociocultural exchanges well beyond the economic sphere. During the eighteenth century, the island's diverse inhabitants would continue to cruise to the most advantageous places, largely with the approval of the WIC, but they would do so increasingly on their own terms and with their own interests foremost.

PART II

SOCIOCULTURAL INTERACTIONS IN A MARITIME TRADE ECONOMY

On 1 September 1753, Captain Mosseh Henriques Cotino freed a male slave named Primero, one of forty-two manumissions that were recorded in Willemstad that year. But this was no routine emancipation. A note at the bottom of the document indicated that the freedom paper was "granted pro forma to sail."[1] It would be revoked when Primero returned to port. Henriques Cotino was a prominent member of the local Sephardic community and treasurer of the synagogue. He owned at least ten sailing vessels at midcentury, which he used to trade around the Caribbean.[2] Maritime trade was so important to Henriques Cotino that his 1762 tombstone in Curaçao's Beth Haim cemetery bears a carving of a two-masted sailing ship.[3] Six years earlier, on 27 July 1747, Mosseh's brother, Abraham Henriques Cotino, had freed a slave named Mattheuw using the exact same wording.[4] On 6 November 1760 another Sephardic merchant, Aron Henriques Moron, freed one of his twenty slaves, Juan Domingo, upon payment of two hundred pesos. Again, using almost identical language, Juan Domingo's freedom papers stated that they were "given pro forma so that he be allowed to sail."[5] Henriques Moron had become one of the island's most prosperous ship owners and shipping insurance agents after he arrived in Curaçao in 1730. At midcentury he owned over two dozen vessels, which he regularly rented to other Sephardim to use in trade around the region.[6] Henriques Moron was also a prominent member of the synagogue, where he served in several governing positions.[7] As well-established merchants, Henriques Moron and the Henriques Cotino brothers knew firsthand the risks association with maritime trade. French privateers seized three of Mosseh Henriques Cotino's vessels in 1747; ten years later the English confiscated another.[8] Aron Henriques Moron's maritime business teetered as English and Spanish privateers repeatedly attacked both the vessels he owned and those he insured. The year he manumitted Juan Domingo, Henriques Moron paid 7,000 pesos to an English privateer supposedly for the return of the *Abigail*, although the vessel itself was only registered as being worth 550 pesos.[9] (The payment was likely for contraband goods that he had purchased from the English.)

The temporary manumissions of Juan Domingo, Mattheuw, and Primero were not isolated cases. Between 1741 and 1776 Curaçaoan merchants freed at least 153 slaves temporarily so they could go to sea, bestowing on them a peculiar intermediary legal status between freedom and enslavement that was revoked once the sailors returned to port.[10] The circumstances that allowed for this form of quasi-freedom reveal much about the particular role of Curaçao's port city of Willemstad as a Dutch entrepôt situated in Caribbean and Atlantic maritime commercial systems. Within the port two conflicting socioeconomic regimes coexisted and sometimes clashed with each other—one based on free trade and the other based on enslaved labor. Willemstad's rising merchant class and the West India Company authorities grappled with the contradictions of living and working in a place that was bound by the conventions of a colonial American slave society even while the economy was based on intercolonial trade, which required the free movement of commodities, vessels, and workers (many of whom were enslaved). This dichotomy had an impact on the port, well beyond the economic realm, as it developed throughout the eighteenth century. Willemstad was simultaneously a Dutch entrepôt and a Caribbean port city, and these dual roles shaped the very character of town life.

Caribbean and Atlantic Entrepôt

As a center of free trade Willemstad occupied a vital role in the Caribbean and Atlantic port systems, alongside its position in the Dutch imperial structure. Although the WIC was well past its prime by the eighteenth century, Curaçao did well as the company's colonial seat in the Americas. Willemstad was an integral part of a wider trade and communications system. The port received and dispatched a constant flow of people and information as well as commodities and ships

FIGURE 2. Van Walbeek's sketches of Curaçao in 1634 included the harbor entrance, St. Anna Bay, and a plan for a simple pentagonal fort on the Point. (National Archives of the Netherlands VEL 595)

FIGURE 3. This 1640 Dutch map shows sites of springs and Spanish settlements, with livestock roaming the entire countryside. (Leiden University Library COLLBN Port 63 N 21)

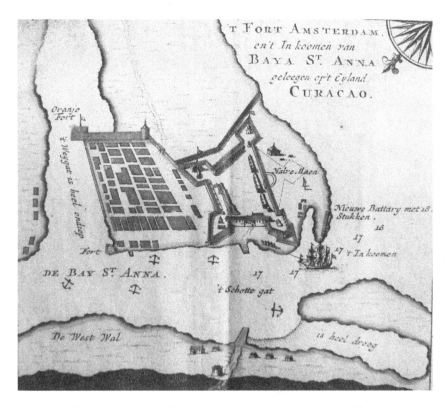

FIGURE 4. Leupenius's 1676 image was reproduced on maps well after
Willemstad expanded, including this one from 1715. (Leiden University
Library COLLBN 001-11-082)

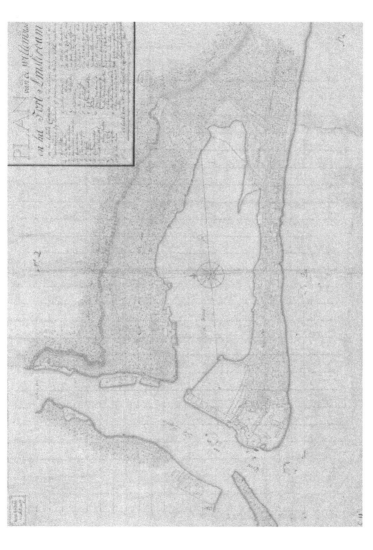

FIGURE 5. Typically, this 1742 map of Willemstad has rich detail for the Point and environs, but ignores the Other Side, then the port's largest and most populous neighborhood. (Leiden University Library COLLBN 002-09-020)

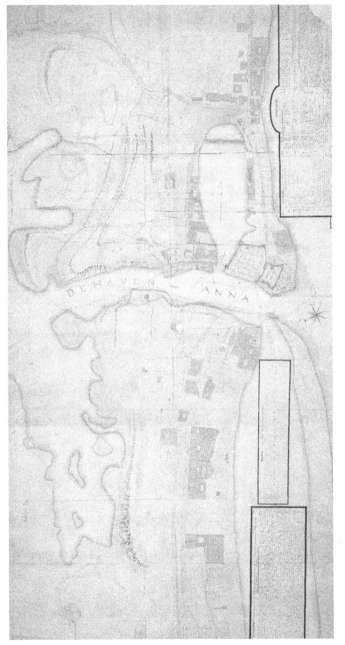

FIGURE 6. Geertz's 1754 map of Willemstad is one of the few that fully depicts Otrobanda, then the largest neighborhood. (National Archives of the Netherlands VEL 1454)

FIGURE 7. The small, sheltered coves on Curaçao's calm southern coast easily accommodated small seacraft. (Courtesy of Ellen Spijkstra)

FIGURE 8. The island's rocky north shore is pounded by vigorous waves and currents and was inhospitable to sailing vessels. (Courtesy of Jan Beaujon)

FIGURE 9. Curaçao was too arid to support plantation agriculture. (Courtesy of Ellen Spijkstra)

FIGURE 10. St. Anna Bay and the Point, as seen from the Other Side. (Courtesy of Ellen Spijkstra)

FIGURE 11. Ft. Amsterdam, at the harbor entrance, was both the seat of government and headquarters of the Dutch West India Company. (Courtesy of KITLV/Royal Netherlands Institute of Southeast Asian and Caribbean Studies)

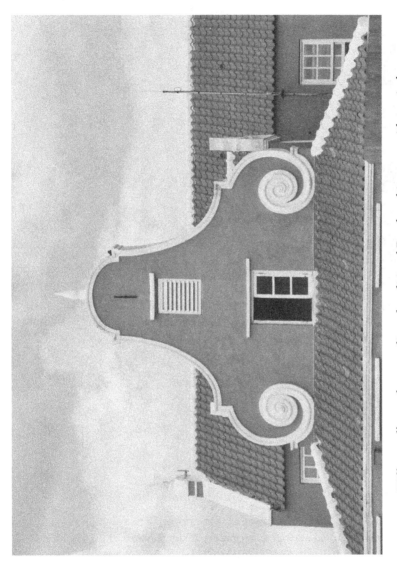

FIGURE 12. Willemstad's merchants replicated traditional Dutch architecture, with tropical modifications. (Courtesy of Jan Beaujon)

FIGURE 13. The new synagogue was completed in 1743 and is still home to an active congregation. (Courtesy of KITLV/Royal Netherlands Institute of Southeast Asian and Caribbean Studies)

FIGURE 14. The image of sailing vessels on many Sephardic gravestones is clear indication of the important role this group had in the island's trade. (Courtesy of KITLV/Royal Netherlands Institute of Southeast Asian and Caribbean Studies)

FIGURE 15 The neighborhood of Pietermaai developed along the southern coast, just east of the walled town. (Courtesy of KITLV/Royal Netherlands Institute of Southeast Asian and Caribbean Studies)

FIGURE 16. Rural estates like Landhuis Kenepa (site of the 1795 slave uprising) were primarily a status symbol for the island's merchant elite. (Courtesy of the author)

FIGURE 17. Coro's isolated desert coast attracted traders and runaway slaves from Curaçao. (Courtesy of the author)

FIGURE 18. The dense mangrove swamps around Tucacas and elsewhere provided excellent cover for contraband trade. (Courtesy of the author)

FIGURE 19. Architecture in Puerto Cabello and other Venezuelan coastal towns shows a clear Dutch influence, evidence of the close ties with Curaçao. (Courtesy of the author)

FIGURE 20. José Caridad Gonzalez, a fugitive slave from Curaçao, has become a Venezuelan folk hero for his supposed role in the 1795 uprising. (Courtesy of the author)

that circulated around the Caribbean and beyond. The island's inhabitants forged commercial ties throughout the Caribbean, the Americas, and the wider Atlantic world. Unlike most other Caribbean port cities, Willemstad was exclusively a regional transshipment center rather than the international nexus for local plantations. Intercolonial and transatlantic trade out of the port, Curaçao's only urban settlement, drove the entire island economy. Nevertheless, Willemstad's growth in the eighteenth century was similar to that of regional ports that were tied more directly to a local plantation economy, such as Charlestown, South Carolina, and Bridgetown, Barbados.[11] Town residents from every socioeconomic sector depended on this trade for their very survival. Curaçao had no landed gentry or planter class. Instead, the island's most powerful denizens were urban merchants who were tied to extra-island trade. Similarly, slavery centered on maritime commerce. Virtually all the products that were handled on the docks were unloaded from vessels that came from elsewhere—from other Caribbean islands, from the mainlands of North and South America (especially Tierra Firme), and from across the Atlantic.

Throughout the eighteenth century Curaçao's transatlantic trade was based on seven major colonial commodities—cacao, sugar, coffee, tobacco, indigo, dyewood, and hides—as well as small amounts of other American agricultural products. All of these were obtained from a robust contraband trade with the American colonies of rival European powers. Tierra Firme produced the lion's share of cacao, tobacco, and hides. Sugar and indigo came especially from the French islands, with lesser quantities from the English islands. Dyewood came primarily from Central America.[12] Trade was highly volatile, and dependent on the interrelated factors of geopolitics and the vicissitudes of the Atlantic economy. Precise statistics are hard to come by. The total value of Curaçao's trade to the Netherlands in the first half of the century was approximately 68 million guilders, and averaged 1.2 million guilders per year.[13] During the first quarter of the eighteenth century the Dutch transit trade via Curaçao was worth between 10 and 15 million guilders, which represented half the total value of all Dutch Atlantic commerce in this period.[14] The average annual value fluctuated from a low of about 900,000 guilders per year (during both the War of the Spanish Succession and the Seven Years' War), to a high of just over 2 million guilders per year in the 1740s (during the War of Jenkins's Ear). The trade was rather more constant during the 1710s, '20s, and '30s, when it averaged just over 1 million guilders per year.[15] Curaçao's transatlantic trade was highest throughout the 1740s, peaking at 5.6 million guilders in 1748. In spite of these fluctuations, the overall value of Curaçao's trade to the Netherlands rose steadily throughout the century, from approximately 9.7 million guilders in the first decade to over 25 million guilders by the 1740s, an increase of 39 percent.[16] Trade to the Netherlands continued to rise in the second half of the century (when trade statistics are less complete), to an average annual value of 2.75 million guilders, more than double the average of the first half of the century.[17]

By far the single most important commodity shipped from Curaçao to the Netherlands was cacao. Virtually all of it came from Tierra Firme. Cacao exports represented 55 percent of the value of Curaçao's total shipping to the Netherlands in the first half of the eighteenth century.[18] Island merchants transported an average of 1.4 million pounds of cacao per year in the first five decades of the eighteenth century, reaching a high of 2.6 million pounds per year in the 1740s. In the same period they exported an average of 1 million pounds of hides per year, 883,000 pounds of dyewood, and 351,000 pounds of tobacco.[19] Venezuelan tobacco was less important than that of Virginia for the total Dutch transatlantic trade. However, it was the second most valuable export from Tierra Firme to Curaçao. There were many varieties of different taste and quality. Especially coveted was Venezuela's Barinas tobacco, which the Netherlands reexported around Europe.[20] Seventy-two percent of all the hides shipped across the Atlantic from Curaçao in the first half of the eighteenth century came from Tierra Firme. The rest came from Santo Domingo (24 percent), Cuba (2 percent), and very small quantities from Puerto Rico, Rio de la Hacha, and Jamaica.[21] Vessels returned with a variety of European manufactures to be redistributed throughout the region. Rather less is known about the Dutch commodities that were shipped to the island, mostly for reexport, especially to Tierra Firme. A variety of textiles seems to have predominated, especially linens, as well as some cottons, silk, and lace.[22] Other European products included various types of alcohol, ironwares, housewares, tools, spices, arms, and gunpowder.[23]

The vessels that sailed across the Atlantic were larger and sturdier, with more complicated riggings, than those that engaged in regional commerce. They required larger crews and much more space for provisions and cargo. Most were frigates, but they also included brigantines, snows, and the occasional two-masted howker. According to Wim Klooster a total of 791 merchantmen sailed from Curaçao to the Netherlands between 1701 and 1755, an average of 14 to 15 vessels per year, ranging from a low of 7 (in 1703, 1704, and 1754) to a high of 29 (1749).[24] Of these, 86 percent went to Amsterdam, 13 percent to various ports in Zeeland, and less than 1 percent to Rotterdam.[25] The average annual tonnage of the vessels making the Atlantic crossing in this period was 2,330. This remained fairly consistent throughout the first half of the century, with a low of 1,863 between 1701 and 1710 and a high of 3,248 in the 1740s. In two typical years at midcentury, a total of 360 vessels arrived and 333 departed in 1743 (a relatively prosperous year), compared to 233 vessels in and 310 out in 1755 (a depression year).[26] Incoming traffic clearly was more influenced by economic vicissitudes than was shipping that originated from the island. The transatlantic traffic became more intense in the second half of the century, especially in war years, most notably during the Seven Years' War. For example, between 1759 and 1761, 49, 39, and 62 vessels made the crossing, respectively; the peak year may well have been 1783, with 80 vessels.[27] (Transatlantic shipping records from Curaçao are virtually nonexistent after the 1760s.)

Trade with the Netherlands was just a fraction of the total vessel traffic into Curaçao, although the overall tonnage was substantially larger. In peak years well over a thousand vessels officially called at the Willemstad harbor.[28] This did not include the numerous unregistered small craft that traded regionally. Most of the commodities that were obtained in the regional traffic were subsequently shipped across the Atlantic. The West India Company accounted for only a small proportion of Dutch trade in the region, much of which was carried out by smaller firms and individual merchants.[29] According to Wim Klooster, most Dutch transatlantic trade was in the hands of independent merchants who were not affiliated with the WIC.[30] Most of the island's regional trade, while fully sanctioned by the Dutch, violated the mercantilist policies of other European powers. This did not go unnoticed by the relevant authorities. In 1725 the lieutenant governor of Bermuda complained that "pyracys and illegal trade has been the custom" of the Dutch islands, and noted that Curaçao was a port "where they always are well receiv'd without any questions ask'd."[31] These officials also were well aware of the widespread economic benefit of such trade for their denizens, in spite of its illegality. "There is hardly any Plantation in America that belongs to H. M. but has a correspondence with Curaoa [sic], and not many but what have raised themselves by it," the British Council of Trade and Plantations in the Americas lamented in 1711.[32]

Sixty-five years later, observing the prosperity of the two Dutch Caribbean entrepôts, Curaçao and St. Eustatius, Adam Smith noted that "this freedom, in the midst of better colonies whose ports are open to those of one nation only, has been the great cause of the prosperity of those two barren islands."[33] St. Eustatius (or Statia) was Curaçao's counterpart to the north. Significantly smaller than Curaçao, both physically and demographically, Statia had an area of just twenty-one square kilometers and a total population of 1,245 in 1720 (which increased to 7,830 by 1789), over one half of whom were slaves.[34] Its small size and barren, rocky landscape made Statia even less suited to agriculture than Curaçao. By the early eighteenth century trade had eclipsed agriculture as the foundation of the island's economy.[35] Unlike Curaçao, Statia also lacked good natural harbors, meaning that lading had to be done offshore with canoes and launches, a labor-intensive task that was at the mercy of weather and seas. Throughout the second half of the seventeenth century, the period when Curaçao was developing as a regional trade center, Statia passed repeatedly between the French and English, before finally returning to the control of the West India Company.[36] Statia's location, nestled among the many small islands of the eastern Caribbean, gave it a particular trade advantage with English and French possessions, with which its merchants conducted a vigorous contraband trade, similar to Curaçao's illicit relationship with Tierra Firme. The many wars of the eighteenth century were a boon to Statia's commerce. The War of Jenkins's Ear stimulated the island's contraband trade with the English and French islands, as it boosted Curaçao's trade with Tierra Firme. Unlike Curacao, Statia's commerce also got a similar boost from the Seven Years' War (1756–63). Its trade with British North America grew significantly after midcentury and was especially intense during the American War of Independence.[37] Compared to Curaçao, Statia's merchants conducted much more intra-Caribbean trade.[38]

Throughout the eighteenth century both islands exported large quantities of the same seven colonial agricultural commodities to the Netherlands. Most of these were obtained illicitly from the possessions of rival powers. The combined value of the transatlantic trade from the two barren islands, virtually all of it contraband, consistently outstripped that of the locally grown products that were sent to the Netherlands by the Dutch plantation colony of Suriname. (The only exception was the 1760s, when Suriname's trade averaged 53 percent of total Dutch transatlantic trade with its colonies.)[39] This was due, in part, to the fact that the Dutch, unlike their competitors, did not give preferential treatment to plantation products from their own colonies. Thus, Surinamese cacao, cotton, and sugar had to compete with the same products from English and French colonies that were shipped via Curaçao and Statia.[40] Between 1738 and 1751 (the only years for which there are relatively complete trade statistics for both islands), the annual value of Curaçao's exports to the Netherlands outstripped that of Statia every year except 1746, and Curaçao's total for the period was greater by a factor of almost two to one (26.9 million vs. 13.8 million guilders).[41] Owing in no small part to the opportunities that were created by the War of Jenkins's Ear (1739–48), Curaçao's share of the total transatlantic trade peaked in the 1740s, when it reached an average of 3.4 million guilders per year, compared to 1.3 million for Statia. The roles were almost completely reversed the following decade.

Beginning in the 1750s, and continuing throughout the second half of the century, Statia's trade to the Netherlands surpassed that of Curaçao, even while that of the latter continued to increase overall. In 1779 Statia exported over 457,000 pounds of cacao and 766,000 pounds of hides.[42] By 1780 it had become the Netherlands's single greatest source of tobacco, even though Curaçao had exported six times as much tobacco as Statia in the 1740s.[43] By the 1770s Statia had earned the nickname, the "Golden Rock."[44] But the contraband trade had a seedy side; Statia attracted "the scum of many nations," according to one historian, and the island had no regular police force, making for an ad hoc enforcement of laws, at best; outright theft was a serious problem.[45] In contrast to Curaçao, Sephardim had an insignificant role in Statia's trade—or that of any of the Dutch Leeward islands—and they had little impact on local society in general.[46] Statia's regional trade burgeoned to supply the transatlantic trade, especially contraband with nearby English and French islands.

Statia's regional trade went hand in hand with a marked Anglicizing of local culture, including language, reflecting the island's insertion into British colonial trade networks. Throughout the second half of the 1700s, English edged out Dutch as the preferred vernacular, and there was a corresponding decline in the Dutch influence on architecture, religion, and cultural life in general.[47] Saba and St. Maarten went through a similar Anglicizing process on local culture, language, and architecture.[48] In contrast, the Dutch retained a major economic and cultural presence on the small Danish entrepôts in the northeastern Caribbean. As late as 1765 the Dutch remained the largest European group on St.

Thomas, where they outnumbered Danes two to one. There were also many Dutch on the other Danish entrepôt, St. John.[49] Their influence extended far beyond the economic realm. By the eighteenth century inhabitants had developed a creole language that was based on Dutch (rather than Danish) and several African tongues.[50]

None of the other Dutch islands came close to Curaçao and Statia in economic importance. The inhabitants of St. Maarten engaged in some regional trade, although commerce never surpassed agriculture in importance. Saba's economy remained agricultural.[51] By the mid-eighteenth century, both Aruba and Bonaire had assumed important supporting roles in Curaçao's trade. Sparsely populated Bonaire had warehouses for storing contraband from Tierra Firme and was frequently and surreptitiously visited by Spanish American traders. Aruba similarly served as a way station, especially for trade with Nueva Granada to the west.[52] Both islands had plenty of undeveloped land for grazing and thus were convenient for temporarily putting up mules to be shipped to French and English islands.[53]

The Port beyond the Fort

Spurred by the island's role in regional and transatlantic commerce, the town of Willemstad underwent a major transition in the first decades of the eighteenth century, from being a mere appendage of the adjacent military base to assuming an independent identity as a full-fledged Caribbean port city. Willemstad's role in regional commerce shaped its physical growth. Fort Amsterdam, guarding the harbor entrance, continued to anchor political and economic power, as both the seat of government and the headquarters of the West India Company. (Even today, the renovated fort complex houses the offices and the official residence of the island's governor.) But the motor of the economy lay outside the narrow confines of the fort, in the bustling, cosmopolitan port. The burgeoning intercolonial trade transformed Willemstad. It became a vibrant nexus in the Caribbean maritime system that was an integral part of complex webs of trade and communications that stretched around the region and beyond. The port received and dispatched a constant flow of people, information, and commodities that arrived on the many incoming vessels.[54] Willemstad's transformation into a thriving Caribbean and Atlantic port included a demographic diversification in which race/ethnicity and religion played central roles. Well-established merchants associated with the West India Company dominated the large-scale transatlantic commerce, while small-scale traders of a variety of ethnicities, including members of the island's two major diaspora groups, were active in regional trade. Sephardic Jews were a rising merchant class. People of African descent, enslaved and free, provided the labor to run the port and were the majority of the population. Women also were the majority of the population by the first decade of the eighteenth century.[55] This was typical for early modern seaports in the Caribbean and beyond; for example, both Bridgetown, Barbados, and Bermuda had female majorities around the same time.[56]

Although demographic information is incomplete, existing records provide a glimpse into the size and character of Willemstad's population in the early years of the century.[57] In 1702 there were 353 residents who were successful enough to pay income tax, a number that rose to 377 five years later.[58] Willemstad clearly was the lifeblood of Curaçao's economy; 80 percent of the island's taxpayers lived in town.[59] In 1709, 687 white people were registered as living inside the town walls, in 217 different households. Just over half of the inhabitants were adults.[60] The rise of the Sephardic merchant class is evident: In 1707 five of the top eight taxpayers were Jewish; Sephardim made up 28 percent of the taxpayers but contributed 35 percent of total taxes.[61] Sephardim headed 39 percent of Willemstad's households, outnumbering those of other whites, and represented about one third of the total white population. Sephardic merchants were far more likely than other whites to be part of households that included women and children. Within Jewish households men slightly outnumbered women.[62] Overall, women were 60 percent of the port's population but only 16 percent of the registered heads of household.[63] However, with many men temporarily away at sea for extended periods of time, women likely were the de facto heads of many more households. Almost half of the female heads-of-household were widows, and 11 percent of the taxpayers in 1702 were widows (forty women). Women also were significant property owners in town, although not in equal proportion to their total numbers. Twenty-five percent of Willemstad's houses were owned by women (85 percent of whom were widows).[64]

The maritime economy influenced the port's demography. Among those earning enough money to be taxed in 1702 were a sailmaker, two ship masters, a carpenter, and two tailors, indicating that maritime-related trades could pay a decent wage.[65] Eighteen percent of Willemstad's households were entirely male.[66] The small average size of households

(3.2 people per residence) is particularly noteworthy, due, in part, to the relatively large number of one and two person households.[67] Many merchants and sailors did not set up large households with numerous dependents, even if they lived on the island long enough to establish a residence and be counted. In 1715, at least five dwellings were used as multiple residences, and their occupants were listed as "various."[68] These may well have been boarding houses for sailors and other itinerant visitors, which would be expected near the wharves of a port city. It is possible that one or more was a brothel. Commerce also affected the look of the town. Within the small, walled town, commerce and residence were closely intertwined. Following Dutch tradition, the lower floors of merchants' homes were used as a warehouse, offices, and store, and families lived on the upper levels. By the first years of the eighteenth century free blacks were making their presence felt in the port. Occasionally they made it into the official records. In 1702, four people who were identified as free blacks earned enough money to pay taxes: a woman named Marta, and three men—Nicolaas (a tailor), Juan Bastiaan, and Nicolaas Morena. All of them paid two pesos in taxes, which was twice the minimum amount.[69] Some free blacks already owned slaves by this time. They occasionally appear as buyers in the records of the regular auctions that were held to dispose of slaves who could not be sold on the regional market. In May 1703, a black man named Anthonij purchased a slave woman for 100 pesos, a relatively high price.[70] Later that year a free black woman named Clara bought two slaves in another auction.[71] The 1715 tax list of slave owners identified men named Juan, Domingo, and Anthonij among the taxpayers (all common names among people of African descent, but not among Europeans), as well as two free black women, named Grasie and Martha, both of whom paid two pesos, and a woman named Dominga, who paid three pesos in slave taxes.[72] Although Dominga is not identified as a free black in the 1715 slave tax list, there is powerful circumstantial evidence that she was. A free black woman of the same name appears in the town housing list of the same year as the owner of two residences.[73] At least one of these may have had a commercial function as a bar, store, inn, brothel, or perhaps a combination. It was common practice to identify women of African descent only by their first names, while white women were dignified with a surname. Several more names of owners that appear in this slave tax list, while not explicitly identified as free blacks, are names commonly associated with people of African descent in that period. For example, the list includes five different

Juans and three different Domingos, all of whom paid minimum slave taxes, indicating that they owned only a few chattel. Such references to Willemstad's black majority are relatively rare, however. The censuses provide essentially no information about the free blacks and slaves who lived in outbuildings around the established houses or in settlements just outside the walled area. These households were ignored by the census takers. Their residences are also missing from town maps of the period, as are any settlements outside the walled area. Also missing are accurate records of the port's large itinerant population, including sailors, visiting merchants, visiting priests, and the motley assortment of transients who did not have a permanent residence.[74] At the other end of the socioeconomic spectrum, the numbers and descriptions also do not include the area inside the fort, which housed the residences of West India Company officials, high-ranking members of the military, clergy employees of the Dutch Reformed Church, and the families, domestic slaves, and support personnel for all these groups. The fort complex is, however, portrayed in detail on some town maps.[75]

The walled town was filled to capacity by the second decade of the eighteenth century. Its twenty-seven small square blocks were tightly packed with 218 tall, narrow buildings, which closely resembled those that lined the canals of Amsterdam.[76] No new buildings were constructed in the area between 1709 and 1715.[77] That Willemstad remained well protected behind its walls but had little room for further construction is visually evident from a map published in 1715 by the prestigious Dutch mapmaking firm, van Keulen.[78] As the population continued to grow, options were limited: tear down the walls, move them, or allow settlement outside their perimeter. Authorities missed an opportunity to enlarge the enclosed area when part of a wall crumbled in 1690 and they rebuilt it in exactly the same place.[79] The walls were repaired again in 1702–3 and periodically throughout the eighteenth century.[80] Throughout the eighteenth century authorities drew up several detailed town expansion plans, the first one as early as 1705–7, but apparently they never were carried out.[81] Instead, Willemstad expanded into three new districts over the coming decades. The Point remained the port's economic center and home to many members of the merchant elite. Fort Amsterdam continued to anchor economic and political power. (By the end of the eighteenth century this area was becoming known by its creolized name, Punda, which is the term used today.)[82] As the eighteenth century progressed the real dynamism of the town increasingly moved beyond the small peninsula. The new urban areas were outside the immediate supervision and protection of the fort. They could develop unhampered by the physical barriers and geographic limitations of the walled area. The urge to expand trumped the need for security. The port was moving beyond the fort.

One logical area of expansion was across the narrow harbor entrance, which the Dutch had named the Other Side (*Oversijde*) and eventually became known in Papiamentu as Otrobanda.[83] Geopolitical developments pushed this option. Just after the outbreak of the War of the Spanish Succession in 1702 the Dutch built two forts there to help defend the harbor from enemy attack. Although the WIC initially forbade any other building along the adjacent waterfront, in 1707 Governor Beck authorized permits for fourteen lots, initially with the restriction that dwellings could be only one story high so as not to impede the line of sight from Fort Amsterdam into the countryside.[84] (Such security concerns proved to be justified when a French privateer, Jacques Cassard, attacked the island in 1713; he landed at a bay on the southwestern coast, but was unable to penetrate fort defenses in town. He did, however, extract a substantial ransom from concerned denizens.) Apparently settlement predated official approval by at least several decades. There already were people living in the area by the late seventeenth century. Leupenius's 1676 map showed a few small thatched huts there, which may have been occupied by enslaved people and/or free blacks, and a small road leading westward from the waterfront toward the countryside.[85] (Interestingly, Leupenius's image of Otrobanda was repeated on maps well after the area had become urbanized.)[86]

The new settlement on the other side of the bay grew quickly following the end of the War of the Spanish Succession, when authorities loosened building restrictions. By 1715 there were fourteen houses standing along its waterfront.[87] The Other Side had a completely different character from the settlement on the Point. Unencumbered by confining walls, it soon occupied a much larger areas. Its streets and alleyways were more open, its buildings more spacious and spread out. Many of the homes were surrounded by gardens and small yards, a rare luxury within the walled town. (According to the 1715 census only six residences behind the walls had a garden.)[88] Buildings on the Other Side retained some of the overall Dutch architectural influence, but they were further modified to reflect the relative openness of the neighborhood and the tropical climate.[89]

This expansiveness carried over into the area's more varied ethnic composition. Although it had its share of elegant merchant mansions, the Other Side also was attractive to middling, up-and-coming independent merchants, who were not closely tied to the WIC. They found its real estate less expensive than that of the Point. The Other Side also became home to a growing free black and mulatto population, as well as to small groups of urban slaves who worked for wages as artisans or in the maritime economy, and lived away from their masters at least part of the time. In contrast, the walled settlement on the Point remained a predominantly Dutch enclave, with its elegant residences belonging to well-established merchant families. Many of the wealthiest Sephardic families also lived here, their ability to purchase the island's most expensive real estate testimony to their rising success. The walled town had a decidedly Dutch style and character, with its tightly packed merchant buildings perched on narrow streets adjacent to the water.

In subsequent decades, as the port's population grew and continued to prosper, two new neighborhoods developed adjacent to the walled area. Pietermaai (named after one of its first residents, a Dutch ship captain named Pieter de May[90]) developed along the narrow strip of land on the southern coast east of Fort Amsterdam. Scharloo was immediately north of the Point, across the Waigaat ("Windy Hole") inlet.[91] There had been a scattering of dwellings along the spit due east of town even before the turn of the century, likely an early settlement of free blacks.[92] Unlike the other two neighborhoods, both Scharloo and Pietermaai were predominantly residential, with no commercial buildings or wharves, although some homes on the waterfront had their own small docks for private vessels, similar to canal-side residences in the Netherlands. Scharloo and Pietermaai were primarily home to up-and-coming merchants who eschewed the expensive, scarce, and cramped real estate in the narrow confines of walled Willemstad, and preferred the quiet elegance of a nearby residential area to the boisterous multiuse district across the water. Homes in Pietermaai and Scharloo combined the cachét and elegance of Punda with the spaciousness of Otrobanda. Both neighborhoods were relatively smaller and remained less populated than either the Point or the Other Side.[93]

As the gains from trade poured back to the island, Willemstad was transformed. By midcentury, to accommodate the expanding shipping traffic, wharves were built on both sides of the bay deep into the interior, well past the fort and port complex at the harbor entrance.[94] At least one widow owned wharves along the east side of St. Anna Bay in 1768.[95] While the area around the Point developed infrastructure for shipping, the new neighborhoods outside the walls became the locus of residential expansion. Many homes in the Other Side, Scharloo, and Pietermaai had gardens and even small yards, something that was not possible for residents who lived in the tightly confined area behind the walls.[96]

By midcentury, the Other Side had become the largest part of town both in terms of physical expanse and demographics By 1753, the Other Side had more dwellings than the Point.[97] Twenty years later, in 1774, Otrobanda had over three hundred houses and occupied an area that was several times the size of the Point.[98] (Nevertheless, depictions of the town often downplayed the size of Otrobanda, making the walled town and surroundings seem bigger.)[99] The neighborhood included not only a concentrated urban core at the waterfront, directly across the harbor from Willemstad, but also an area that extended west from the harbor along a broad avenue that ran from the docks on St. Anna Bay westward through the urban neighborhood and to the countryside beyond. The Other Side thus also was the link between rural, western Curaçao and the port. The neighborhood's major street, Breedestraat, was an extension of the same street on the eastern side of the harbor within the walled town. The two streets were clearly part of the same urban unit even if they were in two very different neighborhoods and separated by a wide canal.[100]

As Willemstad grew and prospered, its wealthy merchants clearly no longer felt the need to build their homes in the protective shadow of the fort. Instead they built up the surrounding areas. A 1741 map shows over two dozen houses in Pietermaai; one published ten years later has almost double that number, extending all the way along the peninsula to roads that led to well-ordered country estates in the east.[101] Several of the homes are depicted with outbuildings, which presumably served as slave quarters. Most of the residences have survived to the present, elegant multistory mansions showcasing the finest Dutch colonial architecture.[102] It is striking how vulnerable the buildings on this strip appear, facing the open sea and well outside the range of fort gunners.[103] Comfort and prosperity clearly trumped security concerns for their owners. This is in marked contrast to the enclosed town that was safely nestled inside the harbor entrance, ensconced behind thick walls, and well protected by the sturdy fort ramparts. Even the neighborhoods of Scharloo and Otrobanda were well inside the harbor, securely protected by the fort. By 1753 Pietermaai had about fifty houses, almost one quarter of the number in the enclosed area.[104]

The fort complex remained a somewhat separate, self-contained entity. It was practically a mini-town of its own, simultaneously the seat of government, the site of the West India Company offices, and home to the principal garrison, the Dutch Reformed Church, and the governor's residence. Its multipurpose role clearly demonstrated the intertwined political, economic, military, and religious power that was concentrated in the West India Company. From its headquarters at Fort Amsterdam the WIC controlled both the economy and the government of Curaçao. The well-protected fort had the offices and residences of the island's top Dutch denizens. It also contained a school (for children of the Dutch elite), homes for WIC employees and factors, a cemetery, assorted workshops and residences for carpenters, coopers, bakers, and smiths, and slave quarters.[105] Together, the privileged residents of the fort formed a tight-knit ruling elite who met for Sunday worship at the Dutch Reformed Church and whose sons and daughters frequently intermarried. The church was repeatedly expanded and renovated throughout the eighteenth century to reflect the growing wealth and prestige of its members.[106] By midcentury, the Fort Church had become a splendid example of Dutch colonial architecture. Within the confines of the fort, the island's Dutch elite were surrounded not only by their peers, but also by a group of service workers, white and black, enslaved and free, who supported their lifestyle. The clear depiction of the dwellings of black servants within the fort complex (labeled *neegerhuisen*) on Geertz's 1754 map of the town is one of the very few explicit references to people of African descent on any map of Curaçao.[107] Perhaps not coincidentally, Geertz's map is also one of the only ones that fully depicts the neighborhood of Otrobanda.

Island defense remained a high priority of the WIC at midcentury. With almost continuous interimperial warfare, pirates and privateers swarmed in Caribbean waters, and anticontraband vessels patrolled along the nearby coast of Caracas and beyond. There were multiple plans to repair, upgrade, and expand the forts throughout the century.[108] The open land between Fort Amsterdam and the sea remained important for defense and was the site of several lines of cannon.[109] It was also a convenient location for the gallows and the cemetery.[110] By the 1750s there was also a gallows in Otrobanda, as well as a leper house.[111]

As the town expanded, it developed its own identity. This is reflected in the developing use of its name. The 1715 census clearly identified the walled area as Willemstadt.[112] By the mid-eighteenth century the name usually appeared on island maps.[113] The dateline of official documents, however, continued to favor the designation, Fort Amsterdam.[114] This is not surprising, given that the fort was, in fact, the seat of government, and thus the physical site where laws were made. Throughout the eighteenth century, of the hundreds of laws that the WIC issued from Fort Amsterdam only a handful appear to have included Willemstad in the dateline.[115] Reports by the island governor, on the other hand, often mentioned Willemstad in the dateline (often along with Fort Amsterdam), or in the text.[116] Occasionally, documents were more generally described as originating from "the Point."[117] By midcentury, if not before, the new districts were referred to by their respective names, and Willemstad usually (but not always) referred exclusively to the walled area.[118] Occasionally the name Willemstad was used to refer to the entire urban area.[119] Other times the town simply was called *de stadt* ("the town").[120]

By the end of the century the process of creolization also was reflected in neighborhood names. Both *de punt* and *de overzijde* acquired Papiamentu versions, Punda and Otrobanda, respectively. The official name, Willemstad, was used only sporatically, and even then primarily in official documents to refer to the walled town. (Even today the names Punda and Otrobanda are much more common, and the term Willemstad is rarely if ever used in popular parlance.) The creolized name, Punta—a transition between the Dutch and full Papiamentu—appears in writing as early as 1775 in a clandestine love letter between two Sephardim who were having an illicit love affair.[121] Its rather cavalier use as a reference to town (as opposed to Willemstad or *de stadt*) indicates that it was already a well-accepted place identification by then. The Dutch continued to use the term *oversijde* throughout the eighteenth century to refer to the neighborhood across St. Anna Bay, often employing variations of the phrase, *de overzijde van de haven* ("the other side of the harbor").[122] The transition to the creolized name, Otrobanda, would appear to be more straightforward, since, unlike Punta or Punda, it clearly has Iberian roots. By the mid-eighteenth century, Sephardic documents in Portuguese refer to the neighborhood as *da banda*.[123] Testimony in a 1751 case in Venezuela, concerning fugitive slaves from Curaçao, noted that a free black from the island lived in "Otra Banda."[124] By the 1830s, maps of Curaçao produced and printed by well-established Amsterdam firms consistently were labeling the other side of the harbor as "Otrabanda."[125]

By the end of the century Willemstad had become one of the largest and most cosmopolitan ports in the Caribbean. A detailed census conducted in 1789 found that the port contained a total of 914 houses and 11,543 people, out of a total island population of 20,988.[126] (Interestingly and atypically, in this census the name Willemstad referred to the greater urban area, including all the neighborhoods outside the walls.) Willemstad was smaller than the major Spanish American maritime centers at Havana, Cuba, and Vera Cruz, Mexico, about the same size as Cartagena, Colombia, and Kingston, Jamaica, and significantly larger than the French ports in Saint Domingue and Guadaloupe.[127] By 1789 the town's four districts were home to 55 percent of Curaçao's total population, and 42 percent of all the island's slaves, clear testament to the port's centrality in the local economy.[128] Not surprisingly for the eighteenth-century Caribbean, slaves were the port's largest single demographic group, constituting 47 percent of its population. Free people of color were the second largest group. They outnumbered both white Protestants and Sephardim, and represented 43 percent of the port's total free population. Together, people of African descent were the clear majority, 70 percent of Willemstad's inhabitants. Sephardic Jews made up 35 percent of Willemstad's entire white population. (See table 4.1.) The spatial distribution of the port's population is revealing. White Protestants were the most evenly distributed between the neighborhoods, Sephardim the least so. The walled area contained the most people—almost 43 percent of the town's total population—due to the fact that so many slaves and servants lived there and that it was overwhelmingly the residential choice of Sephardim (84 percent). Only 7 percent of free blacks lived within the town walls, while the Other Side was home to over half of the port's free blacks. Together, people of African descent, enslaved and free, made up 80 percent of Otrobanda's population. Otrobanda also had the largest number of buildings and households (392 and 629, respectively). In spite of this fact (or perhaps because of it), eighteenth-century maps and townscapes often left Otrobanda almost blank, even when their depiction of the rest of town, including Pietermaai, was highly accurate.[129]

Religion, Social Class, and Ethnicity

Flush with money from their lucrative commercial activities, Curaçao's traders transformed the look as well as the size of the town throughout the eighteenth century. Upper-class merchants tied to

TABLE 4.1
Population of Willemstad, 1789

	Punda	Otrobanda	Pietermaai/ Scharloo	*Total*	Percent of total
White Protestants	658	593	750	*2,001*	17.3
Sephardic Jews	860	80	83	*1,023*	8.9
Free white servants	223	134	126	*483*	4.2
Free blacks and coloreds	401	1,495	719	*2,615*	22.7
Slaves	2,773	1,598	1,048	*5,419*	47.0
Total	4,915	3,902*	*2,726*	*11,543*	
Percent of total	42.6	33.8	23.6		100

SOURCE: Calculated from Nationaal Archief Nederland; The Hague, the Netherlands, Nieuwe West Indische Compagnie, *1176: 430–47, 9 August 1790.*
*This number includes two people who did not specify if they were enslaved or free.

overseas commerce built elegant dwellings in all four neighborhoods. Along the docks of St. Anna Bay on the Point, elegant, multifunctional buildings imitated the practical yet graceful style of the stately merchant houses that lined the canals of Amsterdam and other major Dutch cities, where real estate was similarly scarce.[130] From wide windows overlooking the harbor, merchants could monitor vessels that returned from regional trade, and oversee the lading of transatlantic ships bearing their cargoes, or catch a glimpse of family members riding the ferries home from a visit to the Other Side.[131] Residences in Willemstad's unwalled neighborhoods were more spacious and had room for small gardens.[132] The island's architecture reflected its dual status as both a Dutch and a Caribbean commercial center. Local builders modified traditional Dutch architecture into a unique colonial style, to reflect the specifics of the tropics and the local island reality. For example, the early merchant houses were narrow with step gabled roofs. Later builders and residents added open galleries with windows, roofed verandas, and porches encircling the buildings. These all protected the interiors from the penetrating rays of the intense tropical sun. They repositioned windows to allow the steady, cooling trade winds to blow throughout the house.[133]

Beyond the port, merchants owned rural estates whose main houses somewhat resembled the great Caribbean sugar plantations, with spacious, breezy rooms occupying one or two floors, and expansive verandas giving panoramic views of the surrounding property. They, too, followed a basic Dutch architectural style, with similar adaptations made for the tropical climate and for the exigencies of rural living.[134] The fact that most of Curaçao's rural estates were more for show and relaxation than sites of significant agricultural production gave them a somewhat different layout and style compared to typical Caribbean plantation houses. At the same time, merchant owners were keen on preserving the overall feel and style of these landholdings as a visible marker of their wealth.[135] Many of these rural estates initially had been built and owned by the WIC. By the early eighteenth century, however, most of them were transferred to private hands.[136] In 1717 the WIC sold all its rural holdings except for Hato on the northern coast, dismissed its white employees who worked on them, and reduced its rural work force to about two hundred slaves.[137] Thereafter, Curaçao's so-called plantations were primarily a sign of prestige for wealthy town merchants, and a source of basic foodstuffs for local consumption.

In spite of their localized production regime, Curaçao's rural landholdings were called plantations (*plantages*) by contemporaries. This likely was a deliberate reference to the status that full-fledged plantations had throughout the Caribbean. These holdings were a marker of wealth and prestige of Curaçao's rising merchant elites, even if their owners could not reproduce the particular conditions of the region's great sugar estates, and their prosperity was tied to the very different (albeit related) economic activity of intercolonial trade. Members of Curaçao's rising merchant class were well aware that export-oriented plantations sustained their counterparts in other parts of the Dutch colonial realm, including the Wild Coast of South America, and also supported the elites on the much closer French and English Caribbean islands, with whom they engaged in a vigorous contraband trade.

On both sides of the harbor, Willemstad's diverse inhabitants from different socioeconomic, ethnic, and racial groups lived and worked in close proximity, even as they maintained somewhat separate lives. In their work and daily lives they could not help but cross paths in the crowded streets, along the wharves, in the market, and in the many commercial establishments in the streets and alleyways. In their interactions they developed multiple social and cultural as well as economic bonds. Alongside the merchants, seafarers of a variety of ethnicities and races worked in the port city of Willemstad. These included itinerant sailors from different European countries and their American colonies, and a relatively stable core group of local seamen, especially free blacks, mulattos, and slaves. While men were at sea, women anchored the port, with numerous opportunities for close contact as they sustained the local society and economy in the home, marketplace, and local port businesses, and managed shops, inns, bars, and brothels, as well as the finances of their absent merchant husbands.[138] The narrow streets and alleyways, with dwellings, wharves, and commercial establishments all in close proximity, also encouraged children of different social classes, ethnicities, and language groups to play and speak together.[139] The character of these interactions and relationships was fundamentally unequal in a slave society. Most Sephardic and Dutch merchants owned slaves. People of African descent, including free men and women, occupied a decidedly inferior position in the local society, even when they were pillars of the maritime economy.

The port's population was both highly cosmopolitan and highly stratified. As Dutch sociologist Harry Hoetink has noted, the majority of Curaçao's inhabitants were divided into three groups that were defined along clear, intertwined lines of social class, race/ethnicity, and religion. The small Dutch Protestant merchant elite was at the top, up-and-coming Sephardic Jewish merchants in the middle, and Catholic Curaçaoans of African descent, enslaved and free, black and mulatto, at the bottom.[140] In spite of the sometimes irregular evangelization process, almost all of the island's population of African descent professed Roman Catholicism by the end of the seventeenth century and thereafter.[141] Hoetink's model is accurate and useful overall, and helpful for understanding the nexus between religion, race/ethnicity, and social class in Willemstad. However, it is rather oversimplified, in that it does not allow for the ethnic and religious diversity of the many small-scale merchants and itinerant white seafarers and merchants who passed through the cosmopolitan port of Willemstad, or for the island's small but influential group of European Catholics, especially those of Dutch, French, and Spanish extraction.

Willemstad was also home to a relatively small but highly visible group of poor and lower-class whites, including transient sailors, soldiers, and servants, and an international group of middling sectors made up of Dutch, Germans, Scandinavians, Poles, Frenchmen, and Spaniards, who were attracted by the island's commercial opportunities. The maritime economy facilitated the development of lower and middle-level white sectors. Sailors, ship captains, and small-scale traders who arrived on the island found it relatively easy to become permanent residents. Any man who married a local woman, or who joined the guard and promised to obey all laws, could become a permanent resident.[142] Although they were not part of the elite, these whites developed a certain identification with the uppermost strata, based on race. This was typical for the times. Over the generations many successfully established themselves as middle-level merchants. Some successfully married their daughters to high-level company officials.[143] By the mid-eighteenth century some Spaniards who had moved to Curaçao from Tierra Firme had found profitable opportunities in contraband trade. For example, the owner of the cargo of the sloop *Ufro Sarah* was a well-established Spanish merchant who was "always allow'd to be the Richest Man upon the Spanish Main" before he had emigrated to Curaçao.[144] The crew of another sloop, the *Polly*, included four or five Spaniards who had been living on the island and engaging in maritime trade for at least five years, the vessel's captain testified in 1746.[145]

Curaçao's religious, socioeconomic, and ethnic division also had a linguistic component. The island's Protestant elite spoke Dutch, as did the middling white sectors and merchants who were tied to transatlantic trade. Sephardic Jewish merchants communicated among themselves in the two major commercial languages of the Atlantic and Caribbean, Portuguese and Spanish. Most Sephardic merchants also were conversant in Dutch. Hebrew was the language of the synagogue. Many Sephardic women never learned Dutch, but they were fluent in both Portuguese and Papiamentu, Curaçao's emerging creole tongue, which they often learned from their domestic slaves.[146] Many Afro-Curaçaoans, especially urban artisans, traders, and seafarers, were polyglot, and had at least a working knowledge of Spanish, Portuguese, and Dutch. Those living in the port spoke Papiamentu, while rural slaves spoke another Afro-Portuguese creole known as Guene, which retained much more African influence than did Papiamentu.[147] First generation African immigrants spoke a variety of other languages depending on their point of origin and their transatlantic trajectory. In the course of the eighteenth century increasing numbers of Afro-Curaçaoans and Sephardic Jews began to communicate among themselves and with each other in Papiamentu, although Dutch remained the official language.[148] The merchant elite spoke Dutch, although some of the middling Dutch sectors, especially women, also became conversant in Papiamentu. There were also a small number of French- and Spanish-speaking white immigrants who lived in town.

Women dominated Willemstad demographically. By the first decade of the eighteenth century women were over half the port's adult white population. They formed the majority of every major social and ethnic group except slaves until well into the nineteenth century.[149] Protestant and Sephardic women sometimes owned businesses or participated in regional trade ventures.[150] Dutch and Sephardic widows were overrepresented in many ventures.[151] For example, there were many widows among the Sephardic insurance underwriters, many of them of relatively modest means.[152] This demographic overrepresentation of women was typical of many early modern Atlantic and Caribbean ports.[153]

Sephardic merchants were an up-and-coming group. Although their commercial exploits, wealth, and power paled compared to those of the powerful Dutch merchants aligned with the transatlantic trade of the WIC, they were at least on a par with, and often wealthier than, other independent white merchants.[154] Most of Curaçao's Sephardim were of relatively humble origin. In spite of their Atlantic-wide connections, they were not yet an established merchant elite. Curaçao's Sephardic Jews played a particularly important role in regional trade. Wim Klooster has suggested they "may have been the single most important impetus to Curaçao's rise as a regional entrepôt."[155] Already by the 1720s Sephardim dominated Curaçao's navigation, especially Caribbean shipping, and they owned over two hundred seacraft.[156] In 1734 forty of the island's forty-five marine insurance brokers were Jewish; similar numbers held throughout the century.[157] The importance of seafaring for Sephardic merchants is obvious from the tombstones with maritime images that are dispersed throughout the Jewish cemetery.[158] Women as well as men owned vessels. Between 1721 and 1787 eight Sephardic women, four of them widows, owned eleven ships.[159] Sephardim also became active marine insurance underwriters, a particularly lucrative business because of the risky character of Curaçao's interimperial maritime trade, and the presence of pirates and privateers in regional waters.[160]

Drawing on an interconnected network of family members and associates in port cities around the Atlantic basin, Curaçao's Sephardic merchants traded regularly with almost two dozen different places throughout the Americas, including the northern littoral of South America, the Gulf coast of Mexico, and the Caribbean islands of Santo Domingo, Puerto Rico, Jamaica, Barbados, Trinidad, Cuba, and the smaller French and Danish Antilles.[161] They had especially close commercial ties with English New York, drawing on contacts that had been established during the Dutch tenure.[162] For example, between 1715 and 1722 Nathan Simson of New York organized a total of twenty-three trips to Curaçao, which represented 13 percent of all outgoing shipping traffic from Manhattan in that period; between 1739 and 1772, Daniel Gomez of New York sent a total of 133 ships to the island.[163] Curaçao's Sephardim also traded with coreligionists in Charlestown, South Carolina; Newport and Providence, Rhode Island; and New Orleans.[164] The nearby mainland of Spanish South America was another important trade area.[165] By the early eighteenth century there were Sephardic enclaves in several parts of Tierra Firme, including Santa Marta, Colombia to the west, and Tucacas, at the mouth of the Yaracuy River.[166] This does not include the undocumented conversos who lived throughout the area. Both Santa Marta and Tucacas had especially close trade ties with Curaçao. Curaçao's merchants and seafarers established contact with communities of conversos throughout Spanish America, adding an additional layer of clandestinity to their activities.[167] In many cases Sephardim would travel in small vessels that engaged in contraband trade with Tierra Firme as masters, supercargos, agents, or translators. For example, two well-established Sephardic merchants were on board the sloop *Polly* when it was captured by British privateers near Caracas in 1746.[168] Sometimes the Sephardic owner of smaller vessels would serve as captain.

Although they were a rising merchant class, Curaçao's Sephardim still were not, overall, an elite. Most were of relatively modest means. Between 1719 and 1765 70 to 80 percent of Curaçao's Jews paid third-class family tax. In 1775 between 70 and 75 percent of Curaçao's Jews were assessed in the two lowest tax brackets; none were in the top three brackets (out of seven).[169] Even many of the marine insurance underwriters were of relatively modest means.[170] This parallels the situation of the majority of Amsterdam's Sephardim in the same period.[171] Curaçao's Jews did not gain full political freedoms, including the right to hold public office, until 1825.[172] As an up-and-coming merchant group they were not immune to the trappings to show their success. By the early eighteenth century Jews owned over twenty-five plantations in the areas around the old Jewish cemetery on the northern edge of the

Schottegat Harbor and elsewhere around the island.[173] Their cohesiveness as a group that was separate and distinct from the Dutch Protestants (and even from other mid-level European groups) is evident from the frequent reference to them as "the Jewish Nation" or "the Portuguese Jewish nation" in WIC documents.[174]

Although few eighteenth-century baptismal records have survived, contemporary observations by visiting priests indicate that the majority of the island's black and colored population, enslaved and free, professed Roman Catholicism.[175] As early as 1704 Father Schabel noted that "no black ever visits the Protestant church or Jewish synagogue. No minister or rabbi has ever baptized or circumcised the child of a slave."[176] In the early 1750s Father Grimón wrote to his superiors that local slave owners "have never prevented that their slaves exercise their religion. . . . Their very owners send for me to hear their confession and attend to them according to their Catholic religion."[177] A few years later, in 1758, Father Navarro reported that the fact that the island had been without a priest for a couple of years had thrown the local Catholic population into spiritual disarray, and that over three thousand people were desperately in need of baptism.[178] (His numbers may have been somewhat exaggerated.) Throughout the eighteenth century political and religious authorities in Venezuela repeatedly noted that blacks from Curaçao who had settled there were faithful Catholics.[179] At the end of the century an extensive report to the Spanish Crown about historic ties between Curaçao and Venezuela noted that the overwhelming majority of the island's population was made up of free blacks and coloreds and slaves, "all of them Catholic," and that such a situation had been true for a very long time.[180] Apparently neither Dutch Protestants nor Sephardim on the island were interested in converting their chattel.[181] Sephardim did not circumcise their slaves and allowed them to be baptized by Roman Catholic priests.[182] It was not until 1741 that Curaçao's Dutch Reformed Church accepted people of color. Even then, membership was restricted to free-born mulattos; anyone who had been born in bondage was excluded.[183]

Although conventional wisdom has it that the Dutch Protestants were completely uninterested in converting their slaves, Curaçao provides some evidence to the contrary. In 1741 superiors in the Amsterdam Reformed Church criticized Pastor Wigboldus Rasvelt for not converting any blacks, noting the successful efforts of the Roman Catholic Church, and urged him to begin evangelizing actively. Rasvelt replied that he accepted mulattos who were born free, but not slaves or mulattos who had been born enslaved; that Protestant pastors had never accepted slaves, blacks, or mulattos into the Reformed Church; that white masters did not evangelize among their slaves; and that "it is well known that mulattos and blacks . . . are Catholics or were inclined to Catholicism."[184] Apparently there was a division between, on the one hand, colonial political and religious authorities, including the WIC directors, who were not terribly interested in evangelization, and the religious leaders of the Dutch Reformed Church across the Atlantic, who seemingly were concerned about the success of the Roman Catholic Church in the Dutch territory and the company's seeming spiritual neglect of the island majority.

Curaçao's role as an entrepôt, and the pivotal role of its port city in the island economy, shaped the character of local slavery. The port depended on the work of relatively mobile enslaved artisans, craftsmen, market vendors, dock workers, and seafarers, rather than on plantation laborers who were place-bound. Although Curaçao was no longer a major slave-trading station by the early eighteenth century, it soon matured into a full-scale slave society.[185] The particularities of Dutch participation in the transatlantic slave trade and the wider Atlantic commercial system, and Curaçao's role as a trade hub in this system, shaped the character of enslavement in Curaçao. Enslaved labor was vital to the functioning of Curaçao's developing maritime trade system, both in the port and on the vessels that plied regional waters. Enslaved and free men of African descent worked on the docks, and they served as boatmen to ferry people back and forth across St. Anna Bay.[186] Ferrymen were often the first people to visit a vessel that arrived in the harbor, and they sometimes engaged in small-scale trade with the sailors.[187] Black men also dominated the labor force on regional sailing vessels. In a typical example, at least half the crew of the Curaçaoan sloop *Catharina*, which traded cacao, hides, and mules from Tierra Firme in 1746, was black; in 1747 half the crew of a similar sloop, *de Jonge Johannes*, was made up of free blacks.[188] By midcentury two-thirds of Curaçao's seafarers were black, and almost all sailors of African descent were locally born.[189] Enslaved sailors often earned the same as freemen. Monthly pay in the 1760s ranged from 23 to 30 pesos.[190]

Curaçao's seafarers of African descent traveled around the region on sailing vessels with small but highly diverse crews. For example, the sloop *Polly*, caught smuggling near Caracas, was manned by "one Dutchman, one Dutch boy, two Jews, three Negroes, and fourteen Spanish Indians and Molattoes, one of which was a merchant."[191] The two Sephardim were well-established Curaçaoan merchants. One of the Sephardic merchants on board the *Polly* testified that the Indians on board were natives of Curaçao. This indicates that even in the mid-eighteenth century Caquetios still were active in the island's maritime life, despite their very small numbers. Several Curaçaoan vessels that were captured by the British off the coast of Tierra Firme in the first half of the eighteenth century had several Indians among their crew, although records do not specify their origins or ethnicity.[192] In 1743 Caquetios who were living on Curaçao were ordered to help hunt for fugitive slaves in the countryside.[193]

Slaves were distributed around the town neighborhoods according to the living patterns of their owners. By the end of the century 51 percent of Willemstad's slaves lived within the town walls, 29 percent on the Other Side, and 19 percent in the neighborhoods of Scharloo and Pietermaai.[194] Many urban slaves were skilled workers who labored for wages and/or were rented out by their owners.[195] Some of them enjoyed great autonomy in their daily lives, and even lived separately from their owners. Those who lived independently found quarters outside the town walls, especially in the neighborhoods of the Other Side and Pietermaai.[196] Enslaved laborers also toiled on the rural landholdings that provided food for the island's inhabitants and for the slaves who were in transit. They also worked in the island's salt pans. Because work in the salt pans was particularly grueling, slaves often were sent there as punishment, or they were banished to work the larger salt pans on the neighboring island of Bonaire.[197] As the eighteenth century progressed, many slaves were manumitted and entered the ranks of Willemstad's growing free black and mulatto population, who also labored primarily in occupations related to maritime trade. In the second half of the century at least 2,224 adult slaves received their freedom.[198]

The precise number of enslaved Africans who lived in Curaçao during the eighteenth century is difficult to ascertain. The first tax on slave ownership was introduced in 1680. The tax was steadily increased over the years, from 4 *reales* per head in 1680, to 6 *reales* in 1700 and then to one *peso*. Since the fine for noncompliance was relatively low (10 *pesos*), under-reporting was rampant, especially among people who owned more than ten slaves.[199] Historians agree that slave tax records are not a reliable measure of the actual number of enslaved people who lived in Curaçao throughout the eighteenth century.[200] The tax of 1719 listed 2,072 privately owned slaves, while that of 1748 included just 55 more

(2,127), even though the island had experienced major demographic and economic growth in the interim.[201] In the 1760s the WIC reduced the tax on slaves to 4 *reales* in an attempt to improve the accuracy of reporting.[202] Han Jordaan estimates that the number of slaves was relatively constant throughout the eighteenth century, somewhere between 8,000 and 13,000 people, including both those in Willemstad and rural laborers.[203] The 1789 census listed a total of 12,864 slaves, 42 percent of whom lived in the port city of Willemstad (5,419 people).[204]

The slave tax records of 1764 provide insight into the character of slave ownership in eighteenth-century Curaçao.[205] According to the records, 551 people owned a total of 5,534 slaves. In contrast to the plantation economies of the Caribbean, slave ownership in Curaçao was small scale. Only 9 people owned 100 slaves or more, and no one owned more than 200 slaves. Eighty-one percent of all of Curaçao's slave owners had 10 or fewer slaves. This was typical for a Caribbean entrepôt. For example, whites in eighteenth-century Bermuda owned an average of just 6 slaves, and only 10 percent of households owned more than 10 slaves.[206] The average holding was about 10 slaves, but the range was large. As in all colonial Atlantic slave societies, ownership of chattel was concentrated. Only 107 people owned more than 10 slaves. Although these individuals represented just 24 percent of all the slaveholders, they owned 4,072 slaves, or 74 percent of the total. As table 4.2 shows, women were not insignificant slaveholders. A total of 153 women owned 2,055 slaves in Curaçao. Women represented 28 percent of the island's slave owners and they owned 37 percent of the island's slaves. Women represented just over half of Curaçao's large-scale slaveholders. The person who owned the largest number of slaves (200) was a woman, the widow of Jan Martin.

Many of the Africans who arrived in Curaçao but were not shipped out for resale in Tierra Firme and elsewhere had some type of physical or mental defect, illness, or disease that made them unsalable on the regional market. These slaves, known as *mancarones*, were sold at regular local auctions, which provided opportunities for small-scale buyers and investors to purchase a few slaves, which they either kept for their own use or resold at a profit when they had recovered from their illness.[207] There was also demand on the Spanish American mainland for such slaves who were sold individually and clandestinely in small numbers at reduced prices. On the mainland a strong healthy young woman could fetch as much as 300 pesos and a man 400 or more. Older,

TABLE 4.2

Slave ownership in Curaçao, 1764

Number of slaves owned	Total owners	Female owners (percent of all owners)
under 10	444	122 (27%)
10–49	79	15 (19%)
50–99	19	11 (58%)
100–200	9	5 (56%)
Total	*551*	*153*

SOURCE: Compiled from Oude Archief Curaçao, *907:197–208*, reproduced in Isaac S. Emmanuel and Suzanne Emmanuel, *History of the Jews of the Netherlands Antilles* (Cincinnati: American Jewish Archives, *1970*), 2:*1036–45*, Appendix 22.

sickly, or handicapped slaves sold for less.[208] Locally, the price of sick or handicapped slaves ranged from 15 to 118 pesos at the beginning of the century, with most in the 50–60 peso range.[209]

Information about the African origins and ethnicity of enslaved Curaçaoans is incomplete and sketchy. According to Harry Hoetink the names in slave baptismal records from the mid-eighteenth century indicate seventeen different ethnic origins, ranging from areas in Kongo to Sierra Leone.[210] Spanish colonial records from Tierra Firme for the eighteenth century indicate that many enslaved Africans who had come from Curaçao originally were from western and southwestern Africa, especially the regions of Kongo, Angola, Elmina, and Guinea.[211] The term "Loango" was widely used throughout Tierra Firme as a synonym for slaves who had come to the area via Curaçao, especially fugitives, although it is difficult to know how accurate this was as an ethnic descriptor.[212] Captives from the area around Elmina may have been exposed to the proselytizing efforts of Protestant clerics who were employed by the WIC by the mid-eighteenth century.[213]

Free blacks and coloreds were an integral part of the port, demographically, economically, and socioculturally. Their numbers increased substantially throughout the eighteenth century, from just 48 in 1717 (5.6 percent of the island's total population) to 540 in 1742, to 3714 (17.7 percent of the island population) in 1789. This represented the highest percentage anywhere in the Caribbean, according to Wim Klooster.[214] By the end of the century they represented 23 percent of

Willemstad's total population, 33 percent of the population of African descent, and 43 percent of all free people, white and black, and they outnumbered whites.[215] Manumissions also increased dramatically during the second half of the eighteenth century. Although records are incomplete, existing manumission petitions show an increase from at least 340 in the 1750s and 275 in the 1760s to 518 in the 1770s, 525 in the 1780s, and 566 in the 1790s.[216] Compared to other slave societies of the Americas manumission was relatively easy to obtain in Curaçao. Although owners did not have to pay a manumission fee, slaves who sought to free themselves had to pay a self-purchase fee, which varied between 10 and 1,000 pesos (with the average being 218 pesos). Payment was flexible; it might be in kind, in installments spread out over many years, or paid by someone else.[217] In some cases manumitted slaves were required to continue to work for their former masters. In 1750, concerned about the growing free black population, the local government instituted a tax of 100 pesos for every adult over a certain age who was freed.[218]

Like slaves, free black men found ample work in the maritime trade economy, as sailors, dock workers, ferrymen, and sometimes also as ship captains.[219] Many were involved in the contraband trade with Tierra Firme and elsewhere.[220] Others were fishermen, an occupation that also was common among slaves.[221] Free black and mulatto women worked in a variety of occupations. Sometimes they operated their own small-scale businesses.[222] Free blacks, male and female, also owned small numbers of slaves, some of whom participated in the contraband trade.[223] Although they lived in all parts of town, by the end of the century 57 percent of the town's free blacks made their home on Otrobanda, where they accounted for 38 percent of the neighborhood's total population.[224] Many, including women, owned property in town, especially in Otrobanda.[225] Others purchased and/or leased rural landholdings, including, sometimes, estates.[226] Beginning in 1719 free people of color were assessed the same taxes as whites; they all paid the lowest category of 2 pesos.[227]

In spite of their legal freedom, Curaçao's free people of color suffered multiple levels of discrimination and restrictions by virtue of living in a colonial slave society. Curaçao's eighteenth-century legal codes were based on race rather than on legal status; that is, the restrictions that were placed on free people of color more closely resembled the statutes applicable to slaves than the regulations governing whites. Despite some of the freedoms that the maritime economy provided, Curaçao was a full-scale slave society.[228] In court, free men and women of color did not have any more rights than slaves.[229] Throughout the eighteenth century a series of regulations were put into place which greatly curtailed the activities of free blacks and coloreds. Of special note are the restrictions that Governor Faesch imposed in the 1740s. A 1740 regulation noted that "the insolence of the Coloreds and Blacks, freemen as well as slaves, is becoming intolerable." It instituted a curfew for all people of color, and prohibited them from playing instruments in public or pouring alcoholic beverages. Soon thereafter, another regulation further restricted the activities of all blacks, regardless of their legal status, and forbade groups of more than three or four people to congregate. Even funerals could not be attended by more than six people. The penalty was severe: branding, flogging, or banishment to the salt pans of Bonaire. There were no such restrictions on the assembly of whites.[230] Also in 1740, the governor sought to impose a special tax on free blacks, although apparently it was not enforced. Twenty-nine years later the tax was reimposed, and this time it was collected regularly.[231] In 1745 the governor issued a decree limiting the movement of free people of color. Among other restrictions, free blacks and mulattos could not testify in court against a white person. Penalties for black people who approached a foreign vessel before it had cleared customs were downright draconian. (Soldiers had permission to shoot nonwhites who did so, while whites were only fined.)[232] This may have related to fears of collusion with foreigners and/or gaining economic advantages in trade. As of 1749 they were prohibited from keeping shops, although they were allowed to conduct commerce from their homes. They also had to perform menial tasks such as supplying clay and stones for fort repairs.[233]

Ironically, even as the rights of free blacks were being curtailed, local colonial society depended on free black militias for local defense and to maintain public order. Curaçao's slaves and freemen were organized into militias during the War of the Spanish Succession. In 1710 there were three companies of free blacks.[234] By the 1740s there were two militias of freemen, one of blacks and one of mulattos. A 1749 decree required all free blacks and coloreds to participate in guard duty.[235] The militias played an important role in putting down a one-day slave revolt on the Hato Plantation in 1750. Thirty-four slaves were executed, including thirteen women.[236] Following the uprising further restrictions were put on free blacks and coloreds.[237] The militias patrolled Otrobanda every night after dark to keep order. They also patrolled the southern shores in an effort to stem marronage, hunted fugitive slaves on the island, and guarded the entrance to St. Anna Bay.[238] Apparently by midcentury there were enough foreign-born free people of color to attract the attention of local authorities. A 1754 law required that free blacks and mulattos from the French, British, and Spanish colonies enlist in the local militia.[239] No doubt most had arrived in trading vessels.

In spite of the restrictions imposed on free people of color, and the overall poverty of most of them, some individuals did quite well. Maritime trade was often the key to prosperity. For example, Gaspar Antonio Quirigazo was one of several free black captains who made a good living off of contraband.[240] He parlayed his intercolonial connections into a lucrative side job hunting down and returning fugitive slaves who fled to Venezuela. In October 1748 he was in Coro at the behest of island authorities to find fugitive Afro-Curaçaoans and return them to the island; he even testified in a Venezuelan court on behalf of the Sephardic owners of one Curaçaoan runaway.[241] A month later he returned ten slaves to Coro who had escaped to Curaçao, and sought to exchange them for fugitive Curaçaoans who were living in the area.[242] In 1752 he once again appeared in Coro. This time he captured eight Curaçaoan fugitives and returned them to their owners.[243] Quirigazo also dabbled in the slave trade, although his purchases and sales seem to have been limited to no more than two or three individuals at a time.[244] Apparently this work was profitable enough to allow him to purchase real estate; he bought and sold several rural landholdings throughout the 1740s and '50s.[245] Antonio Beltrán, who was head of the free black militia beginning in 1747, also was affluent enough to purchase expensive property, in his case a large, stately mansion in Otrobanda.[246] At least part of his wealth may have derived from transcolonial activities similar to those of Quirigazo. In 1746 Beltrán was in Caracas testifying in the case of three fugitive slaves from Curaçao.[247] Such individuals were relatively rare, however. Most of the island's free blacks and mulattos were poor.[248] There was also division, competition, and conflict among these groups. At midcentury some were organized into rival gangs.[249]

"The Catholics now have a great church"

Religion played a major role in the dynamics of the port city, and it was closely tied to the town's spatial layout, as well as to social class and ethnicity.[250] There was a close association between the island's political/economic and religious power apparatuses. The WIC director was also *qualitate qua* president of the Council of the Reformed Church. One of his official duties was to defend and protect the Dutch Reformed Church.[251] The church itself was located within the enclave of Fort Amsterdam, testimony of the close ties between the island's religious and secular authorities.[252] The Dutch Reformed Church was the hub of social and religious life for the Dutch merchant class, WIC administrators, and members of the military. Similarly, the synagogue in the adjacent town was the focal point for the life of the local Sephardic community, the great majority of whom lived within the walled town.[253]

For the island's Catholic majority of African descent, there was not such a clear physical demarcation of their religious life in the early years. Religious worship was not as centralized, although it remained narrowly circumscribed by town limits. Throughout the eighteenth century the Spanish Roman Catholic Church continued to exercise de facto religious jurisdiction over the island's black Catholic majority via the Bishopric of Caracas. The requirement of the Dutch States General that a Catholic priest must have a permit from the WIC to settle on the island, first issued in 1661, was reissued in 1705. That, along with the terms that the bishop of Caracas had laid out in his 1677 pastoral letter, served to ensure that itinerant priests would continue to play a major role in evangelization on the island.[254] Throughout the eighteenth century dozens of priests visited Curaçao temporarily, staying between a few months and several years at a time. Many were in transit between the Americas and Europe, and found themselves temporarily on the island because of its excellent maritime connections. Thus, the island's role in regional and Atlantic commerce helped to shape the religious contours of local society and the particular way that religious jurisdiction was exercised over the black majority.

Major Catholic religious orders, especially the Jesuits, Augustinians, and Franciscans, began to have a regular presence on the island in the first years of the eighteenth century. This added another layer to the complex issue of religious jurisdiction. These orders had an important role in shaping Curaçao's Catholic Church and the religious life of its black denizens throughout most of the century. Jesuits had a continuous presence on the island from 1704 until 1742; Augustinians between 1715 and 1738; and Dominicans from 1776 until 1820.[255] In order to exercise their duties openly on the island these clergy required multiple levels of approval—from the Dutch States General in the Netherlands, WIC authorities in Amsterdam and Curaçao, the bishop of Caracas, and the heads of their own orders. There was not always agreement between the different authorities. Sometimes parties appealed their cases all the way to the Holy See in Rome. Thus, individual priests and their superiors required finely honed diplomatic skills to effectively carry out evangelization on Curaçao, and sometimes just to be able to stay on the island.[256] Sometimes members of these orders also found themselves in conflict with visiting secular priests or with the local laity.

The location, size, and importance of Catholic houses of worship reflected the changing configuration of the port, and the consolidation of Roman Catholicism as the accepted religion of the island's black majority. In the first decades of the eighteenth century ministry to the black majority was carried out in small, discreet spaces that were part of merchant houses firmly ensconced behind the town walls. The arrival of Miguel Alexis Schabel in 1704 marked the beginning of the Jesuits' continuous four-decade presence on the island. Schabel was a multi-lingual Bohemian who had spent time in Tierra Firme. He fled to Curaçao during the War of the Spanish Succession, when his outspoken support for the Austrian claimant to the Spanish throne threatened to get him imprisoned.[257] Schabel rented a small dwelling on a merchant street in town, which he also used as a chapel between 1705 and 1708.[258] There was another chapel, located in a merchant house on the wharves, that originally had been operated by Capuchin priests for the asiento in the last decades of the seventeenth century. Later the Jesuits also took it over. Throughout his official tenure on the island (1704–13), which roughly corresponded with the War of the Spanish Succession, Schabel maintained good relations with WIC authorities. He also continued to baptize Africans who arrived via the slave trade.[259] (Apparently he was still living in the walled town in 1715, where he rented a house on a major commercial street from a Dutch widow, two years after completing his official religious duties.)[260] After Schabel was recalled, Flemish Jesuits supervised the Curaçao mission for the next thirty years. Sometimes they worked under assumed names or posed as secular priests so as not to attract undue attention.

Under Father Agustín Beltrán Caicedo y Velasco, an Augustinian, the locus of Roman Catholic worship crossed St. Anna Bay to the Other Side of town. Caicedo was appointed as the first apostolic prefect of the newly created Curaçao mission in 1715, a task he shared with the Jesuits, not always amicably, until his death in 1738.[261] The mission remained under the official jurisdiction of the Bishopric of Caracas. Prior to this appointment Caicedo had performed his ministerial duties in a semiofficial capacity, taking advantage of the carte blanche authorization granted by the bishop of Caracas. Born into a wealthy Spanish creole family in Bogotá, Caicedo was the first American-born and the first American-educated priest to serve in Curaçao, a true creole in the Spanish sense of the term. Previously he had run afoul of Spanish authorities for smuggling tobacco from the Orinoco to Curaçao. As a result he was expelled from all Spanish territories. Perhaps not entirely unrelated to his involvement with contraband, Caicedo also had some doctrinal disagreements with the Roman Catholic Church. This led to orders that he be imprisoned and sent to Spain in 1714. However, nothing seems to have come of this, although questions continued to be raised about his behavior for over a decade after his death. Such controversy did not seem to preclude his eligibility to minister, however, especially after Caicedo absented himself from the island for a few years to travel to Rome and Amsterdam, where he presumably made nice with the relevant sacred and secular authorities. Caicedo's most important legacy is that he moved his ministry from the walled town to the Other Side, where he established the island's first permanent, free-standing Catholic Church since Spanish times. Previous Catholic worship spaces all had been makeshift chapels located in merchant houses on the Point. Initially Caicedo had lived in the Jesuit mission in Willemstad, in a dockside merchant building that was owned by a Dutch widow. [262] In 1731 he bought a house in Otrobanda, which he converted into a church.

By the early 1730s there were two active Roman Catholic houses of worship on Curaçao that vied for the souls of the black majority: the former Capuchin chapel, now run by the Jesuits, on the docks of the Point, and a small free-standing church manned by Father Caicedo for the Augustinians, in the growing, multiethnic settlement of Otrobanda. There was ongoing rivalry between the two for control of Curaçao's church, both on the ground and at the institutional level. In 1731 Caicedo petitioned the Holy See and the bishop of Caracas for his church officially to become the island's only parish. Both demurred, however, indicating that they did not want to favor him over the Jesuits. The latter soon found that their cramped chapel had become too small to accommodate all their parishioners, even after they added multiple Sunday services. In 1734 the Jesuits purchased a large house within the walled town, apparently as a real estate investment, which they then traded for three houses in Otrobanda. They closed the small harbor-front chapel in 1735.[263] Thus, by the second half of the 1730s the seat of Roman Catholic evangelization had shifted from the Point to the Other Side, reflecting the changing demographics of the port. There it was to remain. But all was not clear sailing for Curaçao's Catholic Church, even after it had moved beyond the walls. When Caicedo died in 1738, with no clear successor within his order, the Jesuits took possession of all the Augustinians' properties. (Caicedo's move to Otrobanda was permanent; he was buried under the Roman Catholic house there.)[264] By 1742, there were no longer any Jesuits remaining on the island, either. The churches on the Other Side fell into disuse. The Jesuit house of worship was transformed into a warehouse for the nearby mill. Apparently there was no official, permanent Roman Catholic clerical presence on the island at all for the next decade. This left the lay leadership largely in charge, supplemented by the occasional arrival of itinerant priests, with whom they were sometimes embroiled in elaborate power struggles.[265] The entire issue of religious control within the local church remained unclear for over three decades. During this time, the island's Catholics depended exclusively on visiting priests, until Dutch Franciscans took over the apostolic prefecture in 1776.[266]

During the decades at midcentury when Curaçao's church was without regular clergy, increasing responsibility fell to the laity. The church council developed significant power, which it exercised along largely racial lines. The rising power of the council reflected an important division within the local Catholic Church. First established in 1731, the council was made up of whites, predominantly Dutch, Belgian, or German Catholics, but sometimes midlevel French and Spanish merchants. All of them lacked the political, economic, and religious pedigree to gain access to the island's uppermost power structures affiliated with the WIC.[267] Instead, they carved out a space for themselves within the lay leadership of the Roman Catholic Church, where they easily trumped the status of slaves and free blacks and mulattos.[268] The council—and the laity in general—kept Curaçao's Roman Catholic Church running on a daily basis, and exercised de facto control when there were no priests on the island. As its power entrenched, the council frequently came into direct conflict with visiting priests, who were more apt to advocate for the black majority, and who often were insensitive at best to the established lay power structures that sustained the church in their absence and that were not simply abolished upon their arrival. Roman Catholic clergy, after all, were part of an ecclesiastical hierarchy that did not recognize formal power for laity. Curaçao's church council, in contrast, took full advantage of the irregular and haphazard clerical presence, as well as the fact that they were physically distant from higher church authorities in Tierra Firme and Europe. Power on the ground frequently trumped established hierarchies. On at least several occasions the council seems to have had the stronger hand, at least initially. For example, when a visiting French Dominican sought entry to the former Jesuit chapel in Otrobanda, his access was blocked by the head of the church council, who, not coincidentally, also owned the nearby mill (which, at the time, was using the defunct chapel to store grain).[269] The conflict ended up reaching the island governor. It was not the last time that secular Dutch Protestant authorities had to intervene in Catholic matters. In 1756 Governor Faesch issued a thirteen-point set of regulations detailing the respective powers and responsibilities of the council and the clergy.[270] Besides specifying terms of payment and the management of money, perhaps the most revealing aspect of the document is that it explicitly prohibited Roman Catholic clergy from issuing any publications without first consulting the church council. Faesch, by all counts a skilled administrator, was well aware that he would have to deal with council members and their families long after visiting priests had moved on to the next venue. Once again, local colonial practicalities trumped institutional hierarchies that had developed in distant Europe.

Throughout the second half of the century there were also conflicts among the laity, which usually broke down along racial lines.[271] On several occasions when jurisdiction over the island's Catholics was disputed between priests from northern Europe and those from Spanish America, the white laity usually sided with the former, and free blacks with the latter.[272] (See Chapter 5.) Priests who came through the Spanish system and had spent time in the colonies usually were much more attuned to American racial realities and more sensitive to the needs of the island's black majority, while those who came directly from northern Europe had a keen appreciation for the struggles of middle-sector white Catholics who lived as minorities in Protestant states. As Curaçao's free black population grew in number and influence, WIC authorities realized that it was in their interest to support the council, for the sake of overall racial stability in the colonial slave society. The racial dimensions of conflicts among the laity came to a head in 1759, when the captain of the free black militia, Antonio Beltrán, tried unsuccessfully to establish a Catholic church in Pietermaai. This was a clear indication of the rising power of free blacks, both within the

Roman Catholic Church and in local island society in general.[273] The case also suggests that there was a significant free black population in neighborhood of Pietermaai by midcentury.

After a tumultuous decade, the arrival of Father Miguel Grimón, another Augustinian, in 1752 brought some stability to the local Roman Catholic Church. Duly appointed by the bishop of Caracas, Grimón promptly petitioned for permission to build a larger, more permanent structure in Otrobanda, lamenting that the existing building was unsuitable because it was no more than "a small hermitage."[274] Church officials initially were not inclined to accept his request, as they were fearful that it would "open the doors to contraband."[275] Nevertheless, ground was broken on the Santa Anna Church in 1752. It was completed in 1768. Much of the building material was, in fact, imported illicitly from Tierra Firme, thus fulfilling the prophecies of Grimón's superiors.[276] The building was impressive, with three naves held up by multiple columns and three separate chapels. One visitor described it as "sumptuous . . . very capacious and in excellent taste."[277] The construction of this substantial and permanent Catholic church building in the expanding neighborhood marked a significant turning point for the Roman Catholic Church on Curaçao. As a visible landmark, it testified to the presence and cultural influence of the black Catholic majority, and also to the success of the Roman Catholic Church in maintaining religious jurisdiction in a Dutch Protestant territory. It also provided a suitable home for clergy.[278] Grimón's presence in the port proved much more transitory. He did not live to see the completed structure. He perished in a shipwreck in 1755 while fleeing the island in a small vessel en route to Coro, after he had been deposed by a German priest sent by the Dutch and backed by the church council.[279] In keeping with the contraband theme, the vessel almost surely was involved in illicit interimperial trade.

The increasing institutionalization of the Catholic presence on Curaçao did not go unnoticed. "The Catholics now have a great church," a group of Dutch Protestants complained in 1753, long before the new building was completed, "much larger than what we have for the exercise of our religion."[280] Catholics were not the only group to expand. The island's other major religious denominations also built significant structures at midcentury, attesting both to their dynamism and to the changing configurations of the port. The existing Dutch Protestant and Sephardic houses of worship in the walled part of Willemstad were enlarged and given a much more imposing and prosperous look.

Protestants and Jews also built houses of worship across the water. By the second half of the century the Other Side was home to thriving congregations representing all three of the island's major religious groups.

Curaçao's growing Sephardic community quickly outgrew the small synagogue built in 1703. In 1729 the congregation decided to build a larger house of worship. They demolished the existing one and acquired adjacent buildings and land in the walled town. The building's style was highly influenced by the architecture of the Sephardic synagogue in Amsterdam. In fact, the Curaçao congregation hired a master carpenter who was familiar with both the building tradition of Amsterdam and the particularities of the synagogue there (although apparently he proved less than reliable). The Amsterdam synagogue incorporated design elements of Iberian tradition into the Dutch style, which, in turn, were carried over the Atlantic to Curaçao, where they were adapted to the tropics and infused with some local flavor.[281] For example, the building boasted impressive double curved gables, a decided departure from the cleaner lines of the Amsterdam structure.[282] In contrast to the Catholic church across the bay, all the building materials, including the timber, were imported directly and legally from Amsterdam. The imposing new synagogue was built in the heart of the walled town of Willemstad, a stone's throw from the Fort Amsterdam complex. This is a clear indication that Curaçao's Sephardim had become a cornerstone of the local economy and society. Today the same building remains an active house of worship. It is home to the longest continuously operating Jewish congregation in the Americas. The small but growing Sephardic population on the other side of the bay required their own house of worship, since rabbinical laws prohibited them from using boats on the Sabbath. The much more modest Jewish synagogue there was consecrated in 1743.[283]

In 1762 members of the island's small but significant Lutheran community began building a large stone church in Otrobanda. The congregation was composed primarily of prosperous German and Scandinavian merchants who were not affiliated with the WIC. The building was completed in 1763. The congregation remained active until 1804.[284] The new Lutheran church sparked the rivalry of WIC officials. The following year they broke ground on a larger, more impressive edifice on the site of the original modest Fort Church, inside the confines of the Fort Amsterdam complex. It was completed in 1771. Like the nearby synagogue, no expense was spared to make this an impressive edifice. It, too, continues to be an active house of worship today, welcoming descendants of some of the same families who first worshipped in its pews. The same carpenter who carved its mahogany pulpit and the governor's pew also made the synagogue's Holy Ark, evidence that the Dutch and Sephardic merchant elite shared both similar tastes and access to the same small pool of skilled workers. Like the synagogue, all building materials for the Fort Church were brought from the Netherlands, shipped in WIC vessels on their regular transatlantic routes. Oddly, the church was paid for out of the Relief Fund for the Poor, and there was some suspicion of embezzlement. Even as it was cloistered within the fort complex and served as the religious home of the local ruling class, the Dutch Reformed Church could not entirely escape the island reality in which it was situated. Thus, extensive vaults under the floors stored foodstuffs in times of war, since blockades and trade disruption quickly could lead to island-wide famine. (The original Fort Church, a simple wooden structure located on the same site, had been built over the military storehouse.[285]) Similarly, the high roof provided ample space to dry the waterlogged sails of transatlantic vessels that had battled fierce storms.[286]

Free Trade versus Slavery

Enslaved workers were a vital cog in the maritime commercial system. Their labor was necessary at every stage of intercolonial trade.[287] Their enslavement benefited their merchant owners, by ensuring a labor force and maximizing profits. Within the port slaves who worked in the maritime economy found a relatively higher degree of freedom; they often lived separately from their masters and were hired out for wages. Enslaved seafarers also experienced relative freedom as compared to plantation workers elsewhere in the Caribbean. But they posed a serious challenge for their owners, as they encountered numerous opportunities to escape at virtually every port of call where they had chances to obtain personal freedom even as they engaged in free trade.[288] Wim Klooster has calculated that enslaved sailors represented at least 16 percent of all runaways from Curaçao throughout the eighteenth century.[289] This does not include men who found work on board ship but were not registered as seafarers or those who found maritime-related work in the port. Merchants and authorities faced a dilemma: How were they to control the mobility of enslaved maritime laborers without impeding their participation in trade? Smugglers required freedom of movement so that they could make the most of changing market conditions, seize unexpected opportunities, flee their pursuers, or ride out bad weather. Yet even as vessels sailed between multiple jurisdictions, owners, masters, and crews were bound by at least some of the laws and conventions that governed their home ports and empires.

Enslaved seafarers were particularly vulnerable if their vessel was caught, especially during wartime. Slave sailors could be confiscated as property and sold alongside goods such as hides, cacao, and tobacco.[290] In contrast, maritime convention usually allowed nonenslaved seafarers to be set free (sometimes upon payment of a ransom). Sometimes free black men on board vessels that were seized by privateers struggled to provide evidence of their status. Some cases dragged on for months or even years, as it was not in the interests of either the privateers or of the corresponding authorities to acknowledge the freemen's rights. For example, when a Curaçaoan vessel was seized by British privateers in 1746 the Vice-Admiralty Court noted with some skepticism that the crew included "One Negro Named Henry Who pretends to be free," and granted him three years to provide supporting documentation. If he did not, he would become part of the prize, along with the confiscated goods.[291] The records do not indicate where he would spend those years, or whether he would be allowed to travel back to the island to procure the necessary paperwork. In the many cases of mixed crews, authorities had to sort through sometimes contradictory evidence to determine which black seafarers were freemen who should be released and which ones were slaves that could legitimately be kept as prizes.[292] Perhaps in an effort to head off lengthy and costly court battles, which might tie up the vessel and its sailors, fellow crewmen sometimes testified that some or all of the black men on board were free, their lack of appropriate paperwork notwithstanding.[293] Enslaved sailors also were at risk of mistreatment and abuse by unscrupulous captains and fellow crewmen.[294] In this context, merchant slaveholders had complicated legal requirements. They needed to allow their sailor slaves to trade freely in order to return maximum profit; they had to protect their chattel from seizure as property; and they had to safeguard their ownership rights and minimize the many opportunities for escape that slave sailors found at almost every port of call. Curaçao's merchant slaveholders thus balanced opposing needs, on the one hand as slave owners who needed to control their chattel and on the other as traders who required free reign to maximize their profits.

WIC authorities, many of whom were themselves merchant slaveholders, struggled with these contradictory requirements throughout the eighteenth century. Between 1710 and 1766 the WIC issued nine different laws that addressed the ongoing problem of meeting shipboard labor needs—and thus supporting trade—while attempting to limit

TABLE 4.3
Laws regulating the maritime movement of slaves, 1710–66

Year	Major provisions
1710	Required that blacks as well as whites must have personal passports (identity documents) provided by the West India Company in order to be transported off the island or put into service onboard ships. (A similar requirement already applied to artillerymen, sailors, and soldiers.) Enslaved blacks and mulattos additionally required letters of permission from their masters to work at sea. Ship captains faced a fine of 50 pieces of eight for transporting anyone, white or black, without the requisite documentation. The phrase "in spite of the strong prohibitions of our predecessors" indicates that there may have been an earlier law aimed at controlling maritime marronage.
1714	Prohibited ship captains from transporting slaves off the island without the knowledge of their masters. Raised the fine to 200 pieces of eight for each slave who was so transported.
1741	Required Curaçaoan slaves who went to sea to carry passports. (Not found in the archives, but referenced in the 1742 law.)
1742	Required that all blacks and mulattoes who wanted to work as crew onboard any vessel first document that they were free. Set forth detailed procedures for how they were to prove this freedom and established a standardized passport system for all people of African descent. No blacks or mulattoes would be allowed to board a vessel or leave the island if they did not present a passport when they signed on as crew. Captains who sailed from Curaçao were prohibited from taking into service blacks or mulattos who failed to show this passport, or whose names as written on the crew list did not indicate that they were free. The fine to captains was reduced to 100 pieces of eight for each black or colored crew member who lacked such documentation. Reissued in 1743 and 1744.
1754	Required all boats (including canoes and fishermen's vessels) to obtain a written permit before sailing and to list the names of any slaves who would be departing on the craft. Also required free blacks and mulatto crew to give written proof of their freedom to the authorities and suggested ways that fishermen could secure their boats so that they would not be stolen by runaway slaves.

TABLE 4.3

Laws regulating the maritime movement of slaves, 1710–66 (continued)

Year	Major provisions
1755	Stipulated that slaves could go to sea only if they had both a passport and permission from their masters. Retained the fine of 100 pesos to be levied on vessel captains for each slave who they took on as crew without the requisite passport.
1761	Two laws:
	1. Tightened the documentation required of slaves, free blacks, and mulattos who sought to work as sailors on vessels and set clear procedures for acquiring this documentation. Republished in 1780.
	2. Prohibited fishermen from leaving the island without passports, from taking their boats across land belonging to the West India Company, or from fishing within range of the artillery of forts and beaches, under pain of having their vessels confiscated or shot upon.
1766	Modified the procedure by which slaves, free blacks and mulattos could sign on as crew, requiring that they be physically present before their names could be added to the official crew list. Captains who did not follow the stipulated procedure were fined 100 pieces of eight, plus the value of the slave.

SOURCE: Compiled and summarized from J. A. Schiltkamp and J. T. Smidt, comps. *West Indisch Plakaatboek: Publicaties en andere Wetten alsmede de oudste Resoluties Betrekking hebbende op Curaçao, Aruba, Bonaire.* 2 vols. (Amsterdam: S. Emmering, *1978*), passim. Richenel Ansano provided valuable translation assistance. Reproduced from Linda M. Rupert, "Marronage, Manumission, and Maritime Trade in the Early Modern Caribbean," *Slavery and Abolition 30: 3* (September 2009): 361–82, accessible at http://www.informaworld.com . Used with permission.

opportunities for maritime marronage from Curaçao. Table 4.3 summarizes the major provisions of each law. The earliest, issued in 1710 in the midst of the War of the Spanish Succession, required that both blacks and whites have passports (or personal identity documents) provided by the WIC before they could be transported off the island or put into service onboard ships. Enslaved blacks and mulattos additionally required letters of permission from their masters to work at sea.[295] Four years later the WIC prohibited ship captains from transporting slaves off the island without the knowledge of their masters.[296] There was a thirty-year legis-lative lull, even as smuggling reached new heights. Then, in the twenty-five-year period between 1741 and 1766, the WIC enacted seven laws re-lated to the maritime mobility of Curaçao's enslaved inhabitants. These laws were promulgated during a time of almost continuous warfare and interimperial rivalry, as the War of Jenkins's Ear (1739–48) and the Seven Years' War (1756–63) played out at midcentury with particular intensity in Caribbean waters. Illicit intercolonial trade figured prominently in both these disputes. Spanish efforts to curb contraband trade with Tierra Firme were also at their zenith in this period. They were spearheaded by the Basque-owned and -managed Real Compañía Guipuzcoana de Ca-racas (or Caracas Company, as it is known in English), which patrolled the northern coast of Venezuela for over fifty years (1730–84) and sig-nificantly disrupted the activities of Curaçaoan traders.[297] Two laws were issued in the early 1740s, in the midst of the War of Jenkins's Ear, when both privateers and the Caracas Company were attacking smugglers throughout the Caribbean with particular intensity. A 1741 law required all Curaçaoan slaves who went to sea to carry passports, in an apparent attempt to regularize the ambiguous political status of enslaved seafarers under Dutch colonial jurisdiction.[298] In 1742 the WIC required all blacks and mulattos who sought work as crew onboard any vessel to document that they were free It set forth detailed procedures for how they were to prove this freedom, and established a standardized passport system for all people of African descent. Captains were prohibited from taking into service blacks or mulattos who failed to show the required papers, or whose names as written on the crew list did not indicate that they were free. They were fined for each violation.[299] The problem was that the great majority of Curaçao's black seafarers were not, in fact, free. Five subsequent laws issued in a twelve-year period between 1754 and 1766 fine-tuned the passport requirements and further addressed the issue of maritime marronage, which had become both an enormous problem for island authorities and a significant opportunity for Afro-Curaçaoans.[300]

These increasingly strict laws raised significant hurdles for merchants who depended on the labor of enslaved seafarers to carry out intercolo-nial trade. The 1742 law was particularly problematic since the majority of the island's seafarers were enslaved, and it was not in the interests of their owners to manumit them. Authorities, however, were increas-ingly reluctant to grant slaves permission to leave the island, knowing that many would seek freedom in nearby Tierra Firme and perhaps never return. The law's detailed provisions had the potential seriously to curtail merchants' access to the workers on whom they depended to man their vessels. It contained a fundamental contradiction: How could the island's black seafarers document that they were free when, in fact, the majority were not? Was it really in the interests of merchants to free enslaved sailors? To circumvent this problem, at midcentury Curaçao's merchants apparently developed a temporary form of manumission that freed enslaved sailors only when they were at sea, and was revoked when they returned to the port of Willemstad. In the thirty-four-year period between 1741 and 1775 at least 153 slaves were manumitted "pro forma, to go to sea." The wording is almost identical in all 153 cases.[301] Such temporary manumission offered enslaved sailors the document they needed to board outgoing vessels. It also provided some measure of protection in the turbulent years at midcentury, when Caribbean waters were teeming with pirates, privateers, and freelance smugglers, and representatives of rival European powers were intent on curbing clandestine commerce. It also benefited their owners. By temporarily manumitting their enslaved maritime workers Curaçaoan merchants could circumvent the new legal requirements that seafarers be free—or at least they could provide papers to that effect—while not permanently forfeiting ownership of their chattel. Paradoxically, some merchants discovered that temporarily manumitting their enslaved workers was the best way to ensure their long-term bondage, while also promoting the merchants' commercial success. Merchant owners thus manipulated to their own ends legal codes that were designed to uphold the rules of colonial slave societies.

Less than four months after the 1741 law went into effect a Dutch merchant named Willem Meyer granted temporary manumission, "pro forma, to sail," to his slave named Claus. Later that same year Jurgen Woodgars of neighboring Bonaire (also under Dutch control, and administered by the WIC from Curaçao) freed his slave Marco using almost identical wording.[302] The 1742 requirement that seafarers provide written documentation of their liberty before setting sail apparently opened the floodgates for temporary maritime manumissions. Between 1742 and 1754 (the year of the next relevant law), Curaçaoan slaveholders temporarily manumitted 97 enslaved men specifically to go to sea. This represents 63 percent of all 153 known pro forma manumissions that occurred on the island. Another 39 such manumissions (25 percent) occurred between the laws of 1754 and 1761. Thereafter, it appears that pro forma manumissions decreased significantly. There are records for only 13 such cases after the 1761 law went into effect, and only 5 after the 1766 law. The last recorded one occurred in December 1775, when a Dutch preacher, Johannes Ellis, manumitted Juan Nicolaas Roubio.[303] Given the gaps in the historical record (several entire years are missing from the overall manumission records; information from other years is incomplete) one must be cautious about drawing hard-and-fast conclusions about the total number of these pro forma manumissions, their timing and distribution, their concentration (or lack thereof) around certain years, and their relationship to the laws discussed above. That said, it is notable how the phenomenon appears to be concentrated in a three-decade period at midcentury and corresponds closely to the promulgation of laws aimed at restricting the mobility of enslaved maritime workers. A full 89 percent of the known pro forma manumissions occurred in the period between the promulgation of the 1742 law, which required enslaved seafarers to prove their freedom before setting sail, and the 1761 law, which tightened the requisite documentation. Also notable is the fact that some of these manumissions were issued retroactively, several years, or in some cases decades, after the fact.

The particular exigencies of illicit intercolonial trade permeated social relations in the port city of Willemstad throughout the eighteenth century, shaping the character of local society and even the terms of enslavement. In turn, the specific ways that enslavement played out in the legal and sociocultural worlds of Willemstad influenced the development of maritime commerce. Curaçao's pro forma manumissions stretched the conventional parameters of enslavement and freedom, even as they provided merchants with an easy way to meet the letter, if not the spirit, of the new laws. Local merchants devised a gray area along the continuum between enslavement and freedom by establishing a new class of temporary freemen among sailors, a status that was valid only for the limited time they were at sea, and was revoked when they returned to port. Paradoxically, some Curaçaoan merchants found that temporarily manumitting their enslaved maritime workers and thus briefly acknowledging the men's full humanity was the best way to protect ownership of their chattel in the long term. These pro forma manumissions responded effectively to the contradictory exigencies of two interconnected regimes: a maritime economy based on free trade undergirded by a colonial American slave society. Apparently Curaçao was not unique here; similar temporary maritime manumissions also occurred in the British Caribbean and perhaps elsewhere.[304]

As the eighteenth-century laws regulating the movement of enslaved seafarers make clear, flight to Tierra Firme was an ongoing temptation for Curaçao's enslaved workers. As trade burgeoned, maritime marronage increased dramatically throughout the eighteenth century, along with other types of ties to the mainland. Curaçao's small-scale traders forged close ties with people in Tierra Firme, building on geographic, cultural, and economic ties that dated from the pre-Columbian and Spanish eras. There, too, the maritime economy interacted dynamically and dialectically with the realities of a colonial slave society, and commercial relations also developed sociocultural dimensions.

5 /   Curaçao and Tierra Firme

In 1729 an enslaved woman named Juana Isabel Curazao fled the island in a small vessel and made her way to the northern shores of Tierra Firme. After ostensibly converting to Catholicism, she obtained her freedom and acquired a small plot of land in Curiepe, a town of free blacks on the coast east of Caracas. On her small plot Juana Isabel planted cacao trees. Defying Spanish law, locals sold sacks of cacao beans from thousands of such landholdings to Curaçaoan traders, usually Sephardic Jewish merchants or black seafarers, who then smuggled the beans to Curaçao. There, dock workers of African descent loaded them onto large ocean-going vessels owned by Dutch merchants, which carried them across the Atlantic to the Netherlands, where they were processed into chocolate. By the mid-eighteenth century chocolate was becoming an increasingly popular drink among middle classes and elites around the Atlantic world. In 1765, thirty-six years after Juana Isabel escaped from Curaçao, her niece and heir, a free black woman named Ana María Motete, began a long legal battle to retain the cacao grove which, by then, had grown into a thousand-tree holding. Spanish colonial authorities challenged Ana María's ownership of the land, charging that Juana Isabel had acquired both the land and her freedom under false pretenses. After a court case that dragged on for two years, authorities confiscated half the property, allowing Ana María to keep the rest.[1]

The cases of Juana Isabel Curazao and Ana Maria Motete highlight the particular opportunities that were open to people of African descent and others in the intercolonial exchange zone that had developed between Curaçao and Tierra Firme by the mid-eighteenth century. The centuries-old ties between people in the two areas that had existed since pre-Columbian times took on a new character in the eighteenth century, with Curaçao's consolidation as a Dutch and Caribbean commercial hub, the development of cacao plantations on the mainland, and the emergence of a well-integrated Atlantic commercial system. Throughout the century a variety of people took advantage of opportunities that were opened by the burgeoning contraband trade and the regular transit of dozens of vessels and seafarers between Curaçao and Tierra Firme. People on both sides of the imperial divide participated actively in smuggling. They included not only well established merchants but also small-scale traders, sailors, ship captains, runaway slaves, free men and women of African descent, indigenous people, government officials, Sephardic Jews, and members of the Roman Catholic clergy. Contraband facilitated contact between people in Curaçao and Tierra Firme that extended well beyond the economic sphere and opened opportunities for a wide variety of social and cultural interactions.

The lives of Juana Isabel Curazao and her niece also reveal the changes that were occurring in this corner of the Atlantic world throughout the mid-eighteenth century. During the 1720s a foreign-born fugitive slave woman was able to obtain a plot of land in Tierra Firme and establish herself as a minor player in the global cacao economy. Forty years later her legitimate, locally born heir, free from birth, lost half the grove to authorities who were well aware of the increasing value and scarcity of such holdings and sought to bring them under more direct control. By the end of the century legal parameters had tightened, and Afro-Curaçaoan fugitives were no longer able to obtain either land or freedom in Tierra Firme. The interactions between the inhabitants of the Dutch island and the Spanish American mainland were shaped, in part, by the relative roles that Curaçao and Tierra Firme occupied in their corresponding imperial spheres and in the emerging Atlantic system. By the eighteenth century inhabitants of the two areas had developed close ties across the imperial divide, ties that were based on, but went well beyond, illicit trade. Smuggling opened up possibilities for a wide variety of sociocultural exchanges among women and men of many different social sectors. As the century progressed, inhabitants of the two areas created a well-integrated intercolonial system based on smuggling, one that responded to, but was also somewhat independent of, wider imperial and global dynamics.

Dutch Port/Spanish Hinterland

By the early eighteenth century, Curaçao was a colonial center, an important regional hub in the Dutch Atlantic commercial system that linked buyers and sellers in the Americas, Africa, Europe and beyond.[2] Lacking the basic resources to sustain agricultural production, Curaçao's merchants sought markets throughout the Caribbean and the Americas that would provide them with agricultural commodities they could sell in the wider Atlantic system. "The land is poor quality, sterile, and rocky. . . . It produces nothing except some grass, lemons, and coconuts. . . . There are no rivers nor springs," one observer wrote in the 1720s. "In spite of all this sterility, foodstuffs are so abundant, merchandise so common that it seems like one of the best cities of Europe."[3] Locals depended on trade not just for prosperity but to meet their most basic necessities. Even fresh water was so scarce that sometimes it was imported from Tierra Firme.[4]

Nearby Tierra Firme, especially the province of Venezuela, was a particularly attractive market for Curaçaoan traders. It was easily accessible by boat and filled with eager trade partners because of ongoing Spanish neglect. Tierra Firme's numerous fertile valleys along the coast produced a variety of marketable crops, especially cacao and tobacco, which were cultivated along navigable rivers that stretched from deep in the interior to the Caribbean Sea.[5] "In all of these valleys there are lovely ports which attract foreigners," according to another eighteenth-century observer; "They enter via the navigable rivers through which they provide the population with many articles."[6] According to official registers, trade with Tierra Firme made up fully half of Curaçao's total shipping throughout the second half of the eighteenth century.[7] By midcentury entire areas of Tierra Firme were much more closely tied to Curacao than to Spain.[8] Contraband trade penetrated the local economy of at all levels and provided opportunities for many people across the socioeconomic spectrum.

As the American seat of the West India Company, Curaçao was economically and politically important for the United Provinces. Tierra Firme, in contrast, was one of what John TePaske has called Spain's "vital peripheries."[9] Largely marginal to the central economic interests of an empire that focused its attentions on the far wealthier possessions of Mexico and Peru, Tierra Firme nevertheless produced crucial agricultural commodities for Atlantic markets. Moreover, its Caribbean coast was important strategically as a buffer against the incursions of privateers and other interlopers, preventing them from penetrating farther inland to the colonial heartland.[10] Since the 1520s, when Holy Roman Emperor Charles V had granted exploration and settlement contracts to the German financial family of the Welsers, Spain had allowed a variety of foreign colonists to settle in Tierra Firme in an effort to populate the area with Europeans and so bolster royal jurisdiction. One unintended consequence of this policy was to open contact and commerce between the area's inhabitants and non-Spaniards, expediting close political and economic alliances between these groups against the Spanish Crown and its representatives.[11]

Tierra Firme's physical geography facilitated its illicit economic relationship with the Dutch entrepôt. Coastal topography aided maritime trade and provided ample cover for discreet encounters.[12] To the east the long Caribbean coastline was broken by small bays and narrow, unobtrusive coves that provided havens for small vessels. High mountain peaks were interspersed with lush, narrow river valleys that opened onto the Caribbean at sheltered, isolated harbors. Numerous river valleys stretched from the shore deep into the interior, allowing easy transport of commodities and providing access to inland markets far upriver. The little-traveled, poor-quality roads that traversed remote parts of the coast also were well suited for transporting goods between the sea and points inland.[13] To the west, the terrain gave way to a desolate, windswept desert coast that impeded all but the most intrepid traders. Geography was a vital element in the selection of appropriate rendezvous points. Captains of larger vessels easily overlooked the tiniest cays, making them particularly appropriate for storing contraband goods.[14] Thick mangrove swamps such as those around Tucacas, at the mouth of the Yaracuy River, were ideal smuggling centers. The narrow channels between islets could be navigated by only the smallest seacraft, while the dense, tangled roots and branches of the mangrove clusters provided ample opportunities to hide canoes, people, and sacks stuffed with contraband wares. Small vessels could lay in wait and quickly lade in shallow harbors that were inaccessible to larger craft.[15]

Dugout canoes such as those favored by the Caquetios carried small amounts of goods. They could land almost anywhere along the coast or among mangroves and could make swift getaways if they were pursued by larger vessels, quickly and quietly disappearing into the dark.[16] For Curaçaoans, sloops were the preferred trade vessel in the first half of the eighteenth century. The use of schooners increased thereafter. Sloops were manned by fourteen to twenty-five men; schooners, being larger, had crews ranging from thirty or forty to as many as ninety men.[17] Crews were usually multiethnic; those of several Curaçaoan sloops that were captured by British privateers in the mid 1740s, for example, included Frenchmen, Dutchmen, Englishmen, Spaniards, Sephardim, Italians, blacks (free and enslaved), mulattos, and Indians.[18]

Tierra Firme's varied inhabitants depended on smuggling for their livelihood. The two Spanish fleets that plied the Atlantic between Spain and its New World colonies, the *flotas* and *galeones*, served the much more lucrative markets of Mexico and Peru, and largely ignored Tierra Firme.[19] Between 1713 and 1763 the fleets visited Cartagena, the principal mainland port in the southwestern Caribbean, only four times.[20] Even these bypassed the coast of Venezuela. Only one register ship from Spain and another from the Canary Islands were authorized to visit Tierra Firme annually. Many years neither made the trip.[21] Even as early as 1715 one report to the Crown suggested that there was enough demand for products from abroad, and enough locally produced crops, to support the arrival of four large register ships annually.[22] As a result of this neglect the entire Caribbean coast of Spanish South America depended on foreign suppliers and markets. "If the governing Ministers had facilitated commerce, it would not be so abandoned and deteriorated as it is," Pedro José de Olavarriaga reported to the Spanish Crown in 1722. Olavarriaga spent eighteen months traveling throughout Tierra Firme at the behest of the Crown to document the extent of smuggling. His book-length report provided ample evidence that it had become epidemic.[23] The entire northern coast of Tierra Firme—or the Coast of Caracas as contemporaries called it—was open to foreign traders.[24] The area around Coro, located on the narrow eastern base of the Paraguaná Peninsula, was an especially favored destination for Curaçaoan traders. Even simple canoes could make the journey in just a few hours, as they had been doing since pre-Columbian times.[25] Larger vessels found ample mooring in the spacious natural harbor.[26] Coro was a center of intercolonial trade already by the 1650s. It was particularly favored by small-scale merchants and seafarers.[27] Sometimes Coro was even within sight of the Dutch island, if barely. "It has happened to me that on clear days I could see [Coro's] hills from the island's fort," one visitor commented in 1764.[28] Another favorite destination was the Barlovento area of the coast several hundred miles to the east, which included the town of Curiepe, site of Ana María Motete's cacao groves.

The major agricultural commodities that were traded from Tierra Firme to Curaçao were cacao, tobacco, and hides. Of these, by the eighteenth century cacao was by far the most valuable. It was the region's premier cash crop, and the one that the Spanish Crown tried the hardest to regulate. Although it was native to the area, serious cultivation did not begin until the end of the sixteenth century, with the first documented export of pods occurring in 1607.[29] (The trees take four to five years to bear fruit.) In the course of the seventeenth century cacao gradually edged out both tobacco and hides, both of which had been exported in the 1500s. To keep up with the sky-rocketing global demand, cacao groves were planted in virtually all of the province of Venezuela, which became known internationally for the high quality of its product.[30] Cultivation occurred both in small holdings and on large plantations that depended on slave labor. As cacao became an increasingly important export crop throughout the eighteenth century, the larger holdings began to overtake the smaller ones. Even on large-scale holdings, slaves often cultivated their own small plots of cacao and other products for sale, usually to foreigners.[31] Indians, free blacks, people of mixed race, and poor whites all made money from cacao throughout the eighteenth century.[32]

By the mid-eighteenth century as much as 50 percent of all the cacao that was produced in Venezuela found its way to smugglers.[33] Although reliable, exact numbers are virtually impossible to obtain for such a widespread contraband item, the province of Venezuela exported at least 24,500 fanegas of cacao in 1720/21. This amount increased steadily throughout the next decades, peaking at 59,500 in 1765 and then decreasing to 56,700 a decade later.[34] In the first half of the eighteenth century at least 30 percent of the cacao Venezuela exported found its way to Curaçao, with 42 percent shipped legally to Nueva España and 28 percent to Spain.[35] With the establishment of the Caracas Company, much more cacao was exported through legal channels. The lines between legal and illicit commerce were not clearly drawn, however, even after the pods left Tierra Firme. In the 1760s and '70s, as much as 90 percent of the cacao that Venezuela shipped to Mexico in the officially sanctioned intracolonial trade may have been resold to foreigners.[36]

Tobacco, another native crop, was Tierra Firme's first export under Spanish rule. Already by the end of the sixteenth century, locals widely traded it with visiting corsairs.[37] Although by the early eighteenth century tobacco exports had been overtaken by cacao in both quantity and value, nevertheless the leaf continued to be an important export in both the legal and illegal sectors. Tobacco had several advantages which made it particularly well suited for small-scale independent growers who did not have access to a large pool of slave labor: It grew quickly and was ready to harvest after just a few months; its cultivation required minimal attention and was not labor intensive; it did not require major capital investment; demand, both local and in overseas markets, was strong and constant. Tobacco had been cultivated and used by the area's indigenous population pre-Conquest; many continued to grow and sell small quantities to foreigners throughout the eighteenth century.[38] Although tobacco was produced by many other colonies across the Americas, the Venezuelan variety was known for its quality and taste. "It is much appreciated by foreigners," as one observer noted in 1764.[39] In comparison with cacao, tobacco cultivation and trade was much less regulated by authorities. As a result, virtually all the tobacco that was exported went through contraband channels.[40] Between 1731 and 1756, the province of Venezuela exported an estimated 17.8 million pounds of tobacco, 58 percent of it to Curaçao.[41]

Venezuela's export of hides, dried meat, and livestock dated from the days of Juan Ampíes and the Welser grant.[42] Cattle, sheep, goats, and pigs brought by the Spaniards flourished in the tropical climate. Runaways soon were breeding profusely, especially in the vast llanos (central plains) of the interior. By the late eighteenth century, there were an estimated 1.2 million cattle, 180,000 horses, and 90,000 mules inhabiting the llanos between Caracas and the Lake of Maracaibo.[43] Hides were there for the taking from the hundreds of thousands of feral cattle that roamed freely. They also were harvested from privately owned herds.[44] Throughout the seventeenth century, hides competed with tobacco and cacao as the region's most important export, representing a full 75 percent of the value of shipments to Spain.[45] By the early eighteenth century, exports to Spain and the Canary Islands via the register ships had fallen off, although both production and international demand remained robust.[46] Hides were used throughout Europe to make shoes, hats, saddles, harnesses, and chairs.[47] Apparently Spanish authorities never seriously tried to curtail the illicit export of hides, which would have been virtually impossible owing to the sheer numbers of wild herds that roamed the province's most remote and least governed areas. Some privately owned herds were so large that their owners did not keep reliable numbers, which facilitated pilfering.[48] Locals who could assemble a batch of semicured hides easily traded them for much-needed slave labor.[49] In years when authorities cracked down on the clandestine commerce of cacao and tobacco, the relative importance of the hide trade grew dramatically.[50] Venezuela legally exported some 190,000 hides to other parts of the Caribbean at the end of the eighteenth century; the contraband trade may well have been several times that.[51]

The abundant livestock also stimulated the breeding of mules, not just in the llanos but throughout the countryside. At midcentury a single rancher might produce between eighty and four hundred mules per year.[52] Sturdy and steady on their feet, the beasts were ideal for carrying contraband goods between the coast and the interior. Muleteers were an iconic image of smuggling. They made a handsome living, although their work depended on the passability of the poor roads of the interior.[53] Muleteers and canoemen transported contraband goods between the coast and the hinterland. Both earned an average of six pesos per cargo at midcentury.[54] Mule production far outstripped legal demand, both for local use and in the limited external commerce that the Crown allowed to other Spanish American colonies. Widely used throughout the Americas as beasts of burden, mules also were the motor of choice in Caribbean sugar mills (including the small-scale ones in Venezuela). There were ready markets in the English and French islands, especially Saint Domingue, which by the mid-eighteenth century had becomes the world's largest sugar exporter.[55] Because mules are sterile and have a short lifespan, plantations required a regular supply to keep the mills turning. Venezuelans often circumvented the trade restrictions by purchasing young mules at local fairs in the interior, ostensibly for their own use or for sale elsewhere in the province. In other cases the contraband trade was brazen, with no attempt at dissimulation. Mules bred in the interior were either walked or carried by river to the coast, where they could fetch up to four times the purchase price.[56] Along the way, they also carried other contraband wares, thus increasing their value. Payment was either in pieces of eight or in kind, in exchange for European textiles, alcohol, and slaves.[57] Local authorities became creative in developing maneuvers that circumvented export restrictions while allowing them to reap some economic gain for local coffers. In Coro, for example, boat captains often would serve as intermediaries, purchasing the beasts and duly paying the requisite tax, before loading the animals on board and then transferring ownership.[58] Compared to sacks of cacao or tobacco, or bundles of hides, these active, noisy, smelly, unpredictable living commodities presented particular challenges for an illicit trade that thrived on some level of discretion. "Mules and other livestock are not easily hidden wares," observed the author of a report on the contraband trade out of Coro. "Nor can they be removed suddenly when a boat appears."[59]

The reliability of merchant intermediaries, who could link sellers in Venezuela with markets hundreds of miles away, was critical. Given their extensive regional connections, Curaçao's Sephardic merchants were especially well suited to this role. They brokered the trade from their bases at Tucacas and Coro, which were the most common embarkation sites.[60] This was especially convenient because the hills around Coro were also a major breeding site.[61] The mules rarely set hoof on the Dutch entrepôt. They either were dispatched directly to their final destinations or kept temporarily on Aruba, where they could graze freely until a suitable vessel was available to carry them across the Caribbean.[62] Sometimes the vessels stopped at one of the smaller, uninhabited islands near the coast, such as Klein Curaçao, to gather fodder for the trans-Caribbean trip.[63] Occasionally, Venezuelans themselves transported the animals across the sea.[64] By midcentury, St. Eustatius sometimes served as a distribution center in the northeastern Caribbean for the animals, which arrived from Tierra Firme in Curaçaoan vessels. In 1746, for example, the Curaçaoan Sloop *Catharina* carried twenty-eight mules from Tierra Firme to St. Eustatius and returned with a cargo of Madeira wine, coffee, and sugar.[65] Lading the livestock was cumbersome. "It is a most curious spectacle to see these animals being embarked," Alexander von Humboldt remarked at the turn of the century. "They are felled with lazos and then lifted onto the vessels with an apparatus that resembles a crane."[66] Specially designed boats typically carried fewer than two dozen beasts at a time, although larger cargoes of up to forty-three animals appear in the records.[67] Transport logistics were challenging and bordered on the comical. The beasts often were distributed in two separate rows along either side of the vessel for balance, and they had to be kept upright and separated during the regular swells and the frequent squalls that rocked the vessel from side to side. They also had to be securely tied up, and kept as calm as possible, to avoid panic and the resulting mayhem. "To intimidate them and make them more docile, a drum is played almost all day and night," Humboldt noted. "Judge for yourself how much tranquility there would be for a passenger who had the courage to set sail for Jamaica in one of these schooners loaded with mules."[68] Sometimes small vessels carried just a few animals, which obviated some of the logistical problems.[69]

This trade was not insignificant; already by 1720 between one thousand and two thousand mules were sold in Coro annually, at least half of which were purchased by Curaçaoan merchants.[70] Fifty years later, authorities on the Paraguaná Peninsula recorded similar numbers, noting that the animals were exchanged for between five and six hundred slaves.[71] A 1793 report to the Crown estimated that a total of eight thousand mules were exported annually to foreign colonies, generating income of 400,000 pesos. An even greater number was shipped to Spain.[72] At the turn of the century, Puerto Cabello alone exported ten thousand mules, and the entire province of Venezuela sent as many as thirty thousand, worth a total value of 1.2 million pesos, or about half the value of cacao exports, to various Caribbean islands.[73] This represented only about one third of the mules that were then being bred in the llanos.[74]

In exchange for cacao, tobacco, hides, and livestock, Venezuelans sought a variety of basic consumer goods from Europe. First and foremost were textiles. Cloth produced from local cotton was of poor quality and used primarily for Indians, slaves, and other members of the lower classes. High quality textiles from elsewhere in Europe were coveted and cheaper than Spanish imports, which, moreover, were rarely sufficient to meet demand.[75] These included linens and woolens, laces, and silks, as well as finished clothing, especially but not exclusively high end.[76] Imported garments made their way far into the interior of the country.[77] Locals also needed basic goods for the home (scissors, knives, pots and pans, lamps, dishes, mirrors, candles, etc.), tools, agricultural implements, arms, and ammunition.[78] Semiprocessed foodstuffs, such as flour, cereals, and cooking oil, and alcoholic beverages, especially wine, brandy, and rum, also were popular.[79] Shortages of basic foods occasionally provoked crises as, for example, in the early eighteenth century, when a widespread scarcity of flour forced locals to rely on imports from Curaçao and Martinique so they could bake their bread.[80] Although Spanish register ships from the Canary Islands brought some spirits, these were more expensive and of inferior quality to those supplied via Curaçao.[81] Books and other printed matter were another coveted import, their scarcity sometimes owing at least partly to censorship and to the activities of offices such as the Inquisition, as well as to trade limitations. Repression frequently increased during wartime. At the outbreak of the War of the Spanish Succession, Father José Pimentel smuggled "books in Latin, French, Italian and Spanish" into Venezuela, along with a large cache of precious stones, fine clothing and textiles, gold, and silver.[82] Contraband trade gave the inhabitants of Venezuela access to a greater variety of products at much lower prices. "Not even in [the major Spanish Atlantic port of] Cádiz can such goods be had at the prices which foreigners offer here," noted one early-eighteenth-century observer.[83]

Perhaps the most important commodity that was supplied by clandestine commerce was slaves, who were needed to work the province's extensive, bountiful, and sparsely populated lands. Traders who arrived with enslaved Africans always found willing commercial partners. The *asiento de negros* continued to be a lucrative opening for contraband trade between Curaçao and Venezuela, long after the island had ceased to be a major slaving station. At the end of the War of the Spanish Succession, when the asiento came under French control, slaving sloops regularly stopped in Curaçao en route to Venezuela, where they acquired clothing that they exchanged for cacao on the mainland.[84] By facilitating contraband, the asiento was "one of the greatest sources of damage to the commerce of Spain," according to one report.[85] The ongoing need for slaves throughout the province of Venezuela, along with the abundance of mules, created an especially close symbiosis in the clandestine commerce of these two living commodities, both of which required much more complicated transportation logistics compared to agricultural products. For example, in 1717 the sloop *Abigail* loaded twenty-five mules in Coro in exchange for the cargo of slaves it had brought from the English asiento via Curaçao.[86] In 1777 the Crown opened up trade somewhat. For the first time, it allowed a limited legal trade in African slaves that were not brought through the *asiento de negros* It also permitted the export of mules and other livestock to the colonies of rival powers.[87] Both trades, of course, already had been thriving for decades, illicitly but brazenly.

Smuggling between Curaçao and Tierra Firme experienced several cycles throughout the eighteenth century. It responded to a variety of forces. Variations in overall trade patterns are much easier to identify than the absolute quantities and value of the goods that were exchanged. Major Atlantic wars sometimes disrupted this trade but sometimes spurred it. Throughout the first decade of the century, the presence of English privateers in surrounding waters during the War of the Spanish Succession seriously disrupted trade, which then rebounded and enjoyed two solid decades of growth until the early 1730s, followed by a decade of stagnation due to patrols of the coast by the newly established Caracas Company. The outbreak of the War of Jenkins's Ear (1739–48) was a boon to area smugglers, as it pulled Venezuelan vessels away from the more remote coastal areas to defend the major ports of La Guaira and Puerto Cabello, leaving hundreds of miles of the shore unpatrolled. The end of the war saw another period of stagnation, lasting about a decade, as the company reasserted itself along the coast. The slump continued through the Seven Years' War. This was followed by a resurgence in smuggling in the early 1770s, spurred by the American War for Independence, and then another decrease in the 1780s after England and the Netherlands went to war and large numbers of English privateers once again plied regional waters.[88] The 1790s saw further decline, both in Curaçao's over-all trade and in that with Tierra Firme, first as the rebellion that broke out in French Saint Domingue in 1789 all but shut down one of the is-land's important markets, and then as the English successfully block-aded all Dutch shipping to Curaçao following the French invasion of the Netherlands in 1795.[89] It was a blow from which Curaçao would never recover, and marked the end of an era.

Competing Political and Religious Jurisdictions

Tierra Firme's ambiguous and shifting political affiliation within Spanish America throughout the eighteenth century confused lines of imperial authority, diminished local inhabitants' sense of allegiance to the Spanish Crown, and further facilitated illicit trade. During the earli-est days of Spanish settlement Tierra Firme came under the control of the Royal Audencia of Santo Domingo, located on the Caribbean island of Hispaniola far to the north. Contact between Tierra Firme and His-paniola was sporadic at best, and encumbered by unfavorable patterns of Caribbean currents and winds. Vessels carrying official communiqués between the two areas were often intercepted by pirates and privateers who roamed the open sea. (Or so it was claimed. On at least some occa-sions, colonial officials in Tierra Firme may have protested that offi-cial correspondence did not arrive as an excuse for ignoring directives they did not wish to carry out.) Officials in Tierra Firme largely were left on their own, with extensive paperwork the only evidence of their local dealings and their supposed compliance with royal policies. Direct supervision was virtually impossible.

In an effort to improve contact with representatives of the Spanish Crown, and so discourage their open trade with foreigners via the Ca-ribbean coast, Spanish authorities transferred Tierra Firme to the newly created Viceroyalty of Nueva Granada in 1717. However, the effect was just the opposite. Nueva Granada was an enormous, varied jurisdiction. It encompassed all of northern South America from the dense jungle bordering the Orinoco on the continent's northeastern Atlantic shore, westward through the Andes to Quito and the Pacific, and even north through the swamps of Panama.[90] Overland communication within Nueva Granada proved even more unreliable than the maritime connec-tions between Tierra Firme and Hispaniola. Contraband trade in east-ern Nueva Granada—present-day Colombia—was particularly intense in the early years of the new Viceroyalty.[91] The decree that transferred command did not become known in Tierra Firma until 1719, two years after it went into effect. Throughout the eighteenth century, Venezuela vacillated between the two jurisdictions: It was reinstated to Santo Domingo in 1726, temporarily reassigned again to Nueva Granada between 1739 and 1742, then transferred back to Santo Domingo. Finally, in 1777, the entire territory of present-day Venezuela was unified under its own set of colonial political boundaries, which roughly corresponded to the contours of the eventual nation-state.[92] That during this period the Spanish Crown and other European powers were struggling to reconcile ambitious geographic imaginings with more mundane aspects of effective on-the-ground governance is evident from the shifting eastern border of the area on eighteenth-century maps. For example, a French map from 1705 clearly demarcates Tierra Firme as ending at the western shore of the Orinoco River; a Dutch map published twenty years later extends the area hundreds of miles eastward to include most of the Wild Coast and its jungle interior, and south almost to the Amazon; but another Dutch map dated 1765 significantly retracts these boundaries, showing the eastern border of Nueva Granada ending just east of the mouth of the Orinoco, and extending much less farther south.[93] In the intervening decades, the French, Dutch, and British all had established viable and even thriving settlements in the onetime no-man's-land of the Wild Coast.

Owing in part to this fluctuating jurisdiction and also to the difficult, unreliable communications with either colonial seat of power, governance of much of Tierra Firme was chaotic throughout the mid-eighteenth century. Lines of colonial authority often were unclear over the sparsely inhabited coast.[94] Such administrative confusion further facilitated participation in the contraband trade by a variety of people across the socioeconomic spectrum. This included local officials, who often were uncertain about the precise imperial chain of command and their own authority and position in the hierarchy, but were eager to placate their local constituents and to seize lucrative opportunities to improve their own lot. Colonial authorities were particularly anxious to strengthen their claim over isolated northern coastal regions that were in the hands of indigenous groups and frequently visited by foreign traders—and to get a piece of the lucrative contraband trade.

If Tierra Firme functioned de facto as Curaçao's economic hinterland, the roles were somewhat reversed, and much more complicated, in the religious realm. Here again, this was not entirely because of carefully devised policies but also because of the realities of colonial life. Colonialism often led to messy situations on the ground, ones that did not always fit into the neat political categories devised by imperial authorities in distant Europe. Such was the case with the religious ties between Curaçao and Tierra Firme. The Bishopric of Caracas continued to maintain some direct control over Curaçao's Roman Catholic Church throughout the eighteenth century, even after the island became an apostolic prefecture in 1715. A steady stream of priests from Spanish America continued to visit the island sporadically, punctuated by more regular control on the part of religious orders.[95] Spanish and French priests, among others, regularly came through the island en route to other destinations, taking advantage of the island's excellent transportation links. During their often brief presence they ministered to local Catholics under the umbrella of the bishop's 1677 decree that allowed all visiting priests to evangelize and perform sacraments without seeking specific authorization.[96]

The presence of religious orders added another layer to the claims of the bishop of Caracas and the haphazard presence of itinerant priests. Members of orders brought their own loyalties and responded to their own superterritorial hierarchies. Sometimes they melded smoothly with the secular church structure, and sometimes they were in varying degrees of conflict with it. The priests' varied nationalities, and their experience in a variety of jurisdictions, further complicated their allegiances, and also facilitated their ability to move around and between imperial structures.[97] Miguel Alexus Schabel, the Jesuit who ministered on Curaçao from 1704 until 1713, was by all counts a skilled politician who adroitly used his well-developed connections in both the Dutch and Spanish spheres to maneuver successfully between and around multiple levels of jurisdiction. He had extensive prior pastoral experience in Venezuela and Colombia, and had spent time in Amsterdam before arriving in Curaçao. Despite his access to the inner circles of the WIC on Curaçao (his sister was married to the garrison doctor), Schabel made sure to secure official approval of the bishop of Caracas before taking up his post on the island, thus ensuring that he was in the good graces of the various powers who might claim his allegiance.[98] In 1715, the same bishop officially named Agustín Caicedo as prefect of the mission on Curaçao and the other Caribbean islands, a position he held until his death in 1738, in spite of his previous run-ins with the Roman Catholic hierarchy on matters related both to doctrine and to contraband.[99] Thereafter, Curaçao's church reverted to the control of Flemish Jesuits until 1742.[100] Upon the death of the last Jesuit there followed three decades of confusion. Curaçao's flock was without a regular priest until 1751, when the bishop of Caracas appointed Father Miguel Grimón to the island.[101] In the interim nine years, Curaçao's Catholics once again depended on visits by itinerant priests while the local church council, made up of white laymen, took on the essential administrative duties.[102]

Local lay leaders did not always agreed with the church's transimperial structure. In 1746 Antonio Slijk, a Dutchman who was head of the lay Curaçao church council, directly questioned the authority of the bishop of Caracas over the island's Roman Catholic population. Proximity did not mean "spiritual subordination," he wrote, "considering that the Dutch States legitimately possess the island."[103] It is unclear, however, to what extent this was genuine concern about imperial jurisdiction rather than annoyance that visiting priests from Tierra Firme usually were somewhat sympathetic to the cause of black parishioners, and often sidestepped the white lay leadership.

By midcentury, the northern European hierarchy of the Roman Catholic Church apparently began to reexamine its neglect of the Dutch island. There followed several decades of power-playing at a time when no religious orders had a regular, sustained presence on Curaçao.[104] When Father Grimón requested another priest to assist him in his evangelization tasks, the bishop of Caracas responded with uncharacteristic caution, claiming that he first needed to ascertain the extent of his jurisdiction. Grimón repeatedly and unsuccessfully invited the bishop of Caracas to visit. In 1754, the Spanish Council of the Indies recommended a detailed study of the state of the church on the island, to be carried out "with the greatest caution and discretion."[105] Thereafter, the situation escalated, as multiple parties asserted their sometimes conflicting interests in overseeing the souls of Curaçao's Catholic majority. In 1755 a German priest, Father Petrus Gambier, arrived to depose Grimón, who hurriedly departed for the Spanish mainland on a small boat, probably one that was involved in smuggling, only to perish in a shipwreck near Coro.[106] Soon thereafter, Father Gambier also left the island on direct orders from the Congregation for the Propagation of the Faith in Rome, which cited his lack of proper authorization papers from the bishop of Caracas. (The island laity had engaged in an intense petitions war over Gambier's fate, which broke down along racial lines, with whites supporting him and free blacks seeking his removal.)[107] For the next two years, Curaçao's Catholics once again found themselves without spiritual leadership. Their prayers were somewhat answered in 1758 with the appearance of Father Antonio Navarro, a sick and broken man who arrived from the Yaracuy River valley, an area that had close ties to Curaçao via the contraband trade, on a boat that was captained by a well-known smuggler.

Navarro was in transit to a monastery in Europe to receive medical treatment and initially had no intention of ministering to locals. However, while Navarro convalesced in a country house to gain strength for the arduous transatlantic voyage, one group of Catholic parishioners petitioned the governor of Curaçao to appoint him to administer the local church, a move that was approved by the Spanish Council of the Indies and subsequently by church authorities in Rome. Navarro reluctantly stayed to fulfill these duties. But in 1760 the church authorized Father Theodorus ten Oever from the Netherlands to depose Navarro and assume control of the island's church, with the approval of the local church council. Although ten Oever informed the bishop of Caracas that he carried letters of appointment issued by Pope Clemente XIII, he pointedly refused to appear personally before the bishop to present his credentials. The bishop denied ten Oever the position and ordered Navarro to continue carrying out his duties, "with diligent prudence, cautiously, and with great care," which the latter did until his sudden death in 1763. At that point, appropriately, his body was returned to Coro in another small sailing vessel that probably was on a contraband mission.[108]

Following Navarro's death, the Dutch and Spanish intensified their diplomatic maneuverings to control the island's Roman Catholic Church, as they struggled to redefine an unofficial religious jurisdiction that had held sway for well over a hundred years. Over the next decade, a wide range of religious and secular authorities in both realms weighed in. Spanish authorities asked the Dutch to relieve ten Oever of his duties and to allow the bishop of Caracas to appoint priests to the island, or at least to require that the governor not accept any priest who had not first presented his credentials to the bishop of Caracas. Although this had been the de facto modus operandi for decades, it was an extraordinary request to make officially, considering that the Dutch had held undisputed sovereignty over the island since the Peace of Westphalia in 1648. Not surprisingly, the West India Company demurred. Although conceding that ten Oever lacked the proper credentials for a permanent appointment, company officials insisted that thereafter only Dutch priests be sent to the island. The Spanish Council of the Indies countered that the bishop of Caracas retained the exclusive right to designate priests for the island, citing the extensive historical precedent and, perhaps rather oddly, selected passages in the treaties of Westphalia and Utrecht that guaranteed the free practice of religion to denizens of areas that changed imperial jurisdiction.[109] Continued diplomatic wrangling produced an extensive paperwork trail but no clear resolution. In 1773 Bishop Martí proclaimed in Coro that "the islands of Curazao, Aruba and Bonayre belong to this parish of Coro and to the Bishopric of Caracas."[110] Nevertheless, three years later a group of eight Dutch Franciscans arrived to take charge of the prefecture, which their order controlled continuously thereafter until 1820.[111]

Religious ties between Curaçao and Tierra Firme strengthened throughout the eighteenth century, spurred by the sustained, direct contact between people on the ground as well as by the institutional framework. The handful of Catholic clergy who spent time on the island maintained communication with supervisors, fellow clergy, and parishes in Tierra Firme, as well as with their respective hierarchies and with clerical networks that fanned across the Americas and beyond. In a mirror image of the intercolonial trade that played out in the opposite direction, these religious connections were sanctioned fully by Spanish authorities, and largely ignored—or at least tolerated—by WIC officials in Curaçao. Priests who regularly crossed political boundaries opened an important network between the two colonial areas. Their mobility and flexibility allowed them to parlay religious connections into economic and sociocultural ties. There was also more direct contact at the grassroots level. People of African descent, the great majority of them practicing Roman Catholics, developed their own religious networks and exchanges. For example, in the 1760s and '70s, several religious brotherhoods (cofradías) in Coro had direct ties to similar societies in Curaçao, and some had members who lived on the island. One such society in Coro, the Cofradía del Carmen, even sent a delegation to collect alms from their brothers on the island, where they remained for six months.[112] Sailors, merchants, ship captains, small-scale traders, artisans, fugitive slaves, and other immigrants shared their religious beliefs and practices across the imperial divide.

By the early eighteenth century, having access to the souls of enslaved Afro-Curaçaoans apparently was not enough; authorities in Tierra Firme wanted their bodies as well.[113] During the War of the Spanish Succession authorities issued two royal provisions, in 1704 and 1711, offering freedom and even land to enslaved Afro-Curaçaoans who had arrived in Tierra Firme, provided they converted to Catholicism and were baptized after they arrived on the mainland.[114] This was a bit of a ruse, since Spanish authorities across the spectra, secular and ecclesiastical, colonial and imperial, knew that virtually the island's entire enslaved population already was Roman Catholic.[115] After all, they had been overseeing evangelization efforts there for decades. The manumission process was not automatic; new arrivals had to petition authorities separately for freedom and for land, as well as provide documentation and often third party testimony that they had converted to Catholicism and been baptized after arriving in Spanish territory.[116] What followed was an elaborate dance that played out within the Spanish colonial legal system, sometimes involving years of complicated proceedings, whereby authorities, fugitives, and witnesses (including members of the Roman Catholic clergy) duly certified the conversions and baptisms of people who already were Catholic in order to grant them legal freedom.[117] For example, three men who arrived in Coro from Curaçao in 1740 took six years of legal maneuvering to gain their freedom, and even changed their story several times along the way to enhance their case.[118] In some cases freedom was granted and then revoked multiple times over several years, or even decades. Curaçao was not unique here. Between 1680 and 1764 the Spanish Crown issued over half a dozen royal decrees and royal provisions authorizing colonial officials throughout the Americas to manumit runaway slaves who arrived from the colonies of rival Protestant powers, provided they converted to Catholicism and were baptized.[119] For approximately one hundred years beginning in the late 1600s, hundreds of enslaved people of African descent fled Dutch, English, Danish, and even French possessions in the circum-Caribbean to seek freedom in Spanish American colonies.[120] The Spanish Crown valued fugitive slaves not only for their labor but also as pawns in wider geopolitical maneuverings, including their value for intelligence about the colonies of rival powers.[121] By luring labor away from their enemies they built bases of loyal subjects in sparsely populated, relatively marginal areas, far from the empire's colonial centers. Throughout the eighteenth century, over one thousand Afro-Curaçaoans fled the island to seek freedom in Tierra Firme.[122] Such emigration spiked in times of economic decline, drought, and other crises. Once in Tierra Firme many of these immigrants maintained close ties with Curaçao via the contraband trade.

"Hovering Upon the Coast"

Illicit intercolonial trade was the bedrock of all other exchanges between Curaçao and Tierra Firme.[123] By the mid-eighteenth century this trade had expanded dramatically. Following the War of the Spanish Succession, the realignment of imperial power in the Atlantic world produced major changes in the character of the contraband trade. Colonial commerce increasingly became an end in itself for local merchants and other participants, whose economic interests increasingly diverged from those of the mother country across the Atlantic and large-scale merchants. What had begun in the early years under the first West India Company as a somewhat centralized endeavor, conducted and controlled by government and company officials, by the mid 1700s had become a way for a variety of local groups to promote their own economic interests and develop their own ties. This had social and cultural implications both in Curaçao and in Tierra Firme. Spanish colonial reports in this period abound with references to the wide social net that the contraband trade cast across socioeconomic and racial divides. In 1715, Alvarez Abreu observed that smuggling provided not just employment to the lowest classes of Indians, blacks, and mulattos, but also allowed them access to a wider range of more affordable goods.[124] "It is in no one's interest to block a trade in which almost everyone is implicated," Olavarriaga noted in his 1722 report.[125] With the consolidation of far-reaching networks of independent merchants, smuggling became a tool that formed part of and helped consolidate a much wider, dynamic process of creolization, one in which the interests of front-line participants, including colonial officials, were often at odds with those of more established merchants and imperial authorities.[126]

As Wim Klooster has noted, smuggling in the Americas "made a quantitative leap" in the first decades of the eighteenth century.[127] By midcentury, illicit intercolonial trade had become so prevalent that it was the cornerstone of many economies around the Americas. Local merchants and officials had no difficulty putting their own economic needs above those of distant imperial interests.[128] By the early decades of the eighteenth century, illicit trade across geopolitical boundaries had become a widespread problem for European powers throughout the Caribbean and the Americas, as extensive correspondence between colonial and imperial officials testifies.[129] As American populations grew and became well established, intercolonial trade became increasingly consumer-driven, fueled by demand for products that the European mother country was unable or unwilling to supply. This included not only the basic foodstuffs and manufactured goods that were needed for survival but also items that had been considered luxuries and were gradually becoming affordable to middling sectors.[130] As Governor Worsley of Barbados noted in 1723, "the inhabitants of this Island can't live without chocolate."[131] Across the Americas, smuggling allowed locals to put their own economic interests above those of the metropole, thus forging colonial economic identities that were specific to local circumstances.[132]

As illicit intercolonial trade took on an increasingly important role in local American economies, it also developed sociocultural dimensions.

The creolization of intercolonial trade shaped the societies of Curaçao and Tierra Firme throughout the eighteenth century. As they began to see their own interests as independent of those of their respective mother countries, many traders began to recognize the deep alliances they were forging with supposed foreign enemies across imperial boundaries. The ambivalence of Venezuelan colonial officials is particularly clear.[133] Officials in different areas who were involved in the trade sometimes developed intense political disputes with each other motivated by their divergent economic interests around the contraband trade.[134] Dealing with the trade, whether as participants or as repressors—and often as both—helped local and regional officials consolidate their own power vis-à-vis larger imperial structures. The participation of lower-echelon officials, especially those in more remote coastal areas, may have signified not only the clear and simple economic realities of their marginalized jurisdictions, but also their way of asserting some political and economic independence from regional and imperial seats of government. This was part of the broader process of separate identity formation that was taking place in colonies across the Americas throughout the eighteenth century and which, by the late eighteenth and early nineteenth centuries, spurred by the geopolitical upheavals of the Age of Revolutions and the Napoleonic Wars, eventually fed national independence movements throughout Spanish America, including Venezuela.

Rising demand for chocolate around the Atlantic world stimulated the development of entire new tracts devoted to cacao production in Venezuela. By 1720 there were over 4.5 million cacao trees on plantations across Tierra Firme.[135] Over the next decades the number increased steadily, especially in the valleys around Caracas, where plantings increased at an average of 75,000 trees per year. In the Tuy Valley south of Caracas, for example, the number of cacao trees rose from 300,000 in 1720 to 1.5 million in 1744.[136] The size of holdings varied greatly, reflecting the fact that cacao production attracted both large-scale agriculturalists and small-scale entrepreneurs. According to Olavarriaga's calculations, in 1720 48 percent of Venezuela's 677 cacao holdings contained 2,000 trees or fewer; only 15 percent had as many as 10,000 trees, and just 6 percent had over 16,000 trees.[137] The situation was not markedly different forty-seven years later in the town of Curiepe, site of Ana María Motete's groves. There, forty-nine people owned a total of 276,000 cacao trees. Twelve people, including Ana María Motete, had groves of just 1,000 trees, and twenty-six had holdings of 4.000 trees or fewer. Only ten people owned more than 10,000 trees, with the largest holding being 21,000.[138] Due to the hardiness of the trees, their low maintenance requirements, the relative imperishability of the beans compared to other agricultural products, and the ever-ready contraband market for even small quantities of beans, cacao cultivation was especially suited to small-scale farmers.[139] By the second half of the century, however, larger holdings were increasingly common. For example, in the area around San Felipe, up the Yaracuy River from Puerto Cabello, plantations of 10,000 to 40,000 were the norm by the late 1760s.[140]

The growth in the number and the size of cacao plantations in Tierra Firme spurred Curaçao's rise as a Dutch entrepôt.[141] Growing demand for cacao on the Atlantic market also changed the demographic configuration of Tierra Firme. By the early eighteenth century, settlers from Spain's Canary Islands were arriving in Tierra Firme in great numbers. Some acquired small landholdings and planted cacao; others were landless and turned to trade.[142] As the century progressed, cacao-producing land was increasingly concentrated in the hands of an emerging white elite, which, by the end of the century, was a small, closed group that had intermarried across the generations.[143] Increasingly larger holdings were concentrated in the hands of a smaller number of wealthier families.[144] By 1800, whites together represented only 14 percent of Tierra Firme's population; less than 1 percent of them were large-scale landholders.[145] At the same time, increasing numbers of laborers of African descent, enslaved and free, came to the area to work on the cacao plantations. Cognizant that the cacao plantations served an eager and growing global market, Spanish officials belatedly took steps to try to control the contraband trade and channel more earnings into the Spanish treasury. This was part of the new Bourbon Crown's strategy to control colonial trade in the decades following the Peace of Utrecht that ended the War of the Spanish Succession.[146] Spain's new Bourbon rulers implemented major reforms throughout their colonial possessions, aimed at bringing the colonies under royal scrutiny and addressing some of the problems that developed in the final years of Hapsburg neglect.[147] One strategy was to found new towns in isolated frontier areas to try to stem the contraband trade, especially towns that were made up of free blacks, such as Curiepe and others.[148] In 1720, the Spanish Crown sent Pedro José de Olavarriaga to Tierra Firme to document the scope and impact of the illicit interimperial trade. Olavarriaga traveled throughout Tierra Firme for eighteen months accompanied by an engineer. Together, they amassed a wealth of information on topics ranging from geography to economics to demography, and developed a detailed set of recommendations aimed at curbing contraband. Olavarriaga published his findings in an extensive report in early 1722.[149] Olavarriaga was not only meticulous in his documentation; he also actively tried to disrupt the illicit trade he was sent to study. Six months after he arrived in Tierra Firme, Olavarriaga already had confiscated fifty enslaved Africans as well as significant amounts of cacao, mules, horses, and clothing; driven away forty-four foreign vessels from the coast (the majority of them from Curaçao); and at least temporarily disrupted an active colony of Sephardic merchants at the coastal settlement of Tucacas, at the mouth of the Yaracuy River.[150] Olavarriaga sent to Venezuela's principal port, La Guaira, almost 1,700 fanegas of cacao from around the region, produce that was duly taxed and legally shipped to Spain instead of entering Dutch Atlantic commercial circuits via contraband circuits.[151]

Six years after Olavarriaga published his report, the Spanish Crown granted a newly formed Basque company, the Real Compañía Guipuzcoana de Caracas, or Caracas Company, full monopoly rights to trade in cacao and other commodities in Tierra Firme. Olavarriaga's dedication earned him a stint as the company's first director. The Caracas Company, which functioned until 1784, was one of Spain's most ambitious and comprehensive attempts to limit illicit trade and channel its wealth directly to the royal treasury.[152] The company established a coast guard that was authorized to intercept and repress suspected smugglers and confiscate their vessels.[153] Many of these seacraft subsequently were sold on the Venezuelan market, sometimes after lengthy legal disputes regarding their ownership.[154] Although it was not successful in stopping the contraband trade, the Caracas Company significantly disrupted it, increased the risk of getting caught, and channeled at least some of the profits directly to the Spanish Crown. In doing so, the company also sparked the wrath of the many different social sectors in Curaçao and Tierra Firme who depended on smuggling. It also forced them to become more creative in their endeavors.

Bolstered by the support of the Caracas Company, the Spanish Crown attempted to implement a broad-based policy against contraband, which included a detailed analysis of the routes that vessels were following. A royal decree dated 30 May 30 1734 authorized the seizure of all foreign vessels in the Caribbean found to be *navegando en rumbos sospechosos*, that is, "sailing suspicious routes," where, presumably, only illicit trade would take them.[155] Spanish authorities produced a detailed map that clearly indicated the Caribbean routes that a Dutch vessel conducting legitimate trade might be expected to take, as well as those that were presumed to be "suspicious."[156] A related report described several routes around the Caribbean that Dutch vessels were taking "that should be considered very suspicious in illicit commerce by virtue of not being necessary for the purpose of free navigation."[157] A royal decree issued in 1735 closed all the ports in northeastern Venezuela, thus forcing local producers to send their commodities overland to Venezuela's official port of La Guaira, at great cost and inconvenience.[158] Regular reports from Curaçao's governor to the Amsterdam chamber indicate that the Basque vessels plying the waters off the northern coast of Tierra Firme successfully disrupted enough of the clandestine commerce throughout the mid-eighteenth century to have a negative impact on Curaçao's economy.[159] Throughout the 1730s, the company captured at least fifty-six Curaçaoan slaves who were involved in contraband trade.[160] Repression against people who were caught smuggling often was severe.[161] Measures to curtail smuggling were only partially successful, however, and illicit trade in cacao and other products continued. Paradoxically, by closing the ports, and so further cutting the import of basic necessities to many mainland areas, Spanish officials actually stimulated the contraband trade, forcing smugglers to become even more creative in their activities and to seek out even more isolated rendezvous points. Moreover, they did not address the fundamental market issue. Dutch and Curaçaoan merchants were not the only ones conducting contraband trade in these waters; there are many reports of French and British vessels.[162] Sometimes these smugglers came into direct conflict. British privateers captured at least six dozen Curaçaoan vessels trading with Tierra Firme between 1740 and 1763; the French seized over a dozen more.[163]

Illicit trade required extensive preparations, a high degree of coordination and communication between all parties involved, clear planning as to the site and time of the rendezvous, and a certain degree of mutual confidence between the participants.[164] These mechanisms developed in response to changing circumstances not only in the societies and economies of Curaçao and Tierra Firme, but also within the Dutch and Spanish systems and in wider commercial circuits. As well situated as Curaçao was for trade with Tierra Firme, neither geographic positioning nor detailed policies handed down from above could ensure successful smuggling ventures. Someone had to travel to the lucrative source markets and establish reliable contacts, link the products with the vessels that were available to carry them, and sort out the innumerable logistical details that would guarantee the success of the operation. Much of this occurred outside the official structures of the West India Company. Even when functionaries made the initial contacts, they required not only reliable associates in Tierra Firme but also Curaçaoan counterparts to maintain and extend the trade via dozens of trips across the waters separating the two areas. It was not high-level company administrators or well-established Dutch merchants who carried out most of the trade with Tierra Firme. For this, seafarers and middling merchants were vital. Curaçao's denizens of African and Sephardic descent were on the front lines of such exchanges with Tierra Firme, alongside a variety of other participants.[165]

The owners of schooners and other small to medium-sized vessels that plied the waters between Curaçao and Tierra Firme often stayed in the home port and left their seacraft in the hands of experienced captains. Sometimes owners issued detailed instructions to their captains regarding the place to trade and other specifics.[166] In other cases, captains had leeway and flexibility to cruise along the shores of Tierra Firme in search of markets, often "hovering upon the coast" until they could "find an opportunity of running their goods in some creek, or bay in the nighttime."[167] Once a site was agreed upon, traders on both sides made extensive preparations. In 1742 the crew of a Curaçaoan sloop hired a Spanish pilot in Rio Hacha, who went ashore to make the necessary contacts and arranged for a fire to be lit at night as a discreet signal that, literally, the coast was clear and trade could begin.[168] Ideal coastal rendezvous sites were far removed from the official Spanish American ports and their meddlesome colonial officials.[169] Ports also were centers for the Inquisition, which not only was charged with prohibiting the introduction of heretical material in sailing vessels but also was authorized to inspect incoming cargoes. As a result, captains and merchants experienced delayed shipments and deliveries, and often unfavorable prices as a result, as well as unwelcome scrutiny of their cargo.[170] Vessels that lay offshore could avoid such scrutiny. They also did double duty as floating warehouses, gradually accumulating goods as the crew engaged in multiple encounters, until they were fully laden and could sail back to Curaçao.[171] Sometimes Curaçaoans were more brazen and openly anchored at ports like Puerto Cabello to exchange wares. Spanish authorities were well aware that bad weather or the lack of water or wood were common excuses that captains of foreign vessels used to visit a Venezuelan port, the better to engage in contraband trade. A report to the Crown in 1715 recommended that local officials board such craft and conduct an inspection to ascertain if, indeed, they had suffered storm damage or were low on vital supplies, and even suggested interviewing the crew.[172] It is unlikely that this suggestion was followed with any regularity, if at all, given the widespread complicity of locals.

Enterprising smugglers sometimes took the trade to sea in well-organized vessel-to-vessel encounters. On at least one occasion traders organized an elaborate mock attack by Curaçaoans on a Spanish vessel filled with cacao, so that the Spanish sailors could appear to be surrendering the commodity by force. In November 1735, upon arriving at the established rendezvous point on the Tierra Firme coast, Curaçaoan sailors sought their local contact, who previously had arranged the transfer of several sacks of cacao. The presence of the coast guard thwarted their carefully arranged plans for him to fetch the commodity from their vessel, however. Instead, he told them that "if we wanted to we could board his vessel and do as if we were taking it by force so his people would not catch on and tell the coast guard that he was selling it voluntarily."[173] Such activities required careful and elaborate planning beforehand, and close coordination between all parties.

Most of the trade was conducted by Curaçaoans visiting Tierra Firme. More rarely, Venezuelans sometimes traveled to the Dutch island to purchase small quantities of goods. Traveling in small fishing boats or canoes allowed them to stay well under the radar. More commonly, such traders might surreptitiously visit the warehouses on sparsely populated Aruba or Bonaire, where their selection of merchandise could go largely unnoticed.[174] Occasionally, larger Spanish vessels visited Willemstad to engage in illicit trade, en route to or from other Spanish America possessions.[175] For example, Spanish sloops that engaged in legitimate intracolonial commerce with Santo Domingo and Puerto Rico often stopped in Curaçao en route to dispatch some of their cargo for a more favorable price, and on return to load up on goods to sell in Tierra Firme.[176] It was reported in Venezuela in the early eighteenth century that the vessels that sailed to New Spain regularly carried up to twice as much cacao as they registered, thus allowing the captain and crew to turn a handsome profit in contraband along the way.[177] The cargo list of one vessel bound for Santo Domingo in 1712 was so minimal that it would not even pay for the drinking water on board, according to one report.[178] Sometimes Spanish vessels even visited Curaçao to procure cacao, an especially egregious violation of colonial restrictions given its abundance in Tierra Firme, but one that might be overlooked if they cited the exigencies of bad weather.[179] Most of the trade, however, took place from Curaçaoan vessels that visited the coast.

The intercolonial alliances that developed around the contraband trade often were transient, and they were easily broken when self-interest prevailed. Sailors freely pilfered small amounts of cacao and other contraband goods from the vessels on which they worked, to sell on their own.[180] Participants in joint trading ventures might steal outright from each other or dispute the division of the spoils.[181] There was always the risk of Spanish spies, who sometimes posed as allied merchants to foil contraband traders. Sometimes seemingly reliable contacts in Tierra Firme betrayed Curaçaoan traders.[182] Sailors often deserted en masse when a vessel faced capture.[183] The crew of one smuggling vessel avoided arrest by hiding in a priest's house in Venezuela and then paid the captain of a vessel from Curaçao to return them safely to the island.[184] Occasionally, a Spanish crew would desert upon arriving in Curaçao.[185] Such ambivalent relations between smugglers seems to have been typical in other areas where smuggling was prevalent.[186]

A variety of participants on both sides of the political divide facilitated the illicit movement of goods between Curaçao and the mainland. They included colonial government officials, members of the Roman Catholic clergy, indigenous people, and a motley crew of independent merchants and seafarers of different ethnicities and backgrounds, as well as members of the island's two diaspora groups.[187] In Tierra Firme, landholders large and small were eager to purchase European manufactures to ease their life and work, while seeking an outlet for their agricultural products. Plantation laborers, enslaved and free, often pilfered produce to sell on their own, as did runaway slaves and other "vagabonds," that is, landless people, both black and white. Soldiers, who were particularly open to risk-taking and were highly experienced in crossing political boundaries and navigating dangerous situations, also participated in the trade, especially in Tierra Firme, where they were often paid late or not at all for their military duties and so were anxious to earn additional income.[188]

Women from different social sectors supported the contraband trade in a variety of ways. In Tierra Firme, women across the racial and social class spectrum participated in the cacao economy. In the mid-eighteenth century, a free black woman named Dominga Gemba and the wealthy owner of a large cacao plantation, Doña Mariana Quixán, both opened their homes to clandestine meetings of smugglers in Valencia.[189] By 1767, women owned 11 percent of the 276,000 cacao trees in Curiepe, the Venezuelan town of free blacks where Ana María Motete had her grove.[190] By the eighteenth century, widows were major landholders among Tierra Firme's white cacao elite.[191] Rarely, however, were women on the front lines of the trade. Seafarers and maritime merchants were almost exclusively men. Back in the port, however, Curaçaoan women actively invested in clandestine commerce, albeit on a relatively small scale. Between 1721 and 1787, eight Sephardic women, half of them widows, owned eleven seacraft. Four co-owned their vessels with a man who was not necessarily their husband. Rachel, widow of David Bueno Vivas, owned three or possibly even four different vessels in the 1760s and 1770s.[192] The names of Dutch and Sephardic women, especially widows, appear occasionally on cargo lading lists, indicating that they assembled small lots of goods to ship to Europe.[193] A close inspection of the roster of Curaçaoan slaves who were caught smuggling in the 1730s reveals that thirteen of the forty-four owners of the captured slaves were women. Together, these thirteen women owned seventeen of the fifty-six slaves who were caught.[194] That is, in this single, small window into the intercolonial trade in one seven-year period, women constituted a full 30 percent of the investors, measured either by number of owners or by number of slaves owned. Similarly, women owned 31 percent of the 153 enslaved Curaçaoans who were temporarily manumitted to go to sea between 1741 and 1776.[195] These quasi-free seafarers actively participated in trade to the benefit of their erstwhile owners. In other cases, Curaçaoan women purchased slaves individually or in small lots to sell clandestinely in Tierra Firme.[196]

Local government officials in Tierra Firme played a significant role in intercolonial trade.[197] Spanish colonial authorities faced an intense, perhaps impossible, conflict of interest, as they simultaneously tried to serve the immediate needs of their isolated communities and to represent the economic and political interests of the Crown. Since the mid-sixteenth century, Tierra Firme's inhabitants had depended on trade with pirates, privateers, and independent merchants for the entry of basic manufactured products and as a market for their agricultural goods. A variety of foreign interlopers, in addition to sanctioned settlers, had frequented the coast, which also attracted independent maritime entrepreneurs in search of adventure and booty, and representatives of rival European powers who sought to encroach on the Spanish American empire.[198] Government officials at all levels were complicit in contraband. Some participated directly. Others were negligent in enforcing the relevant laws. Many committed crimes of both commission and omission.[199] The participation of mid-level officials in isolated provincial areas was particularly brazen.[200] "They themselves purchase the merchandise, and then sell it to their neighbors," according to one report.[201] In some areas, imperial neglect, low salaries, and the scarcity of basic goods all but forced officials, along with everyone else, into contraband trade.[202] "Their need obliges/forces them to open their hands to foreign commerce," the report noted.[203]

Large areas of the coast where clandestine commerce thrived remained thinly populated and in the control of several different indigenous groups until well into the eighteenth century. Most of these areas were served by bad roads, where any existed at all.[204] Foreign interlopers found it to their strategic advantage to trade with indigenous locals, who often felt minimal allegiance to the Spanish crown and its representatives.[205] In the eighteenth century, autonomous indigenous communities forged alliances with foreign smugglers in an effort to resist the encroachment of mainland authorities. The inhabitants of the many autonomous Indian villages just outside the town of Coro traded freely with Curaçaoans at midcentury.[206] Indian villages that were ministered to by Capuchin Fathers, who themselves were closely involved in smuggling, traded their agricultural crops to foreigners.[207] West of the province of Venezuela, the Guajiros of Santa Marta (in present-day Colombia) regularly acquired arms and ammunition from Dutch merchants to defend themselves against attempted Spanish domination; they also exchanged livestock, hides, and tallow for European manufactures.[208] Spanish colonial authorities tried repeatedly and in vain to curtail the participation of Guajiros in smuggling.[209] Contraband trade strengthened both the economic and the cultural autonomy of the Guajiros in the area around Rio de la Hacha.[210] Some indigenous groups served as intermediaries in the intercolonial trade.[211]

Roman Catholic clergy, who were allowed to travel relatively freely across the imperial divide, and who also enjoyed widespread respect among large sectors of the population on both sides, were particularly well positioned to make contacts and engage in illicit commerce. Curaçao's continued position under the jurisdiction of a Spanish American diocese, and the fact that most of the Catholic clergy who came to the island were itinerant priests from Tierra Firme, provided a natural conduit through which contacts could be established and the trade could be conducted. Priests traded a variety of commodities, including slaves from Curaçao.[212] Clergy also provided important contacts with indigenous people who were eager to trade.[213] José Pimentel, an apostolic priest, facilitated trade between Guajiros near Santa Marta and merchants from Curaçao.[214] Deep in the interior of Venezuela, in San Felipe, Father Francisco Rodriguez Camejo was arrested and put on trial for squandering over 12,000 pesos on the cacao trade in 1730.[215] The inherently transatlantic, interimperial character of Catholic clerical networks, including the fact that many felt their primary alliance to the Holy See in Rome, and/or to their religious orders, rather than to secular authorities in Madrid or Caracas, spurred economic exchanges outside official circuits. Residents of the various Franciscan monasteries that existed in a half dozen Venezuelan towns and cities were reported to "publicly trade in foreign goods."[216] Catholic clergy in Curaçao maintained close contact with their supervisors, colleagues, and parishes in Tierra Firme, boosting sociocultural contact between the two areas. The role of clergy in the contraband trade sometimes took on an intensely political character in response to changing Atlantic currents. After the Spanish Crown began allowing foreign Catholic priests to work in Spanish American colonies at the end of the seventeenth century, regional clerical networks were made up of a diverse group of men from a wide variety of European backgrounds and locations, men who had varied political sympathies and allegiances. Up to two-thirds of the Jesuits were non-Spanish.[217]

Curaçao's community of Sephardic Jews consolidated their role in contraband trade throughout the eighteenth century. Sephardim had an especially important role in the trade with Tierra Firme. "The Jews (above all) are those who come the most because they are the largest group on the island," Olavarriaga's 1722 report noted, "and because the majority of them are representatives of Merchants or Jews in Holland, they receive their compensation via the Vessels that come almost every day."[218] Sephardim forged close commercial ties with contacts in Tierra Firme from their earliest years on the island.[219] No doubt Curaçao's Sephardim encountered conversos among the mainland inhabitants. Contact between Sephardim in Curaçao and conversos on the mainland may have begun as early as the 1630s, as individuals were in both places even before there was a permanent Jewish settlement on the island.[220] By the early eighteenth century, there were semi-clandestine Sephardic enclaves in several parts of the mainland, including Santa Marta and Tucacas.[221]

Curaçao's Sephardim established a particularly thriving, open enclave in Tierra Firme at Tucacas, on the Yaracuy River east of Coro. They even built a synagogue there. By 1710 Tucacas was such a notorious center for illicit trade that the Spanish authorities tried, unsuccessfully, to eliminate it.[222] Sephardim lived so openly there that one, Samuel Hebreo, was known for a time as "Señor de las Tucacas."[223] A prominent Sephardic merchant from Curaçao, Felipe Henriquez (aka Felipe Senior), was another prominent denizen.[224] The dense mangrove swamp just off the coast, with its numerous islets, made the area especially suited to clandestine commerce. In 1722 Olavarriaga noted that "usually there are fourteen or fifteen Dutch ships in port" near Tucacas.[225] (Typically for such Spanish reports, Olavarriaga referred to all white people and vessels from Curaçao indiscriminately as Dutch, although most of the ships likely were owned and captained by Sephardim and most of the crew was black.) Olavarriaga reported that he burned down all the buildings in Tucacas in November 1720 and then organized a choir to sing the rosary in the smoldering synagogue. He noted that colonists returned to inhabit the three remaining houses as soon as he left. The resilient settlement was burned down twice more during his extended stay in Tierra Firme, in April and September of 1721.[226] These and other repeated attempts to rout the Sephardic merchants were unsuccessful, however, and vigorous trade resumed. The insistence of Curaçao's Sephardim on returning to Tucacas, even after such intense persecution, indicates that they had good connections among the area's inhabitants, and even suggests that perhaps there were local conversos who facilitated their contacts and exchanges. By the 1740s, smugglers were trading over one million pounds of cacao, as well as tobacco, cattle, and mules from Tucacas to Curaçao, often in exchange for enslaved workers whom they brought in clandestinely to work the growing cacao plantations.[227] Two decades later a visitor noted that Curaçaoan merchants were so prevalent, and traded so brazenly, that they acted "as if they were in their own domain."[228] The small town was especially suited to contraband trade: The easily navigable Yaracuy River provided links with fertile agricultural land deep in the interior, while the adjacent mangrove swamps afforded ample opportunities for smugglers to escape detection.[229] So important was the Yaracuy River for contraband trade that local Indians and whites were embroiled in an ongoing legal battle for navigation rights.[230]

As Olavarriaga's exploits make clear, Jews faced particular risks in trading with Spanish possessions. Sephardic merchants were especially anxious to avoid contact with the Inquisition, which might haul them to jails as far away as Mexico or even across the Atlantic to Spain.[231] Enterprising Spanish ship captains sometimes capitalized on this fear, extorting high ransoms from Sephardic merchants in exchange for the promise of not turning them over to the Inquisition.[232] Sometimes Spanish sailors and ship captains carried out atrocities against Jewish traders. The governor of St. Christopher reported in 1726 that he had received notice from the governor of Curaçao that "there were two Jews taken on board" when the Spanish seized a vessel from Curaçao along the coast of Tierra Firme, "who in their barbarous mirth they (the Spaniards) cut into very small peices, [sic] saying they wou'd not be at the trouble of sending them to the Inquisition."[233] Unlike more prosperous Dutch merchants who contracted out their regional trade, Curaçao's Sephardim often captained their own small vessels and traded their own cargo around the region, especially in the earlier part of the century. Sephardim also established close business relations with Protestant and Catholic merchants on both sides of the imperial divide.[234] Sometimes these commercial ties broke gender barriers. In the 1710s Phillip Henriquez, one of Curaçao's most successful Sephardic merchants, had an ongoing business partnership with Clara Catharina Kerckrinck, the Dutch widow of former island governor Jeremias van Collen, for trade ventures with Coro.[235]

Commodities, Laborers, and Traders

Enslaved and free people of African descent were a particularly important nexus between Curaçao's port city of Willemstad and its hinterland in Tierra Firme. They participated in intercolonial trade in three ways: as commodities, as enslaved laborers, and sometimes as autonomous agents acting in their own interests. As we have seen, enslaved Africans were one of the most important commodities in intercolonial trade already in the seventeenth century, and the slave trade helped pave the way for an integrated intercolonial commercial circuit between the two areas. Although the West India Company never regained a major role in the official asiento trade to Spanish America after the War of the Spanish Succession, independent merchants continued to conduct clandestine trade in slaves from the Dutch island to the Spanish mainland throughout the eighteenth century.[236] Their status as one-time commodities in the larger transatlantic slave trade continued to shape the identity of the great majority of blacks living in both Curaçao and Tierra Firme. The labor of people of African descent was vital to the functioning of the entire maritime commercial system in both the Dutch and Spanish spheres, from cultivating cash crops such as cacao and tobacco in Tierra Firme, to manning the vessels that plied regional waters, to working on the docks of Willemstad. Most of these laborers were enslaved. As the eighteenth century progressed, individuals of African descent sometimes found that the connections that the contraband trade opened between the two areas provided them with opportunities beyond their traditional roles as commodities and laborers. Men and sometimes even women of African descent, such as Juana Isabel Curazao and Ana

TABLE 5.1

Ethnicity of Venezuela's population, 1800

Ethnic/social group	Population	Percentage
White Spaniards and Canary Islanders	12,000	1.3
Locallyborn whites	172,727	19.0
Total whites	*184,727*	*20.3*
Pardos (mulattos)	407,000	45.0
Free and manumitted blacks	33,362	4.0
Black slaves	87,800	9.7
Fugitive blacks	24,000	2.6
Total blacks	*552,162*	*61.3*
Tribute-paying Indians	75,764	8.4
Non-tribute-paying Indians	25,590	3.3
Marginal Indians	60,000	6.7
Total Indians	*161,354*	*18.4*
Total population	*898,243*	*100*

SOURCE: Federico Brito Figueroa, *Las insurrecciones de los esclavos negros en la sociedad colonial venezolana* (Caracas: Editorial Cantaclaro, *1961*), *11–12*.

MariáMotete, found ways to participate in and benefit from smuggling on their own terms. Others found that the contraband circuits opened new prospects beyond the economic sphere. Such opportunities, however, occurred within the confines of maturing colonial slave societies. The harsh reality of enslavement remained a defining feature in the lives of people of African descent in both Curaçao and Tierra Firme.

By the eighteenth century, both the Dutch island and the Spanish mainland had a black majority. Although reliable demographic data from the extensive and remote tracts of Tierra Firme is scarce, free blacks and mulattos likely dominated the area demographically by the mid-eighteenth century. There was a particularly high percentage of free men and women. (See table 5.1.) By 1800, free blacks and mulattos made up 49 percent of Venezuela's total population of just under 900,000. Including slaves and maroons, people of African descent constituted over 60 percent of the population.[237] In the towns and cities they were

TABLE 5.2
Ethnic composition of Coro, 1794–95

Ethnic/Social Group	Population	Percentage
Whites	3,750	14.2
Free Indians (Caquetios)	7,443	28.2
Tribute-paying Indians	768	2.9
Total Indians	*8,211*	*31.1*
Free people of color	11,468	43.5
Slaves	2,962	11.2
Total blacks	*14,430*	*54.7*
Total	*26,391*	*100*

SOURCE: Archivo General de Indias; Sevilla, Spain ,Caracas, 426, folio 1, in Pedro A. Gil Rivas, Luis Dovale Prado, and Lidia Lusmila Bello, *La insurrección de los negros de la sierra coriana, 10 de mayo de 1795: Notas para la discusión.* (Caracas: Dirección de Cultura, Universidad Central de Venezuela, 1996), 96.

especially prevalent in commerce and related occupations. Internal marronage within Venezuela was common by the early 1700s, facilitated by the region's physical geography and by the lack of effective control by the Spanish. Olavarriaga calculated that already in the early 1720s there were 20,000 fugitive slaves throughout Venezuela.[238] This number of internal maroons likely represented a substantially higher percentage of a smaller overall population in the early 1700s compared to the end of the century. As table 5.2 shows, Coro's demographic distribution was somewhat similar to that of all of Tierra Firme, although with a higher overall proportion of Indians and a correspondingly lower percentage of whites and blacks. By the end of the eighteenth century, free blacks made up 43 percent of the area's population. Including slaves, people of African descent constituted almost 55 percent of Coro's inhabitants, slightly less than that of the entire province of Venezuela, but still a majority.[239] The second largest ethnic group was Caquetios who, unlike other indigenous people, were not required to live within a tribute-paying *encomienda* system, and so were relatively autonomous compared to other mainland indigenous groups.[240] Many Caquetios, who lived in settlements throughout most of the Paraguaná Peninsula and along the adjacent coast, retained close contact with Curaçao and were involved in inter-colonial trade. Many had maintained close ties with the Spanish since the early sixteenth century, and often sided with them against people of African descent.[241]

Spanish law promoted close relations between enslaved and free people of African descent. Although the Crown's colonial policy in the Americas forbade intermarriage between blacks and whites, intermarriage was common between free blacks and slaves, as well as between people of African and indigenous descent. Because a child's status depended on that of the mother, marriages across the divide of enslavement/freedom always resulted in children whose status was different from that of their fathers, and identical to that of their mothers.[242] Many skilled, relatively autonomous free black men had enslaved wives and thus unfree children. In contrast, the children of an enslaved man and a free black or mulatta woman were free. Frequent intermarriage between enslaved and free people further blurred the boundaries between these two social categories, creating nuanced communities and interactions and sometimes leading to particular social tensions across the lines of freedom/enslavement.

Slave ownership was much more skewed in Venezuela than in Curaçao. In both places it was widespread, but overall numbers were larger in Venezuela. "There are hardly any families in this Province who do not have four or five slaves, most have more than twenty, and many have over four hundred," an observer noted in 1715.[243] Although the largest concentration of slaves were employed on cacao haciendas and in the cultivation and processing of sugar, slave ownership was a status symbol even for middling sectors, who showed off their domestic servants.[244] As we have seen, people of African descent were a majority of Curaçao's population already in the first decades of Dutch rule, and they were the backbone of Willemstad's maritime economy.[245] By the end of the eighteenth century, enslaved and free blacks were 69 percent of Willemstad's population, while free blacks and coloreds made up over a third of the port's total number of free denizens.[246]

In 1741 Curaçao's governor noted that freemen frequently absented themselves from the island for extended periods, presumably to engage in the contraband trade.[247] Afro-Curaçaoan sailors were on the front lines of intercolonial trade. They often were charged with risky ventures such as going ashore to obtain cargo and negotiating the complexities of the exchange.[248] Between 1729 and 1736, Venezuelan authorities captured fifty-six enslaved Curaçaoans who were trading illicitly with the mainland, presumably with the tacit approval of their owners.[249] Enslaved seafarers who engaged in smuggling sometimes absconded when they reached the mainland.[250] Tierra Firme's vast, ungovernable land, including the longest coastline in the Caribbean, was not just ideal for smuggling goods; it also provided an excellent opportunity for enslaved people to escape bondage via self-smuggling. The population of unaffiliated blacks soared in coastal Venezuela throughout the eighteenth century, bolstered by fugitives from within the Spanish realm and those from Curaçao. Runaways from Curaçao had the added incentive of being able to petition the Spanish Crown for their freedom.[251] Many of the fugitives originally may have entered the mainland via the contraband slave trade from Curaçao, or they were the offspring of these forced immigrants. In Tierra Firme local communities of maroons participated in well-established contraband networks.[252] Already in 1722, Olavarriaga's report to the Spanish Crown cautioned that such "vagabonds" were major participants in the smuggling trade.[253] They regularly stole crops from haciendas to sell to foreigners, and often secreted them away to the coast under cover of darkness.[254] Once in Tierra Firme, many fugitive Afro-Curaçaoans also participated actively in the contraband trade. Afro-Curaçaoan runaways often established close links with communities of Afro-Venezuelans who were already involved in smuggling, including maroons, urban free men and women, and enslaved laborers who worked on the cacao plantations. But these relations were not always friendly. Sometimes local slaves could receive their freedom or other perks by denouncing smugglers. Fugitive Afro-Curaçaoans were an easy target.[255]

Coro and environs remained a popular destination of runaway Curaçaoan slaves throughout the eighteenth century and beyond. Some of the fugitives settled in town, especially in the neighborhood of free blacks and mulattos known as Guinea, located on the southern outskirts. Guinea was such a magnet for immigrants that it was the only neighborhood that saw steady demographic increase in the eighteenth century.[256] Others used Coro as a way station for rural destinations, especially in the nearby mountains.[257] Many congregated in the settlement of Macuquita, which was home to at least two hundred fugitives from Curaçao by the end of the century.[258] Periods of economic downturn and drought on the island spurred marronage.[259] The West India Company documented the flight of five hundred and eighty-five Curaçaoan slaves to Tierra Firme, primarily to Coro, between 1729 and 1774.[260] Eighty-nine of them were women (15 percent of the total). The majority of these fugitives were skilled tradesmen and -women. They included eighty-two seafarers and fourteen women whose occupation was listed as vendor. Most of the women probably had worked as market vendors within the port city of Willemstad, where they developed commercial skills that would have served them well in the thriving smuggling networks of Tierra Firme. Among the many occupations listed, no men were identified as traders. The fact that most of these runaways were skilled may be one reason local authorities welcomed them. There likely were many more who escaped not only slavery but also the historical record. The number and impact of the enslaved Curaçaoan runaways concerned colonial authorities in both Curaçao and Tierra Firme. The problem occasionally provoked serious diplomatic tensions, and it generated an extensive paper trail of official efforts to return the fugitives to Curaçao and counterefforts to prevent this in cases that could drag on for years.[261]

Curaçaoans of African descent had a major impact on communities along the mainland littoral. This is clear from the number of last names in Tierra Firme's historical record that are variations of the term Curaçao.[262] By the 1790s there were over four hundred identifiable Afro-Curaçaoans in the area around Coro.[263] Many lived in Santa María de la Chapa, a maroon community which was established in the surrounding mountains at midcentury.[264] By 1767 Santa María de la Chapa had a population of 154 inhabitants, many of whom were registered with last names that were some variation of the name Curazao.[265] Curaçaoans made up such a large percentage of the black population of Coro that they are considered to have made a significant contribution to the area's ethnic composition.[266] The Barlovento area to the east, including the free black town of Curiepe, was another favorite destination.[267]

By the second half of the eighteenth century, intercolonial fugitives had put into place a sophisticated transcolonial network to manage the process of emigrating from slavery on the small Dutch island to freedom in Spanish America, and to assist new arrivals in navigating the unfamiliar Spanish colonial system. This included finding sympathetic ship captains and crew members in Willemstad; safely crossing the waters to Tierra Firme without being captured; identifying, arriving at, and settling into mainland communities; learning a new language and culture; and, for those who sought to obtain their freedom officially, negotiating the complexities of an unfamiliar legal system.[268] Some slaves left the island openly by forging documents or posing as free men and women. Others surreptitiously stowed away on seacraft.[269] Many seafarers simply jumped ship once they reached a mainland port. Some enslaved sailors may have used their temporary manumission papers to try to claim freedom in Tierra Firme. Throughout the eighteenth century dozens of enslaved Afro-Curaçaoans who arrived in the mainland began the complicated legal procedures to obtain their freedom. The voluminous paperwork left by these cases often involved suits and countersuits, testimony for and against the fugitive by a wide range of local people, and a variety of sophisticated legal maneuvers and arguments. Fugitives had to become well versed in the relevant Spanish legal codes, strategies, and precedents (as well as the language), and they often used a variety of tactics to obtain the ultimate prize of freedom and land. Dozens of cases in Venezuelan archives attest to the tenacity and creativity of those who litigated to obtain their freedom. Some Curaçaoan litigants changed their stories multiple times as their cases wound their way through the Spanish courts.[270] We do not know how many fugitives pursued their cases in Venezuelan courts to obtain their freedom, or what percentage was successful in such endeavors. It is likely that the majority of people who fled across the imperial divide never bothered to legalize their status.[271] Legitimately purchased slaves also were sometimes emancipated. In 1721 forty-nine enslaved Curaçaoans who were sold by the Royal Guinea Company in Venezuela were later freed by the Audiencia of Santo Domingo, to the consternation of their owners.[272]

Not all fugitive Afro-Curaçaoan slaves found freedom and prosperity in Tierra Firme. Nor did all benefit from the legal system. Relations between people of African descent from Curaçao and those in Tierra Firme were not always harmonious. Afro-Venezuelans were often hostile to the special privileges the runaways received, especially their access to manumission and land via conversion, options that were closed to locals. Local slaves sometimes testified that an immigrant's conversion was bogus, an accusation that often probably was true. Venezuelan archives are filled with legal proceedings in which Africans from both sides of the imperial divide were pitted against each other.[273] Among the early inhabitants of the free black town of Curiepe, Curaçaoans and locals were embroiled in a bitter long-term dispute over property rights.[274] In 1745 mainland authorities commissioned Curiepe's free black militia to fight against contraband traders, even though the town's founders included many Curaçaoan fugitives who were closely involved in smuggling and retained close ties to the island.[275] The same porous boundaries that encouraged flight also facilitated the capture of fugitives and allowed close collaboration between interested parties across imperial divides. Sometimes runaway slaves were captured and resold into slavery on the mainland or returned to the island.[276] Representatives of the English asiento in Venezuela were authorized to sell runaway slaves and also those who were introduced to the mainland illegally.[277] Curaçaoan slave owners were not without recourse to reclaim their chattel. If a Curaçaoan owner petitioned in a mainland court for the return of a fugitive before the slave had converted, been baptized, and legally filed for freedom, Spanish colonial authorities would proceed with the extradition. Thus, mainland courts could be used to deny freedom to runaway slaves as well as to grant them rights. For example, in 1749 a Sephardic merchant from Curaçao, Moses Henríquez, traveled to Coro in pursuit of his mulatta slave, Mariana, who had fled the island with her infant daughter, Juana. Henriquez legally established his ownership rights to Mariana in a Coro court. His case was bolstered by testimony from several other Sephardim and that of a free black ship captain from Curaçao, Gaspar Antonio Quirigazo, who had been sent to get her. Henriquez then sold Mariana and Juana to a local cleric, Francisco de la Colina, who, in turn, gave them to his sister, who was the wife of a local government official.[278] If, as is highly likely, some members of the Colina family were involved in illicit trade, they may well have hoped to develop lucrative business ties with the Curaçaoan merchants. The records do not indicate whether Mariana had tried to win her freedom with a professed conversion. Cases such as these could drag on for years in mainland courts.[279] For people of African descent, then, the transcolonial exchange circuit could be a mechanism of enslavement as well as a path to freedom.

In all these cases it is notable how easily Afro-Curaçaoans navigated not only the waters between the two colonies but also the legal system of the rival Spanish empire and were allowed to do so. Escaped Curaçaoan slaves, as well as free men and women, were not afraid to use the Venezuelan legal system to fight for their own interests. These cases also demonstrate that the boundaries between freedom and enslavement, like the colonial borders themselves, sometimes were fluid. Complicated transactions linked women and men across geopolitical, geographic, social, and ethnic boundaries, in complex webs of human relations that were woven around intercolonial exchanges.

Marronage occurred in both directions, although archival data about slaves who escaped from Tierra Firme to Curaçao is less frequent and more dispersed. However, it was common enough that several laws at midcentury addressed the issue. In 1731, Spanish slaves who were on Curaçao without clear owners or affiliation with rural landholdings were ordered to work on fort repairs.[280] In 1740, Governor Faesch ordered that fugitive slaves from Tierra Firme be hunted down and returned, preferably in exchange for runaways from Curaçao who were in Coro and Caracas.[281] A 1748 law further stipulated the treatment of runaway slaves from Spanish territory who were caught in Curaçao. Locals were forbidden from offering them protection, lodging, or sustenance; from transporting them clandestinely back to the mainland; or from hindering their arrest, under penalty of a stiff fine of 180 pesos. This was part of an agreement with mainland authorities that the two areas would exchange runaways.[282] That same year, Gaspar Antonio Quirigazo, a free black Curaçaoan ship captain, brought back to Coro ten fugitive slaves who had been living on the island.[283] Three years later, a Coro notary sought the return of two of his slaves who were living in Willemstad, in exchange for two fugitive Afro-Curaçaoans.[284] Slaves from Tierra Firme were attracted by the employment opportunities, the higher standard of living, and the relative autonomy of people of color that existed in the maritime economy of Curaçao's bustling port of Willemstad. In 1745 it was reported that Juan Pedro had been missing from the Venezuelan town of Mitare for at least ten years; the local priest had it on good authority that he was in Curaçao.[285] Such cases were relatively rare, however, compared to successful marronage in the other direction. The lack of legal enticements, Willemstad's relatively compact layout, scant opportunities to work or hide on the rest of the small, desert island, and the reluctance of WIC officials to provoke Spanish colonial authorities unnecessarily, meant that relatively fewer slaves escaped from Tierra Firme to Curaçao. Most of those who did eventually were returned to their owners.

Beyond Trade

By the mid-eighteenth century, smugglers across the socioeconomic spectrum had developed a well-integrated exchange circuit between Curaçao and Tierra Firme. The regular flow of vessels, commodities, and people linked to contraband created opportunities for other types of intercolonial exchanges, ones that built on, but sometimes went beyond, trade. Along with commodities, people who were in regular contact with each other via the smuggling economy also exchanged ideas, perspectives, and languages, and they shared a variety of skills. Evidence of the ongoing contact between Curaçao and the Caribbean coast of Tierra Firme is preserved today in the region's architecture. Contraband trade left its mark on the built environment in both the island and the mainland. Dozens of eighteenth-century buildings in port towns along the Venezuelan coast, from Puerto Cabello to Puerto de Vela to Coro to small settlements on the desolate Paraguaná Peninsula, show clear Dutch influence.[286] This required cultural exchange and the transfer of knowledge at multiple levels, not only interest in the Dutch style on the part of wealthy local merchants, but also technical expertise on the part of carpenters (often of African descent) so they could replicate the structures both physically and artistically using the appropriate materials. Some merchants in Tierra Firme who grew wealthy from the contraband trade built elegant urban dwellings in coastal ports that closely resembled the Dutch gabled houses that lined the streets of Willemstad. Entire streets of Puerto Cabello and Puerto de la Vela have a decidedly Dutch colonial feel. Intercultural contact also influenced interior design. Elite merchants in Venezuela's port towns often furnished their homes with objects such as mirrors, artwork, furniture, and china that bore a clear Dutch rather than Spanish influence. This reflected their access to these commodities via extra-official exchange circuits.[287] Creolization was at work on two separate but interconnected socioeconomic levels here: among the emerging urban merchant upper classes, who desired to imitate Dutch rather than Spanish styles, and had the means to do so, and among lower-class laborers (many of African descent) who possessed the necessary technical skills to reproduce buildings, furnishings, and so on, and so fulfill the aspirations of the upper strata. Both levels spoke to the widespread sociocultural impact of the contraband trade, which influenced not only access but also taste. The influence went both ways. Laborers and artisans from Coro and perhaps also Caracas had a major role in the design and construction of the Roman Catholic Church that was built in Otrobanda in the mid-eighteenth century, as well as in fashioning its furnishings and religious objects.[288] Construction materials that were exported illicitly from Tierra Firme influenced building styles in Curaçao. This was especially true with wood, which was scare on the small arid island.[289]

Ongoing repression of contraband trade shaped patterns of popular resistance and collaboration across the imperial divide. Sometimes smugglers parlayed their transcolonial contact into collusion against those who would limit the trade. Within Venezuela, the formation of the Caracas Company in 1730 met with immediate resistance among the many different people who were involved in illicit intercolonial trade. There were at least six major rebellions in cacao-producing areas during the fifty-four years of the company's existence. These included the one led by Andrés López del Rosario in the Yaracuy Valley (1730–32), a 1740

uprising in San Felipe el Fuerte, one in El Tocuyo in 1744, a slave uprising in Caracas in 1749, a revolt against the Caracas Company led by the
Canary Islander Juan Francisco de Leon in 1749, and a 1781 uprising in
Mérida.[290] Venezuelan historian Carlos Felice Cardot sees these uprisings as helping consolidate an emerging proto-national identity among
Venezuelans, who rallied across divides of race/ethnicity and social class
to defend their common economic interests against those of the Spanish
Crown, so paving the way for the subsequent independence movements
of the nineteenth century.[291] These disturbances provide clear evidence of
the close relations that developed between the very different participants
in the contraband trade. Smuggling sometimes proved to be a unifying
force, trumping race, ethnicity, social class, and even colonial affiliation.

The first of these revolts broke out in 1730, soon after the Caracas
Company began patrolling the Caribbean coast of Tierra Firme. It was
led by Andrés López del Rosario, alias Andresote, a mixed-race Venezuelan of African and indigenous descent who had close ties to the trade
with Curaçao. There is some disagreement among Venezuelan historians
about Andresote's status. Brito claims he was born a slave but had joined
maroon communities years before the uprising. Others say he was free,
either by birth or manumission. His status at birth would have depended
on that of his mother.[292] The uprising of slaves, free blacks, mulattos, and
native people that he led was directed against the Caracas Company and
the colonial authorities who were trying to curtail smuggling. It had the
full support of local whites, including elite landholders. At its height,
participants took over several towns and blockaded roads in the Yaracuy
Valley, a major contraband area and site of the thriving settlement of
Tucacas. (Olavarriaga had devoted several pages of his 1722 report to
cacao production and contraband trade in the Yaracuy Valley. He had
suggested that local fortifications be improved and the river mouth and
port be dredged, so that larger ships capable of making the transatlantic
crossing might arrive directly to purchase cacao, tobacco, and mules,
thus circumventing smugglers and channeling revenue to the Spanish
Crown.[293] These recommendations largely were ignored.) Most of the
Yaracuy Valley's inhabitants, including local officials, enslaved plantation workers, indigenous people, and maroons, as well as white farmers,
rightly felt that their entire livelihood was jeopardized when the Caracas
Company began to crack down on smuggling. Curaçaoan traders, who
also felt threatened by the company's activities, provided critical support to the rebels. They traded arms and alcohol to them in exchange
for cacao.[294] When officials sent in several thousand troops to repress

the uprising, Curaçaoan smugglers whisked Andresote off to the nearby island, where he remained at least until 1739.[295] Venezuelan authorities offered a bounty of six hundred pesos and full immunity to anyone who killed him, with the promise of freedom if his slayer were a slave. They also noted that the incident had occurred in an area that already was rife with smuggling and further "facilitated commerce with foreigners."[296] In the subsequent trials, several residents of Tierra Firme testified that they had taken Andresote to Curaçao several times to purchase goods prior to the uprising.[297] One must read such testimonies with a healthy dose of skepticism, however, since the witnesses would have had little to lose by fabricating or exaggerating such ties, and stood to improve their own situation if they fed authorities the information the latter hoped to hear.

The uprisings in Tierra Firme were also connected to deeper currents related to enslavement and freedom that swirled around the Atlantic world during the second half of the eighteenth century. As early as the 1740s, stories began to circulate among Tierra Firme's black majority that the Spanish Crown had issued an order to free all slaves throughout the empire, and that local authorities simply were refusing to comply.[298] These rumors intensified later in the century. The fact that the Crown had, in fact, offered freedom to fugitives from Curaçao may well have helped to keep this rumor alive by demonstrating that it was not completely outside the realm of plausibility. For almost twenty years, between the 1770s and 1790s an enslaved healer named Cocofío often absented himself from his master and traveled around the mainland countryside, proclaiming that a Spanish royal decree had freed the slaves but was being suppressed by local authorities.[299] The rumors persisted after Cocofío's death in 1792. They allegedly were fanned by fugitive slaves from Curaçao, who brought more reliable news from the port of Willemstad of the French and Haitian revolutions, including reports from black seafarers that slaves had been freed elsewhere in the Caribbean.[300] This social unrest was intensified by local factors. By the end of the eighteenth century, in response to the exploding Atlantic market for chocolate, Tierra Firme's lucrative cacao plantations were increasingly concentrated into larger holdings that were held by fewer families and worked by larger numbers of slaves. By the 1790s, plantations were concentrated among just eight major families; large-scale landowners made up only 3 percent of Coro's white population and 0.5 percent of the total.[301]

By the last decades of the century, the geopolitical usefulness of people of African descent in Tierra Firme also was shifting. Already in 1771 the commander of the Caracas battalion warned of "the suspicion and fear which is being caused by the continued flight of black slaves from Curaçao."[302] When the schooner *La Americana* arrived in Puerto Cabello from Curaçao in September 1790 with a shipment of thirty-one enslaved Africans to sell, local authorities opposed the disembarkation of nine of the slaves who apparently had been born in Curaçao. (The other twenty-two were recent arrivals from Africa.) "It has been observed that creole slaves or those who have been educated in foreign colonies are detrimental to these provinces," a Spanish colonial official wrote a few months later, articulating a sharp break from previous policies that had welcomed fugitives from the Dutch island.[303]

In 1791 Spain and the Netherlands signed an agreement for the reciprocal return of fugitive slaves, "especially between those in which the complaints of desertion have been the most frequent."[304] The accord specifically noted the close relationship between marronage and contraband trade between Curaçao and Coro.[305] Two years earlier, in 1789, Spain finally had allowed free trade in enslaved Africans to some of its American colonies, including Venezuela, Cuba, Santo Domingo, and Puerto Rico.[306] This eliminated, at least in theory, the need both for the asiento and for the parallel contraband trade in slaves. It is not entirely clear, however, how this played out, especially in the short term, and whether, in fact, it immediately led to the cessation of the illicit trade in enslaved labor that had enriched so many people in both Curaçao and Tierra Firme. In the early 1790s, increasingly concerned about the widespread travels of people of African descent around the Caribbean and the potential impact of news of the developing Haitian and French Revolutions, the Spanish Crown rescinded the decrees that had granted freedom to runaway slaves from rival powers.[307] Foreign fugitives were now seen as a threat to Spanish interests, rather than as an opportunity to boost colonial loyalty and manpower.

Spanish fears were not unfounded. In the summer of 1795, sixty-five years after Andresote's rebellion, slaves planned and carried out revolts within three months of each other in Coro (May) and Curaçao (August). Unlike Andresote's 1730 uprising, these revolts garnered no broad-based support across lines of race/ethnicity and social class, although both also involved a significant number of free blacks. In both places, authorities quickly allied with local elites to punish the unsuccessful rebels and executed the leaders. The Coro rebellion began with a series of meetings among slaves and free men and women in the mountains south of Coro, an area with several cacao haciendas.[308] On May 10 the rebels, led by José Leonardo Chirinos, attacked several of the haciendas and killed the owners. A group of them then began marching toward the town.[309] Authorities in Coro were well aware of their own vulnerability. They could not count on the support of the militias that were made up of slaves, free blacks, and Indians. The rebels, however, numbering at least 300 and possibly as many as 450, did not attempt to take the town until the following day. This gave authorities enough time to assemble an adequate defense. They killed over two dozen rebels and caused the rest to disperse. Authorities quickly arrested and killed a freeman who lived in town, José Caridad Gonzalez, whom they claimed was one of the brains behind the plot and was conspiring with a group of twenty-one urban free blacks to join the rebellion.[310] Chirinos was captured in early August, taken to Caracas, and sentenced to death the following December. At least 162 rebels were executed. Another seventy-eight were subjected to a variety of harsh punishments, ranging from flogging to hard labor to prison to public humiliation. These included at least seven Indians, several women, and thirty-three so-called Loangos.[311]

The leadership of the Coro uprising indicates the complex ties that were woven around enslavement and freedom, and across the geopolitical boundaries that nominally separated Curaçao and Tierra Firme. José Leonardo Chirinos was a freeman, the son of an enslaved man and a free Indian woman, who worked as a day laborer on two different cacao plantations so he could be near his enslaved relatives. Chirinos's father labored on one of the plantations, and his enslaved wife lived and worked with their children on the other. Chirinos likely had close ties with people who smuggled cacao off both plantations, and he may well have been directly involved in contraband trade himself. There is evidence that he traveled to both Curaçao and Saint Domingue in the early 1790s with José Tellería, his wife's owner and his employer, who had commercial ties to both islands, and was involved in the mule trade.[312] Ties between the Tellería family in Coro and Curaçaoan runaways had deep roots. In the 1740s another José Tellería purchased three slaves who had escaped from the island but had not succeeded in finding freedom on the mainland.[313]

José Caridad Gonzalez, whom authorities accused of masterminding an aborted simultaneous uprising of free blacks in the town of Coro, was born in West Central Africa, where he was captured and forcibly transported across the Atlantic to Curaçao by Dutch slavers.[314] Records identify him as Loango, although it is unlikely that this was a meaningful indication of either ethnicity or precise African provenance. As a young man, Gonzalez, known in Curaçao as José Kopra, fled to freedom in Tierra Firme and settled in the town of Coro. Thereafter, he facilitated the escape of other enslaved people from Curaçao along a well-established route that he knew well, and which had been used by hundreds of Afro-Curaçaoans since Juana Isabel Curazao's escape in the 1720s.[315] Gonzalez also helped defend the lands of several free blacks against the incursions of the area's major landholders, in cases that bear a strong resemblance to that of Ana María Motete.[316] Gonzalez traveled to Spain to procure a royal decree supporting the small-scale owners, several of whom were fugitives from Curaçao.[317] He also traveled regularly to Caracas to meet with colonial authorities, whom he hoped would appoint him as the leader of a militia made up of free blacks from Curaçao.[318] Sometimes he stayed away for years at a time, according to his wife, who also testified that he had been back from Caracas less than a month before the rebellion broke out.[319] Gonzalez was fluent in French, Spanish, and Papiamentu.[320] He likely also knew at least some Dutch and one or more African languages. In Coro, he maintained close contact with the communities of fugitive slaves from Curaçao. He even proposed to authorities in Caracas that he lead a militia composed of these so-called Loangos, alongside the existing free black militia.

The largest slave revolt in Curaçao's history took place just three months after the Coro rebellion. It began on August 18 on Kenepa, the island's largest and most prosperous rural estate (although such terms are relative), located on the western end of the island, and soon escalated into a full-scale, island-wide uprising.[321] Led by a field slave named Tula, all fifty of the estate's slaves joined in the work stoppage, procured some arms, and marched to the next nearest plantation, Santa Cruz, where Tula's co-conspirator, a black overseer named Karpata, was waiting with another contingent. The entire group then moved steadily toward town. They passed through all the landholdings on the southern coast along the way and rapidly increased their numbers until there were two thousand, including a group of free blacks. As news of the uprising reached town, the governor mobilized soldiers and the various militias, put the corps of free blacks under white command, and forced the rebels to disperse to the countryside. Almost half of the two hundred troops that attacked and captured the rebels were blacks or mulattos. The rebels found few places to hide on the barren island, although some held out for a few weeks. A month after the rebellion started, most had either been captured or returned to work. In the end twenty-nine were executed, the leaders first subjected to brutal torture. Many more had been shot in the field.

Some contemporaries and subsequent researchers have claimed that the slaves and free blacks in Curaçao and Coro had planned to carry out their revolts simultaneously, but that the insurgents in Coro rebelled several months ahead of schedule.[322] Several authorities in Coro testified that at least twenty-one free blacks from Curaçao (so-called Loangos) had conspired with José Caridad Gonzalez in town, and that a number of others had joined the uprising in the countryside.[323] The rural rebels supposedly send two Curaçaoans to town to inform Gonzalez of their plans.[324] However, even at the time, Venezuelan authorities disagreed as to the role fugitive slaves from Curaçao had in the uprising, whether among the rebels in the countryside or as part of the urban contingent in Coro that supposedly was to join them under Gonzalez's leadership. Several contemporary reports noted the participation of Curaçaoans.[325] Others, however, stressed their loyalty. For example, less than a month after the uprising, an official in Coro observed that a contingent of Curaçaoan fugitives had been doing hard labor fortifying the town's defenses "at no more than subsistence wages," praised their "submission to the sovereign," and noted that "at all times and occasions they have been loyal."[326] The leaders of Coro's free black militia, at least one of whom was from Curaçao, pleaded that they were "loyal vassals of his Majesty."[327] Another argued that the Curaçaoans who had been detained in the wake of the uprising were simply "poor souls who have not committed any crime."[328] Among the Curaçaoans who were captured and imprisoned were children and "useless old men."[329] Ultimately, the Real Audiencia of Caracas exonerated all of the Curaçoans, noting that they were "loyal servants of the King," and allowed them to return to Coro.[330] Authorities were aware that there also had been an uprising on the nearby island. In September 1796, an extensive report to the Spanish Crown mentioned the "suspicions which the feared revolution in Curaçao has caused" and discussed in depth the problem of marronage from Curaçao.[331]

Contemporaries and historians alike have raised the possibility of a wider Caribbean conspiracy. One of the leaders of the Curaçao rebellion, Tula, often went by the name of Rigaud, a reference to the mulatto general, Benoît Joseph Rigaud, who was a military leader of the uprising in Saint Domingue. Although some historians have suggested that Tula had ties with the Saint Domingue rebels, hard evidence for this appears to be elusive.[332] However, in his meeting with Father Jacobus Schink, the Roman Catholic priest whom local authorities sent to negotiate with the rebels, Tula demonstrated his clear understanding of the geopolitical context in which the Curaçao rebellion took place, including the French and Haitian revolutions and the French invasion of the Netherlands in January 1795. "We seek to do no one harm, but seek our freedom," Schink reported that Tula told him. "The French blacks have their freedom. Holland has been taken by the French, thus we should also be free here." When Schink insisted that the Dutch retained political control of Curaçao, Tula asked pointedly, "If that is the case, where are the Dutch ships?" This apparently was a reference to the lack of Dutch warships in the Willemstad harbor, rather striking in light of the French invasion of the Mother Country. Tula also indicated that Curaçaoan landholders were deeply afraid of the impact of the Haitian Revolution on local slaves' aspirations for freedom: "Mr. [Heer] Father, the French freedom has served as a torment for us," Tula explained; "if one of us gets punished he is constantly asked to his face, 'Do you also seek your freedom?'"[333] Schink also reported that the rebels sang French freedom songs.[334]

Several Venezuelan authorities claimed that the Coro rebels had not only been influenced by the events and ideas of the French and Haitian revolutions, but that they also were in communication with, and expected assistance from, French vessels that were stationed off the coast.[335] (It is likely that these were either privateers or traders engaged in contraband.) Some historians, however, maintain that authorities and plantation owners invented any such conspiracies to justify heavy-handed repression and to manipulate whites' fears of conspiracy to their own ends.[336] Gil, Dovale, and Lusmila argue that the Venezuelan historiography has overemphasized the influence of outsiders, including the impact of people and ideas from both Curaçao and Haiti, and that it relies too heavily on the hysterical and paranoid testimonies of threatened white contemporaries, for whom a supposed slave conspiracy was useful to further consolidate their political and economic interests. They note that an overemphasis on external influences has overlooked local and regional factors that sparked the Coro revolt. In particular, they point to the intensifying concentration of cacao plantations into fewer and larger holdings that were controlled by an increasingly powerful and smaller local elite, and were worked by larger numbers of enslaved Africans. This situation deprived many lower and middling sectors of the opportunity to profit from the cacao trade. In this view, local elites sought to divert attention away from the increasingly polarized socio-economic situation, including a rise in the number of enslaved people who were tied to plantations. They pointed to supposed outside agitators as a convenient scapegoat that would capture the attention of remote imperial authorities and help increase their own hold over the local society and economy.[337]

We may never know with certainty the exact degree and type of collaboration that existed between the rebels in Curaçao and Coro. But it is clear from the ongoing contact between people of African descent in the two areas, and the involvement of people like José Caridad Gonzalez—who maintained close ties both with Curaçao and with communities of fugitive slaves from the island and their descendants who had settled in Coro—that some of the people who were involved in the two revolts were connected at some level. Throughout the eighteenth century, both the town of Coro and settlements in the surrounding mountains had received hundreds of runaway slaves from Curaçao, who established recognizable communities that maintained both a certain Curaçaoan identity and contact with the island.[338] Enslaved and free women and men who traveled between the island and Coro would have carried news about rising discontent and plans to organize resistance in both places, as would have others who were involved in the contraband trade. Word of the May uprising in Coro, and the subsequent repression, certainly reached Curaçao well before August. Such contact continued after the rebellions. In September 1795, military authorities in Coro reported that at least two groups of fugitives had arrived from the Dutch island since the August uprising there, complaining that increased repression and chronic food shortages made life intolerable.[339] It was the well-established contraband circuits that faciliated the transmission of all this information. The largest slave revolts in the southern Caribbean occurred almost simultaneously in two places that had been closely linked by trade and migration for over a hundred years, processes in which people of African descent had a central role. Whether or not there was a direct conspiracy, the mobility of the area's black majorities across geopolitical boundaries shaped both rebellions. This mobility was intricately linked to smuggling. By 1795, people of African descent in both areas had been part of extensive intercolonial networks for well over a hundred years. They forged deep, multifaceted ties which went far beyond communicating about revolt to encompass economic, religious, and sociocultural connections.[340]

Common language facilitated communication between the rebels of Coro and Curaçao. José Caridad Gonzalez was fluent in several languages, including Papiamentu.[341] Gonzalez was not the only Papiamentu-speaker who participated in the Coro uprising. By the second half of the eighteenth century there were Papiamentu-speaking enclaves of fugitives slaves from Curaçao in the hills around Coro as well as in the town itself.[342] Throughout the eighteenth century, hundreds of

Afro-Curaçaoans like Gonzaléz, fugitive slaves and traders alike, carried Papiamentu to Coro and other communities throughout Tierra Firme, as well as to the Spanish islands with which Curaçao had close trade relations, including Santo Domingo and Puerto Rico.[343] By the late eighteenth century, Papiamentu had become the lingua franca of the majority of people who participated in Curaçao's regional trade, Sephardic Jews as well as people of African descent. Papiamentu's rise and consolidation provides a window into the broader creolization processes that occurred around the intercolonial exchange circuits that sustained Curaçao's maritime economy and society.

6 / Language and Creolization

In 1775 a young man named Abraham de David de Costa Andrade Jr. poured out his heart to a member of his synagogue, Sarah de Isaac Pardo y Vaz Farro: *My diamanty no laga dy skirbimy tudu kico my ta puntrabo—awe nuchy mi ta warda rospondy* ("My diamond, do not fail to write me everything I am asking you—tonight I await an answer"). Apparently Abraham shared more than his feelings with Sarah. She was expecting a baby, probably not fathered by her dying husband, a prosperous merchant who was also her elderly uncle and was, according to the sworn testimony of his doctors, impotent. Abraham's marriage, like Sarah's, was childless. With Abraham's encouragement Sarah tried unsuccessfully to abort the fetus, using herbal remedies provided by her slaves. "Write to me how you are and what that negress says, when you will throw it," her lover implored, to which the pregnant women replied, "Davichy is very tough, he refuses to fall." In due time, Sarah gave birth to a healthy boy, apparently none the worse for his exposure to abortifacients. After the birth, synagogue elders excommunicated the two adulterers. Whether the excommunication should hold and what restrictions, if any, there would be on Sarah and her son, caused a scandal that rocked Curaçao's Sephardic community and led to litigation in secular and religious courts on both sides of the Atlantic for twenty years. It divided the congregation to such an extent that some historians believe it was the catalyst for an eventual permanent split. Several interested parties sought the intervention of the States General of the Netherlands and of the elders of Amsterdam's Sephardic community. A few years after his birth, upon orders from Dutch authorities, Sarah's son finally was circumcised as the legitimate offspring of her long-deceased husband, whose name he bore. Sarah remarried and was whisked off to the Danish island of St. Thomas, at the Curaçao congregation's expense. Abraham, disgraced, moved to Jamaica.[1]

Of greater historical significance than the tragic love story of the young Abraham and Sarah and their successful, if illicit, procreation, is the fact that their letters are the earliest known documents written entirely in Papiamentu. The incriminating correspondence, which was described in court records as being written "in black speech" (negers spraake) or "in creole speech" (crioolse spraake), was the primary legal evidence of the lovers' adultery and the basis for their excommunication.[2] Why did two Sephardic Jews from respectable merchant families choose to communicate their most intimate feelings in a creole language? How were Curaçao's Sephardim involved in the genesis and diffusion of what was to become one of the Caribbean's most successful creoles—a language genre that usually is associated with the transatlantic slave trade, plantation society, and people of African descent? Why did Curaçao's Sephardim and people of African descent speak Papiamentu, which is clearly based on Iberian tongues, instead of a Dutch-based creole? Answers to these questions lie in the specific conditions of the commercial economy and society of the port city of Willemstad during the seventeenth and eighteenth centuries, and in the exchange networks that Curaçao's inhabitants developed via maritime trade. The emergence and consolidation of Papiamentu across lines of social class and race/ethnicity provides clear evidence of the dynamic processes of creolization that occurred around Curaçao's maritime economy at the height of the island's success as an Atlantic and Caribbean trade center. This creolization process took place alongside, intertwined with yet also somewhat independent of, the official Dutch colonial structures, and it imprinted the very character of local society. Like other aspects of creolization in Curaçao, the development and consolidation of Papiamentu was tied to the contraband economy. If creolization by its very nature transgressed clearly marked sociocultural boundaries, then the development of a successful creole language that was accepted beyond the confines of slave society—especially one that was not even based on the dominant language of the colonizer and which was spoken by whites as well as blacks—was a particularly egregious violation.

"In creole speech"

Although there has yet to be a comprehensive historical study of Papiamentu, we can begin to piece together some of the evidence of its early existence in Curaçao. This evidence clearly indicates that Papiamentu already was well established in Curaçao at least by the mid-eighteenth century. There is a steady and reliable stream of references to the language being spoken across a variety of socioeconomic groups throughout the 1700s. The data are especially rich in the religious realm. Roman Catholic priests, who often traveled widely and were assigned to markedly different colonial venues in the course of their careers, often were especially attuned to cultural variations in the Americas. The ability to communicate clearly with their parishioners was vital for their evangelization efforts. Clergy were trained in multiple languages, which facilitated their acquisition of more. Clergy also regularly sent detailed reports to their superiors, which were dutifully archived and well preserved. The earliest known written reference to an emerging creole language in Curaçao is in a 1704 diary entry by Father Alexius Schabel, the Bohemian Jesuit who lived in Willemstad during the War of the Spanish Succession, who noted that "the blacks of Curaçao speak broken Spanish."[3] In 1732, Father Agustín Caicedo, the island's first apostolic prefect, wrote to his superiors that, in addition to Dutch, Spanish, and Portuguese, there was spoken on Curaçao "the language of the country" (*el idioma del pais*).[4] This observation is widely regarded to be the earliest known acknowledgment of Papiamentu as a completely separate language (as opposed to Schabel's reference to it as a variation of Spanish). Caicedo also requested the services of a linguist in order to minister better at his new church in Otrobanda, testimony to the linguistic richness of the port.[5] At midcentury, a priest commented that he had to learn several languages, including the local creole, to do his work on the island.[6] There are also references outside the religious sphere. Already by the 1730s, depositions in legal cases occasionally noted that Afro-Curaçaoans spoke "in the creole language" (*creolse taal*).[7] An ordinance drawn up by the captains and officers of the free militias in 1769 was read out "in the creole tongue."[8] Court testimony in the Andrade/Pardo case includes reference to conversations in Papiamentu that took place between two female slaves in October 1775.[9]

Unlike many other Caribbean creoles, this emerging tongue was not confined to the lower classes. It is abundantly clear from legal documents related to the Pardo/Andrade case that at least some members of the Sephardic community besides the star-crossed lovers were familiar with the language. Sarah and Abraham's letters in Papiamentu were translated into Dutch for the court by a Sephardic Jew.[10] Such simultaneous translation and faithful transcription would have required that the educated court scribe either be fluent in the creole himself, or have access to a reliable, literate, and fully bilingual assistant. The rich cache of sworn testimony in the Andrade/Pardo case provides numerous references to Papiamentu (although not by name). Two Sephardic merchants reported overhearing various conversations in "creole" among female slaves. Apparently the men knew the language well enough to identify it, or at least to distinguish it from Portuguese and Spanish.[11] At least six Sephardic witnesses in the case apparently gave their testimony in "black speech" (*neegers Spraake*) according to court records.[12] Deborah, wife of the merchant Samuel Levy Maduro, testified that Sarah Pardo spoke "in creole speech behind closed doors"—that is, she used Papiamentu as more than just a medium with which to communicate with her illicit lover.[13] Sephardim also helped to creolize the name of town neighborhoods. Abraham's letter to Sarah mentions a rendezvous in "Punta," a hybrid between the Dutch name for the walled town, *de Punt*, and the full Papiamentu version, Punda.[14] Twenty years earlier, regulations regarding synagogue governance referred to the other side of the harbor (known in Dutch as *Oversijde*) as *da banda*, close to its fully Papiamentu name, Otrobanda.[15]

Given the fact that Curaçao was predominantly an oral culture, and most of the lower classes had little or no formal education, one would not expect to find significant written evidence of the language until well after it was established as a spoken tongue. Yet there is a smattering of compelling, if incomplete, written evidence of Papiamentu from throughout the eighteenth century, well before the Andrade/Pardo letters. Several Papiamentu words and phrases appear in official Dutch deeds in the early 1700s, and in fragments of a Dutch diary from 1713.[16] The linguist Frank Martinus argues that the names of at least eight seacraft owned by Sephardic merchants throughout the eighteenth century show clear Papiamentu influences, one from as early as 1706.[17] The most intriguing vessel name is *Awa pasaharina*, which was registered to Manuel Hisquiao Pinedo in 1767 and valued at 800 pesos.[18] According to Martinus, this is the earliest known complete phrase written in Papiamentu.[19] *Awa pasa hariña*, literally, "water over corn meal," is today a well-known Papiamentu expression that means "to be drunk." Although its meaning as a vessel name is unclear, and we have no other possible different interpretation of the phrase in that time, the words and construction clearly are full-fledged Papiamentu. The vessel was registered just eight years before the Andrade/Pardo letters were written. In 1771 a Sephardic Jew purchased a bark called *le'Criole*.[20]

By the time of the Andrade/Pardo case, Papiamentu had become so well established among the island's black majority that the Roman Catholic Church had adjusted its ministry accordingly. In 1776, when Dutch Franciscans took charge of Curaçao's apostolic prefecture, they began preaching to their black parishioners in Papiamentu.[21] Father Theodorus Brouwers, the Franciscan who became apostolic prefect of the island in 1776, was "a man well-versed in languages" (*een man goed bekend met de talen*) and familiar with "the national and foreign languages" spoken on the island, according to the papal nuncio who appointed him to the island.[22] In 1784, Father Brouwers wrote to the prefect of Propaganda Fide at the Vatican that Curaçao's Catholic Church had begun preaching in the local creole, which he erroneously called "a mixture of the Galician, Spanish, and Dutch languages."[23] Following the 1795 slave uprising, Father Schinck, a Dutch Franciscan who had been on the island since 1778 and became apostolic prefect in 1787, was chosen to mediate with the rebels in part because he was fluent in Papiamentu.[24] By the early nineteenth century, there is ample evidence that the local Roman Catholic Church was preaching regularly in Papiamentu.[25] In the late eighteenth and early nineteenth centuries, several Dutch visitors wrote disparagingly that local children spoke an unintelligible language.[26] None of these early local references, however, gave the creole language a name. They simply called it "black" or "creole" speech.

The earliest known written reference to Papiamentu by name occurred in British North America, in a place that was over two thousand miles due north of Curaçao, but closely tied to the island through maritime connections. On September 25, 1737, in the British Vice Admiralty Court at Newport, Rhode Island, Daniel Soorbeek, master of the sailing sloop *de Jonge Johannes*, which had been taken by a British privateer, testified that the language spoken by the sailors on board his vessel was "broken Spanish and broken Dutch, what is called Poppemento Spanish." One of his sailors, a Spanish subject named Torinio Lopes, who had lived on the island for two years, stated that the most common languages spoken on board were "Dutch, Spanish, and Poppemento, but chiefly Poppemento," and that the latter was commonly spoken in Curaçao. It is noteworthy that the vessel's master, a Dutchman born and raised on the island, seems to have dismissed the creole as the bastardization of a

European language, whereas the Spanish sailor recognized Papiamentu as a completely separate language. A member of the crew of the British privateer swore that Spanish was spoken on board the Dutch sloop, although he confessed that he neither spoke nor understood the language; he may well have been hearing Papiamentu.[27]

At least by the 1760s, and perhaps even earlier, authorities in Tierra Firme also were identifying Papiamentu by name in their correspondence about Curaçao. A 1768 report to the archbishop of Caracas, in support of its continued jurisdiction over the Roman Catholic majority in Curaçao, explained that the island's black population did not understand "any other language except that which there they call Papiamentu," and noted that it was used by priests in their daily work, including masses which were said in the church in Otrobanda.[28] Almost thirty years later, in the wake of the 1795 slave uprisings, Governor Pedro Carbonell of the Captaincy General of Venezuela ordered his subordinates to cease importing any slaves who came from or through Curaçao because, among other things, "they intimidate the slaves to speak Papiamentu (which is the provincial language which is used in Curaçao)."[29] In contrast, that same year Governor de Veer of Curaçao referred to the creole as *de landstaal*— "the country's language," roughly equivalent to Caicedo's terminology over sixty years before—rather than using the name Papiamentu.[30] The governor expressed surprise that a mulatto man from Curaçao spoke in French, rather than in the local creole, further evidence that Papiamentu was well established by then and well known to island authorities. To date, mention of Papiamentu by name in written records from Curaçao has been found from the nineteenth century only, and even these earliest reports are not Dutch. The interim British governor of the island, William Carlyon Hughes, mentioned "Papimento" in a letter dated 18 August 1802; in 1805 Governor Pierre J. Changuion wrote that an officer understood "Papiments"; and in 1816 Father Johannes Stöppel wrote that early morning mass was celebrated in "Papiamentice."[31]

The illicit love letters between Abraham and Sarah have provided by far the richest material for linguistic analysis of the emerging tongue. Linguists agree that, by the time the letters were written, the fluidity and complexity of the writing indicates that Papiamentu already was a full-fledged language in its own right, and that it was widely spoken among both Sephardim and people of African descent.[32] They further agree that it clearly has Iberian roots, and that Dutch influence on it is limited. But the letters, and the language itself, also have sparked some debate. There is some disagreement about Papiamentu's underlying roots. Is it based on Portuguese, on Spanish, or perhaps even on some combination of the two? One of the challenges in trying to make sense of the limited historical evidence, beyond its incomplete nature, is evaluating the claims and references of contemporary reports. For example, Father Schabel's reference to the existence of a "broken Spanish" on the island at the beginning of the eighteenth century, while it has been cited by some as evidence of Papiamentu's Spanish base, may or may not be strictly accurate. Did Schabel, a native German-speaker, have the linguistic expertise to discern that the language's roots were Spanish rather than Portuguese? Was that even his intention, or was he simply acknowledging Papiamentu's Iberian character without meaning to comment definitively on its specific pedigree? Similarly, it is unclear whether or not—or at least how well—Father Brouwers, a Dutchman, knew Galician (although his superiors repeatedly commented on his linguistic dexterity), which he claimed to discern in Papiamentu—a claim that apparently is completely untenable linguistically.[33] Might his comment simply mean that he clearly detected non-Spanish vocabulary with some Iberian flavor? In both cases, although the references clearly indicate the existence of a separate language with an Iberian lineage, one should be cautious as to the exact meaning. One must exercise similar caution in evaluating Daniel Soorbeek's claim that sailors on his sloop spoke broken Spanish or broken Dutch. His testimony confirms the prevalence of the creole language on board but is not reliable regarding its precise linguistic lineage.

Unlike most creole languages that took root in the colonial Americas, Papiamentu is not based on the dominant language of the European colonizer. The influence of Dutch on Papiamentu has been minimal, and it is largely limited to vocabulary rather than to structure or syntax. "The number of Dutch-derived functional elements in [Papiamentu] can be counted on the fingers of one hand," according to linguist Bart Jacobs, "and all seem to be relatively recent borrowings."[34] Interestingly, a Dutch-based creole, Negerhollands, did develop in the Caribbean by the end of the seventeenth century, but hundreds of miles to the north, on the islands of the Danish West Indies. By the mid-eighteenth century, Negerhollands had a written form. It was the preferred tongue of slaves and free men and women on the island of St. Thomas; it was also spoken by many whites.[35] This is clear testimony to the important role of Dutch and Sephardic merchants in the society and economy of St. Thomas and the other Danish islands. (Recall that, in the wake of her adultery, Curaçao's Sephardic congregation shipped Sarah de Isaac Pardo y Vaz Farro to St. Thomas.)

Although the influence of African languages on Papiamentu has not been sufficiently studied, there is evidence of Kwa and Bantu in at least fifteen words.[36] This surface influence on vocabulary and grammar is separate from the issue of one or more African languages forming the substrate on which the emerging new language was based. There has been virtually no research on the possible influences of Arabic on Papiamentu or other Caribbean creoles, via the arrival of enslaved and free Muslims from Africa.[37] Amerindian languages had a minor influence on Papiamentu, limited to a smattering of Caquetío vocabulary.[38] Similarly, Papiamentu contains some Hebrew and Ladino vocabulary. Emmanuel and Emmanuel identified nine Papiamentu phrases that clearly were of Hebrew origin and three words that resemble Ladino.[39] May Henriques has analyzed the particular Sephardic usage of close to 1,500 Papiamentu words and expressions in use today, and identified words of Hebrew, Spanish, Portuguese, French, Ladino, and Guene origins that have particular meanings in the present-day Sephardic community of Curaçao.[40] The influence of all these languages is superficial and indicates little more than the fact that Papiamentu-speakers had sufficient regular contact with speakers of these other languages to incorporate some of their vocabulary. To find Papiamentu's roots one must look elsewhere.

Linguists agree that Papiamentu's roots are clearly Iberian.[41] Although there has been some disagreement about whether it sprang originally from Spanish or Portuguese, most scholarly research now seems to favor the latter.[42] The name almost certainly derives from the Portuguese *papear* ("to talk"). Some Curaçaoans have argued vociferously in favor of Spanish origins, no doubt partly due to the island's ongoing, centuries-long close cultural and economic ties with Venezuela, and the corresponding obvious influence of Spanish vocabulary.[43] There is no doubt that centuries of close contact between Curaçao and Tierra Firme have resulted in a major influence of Spanish vocabulary and grammar. However, Lipski's assertion that, due to this influence, Papiamentu "is for all intents and purposes now a Spanish-based creole," is not shared by most linguists, because it focuses on elements which were added later rather than on the language's underlying foundation.[44] Even some linguists who classify Papiamentu as a Spanish-based creole hypothesize that it, like other now-extinct Spanish-based creoles of the circum-Caribbean, likely originated from a proto-Portuguese.[45] At least one expert has suggested that the Spanish and Portuguese elements in Papiamentu may be so intertwined as to be indecipherable.[46] According to John Lipski, well over half of the language's lexical elements cannot "be identified as pertaining exclusively to Spanish or Portuguese."[47] Another creole which exhibits similarly hybrid Spanish/Portuguese elements is Palenquero, which is spoken in a rural community of Colombia descended from runaway slaves.[48]

Although the debate about whether Papiamentu is based on Portuguese or Spanish is important to linguists, it has monopolized the study of Papiamentu's early years, even among nonlinguists, edging out the far more intriguing historical question of the language's successful consolidation in Curaçao. The debate often erroneously posits European languages as static and autonomous foils against which incomplete and inferior creoles such as Papiamentu struggled to emerge. This is the enduring legacy of earlier analysis that unabashedly categorized all creoles as substandard proto-languages rather than as new but fully formed languages that evolved in specific historical settings.[49] The search for Papiamentu's roots in either Spanish or Portuguese is artificially dichotomized, and it ignores the wide spectrum of interconnected languages and the complex linguistic encounters that occurred throughout the Atlantic world in the early modern period.

Most linguists now seem to favor a Portuguese-based substrate, with Papiamentu originating in one or more Afro-Portuguese creoles that developed on the western coast of Africa in the early period of European trade and contact there. Even those who support an Afro-Portuguese substrate do not agree about important details, however, such as the exact chains of development and transmission, the precise location(s) in Atlantic Africa where these occurred, the language(s) out of which Papiamentu developed, and the time frame for all these processes.[50] All agree, however, that the transatlantic slave trade was the mechanism by which either an early version of Papiamentu, or the Afro-Portuguese creole(s) on which it was based, arrived on the island sometime in the mid to late seventeenth century, and that Papiamentu's roots thus should be sought in the areas of Atlantic Africa that were tied to Curaçao via the transatlantic slave trade.

From a historian's perspective, it is not necessary to try to solve the riddles of Papiamentu's origins, or even to engage the debates too closely. Much more relevant is the process of the language's development and trajectory, situated in a particular social, cultural, and economic context. Regardless of their disagreements, linguists provide powerful evidence that Papiamentu developed out of the dynamic processes of creolization that took place in the areas on the western coast of Africa that were major sources for the early forced migration of enslaved Africans to Curaçao via the Dutch slave trade, areas that also had an important presence of Sephardic Jewish merchants. Its later successful development on the island similarly was tied to processes of creolization on the American side of the Atlantic. To understand fully Papiamentu's success on Curaçao, we must expand the analysis to include the genesis and diffusion of creole languages more generally, as part of the wider processes of creolization that occurred throughout the early modern Atlantic world.

Creole Languages and Atlantic Trade

Disagreement over Papiamentu's origins reflects wider debates about the genesis, development, and diffusion of creole languages. Much of the discussion is highly technical and is not easily followed by nonlinguists.[51] The parameters of the debate have shifted markedly over time, reflecting in part the discipline's rather belated recognition that creoles should be studied as full-fledged languages in their own right, rather than as illegitimate stepsiblings of older European tongues.[52] Beyond the narrow field of linguistics, debates about creole languages inform a much wider discussion about the centuries-long processes of creolization that occurred on both sides of the Atlantic throughout the early modern era. The development of new, hybrid languages was part of these wider processes of creolization. What could be more basically human than the need to communicate? What could be more essentially creole than the emergence of new languages, born of the dialectic between brutal economic exploitation and cultural survival that marked the creation of colonial societies under the umbrella of developing European overseas empires ? However, the literatures of creole linguistics (or creolistics) and cultural creolization are rarely in dialogue.

Much creolistic analysis remains ahistorical at best.[53] Almost forty years ago, the historian Peter Wood noted that "a series of ahistorical notions" plagued the study of Gullah, a creole that developed in the slave societies of coastal South Carolina and Georgia.[54] His observations continue to apply to the study of most creoles. The anthropologist Sidney Mintz contemporaneously observed that historical settings "have affected the ways that creole languages arose and took shape." He proposed a framework for analyzing the specific situations and conditions that influenced the development of creole languages in the Caribbean.[55] These calls for historically grounded research largely went unheeded, although in recent years creolistics has begun moving beyond strictly linguistic considerations to incorporate historical data.[56] "Creole linguists depend ultimately on historians for their socio-cultural context," as the anthropologist Richard Price has noted.[57] Although much of the available historical evidence is circumstantial, it adds an important dimension to understanding the context in which creole languages were born and developed.

Debates among historians and social scientists about cultural creolization all too often privilege one side of the Atlantic over the other. But processes of creolization, if not seamless, certainly were fluid as they crossed the ocean with waves of migrations over the decades and centuries, washing around communities in the circum-Atlantic. Creolization occurred on both sides of the Atlantic over many centuries, responding to specific local situations as well as to regional and global currents. In the Atlantic world, it began with the earliest Portuguese explorations along the western African coast in the early 1400s, and continued with the establishment and consolidation of permanent European colonies in the Americas throughout the seventeenth and eighteenth centuries. Analysis that focuses exclusively on only one side of the Atlantic or that is constrained by the rather arbitrary political boundaries that emerging European powers sought to impose misses important parts of the wide historical processes.[58]

Creolization began on the eastern shores of the southern Atlantic, on the coast of Africa and nearby islands, well before the establishment of colonial European societies in the Americas. Cultural and social interactions between Africans and Europeans began on Africa's Atlantic coast with the arrival of regular Portuguese sailing expeditions in the early fifteenth century. Already by the mid-1400s, multiracial, multilingual societies were beginning to develop around the Portuguese trading forts along the Africa coast. Official representatives of the Portuguese Crown were joined by independent traders and private entrepreneurs, known as *lançados*, whose success, like that of the officials, depended in part on their ability to negotiate with local power-holders and their representatives. Many officials and *lançados* married, or had children with, local women. Their offspring and subsequent generations of mixed-race people soon dominated the towns that grew up around the European forts. By the sixteenth and seventeenth centuries, what once had been small, single-ethnic fishing villages along Africa's Atlantic littoral had become thriving multicultural, multilingual, and multiethnic towns with several thousand inhabitants, which were centered on, but also somewhat autonomous from, the European forts. These Luso-African communities already were in place and continued to grow even after the Dutch seized the major Portuguese forts, including Elmina, in the mid-seventeenth century.[59] Although the Dutch displaced the Portuguese politically and economically, they did not do so culturally or linguistically.

People of mixed European and African ancestry played a major role in the economy, society, and culture of the communities that surrounded European slaving and trading forts, and in surrounding settlements that grew up on the western coast of Africa. Their role was disproportionate to their actual numbers. Although such individuals faced the very real possibility of ostracism by both Europeans and Africans, they also were uniquely positioned to serve as intermediaries between these two groups. They were particularly adept at linguistic, cultural, and economic translation and exchange. Luso-African communities developed a wide range of hybrid cultural expressions, including syncretic forms of language, religion, agriculture, architecture, cuisine, music, art, and technology. This creolization involved ongoing exchange between a variety of equally important actors, although not necessarily on equal footing.[60]

As we saw in Chapter 2, Sephardim and New Christians were an integral part of these hybrid Afro-Portuguese communities from the earliest days of European expansion, and they were closely involved in creolization.[61] The Portuguese merchant settlements throughout early Atlantic Africa included both New Christians and those who openly practiced Judaism.[62] Like the mixed race Luso-Africans, they were particularly adept at maneuvering and interpreting across linguistic and cultural divides. They also regularly violated economic boundaries by participating in smuggling and so directly challenged the jurisdiction of the Portuguese Crown. By engaging in contraband trade and openly practicing their Judaism in an area controlled by a Catholic state, Sephardim in Portuguese western Africa transgressed multiple boundaries. New Christians were trading in the Cape Verde islands by the early 1500s. By 1546, local officials in Ribeira Grande complained that they dominated the island economy.[63] Sephardim vigorously engaged in trade, much of it extra-official, along the entire Atlantic coast of western Africa. New Christians were also involved in the early Portuguese slave trade along the western coast of Africa. They continued to participate openly and actively in trade at all levels after the Dutch seized Elmina and other Portuguese forts, and the transatlantic slave trade became a major economic enterprise.[64]

Creole languages developed during the earliest days of this intercultural contact in Atlantic Africa. In these multiracial, multiethnic settlements, Africans and Europeans of diverse origins, ethnicities, and languages all had to communicate. They began to develop new languages that were heavily based on the dominant trade language, Portuguese, mixed with the different tongues that were spoken throughout western Africa.[65] According to some linguists, this *fala de Guine*, or Guinea speech, became the lingua franca of the emerging Atlantic world.[66] Linguists disagree as to whether Afro-Portuguese creoles all derive from a single proto-Portuguese, such as *fala de Guine*, or whether several developed independently in different locations. Most now eschew the so-called monogenetic theory and favor multiple independent origins. Portuguese and Portuguese-based creoles continued to be major trade languages along the western African coast even after the Dutch, and later the English and the French, established footholds there and began trading in enslaved Africans.[67] An Afro-Portuguese-based lingua franca remained the common communications medium at Elmina and other slaving forts even after the Dutch seized them from the Portuguese.[68] Such cultural intermixing also extended farther afield. There is ample evidence of hybrid languages being spoken among new groups of African immigrants on the Iberian peninsula already by the second half of the fifteenth century.[69]

The growth of the transatlantic slave trade in the seventeenth and eighteenth centuries, and the growing participation of non-Iberian European powers, intensified this process of cultural and linguistic exchange. By the mid-seventeenth century, and throughout the eighteenth, the development of plantation societies in the Americas fueled a sharply rising demand for enslaved workers, thus forcibly bringing more diverse groups of Africans into contact with each other, and intensifying processes of linguistic creolization. As the hunt for captives penetrated deeper into the interior, it disrupted the political, social, economic, and cultural organization of entire African societies that were hundreds of miles from the coast.[70] Enslaved Africans from many different ethnic and linguistic groups found ways to communicate with each other and with their captors during the weeks and months that they made their way through the multiple stages of their diasporic experience—first being marched from inland areas to the coast, then waiting in holding pens around the European forts, and finally embarking on the Middle Passage. Many of them learned Afro-Portuguese creoles as they struggled to communicate with each other and with their captors. Large numbers of people from different language groups were crowded together in close quarters for months at a time, providing an opportunity for intense linguistic exchange and breeding grounds for new languages amid the misery.[71] Not only enslaved Africans, but also merchants, ship captains, supercargoes, and seafarers from Europe and Africa who participated in the Africa trades had to find ways to communicate with each other and with locals with whom they did business. They also learned to speak Afro-Portuguese creoles and carried them around the Atlantic.

Such cultural and linguistic intermixing and adaptation was repeated in the new American colonies. The transatlantic slave trade propelled creolization across the Atlantic, where it intensified, intertwined with the cultural mixing between Europeans and Native Americans. The Middle Passage was not the end of the voyage for many enslaved Africans. Those who became contraband commodities to Spanish America once again were forced to wait in holding pens on Curaçao and elsewhere, where they continued to share close quarters with people from a variety of cultures and language groups. When they arrived at their final destinations, they often were thrust again into interactions with people from a variety of cultural and linguistic backgrounds in New World plantations and port cities. Language acquisition and development continued as part of broader processes of creolization across the Americas. New world settlements, especially those with high concentrations of enslaved Africans, also were crucibles for the development of creole languages.[72] The consolidation of European colonies and of plantation agriculture based on enslaved labor shifted the epicenter of the developing Atlantic system to the Americas. Enslaved Africans carried both African languages and Luso-African creoles to their new homes around the slave societies of the Caribbean and North and South America. There, they developed different characteristics in different areas as they were influenced to varying degrees by the many languages that were spoken by European colonizers, enslaved Africans, and Native Americans. Creolization continued in the slave societies of the Americas, as peoples from different ethnic, linguistic, and cultural areas of African and Europe interacted with each other and with Native Americans across highly porous geopolitical and geographic boundaries.

Creoles were not the only languages that were developing in the early modern Atlantic world. European tongues also were evolving. They, too, were influenced by the new cultural interactions and developing power configurations. Iberia is a particularly clear case in point. Early modern Iberians spoke five major languages that were closely tied to specific geographic areas: Portuguese, Castilian, Catalan, Galician, and the Basque language, Euskadi.[73] While Castilian was the early dominant language in Spain's overseas expansion, it did not fully become the language of the Spanish empire at home and abroad until well into the eighteenth century. Castilian's ultimate victory over Galician, Catalan, and Euskadi to become the language of the Spanish empire for law, government, diplomacy, and education was closely tied both to the Spanish imperial project and to the process of nation-building within Iberia.[74] Galician, Catalan, and Euskadi continued to be widely spoken, and they even influenced the development of Castilian, especially in the colonies.[75] Iberian adventurers, explorers, soldiers, and settlers carried their own languages and local variations of them to the Americas. Galician was so widely spoken by Iberian immigrants to the Americas that Apostolic Prefect Brouwers (erroneously) considered that it had an influence on Papiamentu.[76] Speakers of the official Iberian imperial languages, Castilian and Portuguese, influenced both languages' development in the Americas, as did other Europeans, Africans, and Americans of many ethnicities and languages. This occurred especially in the early period of Iberian expansion and continued throughout the period when the Spanish and Portuguese Crowns were united (1580–1640). Dozens of languages influenced each other as different linguistic groups were in close contact with each other throughout the centuries-long processes of conquest, colonization, and creolization of the Americas, and the economic integration of the emerging Atlantic world.[77]

The highly mobile Sephardim were fluent in multiple languages, which they sometimes mixed as they moved across geopolitical borders. Even before they were forced into diaspora in the late fifteenth century, Iberia's Sephardim were multilingual. Fluency in many languages was firmly embedded in Sephardic culture and education. Well-educated Sephardim in medieval Iberia typically spoke more than one Iberian language socially and several other European languages for commercial purposes, as well as Greek, Latin, and Arabic for scientific and literary work, and Hebrew and Aramaic in their religious lives.[78] Because Iberia's Jews were often forced into relatively isolated communities throughout the Middle Ages, some linguists have argued that there already was a distinct dialect of Judeo-Spanish before the expulsion in 1492.[79] A proposal in the early seventeenth-century by an anonymous Sephardic Jew to Dutch authorities to colonize vast tracts of southern North America was written in a "Luso-Hispanic hybrid idiom," according to the Dutch historian who discovered the document.[80]

Perhaps the best-known and most well developed Sephardic mixing of languages is Ladino. The term Ladino refers to two quite different linguistic phenomena. One was simply a device for transcribing scripture into Spanish using Hebrew characters, used when the scribe lacked full

knowledge of the biblical tongue. This technique was common in Sephardic synagogues throughout the diaspora, where rabbinical knowledge
of Hebrew was often limited, and communities struggled to reproduce
their sacred books accurately. Such Ladino was not a language at all, but
rather what linguists term a calque hagiolanguage, that is, a mechanism
for translating religious texts from holy languages into the vernacular.[81]
The term Ladino also refers to a Spanish-based language that was spoken
in much of the Sephardic diaspora, especially in the East. This language
has several other names, including Judeo-Spanish.[82] Spoken Ladino
adapted over the centuries in the specific locations where Sephardic
communities settled. (Ladino took on markedly different characteristics
in the Ottoman realms, for example.) Linguists have noted its high degree of adaptability.[83]

The expulsion of Spain's Jews to Portugal, and their subsequent forced
movement beyond, in several successive waves of human migration, further complicated and enriched the linguistic dexterity of the Sephardim.
Different groups of Sephardic and converso emigrants who fled Portugal
and Spain throughout the early modern era had different linguistic characteristics, with second and third generation conversos relatively less
multilingual.[84] By the time they reached Amsterdam, many Sephardim
already were fluent in Portuguese, which had become a major global
trade language. Many also retained knowledge of Spanish, which they
passed down over the generations, partly out of nostalgia, partly because
it, too, opened commercial opportunities. A working knowledge of both
Portuguese and Spanish was a boon to conducting overseas trade. To
succeed in Dutch society and commerce, men (and, to a lesser extent,
women and children) also learned Dutch. Men studied Hebrew as part
of their reconversion. Dutch apparently did not begin to appear as a medium of Sephardic worship in the Amsterdam congregation until the
late eighteenth and early nineteenth centuries. Spanish and Portuguese
remained the languages of classroom instruction in Sephardic schools
in the Netherlands until well into the nineteenth century.[85] From the
sixteenth through the mid-eighteenth centuries, Dutch printing houses
turned out a steady stream of prayer books, bibles, and homilies in Hebrew (sometimes translated into Latin characters) and schoolbooks in
Spanish and Portuguese.[86]

Multiple language use was an important component of the changing Sephardic identity across the diaspora, in the Netherlands and elsewhere. Linguists have noted the exceptional degree of diglossia in the
Sephardic diaspora—that is, the use of different languages for clearly

defined, specific purposes, as distinct from general multilingualism. One unusual feature of Sephardic diglossia is that there seems to have been no ranking of these different languages; all were held in equally high esteem.[87] This feature proved useful in the colonial societies of the Americas, including Curaçao. Thus, the rise of an Atlantic world promoted not only cultural intermixing but also the evolution of existing languages and the creation of new ones. Sephardim were particularly adept in this area.

Afro-Portuguese creoles, including Papiamentu and its precursor(s), emerged in this context of multiple, dynamic human interactions that influenced the formation and consolidation of new languages as well as cultures throughout the early modern Atlantic world, from Africa to Europe to the Americas. Several linguists have used both linguistic and historical evidence to argue that Papiamentu—or its precursor(s)—developed in western Africa out of existing Afro-Portuguese creoles, in areas where the Dutch and Sephardim were actively involved in the slave trade, and then was carried across the Atlantic in slaving vessels sometime in the mid to late seventeenth century. The argument that Papiamentu traces its roots to a Portuguese lingua franca that arose out of the slave trade in the region of the Gulf of Guinea was advanced almost forty years ago by Birmingham.[88] It has continued to be refined by subsequent generations of linguists, even if the monogenetic theory largely has been abandoned.[89]

Linguists who agree on Papiamentu's origins in an Afro-Portugues creole disagree as to the specifics, however. According to Bart Jacobs, Papiamentu is a relexification of a creole that originated in the Senegambia region of Upper Guinea and was transferred to Curaçao in the second half of the seventeenth century.[90] Jacobs finds the "linguistic fingerprints" of Upper Guinea Creole all over Papiamentu. He hypothesizes that the former originated on the Cape Verdean island of Santiago and was then carried by traders to the nearby mainland, where it became a primary communications vehicle by the time the Dutch began using the area as a major slaving port in the mid-seventeenth century.[91] The language that subsequently was taken to Curaçao was a full-fledged creole that was passed on by native speakers, not a pidgin or proto-creole, according to Jacobs.[92] Like Jacobs, Frank Martinus also argues that Papiamentu is closely related to the creole languages that developed in the Cape Verde Islands, but Martinus maintains that Papiamentu is most closely and directly related to Cape Verdean Creole, rather than to Upper Guinea Creole. According to Martinus, Papiamentu developed out of "a mixture of several Afro-Portuguese dialects" that arrived in Curaçao, perhaps as early as the 1640s, and that subsequently developed into both Papiamentu and another, now extinct creole, Guene, that had more African influences and was spoken primarily in rural areas of the island.[93] Martinus argues that "Papiamentu is basically a Cape Verdean creole," which also shows "Mina, Angolan, and Congolese creole influences."[94] Like Martinus, Philippe Maurer also believes that Papiamentu is not based on a single Afro-Portuguese creole but rather was influenced by several.[95] This linguistic debate no doubt would benefit from further historical research into the specific geographic and ethnic origins of Africans who were enslaved and transported to Curaçao by the Dutch, as well as the role of Sephardim in the Dutch slave trade.

Historical evidence—albeit much of it circumstantial—provides an important complement to the linguistic data. As Derick Bickerton has noted, a viable theory of a language's origins requires, beyond linguistic analysis, "that the right speakers were in the right place at the right time."[96] In the case of Papiamentu, that means both Africans and Sephardic Jews who later found themselves in Curaçao, or at least were part of well-established networks that included Curaçao. Regardless of the linguistic specifics of Papiamentu's exact origins, Upper Guinea's importance for its transatlantic transmission (or that of its progenitors) is backed by historical evidence. The Dutch used Gorée and Cacheu in Upper Guinea as their premier slaving station in western Africa for five decades beginning in the 1620s. These ties were long-standing. At the end of the century, Dutch merchants signed a contract with the Portuguese Company of Cacheu.[97] The Dutch loss of Gorée to the French in 1677 and the subsequent shift of the Dutch slave trade away from Cape Verde and Upper Guinea, south toward Lower Guinea, Congo, and Angola thereafter, means that Papiamentu, or the creole(s) that gave rise to it, must have been carried to the island before then.[98] The close economic and cultural ties between the Cape Verde islands and Upper Guinea in the sixteenth and seventeenth centuries are also well documented, making it historically plausible that Papiamentu's deeper roots could be traced to this connection.

There were enclaves of Sephardic merchants in these areas at the same time. Several Sephardim who spent time in Senegambia also became part of the Jewish community in Dutch Brazil, the first openly Jewish settlement in the Americas.[99] Whether or not some of these merchants also subsequently spent time on Curaçao, or even settled there, is a topic that awaits further research, but it is certainly plausible. Individual

Sephardim in Curaçao also had direct ties with Cacheu. Felipe Henriquez and Juan Moron both traded with the Portuguese Company at Cacheu and transported slaves to Spanish America.[100] Henriquez was a factor for the company.[101] In some cases this connection may have been more circuitous. Already by 1644, just a decade after the WIC seized Curaçao (and maybe even before), there were several black and mulatto members of Amsterdam's Talmud Torah Sephardic congregation who traced their roots to West Africa.[102] They likely spoke, or at least understood, the variety of languages that were spoken in Atlantic Africa, including, no doubt, one or more creoles. Whether any of these African Jews subsequently migrated across the Atlantic, it is not inconceivable that they left a linguistic mark on some of the white members of the congregation who eventually settled in Curaçao.

Most linguists agree that Papiamentu existed in Curaçao by the second half of the seventeenth century, during the island's heyday as a slave transshipment center. We may never know for sure exactly when and where it first developed. Linguists will continue to debate questions related to its origins and the specific forms of transmission. Historians can contribute important archival evidence to this discussion. We now turn to another question: Regardless of its exact linguistic origins, and the precise manner and decade in which it or its precursor(s) crossed the Atlantic, what were the specific circumstances that allowed Papiamentu to develop and flourish in eighteenth-century Curaçao? How was it that Papiamentu became the lingua franca of a cross section of local society, including Sephardic Jews, rather than remaining, like most American creoles, a marginalized tongue that primarily was spoken among people of African descent? Here, too, we do not have a definite answer, but historical analysis situated in the context of wider processes of creolization provides some clues.

Papiamentu and the Port

Smuggling required close interactions across socioeconomic and ethnic divides, including the ability to communicate clearly. An economy based on illicit intercolonial trade provided the type, frequency, and intensity of interactions that allowed Papiamentu to thrive in Curaçao's port city. Willemstad's inhabitants, like those of many Atlantic port cities, were polyglot. Although there was some clear-cut linguistic division along lines of race/ethnicity and social class, the reality of the port economy and society meant that it was not always easy to keep these neat

divisions intact. Dutch was the official language of government administration and trade, as well as the native language of the upper strata. All
business of the West India Company and Curaçao's political and judicial
administration was conducted exclusively in Dutch. Rising merchants
of all backgrounds and ethnicities needed to be fluent in Dutch to conduct business. Court cases also were conducted in Dutch, with translators provided as needed, and duly noted in the margins of official documents.[103] Dutch was also the language of worship in the Dutch Reformed
Church, located with the confines of Fort Amsterdam.

Curaçao's Sephardic merchants arrived from Amsterdam already fluent in the multiple languages they used in trade and worship. Although
they required Dutch to navigate the island's legal and administrative
system, they often used Portuguese in much of their international
commerce.[104] Court cases from the eighteenth century often mention
that Sephardim men and women testified in Portuguese. For example,
in the Andrade/Pardo case, at least eighteen different testimonies by
Sephardim, including that of the rabbi, were taken in Portuguese.[105]
Merchant correspondence was often in Portuguese.[106] Portuguese also
remained a vital component of Sephardic religious life. Sephardim
conducted worship, kept synagogue records, and often wrote epitaphs
in Portuguese.[107] That Portuguese remained a fundamental identity
marker of Curaçao's Sephardim is clear from the fact that, throughout
the eighteenth century, they were often referred to as "Portuguese Jews"
or "the Portuguese Jewish Nation."[108] For contemporaries in Venezuela, the term, "portugués," often was synonymous with Sephardic Jew.
(Similarly, the term, "the Spanish Nation" was often used to refer to
denizens of Spanish America.)[109] The Spanish language was necessary
for trade with neighboring Tierra Firme and other Spanish colonies
throughout the region. Occasionally, Spanish apparently also was used
for synagogue matters.[110] Spanish also may have retained a certain sen-
timental value, a reminder of the deep historical roots that Sephardim
could trace back to their medieval homeland. The multilingualism of
Curaçao's Sephardim is evident from testimony in the Andrade case
and others, where women and men variously testified in Dutch, Portuguese, Spanish, and Papiamentu.[111] Sometimes documents written by
Sephardim seem to be an amalgam of Spanish and Portuguese.[112] Official communiqués with the government related to the community's
affairs also sometimes were rendered in Portuguese or Spanish.[113] Curaçao's Sephardim, like those throughout the diaspora, not only switched
easily from one language to another, but they also apparently ranked

the various languages they spoke equally, without ascribing higher status to one or the other.[114]

It is difficult to document language use and knowledge among Curaçao's black majority, whose culture and communication were predominantly oral. Afro-Curaçaoans may well have been among the island's most polyglot inhabitants. Because Willemstad was the economic center of the island, there was much more regular contact and movement between rural and urban areas than was true in the plantation economies of the Caribbean. Rural slaves, who represented just 58 percent of Curaçao's total slave population by the end of the eighteenth century, regularly traveled to Willemstad to sell produce at market, and they often worked temporary jobs in the maritime economy.[115] Urban slaves who worked in the port would have needed a basic working knowledge of a variety of languages. Domestic slaves no doubt acquired at least a rudimentary understanding of Dutch. Those who worked in Sephardic households also were exposed to Portuguese and perhaps Spanish. It is quite possible that among Afro-Curaçoans there were relatively more women who spoke or at least understood Dutch than men, due to the relative proximity of domestic servants to their owners and families and their regular interactions. Afro-Curaçaoans who were involved in intercolonial trade learned at least some Spanish, as did runaway slaves and others who emigrated to Tierra Firme. (Papiamentu and Spanish are similar enough to be somewhat mutually intelligible, as are Papiamentu and Portuguese.) Afro-Curaçaoan sailors were exposed to a variety of languages as they traveled around the Caribbean. Many likely had a basic understanding of Spanish, English, and French, as well as Dutch, Papiamentu, perhaps other creoles, and some African languages. A ship captain who sought the return of a Curaçao-born slave who had deserted from his schooner in the harbor of Charlestown, South Carolina, in 1783 noted that the man had been employed as a coastal sailor in the West Indies, and "speaks all the languages used there."[116]

Papiamentu was not the only creole language that existed in Curaçao. Apparently there was at least one other, Guene, a now-extinct tongue that was spoken mostly in rural areas, and in which the influence of several African languages was much more prominent.[117] Guene died out as a spoken language in the early twentieth century. By midcentury, fragments of Guene survived only in songs, proverbs, and other snippets of oral tradition that elderly Afro-Curaçaoans recited and sang even though they often could not explain the exact meaning of the words and phrases.[118] Like many other American creoles, Guene retained significant African influence in its syntax, grammar, and vocabulary.[119] It contained lexical items from Hausa, Kikongo and related languages, Twi and related languages, and Yoruba.[120] The name Guene may well refer to *fala de Guine*, the lingua franca that developed in early Atlantic Africa. Whether its linguistic roots can be traced to the actual physical location of Guinea or whether the reference is more cultural or symbolic is unclear. (Recall that by the mid-eighteenth century the neighborhood of Curaçaoans on the outskirts of the town of Coro was called Guinea.)

Most of the analysis of Papiamentu, and the field of creole linguistics in general, has ignored Guene.[121] Not all linguists agree that Guene was a completely independent language. Jacobs suggests that it may have been a ritual language rather than either a full-fledged creole or even a proto-creole.[122] However, Curaçaoan anthropologists and folklorists have assembled an impressive corpus of material that indicates otherwise.[123] Although most of this research remains unpublished, the evidence is well known and widely appreciated in Curaçao. However, it is so little known outside the island that at least one well-established creole linguist apparently doubts whether Guene even existed.[124] Even the Dutch sociologist Harry Hoetink, whose insights have been foundational for understanding the historical dynamics of Curaçaoan society, dismissed Guene as "probably a corrupt form of African [*sic*]," without appreciating either its roots or the role it had in Curaçao.[125]

Guene remained exclusively a language of the enslaved rural population. It was spoken especially on the handful of relatively large rural estates. However, Guene never broke barriers of race/ethnicity or social class in Curaçao.[126] In contrast, Papiamentu thrived in the urban, cosmopolitan port environment of Willemstad, where it was spoken not just by Afro-Curaçoans but also by Sephardic Jews and even by some Dutch people.[127] "Papiamentu became the language of the city and the community in general and Guene the language(s) of only the countryside and the slaves," according to Martinus.[128] Guene also may have been used as a secret language among Afro-Curaçaoans, even those in the port, as a way of communicating with each other beyond the understanding of their Dutch and Sephardic masters and of white Curaçaoans generally.[129] During the slave uprising of 1795, while Papiamentu was the language of mediation between the rebels and government representatives in town, slaves across the island apparently communicated their plans to each other in Guene.[130] Guene's impact in Willemstad seems to have been limited to its use as a semisecret language, which, unlike Papiamentu, was spoken and understood only by the black majority. It is possible that

Guene was carried by runaway slaves to Tierra Firme, where it may have been spoken in the Guinea neighborhood of Coro, and perhaps by José Caridad Gonzalez, one of the alleged leaders of the Coro uprising.[131]

By the end of the eighteenth century, Papiamentu was becoming the island vernacular among most of the island's population except the Dutch elite, successfully edging out Dutch, Spanish, Guene, Portuguese, and a variety of African languages. How did Papiamentu emerge as Curaçao's primary language, transcending barriers of race, ethnicity, and social class in a way that no other Caribbean creole has achieved? The Dutch sociologist Harry Hoetink has suggested that the existence of two upper strata in Curaçao, rather than a single elite group, led to the adoption of the creole that was spoken by the lower class as the island's common lingua franca. According to his argument, because the Dutch and Sephardic Jews each spoke a different, mutually unintelligible language and because they were separated from each other socially, Papiamentu became the default common language.[132] However, Hoetink did not explain the specific ways in which this occurred, nor does his explanation account for the preponderance of the Dutch language in dealings between Dutch and Sephardim. Moreover, Curaçao's Sephardim did not become part of the local elite until the nineteenth century, well after they had embraced Papiamentu. Throughout the eighteenth century, the critical period for Papiamentu's consolidation, they were still very much an up-and-coming merchant group. Through the end of the century most Sephardim were assessed in the lowest tax brackets.[133]

The Roman Catholic Church clearly had a major role in promoting and supporting the development of Papiamentu. Father Caicedo's request that a linguist be sent to the new church he was opening in Otrobanda in the early 1730s indicates that, already by the early decades of the century, the church was aware of the island's language diversity.[134] Language was also part of the larger power struggles in which the church became embroiled throughout the eighteenth century. Papiamentu was one way to reach the masses, but it also separated visiting clergy from the powerful church council, which was dominated by whites. From the earliest days, Spanish had been the language of evangelization. Although this continued under Dutch rule, Papiamentu progressively emerged first to compete with and then to replace Spanish in Catholic worship services.[135] Church authorities in Tierra Firme, as well as the Spanish Council of the Indies, blatantly but unsuccessfully played the language card in their attempt to retain formal jurisdiction over the island's Catholic flock. They repeatedly claimed that the language barrier would make Dutch priests ineffective in their evangelization efforts.[136] West India Company officials countered that Dutch priests' knowledge of Latin would facilitate their learning of Spanish, so they could communicate with their parishioners. When the Dutch brazenly sent Theodorus ten Oever to depose Antonio Navarro and take control of Willemstad's Catholic parish in 1760, Venezuela clergy and the church hierarchy vociferously denounced his inability to communicate with his parishioners, due to his inability to speak Papiamentu.[137]

Communication among children of different social classes and ethnicities in Willemstad clearly spurred the development of Papiamentu. The crowded streets and alleyways of Punda and Otrobanda, with their dwellings, wharves, and commercial establishments in close proximity, encouraged children of different linguistic groups to play and try to speak together.[138] Dutch visitors complained about the unintelligible language that children in Curaçao spoke in the eighteenth century.[139] The role of children in developing and propagating creole languages is a well-established linguistic phenomenon.[140] Linguists have noted the role of the black nanny or nursemaid in bridging the Sephardic and Afro-Curaçaoan communities, as she suckled the master's babies and brought them up alongside her own.[141] The nanny, or *yaya*, as she was known in Curaçao, often was enslaved, but sometimes she was a free black or mulatto woman. Her close contact with white families, women, and children provided a setting that was rich with opportunities for cultural and linguistic exchange.[142] Willemstad's black nannies might have been expected to transmit Guene as well as Papiamentu—unless, aware of Guene's role as a secret language, they intentionally withheld it from their young white charges, sharing only songs and nursery rhymes, and instead taught them Curaçao's interethnic language, Papiamentu.

Women played an important role in developing Papiamentu in both Afro-Curaçaoan and Sephardic communities.[143] There clearly was a gendered dimension to creole language acquisition in Curaçao and throughout Caribbean slave societies. European women who lived in the colonies frequently picked up creole languages faster than the men, at least in part owing to their close association with domestic servants and their children's contact with slave children and nannies. "The Creole language is not confined to the negroes," Maria Nugent commented in early nineteenth-century Jamaica. "Many of the ladies, who have not been educated in England, speak a sort of broken English, with an indolent drawling out of their words, that is very tiresome if not disgusting."[144] The Reverend William Jones made a similar observation in the 1770s.[145]

In order to preserve their daughters' linguistic purity, wealthy planters on the English islands often brought in governesses from England and virtually cloistered the young women.[146] Willemstad's merchants did not have the luxury of isolating women on rural estates. Curaçao's country houses were far from self-sustaining, and they often lacked sufficient activities to keep the women occupied. Even when they resided in the countryside, merchant families in Curaçao were not as isolated as their counterparts in plantation economies. The merchant family business by its very nature required close contact with others, not seclusion. On the small island, most privately owned estates were relatively close to town. In the port, women across the socioeconomic spectrum interacted in both the private and the public spheres, in situations that required communication. Sarah Pardo's use of a black women to set up trysts with her lover, and her desperate recourse to herbal abortifacients provided by her slaves, were typical of such interactions, not only in Curaçao, but in slave societies across the Americas.[147] Women and children clearly were vital in the dissemination and acceptance of Papiamentu. By themselves, however, they cannot account for Papiamentu's unusual success as compared to that of other Caribbean creole languages. Both groups were important in the spread of creoles throughout the slave societies of the Americas.[148]

What, then, made Curaçao different? As John Rickford observed in his comparative analysis of black and white Gullah speakers on South Carolina's Sea Islands, while differences in social class and race/ethnicity can result in diverging linguistic patterns among speakers of the same language, interethnic interactions reduce these anticipated variations.[149] Interethnic interaction was the hallmark of Willemstad's commercial economy and society throughout the eighteenth century. Willemstad's role as both a Dutch trade center and as a Caribbean port facilitated the intersection of the lives of urban blacks and up-and-coming Sephardic merchants across the relatively porous boundaries between race, social class, and ethnicity. This spurred creolization. The years of Papiamentu's emergence and consolidation as Curaçao's lingua franca coincided with the island's heyday as a thriving economic and cultural exchange center. Willemstad was a crucible for dynamic processes of interaction and creolization among its diverse inhabitants. This was crystallized in linguistic innovations. Aonghas St. Hilaire has noted how the Caribbean city has served as a "conduit for cultural exchange" and as a "meeting ground" between cultural influences from around the Atlantic.[150] Throughout much of the Caribbean, urbanization has diminished both the use and the cultural influence of the local creole language, while it strengthened the consolidation of a dominant European tongue. In Curaçao, by contrast, the port played precisely the opposite role in the eighteenth century, serving as a breeding ground for the consolidation of Papiamentu as an interethnic communications medium in the seventeenth and eighteenth centuries. The particular characteristics of Willemstad as a regional maritime exchange center under the rule of the West India Company provided the context in which Papiamentu developed as a communications link between the island's main diaspora groups, Sephardic Jews and Africans, and allowed them to consolidate a common and distinct local creole identity vis-à-vis the Dutch elite. Papiamentu's seemingly idiosyncratic rise is less surprising when we note that Guene, the creole which was spoken in rural areas, followed a similar trajectory to that of many other Caribbean creoles, declining in urban areas and eventually dying out in the twentieth century as the island urbanized.[151]

In the dynamic, cosmopolitan atmosphere of Willemstad's maritime economy, men, women, and children of different ethnicities and social classes were in close contact as they went about the business of the port. Men and women of both Sephardic and African descent sustained the maritime economy, and they forged multiple ties across divisions of race/ethnicity and social class. When men were at sea, women anchored the port, where they had numerous opportunities for close interethnic contact.[152] Occasionally, interethnic groups of women made the intercolonial crossing from Curaçao to Tierra Firme. Recall, for example, the Sephardic Jewish woman who fled to Coro in the company of four women of African descent in 1688, discussed at the beginning of Chapter 2.[153] Whether these five women were only temporary shipmates or had deeper ties, they likely found ways to communicate with each other to discuss the details of the journey beforehand and their plans upon arrival on the mainland (although they died en route). Enslaved Afro-Curaçaoans, male and female, fled to the same parts of Tierra Firme where Sephardic Jewish merchants traded regularly and sometimes established temporary settlements and enclaves. Sephardic merchants likely took some of their chattel with them to communities such as Coro and Tucacas.[154] Afro-Curaçaoan seafarers, enslaved and free, worked the small seacraft that were owned and operated by Sephardic merchants. Men of Sephardic and African descent often traveled around the Caribbean together in small vessels for weeks at a time, where they shared close quarters as they sought and took advantage of trade opportunities.

Shipboard conditions provided the ideal setting for Papiamentu's use as an interethnic tongue. In their ventures around the region, Sephardic merchants and black seafarers shared the conditions and experiences that linguists have identified as leading to the development of the proto-creole languages known as trade dialects or sailors' jargons.[155] Consider, for example, the different groups associated with the sailing sloop *de Jonge Johannes* from Curaçao, which was captured by a British privateer off the coast of Tierra Firme in 1737 and hauled to the Vice-Admiralty Court in Newport, Rhode Island. The vessel owners, who were accused of engaging in contraband trade, were one Sephardic Jew and two Dutchmen; the cargo owner was Sephardic; the vessel master was Dutch; all of them apparently were born and raised in Curaçao. The crew consisted of five Spaniards from Tierra Firme (at least several of whom resided in Curaçao), eight free blacks from Curaçao, and one slave, as well as a boy, boatswain, and gunner, all of unspecified backgrounds.[156] Both the vessel master and a sailor testified that Papiamentu was spoken on board. There are several similar cases of Curaçaoan vessels with multiethnic crew where the Dutch crew members said that the language spoken on board was a form of Spanish that they themselves did not understand, an indication that it may well have been Papiamentu.[157]

It is important to remember that the character of these interethnic relationships was fundamentally unequal in a slave society. Most Sephardic merchant families owned slaves. People of African descent, including free men and women, occupied a decidedly inferior position in the local society and economy, and their choices were markedly limited compared to those of the Sephardim. Nevertheless, within the very real constraints of this slave society, the urban maritime economy created unique opportunities for Papiamentu to flourish as an interethnic communications medium. Here again, contraband trade provided the foundation for specific forms of creolization and required different social groups to be in extended contact and so find ways of communicating.

Curaçao's Sephardim played a crucial role in Papiamentu's diffusion and acceptance, just as they were central in illicit intercolonial trade. The use of Papiamentu by Sephardim bolstered the language's success, and made it much more than just another creole spoken by slaves and other people of color.[158] Because Sephardim generally did not assign a hierarchy to the different languages they spoke, they apparently attached little or no stigma to Papiamentu, even if it was the emerging tongue of the lower-class black majority and largely shunned by the Dutch elite. Rather, speaking Papiamentu became a way of asserting an intrinsic colonial identity on the island, distinct from that of the Dutch. Moreover, Papiamentu's Iberian roots made it relatively easy to learn for someone who already knew Spanish and/or Portuguese. The Sephardim's diglossia—the habit of using different languages for very specific purposes—also benefited Papiamentu. The creole tongue became the language of interethnic dealings in the port, including those related to the local side of extra-island trade, and facilitated dealings with laborers. (Intercolonial trade itself often would require Spanish, sometimes French or English.) Curaçao's Sephardim had a disproportionate role in the development and maintenance of Papiamentu as a vigorous, living language, both within their own community and in the wider island society. This role continued throughout the nineteenth and twentieth centuries and up to the present.[159] As up-and-coming merchants but not yet an established elite, they were in regular, close contact with seafarers and dockworkers of African descent. Sephardim thus were uniquely positioned to stimulate Papiamentu's development and its use as an interethnic communications medium in a way that Afro-Curaçaoans were unable, and the Dutch-speaking elite was unwilling, to do.

Even as Papiamentu began to emerge as the island's lingua franca throughout the eighteenth century, it did not entirely replace the many other tongues that were spoken in the port. One can imagine the cacophony that was heard on Willemstad's wharves on a typical day. Small-scale merchants returned from their trading jaunts. Seafarers from around the Caribbean and beyond tottered ashore. Transatlantic vessels arrived from the Netherlands with their multilingual crews, who spoke Dutch, Spanish, Portuguese, English, French, German, and perhaps other European tongues. Dockworkers unloaded a variety of wares. As prostitutes and bar owners enticed new arrivals to satisfy their hungers and thirst, they no doubt called out carefully learned phrases in a variety of languages. Well-established company functionaries dropped by to eye the selection of goods they would send to Europe and debated the relative value of cargoes in proper Dutch. Perhaps the most multilingual of all were the groups of enslaved Africans who were hauled from the holds of slaving ships. At various times, depending on the provenance of the vessels that docked and the cargoes they carried, the air might be filled with words and phrases in Akan, Dutch, English, Fante, French, Ga, Guene, Hausa, Ibo, Kikingo, Kimbundu, Papiamentu, Portuguese, Spanish, Twi, Yoruba, and perhaps a smattering of Afro-Portuguese creoles. People who regularly came into contact with each other had to develop efficient means of communicating. Many of them already had begun this process in their weeks and months at sea together or in their contact on the western shores of Africa. This ongoing process continued in Willemstad.

Papiamentu did not remain in the port. It traveled on board sailing vessels with Curaçaoans to communities in the circum-Caribbean, where closely related creole languages developed in the eighteenth and nineteenth centuries.[160] Intercolonial exchange circuits carried the creole, literally providing the vehicles on which it traveled, and also creating conditions that encouraged the movement of merchants, workers, and fugitive slaves and spurred their need to communicate. It is possible that some sort of multilingual trade jargon(s) developed in the coastal areas of Tierra Firme most closely tied to Curaçao via smuggling. Maritime workers and small-scale merchants would have needed to develop basic language skills in order to communicate with their contacts. The development of trade jargons is a well-documented linguistic phenomenon.[161] Close ties between people of African descent in Curaçao and those in the Spanish colonies of the circum-Caribbean, especially ties that developed through illicit trade and marronage, stimulated the diffusion and development of creoles.[162] The contraband trade in enslaved Africans between the Dutch island and the Spanish mainland was an especially important conduit for language dissemination, as the human commodities added another layer of linguistic interaction, alongside that of traders and seafarers.[163] Marronage was another important source of transmission. Across the Americas maroon communities were particularly rich settings for the development of creole languages.[164] For example, in Colombia, Palenquero, which has clear linguistic similarities with Papiamentu, developed in maroon communities that were closely tied to contraband trade.[165]

Several Papiamentu-speaking enclaves developed throughout Tierra Firme, with the arrival of hundreds of Afro-Curaçaoans who settled in maroon communities, towns of free blacks, and urban neighborhoods.[166] One was Curiepe, the town of free blacks that mainland authorities had established on the northeastern coast of Tierra Firme as a buffer against enemy attack in 1721, and where dozens of fugitive Afro-Curaçaoans acquired land and planted small cacao groves in the early to mid-eighteenth century.[167] Another was the thriving urban neighborhood of Guinea, on the southern outskirts of Coro.[168] Other immigrants headed to the settlement of Santa María de la Chapa, in the mountains south of Coro, whose growth was fueled almost entirely by the arrival of fugitive Curaçaoans.[169] By the 1770s there were some four hundred documented fugitive slaves from Curaçao living in the rural areas surrounding Coro, according to contemporary reports.[170]

One way to document the presence of Curaçaoans around Tierra Firme is through names. People of African descent whose last names were some variation of Curaçao frequently appear in the historical record of several places in Tierra Firme that were closely tied to the island via smuggling. For example, at least sixteen people with the last name Curazao or Curazado appear in legal cases in the Barlovento area in the mid-eighteenth century.[171] Seven of the twenty-six names of the original inhabitants of the free black settlement at Curiepe are variations of Curaçao.[172] A significant number of the people living in Santa María de la Chapa in the 1700s had a last name which was some variation of Curazao, as did many residents of Coro.[173] Three men with the last name Curazao appear on the list of people implicated in the Coro slave revolt.[174] Among the most common variations are Curazao, Curasau, Curasao, Curazado, Quirizao, and Quirazago. Place-names are also revealing. Many of the same name variations also appear as place-names for the island on various seventeenth and eighteenth century maps of the Caribbean. Variations even appear occasionally in official documents. For example, a petition by Sephardic Jews to the island governor in 1681 is datelined Curasau.[175] Church records from 1767 identified one town as Citio de Sta. María de los Negros de Curazao—"location of Santa María of the blacks of Curaçao."[176]

Many immigrants to Tierra Firme maintained close ties with friends, relatives, and trade contacts back on the island, via the intercolonial circuits that smuggling created and sustained. Papiamentu was no doubt spoken, or at least understood, in all of these communities and along the intercolonial circuits. Such communication often was put to good use. An official report after the 1795 slave uprising in Coro mentioned that one of the leaders, José de la Caridad Gonzalez, was fluent in "Papiamento, or jargon of Curaçao," which he used to communicate with the many runaway Curaçaoan slaves in the area.[177] Gonzalez's Venezuelan wife testified that she could not understand the conversations he had with the other Curaçaoans, "because they were in his language, Dutch, or that of Guinea."[178] In 1795, following the aborted slave uprisings, a local authority testified that the Afro-Curaçaoans who lived in Coro's Guinea neighborhood accompanied their dances "with songs in a language that cannot be understood"; the short phrases he quoted, including the words *plaka* ("money") and *pa semillá* ("to plant"), indicates that it may well have been Papiamentu.[179] (The term "placas" also appears in a case related to fugitive slaves from Curaçao to Coro in 1751.)[180] When a free black man from Curaçao gave testimony in Papiamentu in a Coro court in 1800, authorities apparently had no difficulty finding a translator.[181] There is some evidence of a fragment of a written text in Papiamentu from the area around Coro, as well as the existence of Papiamentu songs and fragments of speech in communities of Afro-Venezuelans.[182] Curaçaoan merchants, seafarers, and migrant laborers also carried Papiamentu farther asea, to Puerto Rico and Cuba, and perhaps even to the Danish islands.[183] Thanks to Curaçao's regional trade networks, and to the prevalence of Afro-Curaçaoan seafarers, by the turn of the century free black men from Curaçao were well dispersed around the Caribbean. There was a community of Curaçaoan blacks numbering 156 on Danish St. Thomas, and a significant contingent in the town of Aquin in French Saint Domingue, as well as a large group among logwood cutters in Spanish Santo Domingo.[184] All of these groups would have spoken Papiamentu. The aborted slave revolts in Louisiana in 1795 and Trinidad, Cuba, in 1798 both included slaves from Curaçao.[185] On the Spanish-speaking islands, the creole language sometimes was incorrectly described as "broken Spanish," an echo of Father Schabel's diary entry from 1704.[186] By the early to mid-nineteenth century, written texts in Papiamentu were appearing as far away as Puerto Rico.[187]

Precisely because Papiamentu emerged as the lingua franca of different ethnic groups and social classes, it was far more than a simple communications vehicle. The language became a fundamental marker of Curaçaoan identity.[188] Linguists and anthropologists have noted how language development is intimately tied to the development of identities. Throughout the colonial Americas, the consolidation of creole languages has been seen as closely tied to the emergence of a coherent local identity among enslaved people of African descent who came from a variety of cultural backgrounds.[189] This phenomenon has been studied most closely in the context of plantations, which were home to relatively self-contained communities.[190] In the case of Curaçao, with its urban maritime trade economy concentrated in the port city of Willemstad, identity formation among people of African descent was not as separated from that of other social groups, especially the up-and-coming Sephardic merchant class. Nor were the boundaries between these groups as rigid, even if they occupied markedly different places in the socioeconomic hierarchy. In the course of the eighteenth century and beyond, Papiamentu emerged as a fundamental marker of local island identity among members of both of the island's diasporic groups.[191] The specific conditions of the port city of Willemstad and its inhabitants created unusual conditions for the development and successful diffusion of Papiamentu, and the island's Sephardic enclave played an unusually prominent role in this process. Illicit intercolonial trade created the conditions in which this could occur. Smuggling was more than the bedrock of the economy, it shaped the very contours of Curaçao's society, culture, and colonial identity during the time the island was governed by the West India Company.

Conclusions

By the time slave rebellions broke out in Curaçao and Tierra Firme in the summer of 1795 new political currents were coursing through the Caribbean and the Americas, currents that would have a major impact on regional politics, economics, and cultures.[1] In January of that same year the French army had invaded the Netherlands, overthrown the Dutch Republic, and installed a puppet government, the Batavian Republic. The Netherlands remained under French control until 1813. The West India Company had been abolished in 1791, four years before the slave revolts, after teetering on the brink of financial ruin for several decades.[2] Following the company's demise, Curaçao and the other Dutch Caribbean islands came under the administrative control of a new body, the Council of the Colonies, which would enact policies in the overseas possessions through the mid-twentieth century. It was the end of an era in the history of both Curaçao and of the Dutch Republic, after both had played pivotal roles in the early modern Atlantic world for some 150 years. The economic and sociocultural legacies of this period would continue to imprint island society thereafter.

Over the next two decades, as new geopolitical tides swept through the Atlantic world, Curaçao would twice come under British control (1800–1802 and 1807–16), before reverting to the Dutch at the end of the Napoleonic Wars.[3] By the early nineteenth century, the rise of the United States as a regional economic power the consolidation of a British economic empire in Latin America. and the independence of most of Spain's American colonies, including Venezuela, were among the factors that contributed to the decline of Curaçao as a major regional trade center.[4] By the time Britain ceded Curaçao back to the Dutch in 1816, the island had lost its place in regional and Atlantic trade. For the next hundred years, Curaçao would be a Caribbean backwater. The relative economic and geopolitical importance of the entire Caribbean region also declined in this period.[5]

With the dismantling of the WIC, Dutch administrators and merchants had less of a presence and influence on Curaçao. Fewer ships, sailors, and merchants visited the island. Free blacks and urban slaves dominated the society and culture of Willemstad, especially the growing multiethnic neighborhood of Otrobanda. Sephardic Jews continued to rise in economic importance, and several well-established families became part of the island elite. Sephardim also took on a greater role in the overall island society after they were granted full political rights in 1825. Papiamentu thrived, promoted actively by the Roman Catholic Church and further stimulated by the arrival of the printing press in the 1820s.[6] The Roman Catholic Church played an important role in sustaining the language, not only via printed publications, but also by proselytizing and preaching in Papiamentu among the island's majority population of African descent.[7]

Curaçao's Sephardic merchants and urban black residents, enslaved and free, continued to depend on regional trade, much of it extra-official, throughout the nineteenth century. They maintained especially close economic and sociocultural ties with inhabitants of the northern coast of South America, which was briefly unified in the federation of Gran Colombia and later became the independent republics of Venezuela and Colombia. Both countries welcomed Sephardic immigrants from Curaçao, who had a generations-old track record of close, mutually beneficial trade ties with the mainland, and for whom emigration was a particularly attractive option whenever (frequent) droughts or economic recession struck the island.[8] Smuggling continued, as did the flight of fugitive slaves, who were attracted by Gran Colombia's abolition of slavery in 1821. (Slavery was not abolished in the Dutch realm until 1863.) They often found refuge in communities that had been established by previous generations of Afro-Curaçaoans.

After a century on the periphery, Curaçao reemerged on the world economic stage with the opening of the Royal Dutch Shell oil refinery in 1918. As tens of thousands of immigrants poured in from throughout the circum-Caribbean and beyond, the island once again became a regional economic center. The Dutch refinery processed Venezuelan petroleum for the world market, annually sending dozens of tankers across the Atlantic.[9] The resulting boom lasted for most of the twentieth century, and it transformed Curaçao into one of the most prosperous islands in the Caribbean.[10] Willemstad (and its new suburban neighborhoods) once again became a multiethnic, cosmopolitan center, and a Caribbean and Atlantic hub. The Dutch flag continued to fly over Fort Amsterdam, which remained the seat of government. (To this day Curaçao remains under Dutch jurisdiction, although the refinery is now in Venezuelan hands.) Dutch expatriates filled new administrative and management positions in the oil business and in government, inhabited swank new suburban neighborhoods, and exercised a renewed influence on local society and culture, as well as dominating the economy and the government. The refinery also strengthened the island's historically close ties to the nearby mainland, since it processed crude from vast oil fields that had been discovered around Lake Maracaibo, Venezuela. Dozens of workers traveled regularly in the tankers that plied regional waters, while a vigorous parallel trade between the two areas developed in the shadow of the Dutch refinery, much of it extra-official. Curaçao's multiethnic inhabitants also forged their own networks around the Caribbean. This included a robust contraband trade with poorer islands that were the source of labor for the refinery.

The inter-island immigration and economic connection spurred by the opening of the refinery also resulted in rich cultural exchanges. Immigrants brought their own religions, foods, music, dances, clothing, and architectural styles to Curaçao, with much cross-fertilization. Once again, one of the most powerful manifestations of this cultural exchange was linguistic. A common language was vital for communication among the island's many different groups. Following the opening of the refinery, Dutch became Curaçao's official language and the required medium of instruction in all local schools for the first time. At the same time, Papiamentu gained new prominence. The creole became a fundamental marker of local identity among the island's established groups, especially Afro-Curaçaoans and Sephardic Jews. It also became a way for the many newcomers and their children to claim a legitimate place in local culture and society.[11] By the second half of the twentieth century, Papiamentu was widely regarded by linguists as one of the Caribbean's most vibrant and successful creoles.[12] Over the centuries, the Iberian language had endured and reemerged as a way to assert an independent creole identity even as the island inhabitants remained under the economic and political jurisdiction of the Dutch. Thus, some of the same processes that had played out during the time that Curaçao had been the regional seat of the West India Company reemerged in the twentieth century, as the Dutch island once again became a nodal point in Caribbean and Atlantic circuits.

* * *

Curaçao's role as a Caribbean trade center in the seventeenth and eighteenth centuries was the product of a particular historical moment, one that was shaped by the presence of the WIC on the island as both the seat of government and as the motor of the commercial economy. Intercolonial trade imprinted not only the economy of Curaçao but also local society and culture. Whether they were trading around the Caribbean, stretching the conventional boundaries between enslavement and freedom, forging multiple ties with people in Tierra Firme, or speaking a dynamic creole language that had only tenuous connections to Dutch, Curaçao's inhabitants made the best of the opportunities that opened up because the island was a Dutch Caribbean entrepôt. They both drew on and moved beyond the specific configurations provided by the Dutch imperial structure as exemplified by the WIC. The contraband economy also had an impact on much broader sociocultural forces well beyond the confines of this small desert island. It was a major force in Dutch overseas expansion, in moving diaspora groups across the Atlantic, and in the linguistic transformations that led to the development of creole languages.

Although the particular historical circumstances of Curaçao under the WIC were unique, the close relationship between illicit interimperial trade and the social and cultural processes of creolization were not. Creolization reflected a dual reality: the raw power that undergirded the slave societies of the early modern Atlantic world and the possibilities that inhabitants of these societies found to develop and express their own cultural responses. Creolization thus was the manifestation of both economic exploitation and cultural creativity in the slave societies of the Americas, as individuals and groups interacted and borrowed from each other regardless of imperial strictures. Similarly, intercolonial trade, although nominally controlled by European powers for their own benefit, was an arena in which many different members of society found a way to pursue their own economic interests, often circumventing and even flouting norms that had been imposed from above. Smuggling was a way for locals not only to assert their economic power but also to exercise some element of cultural power as they made consumption choices and chose trade partners in line with their own needs and interests, ones that often were outside the limits established by imperial authorities. In making these choices, colonials developed a "vehicle for gaining leverage against a state," as Alan Karras has observed.[13] Creolization and contraband thus were interwoven facets of colonial Atlantic societies that, separately and together, reflected the realities of life under empires, not only the limitations but also the possibilities. Transcending economic barriers often went hand in hand with violating sociocultural ones. The trade circuits, both legal and illicit, that bound together the Atlantic world also shaped the character of everyday life and human interactions.[14]

Curaçao under the WIC was in some ways sui generis. The Dutch imperial project gave an especially central role to merchants, had a high tolerance for intercolonial trade, and allowed extensive participation by Atlantic diaspora groups, especially Sephardic Jews. In Curaçao, the two groups most involved in regional extra-official trade were Atlantic diasporas rather than members of the Dutch elite. Not coincidentally, these were the same two groups that developed Papiamentu. Thus, the specific ways that creolization and contraband played out in Curaçao reflected the specific historical circumstances of the colony—most especially, the central and open role of contraband as the motor of the economy. The role of a merchant federation such as the WIC, as the seat of both political and economic power, was not replicated anywhere outside the Dutch realm for such an extended period of time. But in many ways the island was typical. On the ground, the WIC exercised authority in ways that were markedly similar to those of other European powers. Not only Curaçao, but Dutch colonies around the Americas, along the coast of western Africa, and throughout the Indian Ocean basin, bore many similarities to those of other European powers.

The particular ways that creolization and contraband were linked in the early modern Caribbean—and in colonies around the globe—warrants further study. Creolization in the Caribbean is still defined largely in terms of the plantation paradigm, and studies of creolization often focus narrowly on transformations that played out in the small worlds of individual plantations and within single island societies.[15] The evidence from Curaçao indicates that creolization, like illicit trade, was embedded in maritime networks that superseded geopolitical boundaries. Both intercolonial and transatlantic trade were central to the plantation system that dominated so many island economies in this period. Caribbean port cities such as Willemstad were cogs in the Caribbean plantation system

as well as vital nexuses in wide trade systems. They linked local economies and societies to Atlantic and global markets.[16] Human interactions
played out along a spectrum from plantation to port to ships at sea, each
sphere with its own specific characteristics but none entirely separate
from the others.[17]

In tracing the multiple connections between extra-official economic
and sociocultural exchanges that played out in Curaçao in the seventeenth and eighteenth centuries, this book also has explored how colonial
interactions shaped the contours of early modern empires. Throughout
the Caribbean, the Americas, and beyond, smuggling allowed colonial
denizens to circumvent legal and political regimes as well as economic
boundaries. These demarcations often were more imagined than real. As
Lauren Benton has noted, imperial spaces "were politically fragmented;
legally differentiated; and encased in irregular, porous, and sometimes
undefined borders."[18] The disjuncture between imperial borders and
actual spheres of human interaction had broader effects on the social
and cultural configurations of emerging colonial societies, well beyond
the economic and political realms. "Trading and consuming the same
goods . . . created a vocabulary for a cross-imperial Atlantic culture," as
David Hancock has noted.[19] This was true whether the trade was officially
sanctioned or not, although the particular kinds of trade configurations,
and the way they interfaced with specific local societies and cultures,
would give rise to varied and richly textured vocabularies. Contraband
trade thus contributed to processes of creolization. Creolization and contraband both were inherently subversive activities, in that they worked
against and around formal legal structures. By engaging in these activities, locals helped define the parameters of colonies and empires. Neither
creolization nor contraband was marginal. Rather, both were integral
to forming colonies and thus to the construction of empires. These processes shaped early modern colonial societies around the Atlantic world.
In doing so, they also left their imprint on the modern era.

Curaçao's role as a Caribbean and Atlantic nexus was the product of
a particular historical moment. Eventually it outlived its usefulness. By
the early nineteenth century, fewer and fewer Dutch transatlantic vessels
would line the harbor, their sails and flags unfurled in the wind. Yet even
as the island sank into relative obscurity, its economy a mere shadow of
what it had been, traces of the past endured. Even today, the Dutch flag
continues to fly over the tile roof of Fort Amsterdam, while Papiamentu
is the most common tongue, spoken proudly by people of all ethnicities and social classes. Locals maintain especially close economic and

cultural ties to Venezuela; these connections run the full gamut from official to informal to extralegal. The vestiges of both imperial power and colonial agency remain, over two hundred years after the apparatus of the West India Company was dismantled and slaves unsuccessfully rose up to try to claim their freedom.

NOTES

Introduction

1. Greenwich Maritime Museum (hereafter GMM) PAI0334 (1786).

2. An English translation of the charter can be found in Kavenagh, *Foundations of Colonial America*, 739–77; the quote is from 739.

3. I use these and other similar terms interchangeably throughout this book.

4. There are different conventions regarding the capitalization of the word "creole." I use lowercase except when it is part of the name of a specific language.

5. Alvarez Abreu, *Instrucción* (17 June 1715), 75.

6. For succinct overviews from a global perspective see Karras, *Smuggling*, and Karras, "Smuggling and Its Malcontents."

7. Smith, *Borderland Smuggling*, xiii.

8. Studnicki-Gizbert, *Nation upon the Ocean Sea*, 144.

9. For analyses of smuggling in the Spanish, English, and French Caribbean, respectively, that also touch on the breadth of its social and cultural impact, see Grahn, *Political Economy of Smuggling*, especially chap. 1; Zahedieh, "Merchants of Port Royal, Jamaica, and the Spanish Contraband Trade"; and Garrigus, "Blue and Brown."

10. Smith, *Borderland Smuggling*, 1.

11. Karras, *Smuggling*, 111.

12. Jarvis, *In the Eye of all Trade*, 119.

13. Aizpurua, *Curazao y la costa de Caracas*, 121.

14. Ramón Aizpurua has noted this close relationship in the case of the trade between Curaçao and the province of Veneuzela (ibid., 336–37), but I believe it holds true more generally for illicit trade.

15. Ibid., 338. Jeremy Cohen provides ample examples of how this played out in six different regions of the province of Venezuela; see Jeremy Cohen, "Informal Commercial Networks, Social Control and Political Power in the Province of Venezuela."

16. Grahn, *Political Economy of Smuggling*, 4, 12.

17. There is an extensive historiography emphasizing different shades of meaning of the terms creole and creolization. Foundational works include Brathwaite, *Development of Creole Society in Jamaica*; Mintz and Price, *Birth of African-American Culture*; Bastide, *African Religions of Brazil*; Nettleford, *Caribbean Cultural Identity*. For overviews and analysis of the literature on creolization see, among others, Price, "Miracle of Creolization"; Boland, "Creolisation and Creole Societies"; Buisseret and Reinhardt, eds., *Creolization in the Americas*, 3–17; and Carney, *Black Rice*, 2–5. For a survey of the genealogy of the term and its historical evolution see Allen, "Creole: The Problem of Definition," and Palmié, "'C-Word' Again."

18. See, for example, among others, Sweet, *Recreating Africa*.

19. See Boland, "Creolisation and Creole Societies," 39.

20. Ibid., 19.

21. Buisseret, Introduction to *Creolization in the Americas*, ed. Buisseret and Reinhardt, 8; Schwartz, "Formation of a Colonial Identity in Brazil," 16.

22. Boland, "Creolisation and Creole Societies," 35.

23. See, among others, Mark, "Evolution of 'Portuguese' Identity"; Green, "Further Considerations on the Sephardim of the Petit Côte"; Berlin, "From Creole to African."

24. See the various essays in *Creolization in the Americas*, ed. Buisseret and Reinhardt.

25. Grahn, *Political Economy of Smuggling*, 5; Dubois, *Colony of Citizens*, 48–50.

26. Pomerantz and Topik, *World That Trade Created*, xiv, xv. Also see Curtin, *Cross-Cultural Trade in World History*; Bentley, *Old World Encounters*; and Tracy, ed., *Rise of Merchants Empires*, especially the introduction.

27. Hancock, *Oceans of Wine*, xxvii.

28. Dubois, *Colony of Citizens*, 50.

29. Scott, "Common Wind," 4.

30. Welch, *Slave Society in the City*, 139.

31. The overrepresentation of people of African descent and Sephardic Jews in illicit intercolonial trade was not unique to Curaçao; it also occurred elsewhere in the Caribbean. See, for example, Fortune, *Merchants and Jews*, and Welch, *Slave Society in the City*, 125–26.

32. Aizpurua, *Curazao y la costa de Caracas*, 335; Koot, *Empire at the Periphery*, 13. Rather than trying to reinvent the wheel, I have relied on the meticulous work of others here, especially Wim Klooster and Ramón Aizpurua.

33. Alvarez Abreu, *Instrucción* (17 June 1715), 79, 86.

34. Han Jordaan's detailed study of free people of color in eighteenth-century Curaçao will no doubt fill important gaps here. For life on nineteenth-century rural estates, see Renkema, *Het curaçaose plantagebedrijf.*

35. Recent works that have helped shape this perspective and applied it to the study of the early modern Atlantic world include Daniels and Kennedy, eds., *Negotiated Empires*; Games, *Web of Empire*; Benton, *Search for Sovereignty*; Hancock, *Oceans of Wine*.

36. Games, *Web of Empire*.

37. Daniels and Kennedy, eds., *Negotiated Empires*.

38. Benton, *Search for Sovereignty*, 2.

39. Bentley, "Regional Histories, Global Processes, Cross-Cultural Interactions," 3–4.

40. Hancock, *Oceans of Wine,* xvi; Studnicki-Gizbert, *Nation upon the Ocean Sea,* 155.

41. For essays that address various aspects of this in different times and places see Bentley, Bridenthal, and Yang, eds., *Interactions.*

42. Hancock, *Oceans of Wine,* xv–xvi; xvii; Sweet, *Recreating Africa,* 2; Lane, *Quito 1599,* xv.

43. Hancock, *Oceans of Wine,* 394, xxiii.

1 / Converging Currents

1. Transatlantic Slave Trade Database (hereafter, TSTD): www.slavevoyages.org.

2. AGI P 265, R 9:2 (May 1565).

3. AGI P 265, R 9:4 (May 1565); Hawkins, "The voyage made by the worshipful M. John Hawkins," 35–37; Felice, *Curazao hispánico,* 66–70, citing AGI Santo Domingo 50.

4. AGI P 265 R9:1, Guzmán de Silva to Spanish King (February 1566).

5. Hernando de Heredia, license for John Hawkins to trade at Rio de la Hacha (21 May 1565), in Wright, comp., *Spanish Documents,* no. 14, 92–93; Hernando de Heredia, certificate of good conduct for John Hawkins, Rio de la Hacha (19–30 May 1565), in Wright, comp., *Spanish Documents,* no. 15, 94.

6. John Hawkins to Alonso Bernaldez, Governor of Burburata (16 April 1565), in Wright, comp., *Spanish Documents,* no. 11, 82–83.

7. Haviser, "Amerindian Cultural Geography," 145, 148.

8. See, for example, the 1520 report by Rodrigo de Figueroa, in Pacheco, ed., *Colección de Documentos Inéditos,* 379–85; Allaire, "Agricultural Societies in the Caribbean," 215.

9. "Carta del factor de Santo Domingo, Juan de Ampies, á Su Majestad," AGI P 18 R3 (undated); Haviser, "Amerindian Cultural Geography," 78–79, 140–42, 145, 148–49.

10. Haviser, "Amerindian Cultural Geography," 11, 148.

11. Ibid., 51–54; 73–74, 146, 148.

12. Watlington, "Physical Environment," 31–32.

13. Haviser, "Amerindian Cultural Geography," 11, 20–22, 132–33; Allaire, "Agricultural Societies in the Caribbean," 198.

14. Torres and Rodríguez, "Caribbean."

15. Felice, *Curazao hispánico,* 8–9.

16. Haviser, "Amerindian Cultural Geography," 15.

17. Ibid., 33–35.

18. Ibid., 11.

19. See, for example, Resolution (22 July 1644), in Gehring and Schilkamp, comps., *New Netherland Documents,* no. 9b, 43.

20. Cisneros, *Descripción exacta,* 167; author's own experience.

21. Allaire, "Agricultural Societies in the Caribbean," 98.

22. Royal Decree signed in Toledo (26 June 1539), in *Cedularios de la Monarquía Española Relativos a la Provincia de Venezuela,* no. 266, 99–101; Castellanos, *Elegías,* 173; also see Felice, *Curazao hispánico,* 44–45. For a detailed contemporary description of the vessels and how people navigated in them, see Aguado, *Historia de Venezuela,* 52–55.

23. Haviser, "Amerindian Cultural Geography," 57, 143–44.

24. For example, AGI MP Venezuela, 3, 3BIS, and 4; AGI MP Venezuela, 17, 18, and 19; Goslinga, *Short History of the Netherlands Antilles and Surinam*, 10–11. For speculation as to the origins of the name, see Goslinga, *Dutch in the Caribbean and in the Guianas*, 11.

25. See Goslinga, *Dutch in the Caribbean and on the Wild Coast*, 263–64.

26. AGI P 18 R3, "Carta del factor de Santo Domingo, Juan de Ampies, a Su Majestad."

27. Report of 1515 from Hispañola, cited in Sauer, *Early Spanish Main*, 194.

28. AGI P 18 R3; AGI IG 415 L1, "Sobrecarga de la licencia que se dió a juan de ampíe" (November 1526).

29. AGI P 18 R3.

30. For detailed analysis of the context of the Welser grant see Panhorst, *Los Alemanes en Venezuela*, and Friede, *Los Welser en la conquista de Venezuela*.

31. Morón, *Los orígenes históricos de Venezuela*, 1:230–3.

32. AGI MP Venezuela 17.

33. Haviser, "Amerindian Cultural Geography," 149–50.

34. Morón, *Los orígenes históricos de Venezuela*, 138. For more on Ampíes's maneuvers to control Tierra Firme, see Ramos, *La fundación de Venezuela*.

35. "Juicio de residencia seguido por el doctor Antonio Navarro a los Welser" (1538), in *Juicios de Residencia en la Provincia de Venezuela*, 1:97, 106, 163; Cisneros, *Descripción exacta*, 167.

36. For detailed description of the parameters and geography of the province of Venezuela, albeit in a later period, see Cisneros, *Descripción exacta*.

37. Brada, *Bisdom Coro*.

38. Royal Decree, Toledo (8 November 1538), in *Cedularios de la Monarquía Española Relativos a la Provincia de Venezuela*, no. 266, 81–84. Bastidas first organized the church in the area. See Goslinga, *Dutch in the Caribbean and on the Wild Coast*, 264.

39. Two Royal Decrees signed in Toledo (26 June 1539), in *Cedularios de la Monarquía Española Relativos a la Provincia de Venezuela*, no. 266, 99–101, and no. 267, 101–3.

40. LUSC COLLBN 001–11–082, and LUSC MB Portef 63 no. 21.

41. AGI MP Venezuela, 1, 1547; AGI IG 1208, "Expedientes, Informaciones y Probanzas, 1547–1549"; Felice, *Curazao hispánico*, 51, 55–57, 389.

42. Ibid., 51–52.

43. AGI SD Legajo 218, cited in Felice, *Curazao hispánico*, 52.

44. AGI SD 899; "Carta del Licenciado Santiago del Riego (12 February 1571), in Troconis, comp., *Documentos*, no. 6, 49.

45. Felice, *Curazao hispánico*, 60; "Sobre negros llegados en barcos franceses e ingleses" (15 February 1571), in Troconis, comp., *Documentos*, no. 7, 51.

46. AGI SD 221:69 (5 July 1620).

47. Haviser, "Amerindian Cultural Geography," 57.

48. Among others, LUSC COLLBN 002–09–029, LUSC COLLBN 001–11–082, and LUSC MB Portef 63, no. 21.

49. TePaske, "Integral to Empire," 29, 33.

50. Haviser, "Amerindian Cultural Geography," 57.

51. AGI MP Venezuela 17 (1634).

52. Aguado, *Historia de Venezuela*, 22.

53. "The voyage made by the worshipful M. John Hawkins," 36.

54. Ibid.

55. AGI SD 221: 69 (5 July 1620).

56. Felice, *Curazao hispánico*, 72; reports of the town council of Rio de la Hacha to the Spanish Crown (23 June and 9 July 1567), in Wright, comp., *Spanish Documents*, no. 16, 95–100, and no. 17, 101–6.

57. AGI SD 899.

58. "Report of Cumberland's seventh voyage," in Andrews, ed., *English Privateering Voyages to the West Indies*, 248.

59. Felice, *Curazao hispánico*, 70. For firsthand reports of Hawkins's visit to the mainland, see the documents reproduced in Wright, comp., *Spanish Documents*, no. 18–24, 107–27.

60. Diego Ruiz de Vallejo to the Spanish Crown (21 April 1568), in Wright, comp., *Spanish Documents*, no. 21, 114.

61. See, for example, Lazaro de Vallejo Aldrete and Hernando Costilla to the Spanish Crown (26? September 1568), in Wright, comp., *Spanish Documents*, no. 22, 118–19.

62. Hernando Costilla and Lazaro de Vallejo Aldrete to the Spanish Crown (8 January 1568), in Wright, comp., *Spanish Documents*, no. 19, 109–10; my emphasis.

63. Hernando Costilla and Lazaro de Vallejo Aldrete to the Spanish Crown (26? September 1568), in Wright, comp., *Spanish Documents*, no. 22, 118; my emphasis.

64. "Carta del Licenciado Santiago del Riego" (8 July 1568) in Troconis, comp., *Documentos,* no. 3, 29.

65. For extensive treatment of the revolt, see Parker, *Dutch Revolt*, and Israel, *Dutch Republic*, chaps. 7–24. For a briefer account, see Goslinga, *Dutch in the Caribbean and on the Wild Coast*, chap. 1.

66. Israel, *Dutch Republic*, 308.

67. Ibid., 310.

68. Parker, *Dutch Revolt*, 21, 23; Bloom, *Economic Activities of the Jews of Amsterdam*, xiv.

69. Israel, *Dutch Republic*, 309.

70. Bloom, *Economic Activities of the Jews of Amsterdam*, xv.

71. Ibid., 10.

72. Israel, *Dutch Republic*, 311.

73. Cited in Bodian, *Hebrews of the Portuguese Nation*, 1.

74. The classic study in English of the Dutch Golden Age is Schama, *Embarrassment of Riches*.

75. Parker, *Dutch Revolt*, 23; Bloom, *Economic Activities of the Jews of Amsterdam*, xiv.

76. For more information on this point, see Huussen, "Legal Position of the Jews," 25–41.

77. Goslinga, *Dutch in the Caribbean and on the Wild Coast*, analyzes the revolt's impact on Dutch overseas expansion throughout. For a more synoptic analysis, see Israel, *Dutch Republic*, chaps. 14, 15, and 35, and Davis, *Rise of the Atlantic Economies*, 176–93.

78. See, among others, Davies, *Primer of Dutch Seventeenth Century Overseas Trade*.

79. Schmidt, "Dutch Atlantic," 166–71.

80. Israel, *Dutch Republic*, 312; Postma, *Dutch in the Atlantic Slave Trade*, 7.

81. Israel, *Dutch Republic*, 312–13. For the development of the early Atlantic trade, see Emmer, "Dutch and the Making of the Second Atlantic System," 18–19; Emmer, "West India Company," 70–71; and Ebert, "Dutch Trade with Brazil before the West India Company," 49–75.

82. Israel, *Dutch Republic*, 319–20.

83. For the organization and activities of the VOC see Gaastra, *De geschiedenis van de VOC*, or, in English, Akveld and Jacobs, eds., *Colorful World of the VOC*. For a basic overview of the Dutch presence in Asia, see Zandvliet, *Dutch Encounter with Asia*.

84. Goslinga, *Dutch in the Caribbean and on the Wild Coast*, 56.

85. Laet, *Nieuvve Wereldt*, in Hamelberg, comp., *Documenten*, vol. 1, no. 1, 5.

86. Klooster, *Illicit Riches*, 24–31.

87. Olavarriaga, *Instrucción*, 300.

88. Heijer, "Dutch West India Company," 77–78; Goslinga, *Dutch in the Caribbean and on the Wild Coast*, 34–42, 17.

89. The classic study of the West India Company is Menkman, *De West-Indische Compagnie*. Also see Heijer, *De geschiedenis van de WIC*. In English, see Heijer, "Dutch West India Company," and Emmer, "West India Company," 66–75, and, for a longer treatment, Goslinga, *Dutch in the Caribbean and on the Wild Coast*, chaps. 5–18.

90. Heijer, "Dutch West India Company," 85.

91. Goslinga, *Dutch in the Caribbean and on the Wild Coast*, 195.

92. For a full account of this episode, including its impact on power struggles within Europe, see Goslinga, *Dutch in the Caribbean and on the Wild Coast*, 173–202, Appendix 4, 496–99, reproduces Spanish documents describing the type, amount, and value of the cargo.

93. Morón, *Los orígenes históricos de Venezuela*, 42.

94. See Oest, "Forgotten Colonies of Essequibo and Demerara," 325–26; Enthoven, "Early Dutch Expansion," 31–35, and Goslinga, *Dutch in the Caribbean and on the Wild Coast*, 75–81.

95. Bloom, *Economic Activities of the Jews of Amsterdam*, 146; Shorto, *Island at the Center of the World*, 105.

96. Enthoven, "Early Dutch Expansion," 40; Postma, *Dutch in the Atlantic Slave Trade*, 13.

97. Goslinga, *Dutch in the Caribbean and on the Wild Coast*, 275; Klooster, *Illicit Riches*, 41.

98. Goslinga, *Dutch in the Caribbean and on the Wild Coast*, 261.

99. For a detailed treatment of the early Dutch presence in the region, see ibid., chap. 11.

100. Heijer, "Dutch West India Company," 86; Schwartz, "Commonwealth within Itself," 158–200.

101. Heijer, "Dutch West India Company," 86–87; Schwartz, "Commonwealth within Itself," 162, 166. Also see Ebert, "Dutch Trade with Brazil before the Dutch West India Company."

102. See, for example, Enthoven, "Early Dutch Expansion," 17–47, and Seed, *Ceremonies of Possession*, 154–60.

103. Hugo Grotius, *De mare liberum*, cited in Schnurmann, "Wherever Profit Leads Us," 480.

104. Schnurmann, "Wherever Profit Leads Us," 486–87, 489–90.

105. Schmidt, "Dutch Atlantic," 172.

106. Benton, *A Search for Sovereignty*, 3–5.

107. See Goslinga, *Dutch in the Caribbean and on the Wild Coast*, 258.

108. Laet, *Nieuwe Wereldt*, 509.

109. Diego Gomez, Coro (10 August 1632), in Wright, comp., *Nederlandsche Zeevaarders*, no. 54, 181–82.

110. Francisco Nuñez Melián to Pedro de Llovera, La Guaira (12 October 1633), in Wright, comp., *Nederlandsche Zeevaarders*, no. 55, 183–85.

111. Hamelberg, *Documenten*, vol. 1, no. 9, 18–22.

112. Ibid., no. 10, 23–24.

113. Ibid., no. 7, 17; no. 11, 24–25.

114. Felice, *Curazao hispánico*, 237; Goslinga, *Dutch in the Caribbean and on the Wild Coast*, 265–74.

115. Goslinga, *Dutch in the Caribbean and on the Wild Coast*, 267.

116. AGI MP Venezuela 17 (1634); Felice, *Curazao hispánico*, 212, Goslinga, *Dutch in the Caribbean and on the Wild Coast*, 267, 269.

117. Cited in Goslinga, *Dutch in the Caribbean and on the Wild Coast*, 269.

118. LUSC MB Portef 63 no. 21.

119. Governor Matthias Beck to Amsterdam Directors (11 June 1657), in Gehring and Schiltkamp, comps., *New Netherland Documents*, no. 27, 98.

120. Van Walbeeck's report is reproduced in Hamelberg, comp., *Documenten*, no. 12, 25–28. Also see the legend to his drawing of the harbor, NAN VEL 595 (1634).

121. NAN VEL 595.

122. Goslinga, *Dutch in the Caribbean and on the Wild Coast*, 269.

123. AGI IG 2569, Urcas al Curaçao (1634–35); AGI P 274 R4 (1 September 1640).

124. AGI P 274, R2–7; AGI SD 870: Registros de oficios: Isla de Santo Domingo (1626–47), L10 F114–124; for detailed accounts of these expeditions see Castillo, *Las acciones militares*, 36–40, 91–105, 157–176, and Felice, *Curazao hispánico*, 263–339.

125. AGI IG 2569, 134r–136v (January 1635); AGI SD 194: "Cartas y expedientes Gobernadores de Caracas y Venezuela, 1621–39," R3 and R4. Also see the following in Wright, comp., *Nederlandsche Zeevaarders*: Francisco Nuñez Melián to the Spanish Crown (11 February 1635), no. 60, 200; Francisco Nuñez Melián to the Spanish Crown (15 July 1635), no. 62, 211; Domingo Antonio Francisco, Caracas (12–13 July 1635), no. 62 Annex, 215–16; Juan Mateos, Caracas (19 October 1635), no. 62 Annex B, 227–8; Memorandum (July (?) 1641), no. 67, 248.

126. Francisco Nuñez Melián to Pedro de Llovera, La Guaira (12 October 1633), in Wright, comp., *Nederlandsche Zeevaarders*, no. 55, 183–85.

127. Alonso Diaz, Coro (3 January 1635), in Wright, comp., *Nederlandsche Zeevaarders*, no. 58, 193–94; Pedro Ortiz, Caracas (11 February 1636), in Wright, comp., *Nederlandsche Zeevaarders*, no. 65, 239.

128. Juan Mateos to Caracas (19 October 1635), in Wright, comp., *Nederlandsche Zeevaarders*, no. 62 Annex B, 228; Mathias Herman to Caracas (31 January 1636), in Wright, comp., *Nederlandsche Zeevaarders*, no. 64, 237.

129. Peter Stuyvesant et al., Resolution (31 March 1643), in Gehring and Schiltkamp, comps., *New Netherland Documents*, no. 4b, 22; Peter Stuyvesant et al., Resolution (19 May 1643), in Gehring and Schiltkamp, comps., *New Netherland Documents*, no. 5b, 23.

130. Gonzalez, *Antillas y Tierra Firme*, 32.

131. "Reglement voor de West-Indische Compagnie" (26 April 1634), cited in Schunk, "Lost Catholic Houses of Prayer in Curaçao," 129.

132. Felice, *Curazao hispánico*, 391–92.

133. NAN VEL 595.

134. Goslinga, *Dutch in the Caribbean and in the Guianas*, 496.

135. Ibid., 495; Ozinga, *De Monumenten van Curaçao*, 63–118.

136. Buddingh', *Van Punt en Snoa*, 46–47; Goslinga, *Dutch in the Caribbean and on the Wild Coast*, 275.

137. This can be traced in the succession of laws, declarations, and resolutions that were issued from the island and which are transcribed in Schiltkamp and Smidt, comps., *West Indisch Plakaatboek*.

138. WIC Directors meeting (1 December 1634), excerpted in Hamelberg, comp., *Documenten*, no. 23, 42; Minutes of the Zeeland Chamber (30 June 1635), excerpted in Hamelberg, comp., *Documenten*, no. 25, 43.

139. Goslinga, *Dutch in the Caribbean and on the Wild Coast*, 234.

140. Ibid., 270.

141. Peter Stuyvesant Resolution (26 May 1644), in Gehring and Schiltkamp, comps., *New Netherland Documents*, no. 8c, 39.

142. For analysis of the role of the West India Company in the broader Dutch colonial project in the Atlantic, see, among others, Heijer, "Dutch West India Company"; Heijer, "West African Trade of the Dutch West India Company," 139–69; and Goslinga, *Dutch in the Caribbean and in the Guianas*, esp. chaps. 1 and 3.

143. Goslinga, *Dutch in the Caribbean and on the Wild Coast*, 282.

144. Resolution (13 February 1643), in Gehring and Schiltkamp, comps., *New Netherland Documents*, no. 2c, 9; Curaçao Vice-director Matthias Beck to Director Petrus Stuyvesant (21 March 1656), in Gehring and Schiltkamp, comps., *New Netherland Documents*, no. 26, 91; Matthias Beck to Company directors in Amsterdam (11 June 1657), in Gehring and Schiltkamp, comps., *New Netherland Documents*, no. 27, 99; Matthias Beck to Petrus Stuyvesant (23 August 1659), in Gehring and Schiltkamp, comps., *New Netherland Documents*, no. 41, 127; Matthias Beck to Amsterdam directors (4 February 1660), in Gehring and Schiltkamp, comps., *New Netherland Documents*, no. 57, 160; Matthias Beck to Petrus Stuyvesant (16 April 1665), in Gehring and Schiltkamp, comps., *New Netherland Documents*, no. 104, 211.

145. Instructions to Curaçao director J. P. Tolck (15 August 1640), in Gehring and Schiltkamp, comps., *New Netherland Documents*, no. 1, 6; "Resolutions concerning 'freedoms and exemptions' granted to freemen" (10/12 March 1643), in Gehring and Schiltkamp, comps., *New Netherland Documents*, no. 3a, 12.

146. Resolution by Curaçao island officials (26 May 1644), in Gehring and Schiltkamp, comps., *New Netherland Documents*, no. 8c, 34.

147. Hartog, *Curaçao: From Colonial Dependence to Autonomy*, 89.

148. L. Rodenborch et al. (18 May 1644) and P. Stuyvesant et al. (25 May 1644), in Gehring and Schiltkamp, comps., *New Netherland Documents*, no. 8a and no. 8b, respectively, 36.

149. Francisco Nuñez Melián to the Spanish Crown, Caracas (15 July 1635), in Wright, comp., *Nederlandsche Zeevaarders*, no. 62, 213; Mathias Herman, Caracas (31 January 1636), in Wright, comp., *Nederlandsche Zeevaarders*, no. 64, 233; Memorandum (July (?) 1641), in Wright, comp., *Nederlandsche Zeevaarders*, no. 67, 250, 252–53.

2 / Atlantic Diasporas

1. AF CC no. 914 (9 September 1688). For more about the case, see Gonzalez, "Conversiones judaicas," 15–22, and Rupert, "Waters of Faith." I am grateful to Carlos Gonzalez Batista for helping me locate the original document in the Coro archives.

2. Israel, *Diasporas within a Diaspora*, 22.

3. The literature on this subject is vast. See, among others, Rowland, "New Christian, Marrano, Jew," 125–48; Wachtel, "Marrano Religiosity in Hispanic America," 149–71; Levine, *Scattered among the Peoples*, 28, 35–36; Schorsch, *Jews and Blacks in the Early Modern World*, 15; Kamen, *Spanish Inquisition*, ix, 11, and n. 11, 323–24; Bloom, *Economic Activities of the Jews of Amsterdam*, xivn7.

4. Israel, *Diasporas within a Diaspora*.

5. For discussion of the complex issues of Sephardic identity throughout early modern period, see, among others, Israel, "Jews and Crypto-Jews in the Atlantic World," 3–17; Sutcliffe, "Jewish History in an Age of Atlanticism," 18–30; Rowland, "New Christian, Marrano, Jew," 125–48; and Bodian, "'Men of the Nation,'" 48–76. For a discussion of similar issues in Atlantic Africa see Mark and da Silva Horta, "Two Early Seventeenth-Century Sephardic Communities," 231–56, and Green, "Further Considerations on the Sephardim," 165–83.

6. Israel, *Diasporas within a Diaspora*, 4, 38. For extensive treatment of this topic, see Israel, *Diasporas within a Diaspora*, and the articles in *Jews and the Expansion of Europe to the West*, ed. Bernardini and Fiering.

7. Sutcliffe, "Jewish History in an Age of Atlanticism," 28; Bodian, *Hebrews of the Portuguese Nation*, 64.

8. Hereafter I use the term *conversos* to refer to all early Sephardic immigrants to Spanish America, regardless of their actual degree of conversion. I use the term "New Christians" similarly for the Portuguese realm.

9. Israel, "Jews and Crypto-Jews in the Atlantic World," 3–7; Green, "Further Considerations on the Sephardim," 166.

10. Israel, "Jews and Crypto-Jews in the Atlantic World," 3–4. This framework works well for the Americas but is more problematic for Atlantic Africa.

11. Israel, *Diasporas within a Diaspora*, chaps. 3, 4; Israel, *Empires and Entrepôts*, chap. 12; Metz, "Those of the Hebrew Nation," 209–33; and part 2 of Bernardini and Fiering, eds., *Jews and the Expansion of Europe to the West*.

12. Hertzberg, *Jews in America*, 5.

13. Kamen, *Empire*, 343–44; Bernardini and Fiering, eds., *Jews and the Expansion of Europe to the West*, 486–87.

14. AGI SD 764, cited in Borges, *Alvarez Abreu*, 55; Emmanuel and Emmanuel, *History of the Jews of the Netherlands Antilles*, 822, 831.

15. Emmanuel and Emmanuel, *History of the Jews of the Netherlands Antilles*, 83.

16. Israel, "Jews and Crypto-Jews in the Atlantic World," 10–12; Israel, *Diasporas within a Diaspora*, 19.

17. Israel, *Diasporas within a Diaspora*, 19–20.

18. Ibid., 29.

19. Israel, "Jews and Crypto-Jews in the Atlantic World," 13, 16–17; Israel, *Diasporas within a Diaspora*, 30.

20. For extensive treatment of this topic, see Mark and da Silva, *Forgotten Diaspora*.

21. Mark and da Silva, "Catholics, Jews, and Muslims in Early Seventeenth-Century Guiné," 174; Brooks, *Eurafricans in Western Africa*, 61.

22. Heywood and Thornton, *Central Africans, Atlantic Creoles, and the Foundation of the Americas*, 72.

23. Mark and da Silva, "Two Early Seventeenth-Century Sephardic Communities," 232.

24. Ibid., 232, 234, 246–47.

25. Brooks, *Eurafricans in Western Africa*, 89–90.

26. Heywood and Thornton, *Central Africans, Atlantic Creoles, and the Foundation of the Americas*, 72; Mark and da Silva, "Two Early Seventeenth-Century Sephardic Communities," 248.

27. Mark and da Silva, "Two Early Seventeenth-Century Sephardic Communities," 246.

28. Lewin, *La inquisición en México*, 175; Heywood and Thornton, *Central Africans, Atlantic Creoles, and the Foundation of the Americas*, 96; Mark and da Silva, *Forgotten Disapora*, 169–74.

29. Heywood and Thornton, *Central Africans, Atlantic Creoles, and the Foundation of the Americas*, 117.

30. Ibid., 13.

31. Brooks, *Eurafricans in Western Africa*; Mark and da Silva, *Forgotten Diaspora*.

32. Pijning, "New Christians as Sugar Cultivators and Traders in the Portuguese Atlantic," 486–87; Mark, *"Portuguese" Style and Luso-African Identity*, 13–14; Mark and da Silva, "Two Early Seventeenth-Century Sephardic Communities," 252–55; Heywood and Thornton, *Central Africans, Atlantic Creoles, and the Foundation of the Americas*, 72.

33. Mark and da Silva, *Forgotten Disapora*, 178–79.

34. Ibid., 159.

35. Ibid., 160.

36. Green, "Further Considerations on the Sephardim," 179.

37. Mark and da Silva, *Forgotten Disapora*, 182–83.

38. Mark and da Silva, "Two Early Seventeenth-Century Sephardic Communities," 249.

39. Mark and da Silva, *Forgotten Disapora*, 161, 163.

40. Green, "Further Considerations on the Sephardim," 181–82.

41. Israel, "Jews and Crypto-Jews in the Atlantic World," 13.

42. Ibid., 13–14.

43. Huussen, "Legal Position of the Jews," 30–31.

44. Nusteling, "Jews in the Republic of the United Provinces," 46.

45. Israel, *Diasporas within a Diaspora*, 22.

46. For in-depth discussion of the demographics, see Nusteling, "Jews in the Republic of the United Provinces," 48–56; Bodian, *Hebrews of the Portuguese Nation*, 1–2; Israel, *Empires and Entrepôts*, 425; and Bloom, *Economic Activities of the Jews of Amsterdam*, 31–32, 204, 210.

47. Bloom, *Economic Activities of the Jews of Amsterdam*, 11, 15–17; Bernfeld, "Financing Poor Relief in the Spanish-Portuguese Community in Amsterdam," 63–102.

48. Bodian, *Hebrews of the Portuguese Nation,* 64.

49. Bloom, *Economic Activities of the Jews of Amsterdam*, 17.

50. See, among others, Games, *Web of Empire*; Hancock, *Citizens of the World*; Price, *Perry of London*.

51. Sutcliffe, "Jewish History in an Age of Atlanticism," 24.

52. Ibid., 26–27. For analysis of one case of rivalries among Sephardic merchants in early modern Europe see Trivellato, *Familiarity of Strangers,* chap. 10, "'Big Diamond Affair.'"

53. See Garrigus, "New Christians/'New Whites,'" 316–19.

54. A facsimile of the original document is reproduced in Schiltkamp, "Legislation, Government, Jurisprudence, and Law in the Dutch West Indian Colonies," 323–24. Schiltkamp's article also provides useful analysis and contextualization. I am grateful to Henk den Heijer for this reference. For an English translation of the Order of Government see Wiznitzer, comp., *Records of the Earliest Jewish Community in the New World*, 1–2.

55. For population calculations, see Wiznitzer, *Jews in Colonial Brazil*, 130; and Hertzberg, *Jews in America*, 7–8.

56. Benjamin, *Jews of the Dutch Caribbean*, 95; Drescher, "Jews and New Christians in the Atlantic Slave Trade," 450.

57. See Bloom, *Economic Activities of the Jews of Amsterdam*, 128–44, and Wiznitzer, *Jews in Colonial Brazil*. For insights into the internal workings of this community, see the documents in Wiznitzer, comp., *Records of the Earliest Jewish Community in the New World*.

58. Pijning, "New Christians as Sugar Cultivators and Traders in the Portuguese Atlantic," 491.

59. Ibid., 492.

60. Israel, *Diasporas within a Diaspora*, 8.

61. For more on these first Sephardic settlers in New Netherland see Hertzberg, *Jews in America*, 5–19.

62. Letter to directors of the West India Company from leaders of Amsterdam's Sephardic community, January 1655, reproduced in Marcus, ed., *Jew in the American World*, 31.

63. Arbell, "Jewish Settlements in the French Colonies," 290.

64. For British America see Emmanuel and Emmanuel, *History of the Jews of the Netherlands Antilles,* 40–48; Marcus, ed., *Jew in the American World*, 64; Sachar, *History of the Jews in America*, 13–14; Hertzberg, *Jews in America*, chaps. 1, 2; and Fortune, *Merchants and Jews.* For the French colonial Atlantic, see the articles by Gérard Nahon, Silvia Marzagalli, Mordechai Arbell, and John Garrigus in *Jews and the Expansion of Europe to the West,* ed. Bernardini and Fiering; Israel, *Diasporas within a Diaspora*, 245–68.

65. For discussion of trade diasporas see Cohen, "Cultural Strategies in the Organization of Trading Diasporas," and Curtin, *Cross-Cultural Trade in World History*, 1–14.

66. Emmanuel, *Precious Stones of the Jews of Curaçao*, 213, citing *Publication of the American Jewish Historical Society* (Philadelphia, 5:50, and vol. 19), 175 and 176.

67. Emmanuel and Emmanuel, *History of the Jews of the Netherlands Antilles*, 37–38. Because of their fluency in multiple languages, Sephardim often were employed as interpreters in early modern Europe.

68. Ibid., 38.

69. Ibid., 39–42. Also see Bloom, *Economic Activities of the Jews of Amsterdam*, 145–48. His exact first and last names, and their spellings, vary widely in the documents.

70. Böhm, *Los sefardíes en los dominios holandeses*, 170.

71. Governor Lucas Rodenburch to Amsterdam Directors (2 April 1654), in Gehring and Schiltkamp, comps., *New Netherland Documents*, no. 14, 58.

72. Klooster, "Networks of Colonial Entrepreneurs," 42.

73. Ibid., 47; Emmanuel and Emmanuel, *History of the Jews of the Netherlands Antilles*, 51.

74. Amsterdam Directors of West India Company (22 February 1652), in Gehring and Schiltkamp, comps., *New Netherland Documents*, no. 11, 49; Emmanuel and Emmanuel, *History of the Jews of the Netherlands Antilles*, 42–45.

75. Klooster, "Networks of Colonial Entrepreneurs," 43.

76. "Freedoms and Exemptions granted and Awarded by the directors of the West India Company at the chamber in Amsterdam to Joseph Nunes de Fonseca . . ." (no date), in Gehring and Schiltkamp, comps., *New Netherland Documents*, no. 12, 49–51.

77. Ibid., 51.

78. Klooster, "Networks of Colonial Entrepreneurs," 43; Emmanuel and Emmanuel, *History of the Jews of the Netherlands Antilles*, 43, 51. For more about Nassi's other trading ventures around the region, see Klooster, "Networks of Colonial Entrepreneurs," 43–47.

79. Emmanuel and Emmanuel, *History of the Jews of the Netherlands Antilles*, 44.

80. Ibid., 51.

81. Governor Lucas Rodenburch to Amsterdam Directors (2 April 1654); Amsterdam Directors to Governor Lucas Rodenburch (7 July 1654), both in Gehring and Schiltkamp, comps., *New Netherland Documents*, no. 14, 57–58, and no. 15, 61–63, respectively. According to Klooster he also was involved in a trading venture with Tierra Firme, as well as several other largely unsuccessful schemes. Klooster, "Networks of Colonial Entrepreneurs," 42–43.

82. Emanuel and Emanuel, *History of the Jews of the Netherlands Antilles*, 68.

83. For extensive description of the close trade and familial ties between the Sephardim of New York and Curaçao in the early to mid-eighteenth century see Emmanuel, *Precious Stones of the Jews of Curaçao*, 261– 339 passim.

84. Amsterdam directors to Governor Lucas Rodenburch (7 July 1654), in Gehring and Schiltkamp, comps., *New Netherland Documents*, no. 15, 61, 62.

85. Lucas Rodenburch to Amsterdam Directors (2 April 1654), in Gehring and Schiltkamp, comps., *New Netherland Documents*, no. 14, 58.

86. Vice-Director Matthias Beck (21 March 1656), in Gehring and Schiltkamp, comps., *New Netherland Documents*, no. 26, 92.

87. The relevant correspondence, five letters written between September 1654 and October 1655, is translated and reproduced in its entirety in Marcus, ed., *Jew in the American World*, 27–33.

88. West India Company to Peter Stuyvesant (26 April 1655), in Marcus, ed., *Jew in the American World*, 32.

89. Peter Stuyvesant to West India Company (October 30, 1655), in Marcus, ed., *Jew in the American World*, 33.

90. For extensive treatment of the case, see Hertzberg, *Jews in America*, 7–14.

91. "Extraordinary session held in the residence of the honorable vice-director M. Beck" (21 February 1656), in Gehring and Schiltkamp, comps., *New Netherland Documents*, no. 25a, 87–88; and "Session held in residence of the honorable vice-director M. Beck" (23 February 1656), in Gehring and Schiltkamp, comps., *New Netherland Documents*, no. 25b, 88–89. The quote is from the latter, 89.

92. "Extraordinary session held in the residence of the honorable vice-director M. Beck" (21 February 1656), in Gehring and Schiltkamp, comps., *New Netherland Documents*, no. 25a, 87.

93. See Bloom, *Economic Activities of the Jews of Amsterdam*, 146.

94. Emmanuel and Emmanuel, *History of the Jews of the Netherlands Antilles*, 45–48.

95. The da Costa contract is missing from the archives; for a summary of its main points, see Emmanuel and Emmanuel, *History of the Jews of the Netherlands Antilles*, 48–50.

96. Ibid., 49.

97. Ibid., 75.

98. The area is clearly depicted on later maps. See, for example, LUSC COLLBN 002–09–029.

99. Amsterdam directors to Matthias Beck (7 July 1654), in Gehring and Schiltkamp, comps., *New Netherland Documents*, no. 15, 63; resolution concerning Isaac de Fonseca cargo (21 February 1656), in Gehring and Schiltkamp, comps., *New Netherland Documents*, no. 25b, 89; Vice-director Matthias Beck to Petrus Stuyvesant (21 March 1656), in Gehring and Schiltkamp, comps., *New Netherland Documents*, no. 26, 91; Emmanuel and Emmanuel, *History of the Jews of the Netherlands Antilles*, 62–67 and 68–70. For the location of these early rural landholdings, as well as the Jewish cemetery, see LUSC COLLBN 002–09–029.

100. Welie, "Slave Trading and Slavery in the Dutch Colonial Empire," 53; Vos, Eltis, and Richardson, "Dutch in the Atlantic World," 232 Postma, "Reassessment of the Dutch Atlantic Slave Trade," 123; Curtin, *Atlantic Slave Trade*, 85; http://www.slavevoyages.org.

101. Welie, "Slave Trading and Slavery in the Dutch Colonial Empire," 53–55; Vos, Eltis, and Richardson, "Dutch in the Atlantic World," 229–32. Both are based on critical analysis of the numbers in the slave trade database. They provide extensive, compelling arguments for substantially increasing the total of 408,658 individuals listed in the database, and also for increasing Johannes Postma's numbers, which the latter had revised downward from 542,972 to 505,831. For Postma's explanation of the downward revision of his 1990 numbers, which were first published in *Dutch in the Atlantic Slave Trade*, see his "Reassessment of the Dutch Atlantic Slave Trade."

102. Welie, "Slave Trading and Slavery in the Dutch Colonial Empire," 53–44.

103. Ibid., 55, and calculation from table 1, 53.

104. Vos, Eltis, and Richardson, "Dutch in the Atlantic World," 237.

105. Ibid., 233–35.

106. Postma, *Dutch in the Atlantic Slave Trade*, 10, 12.

107. Heywood and Thornton, *Central Africans, Atlantic Creoles, and the Foundation of the Americas*, 19.

108. Goslinga, *Dutch in the Caribbean and on the Wild Coast*, 340–41; Heywood and Thornton, *Central Africans, Atlantic Creoles, and the Foundation of the Americas*, 19.

109. Postma, *Dutch in the Atlantic Slave Trade*, 10, 13; Emmer, "History of the Dutch Slave Trade," 728–29.

110. See Klooster, "Het begin van de Nederlandse slavenhandel," 250.

111. Heywood and Thornton, *Central Africans, Atlantic Creoles, and the Foundation of the Americas*, 15, 22.

112. Ibid., 15.

113. Ibid., 25–27.

114. Heijer, "West African Trade of the Dutch West India Company," 140.

115. Cited in Welie, "Slave Trading and Slavery in the Dutch Colonial Empire," 57n25.

116. Enthoven, "Early Dutch Expansion," 40; Postma, *Dutch in the Atlantic Slave Trade*, 13.

117. Goslinga, *Dutch in the Caribbean and on the Wild Coast*, 341.

118. Postma, *Dutch in the Atlantic Slave Trade*, 12–13.

119. Welie, "Slave Trading and Slavery in the Dutch Colonial Empire," 57n26.

120. Goslinga, *Dutch in the Caribbean and on the Wild Coast*, 353.

121. Postma and Enthoven, eds., *Riches from Atlantic Commerce*.

122. Heywood and Thornton, *Central Africans, Atlantic Creoles, and the Foundation of the Americas*, 42.

123. Ibid.

124. Acosta, *La trata de esclavos en Venezuela*, 4.

125. Postma, *Dutch in the Atlantic Slave Trade*, 33.

126. Ibid., 29–30.

127. See Goslinga, *Dutch in the Caribbean and on the Wild Coast*, 339–70; Postma, *Dutch in the Atlantic Slave Trade*, 33–36.

128. Heywood and Thornton, *Central Africans, Atlantic Creoles, and the Foundation of the Americas*, 1. Information for this paragraph comes from Chapter 2.

129. Berlin, "From Creole to African," 251–88; Heywood and Thornton, *Central Africans, Atlantic Creoles, and the Foundation of the Americas*, chap. 2.

130. Heywood and Thornton, *Central Africans, Atlantic Creoles, and the Foundation of the Americas*, 6.

131. For analysis of the development of Catholicism in Kongo, see, among others, Thornton, *Kongolese Saint Anthony*.

132. Goslinga, *Dutch in the Caribbean and the Wild Coast*, 351–52.

133. Cited ibid.

134. Cited ibid.

135. Postma, *Dutch in the Atlantic Slave Trade*, 27.

136. AGI P 265, R 9:2 and R 9:4, May 1565; TSTD; Heywood and Thornton, *Central Africans, Atlantic Creoles, and the Foundation of the Americas*, 11–12.

137. Heywood and Thornton, *Central Africans, Atlantic Creoles, and the Foundation of the Americas*, 11.

138. "Carta de Bernabé de Oñate" (12 June 1613), "Carta de Don García de Girón" (6 February 1613), both in Troconis, comp., *Documentos*, no. 33, 137–39, and no. 34, 144, respectively.

139. AGI SD 899. The document does not specify whether he was enslaved or free. Pedro may well have been an Atlantic Creole.

140. Emmanuel and Emmanuel, *History of the Jews of the Netherlands Antilles*, 41.

141. "Instructie voor Jacob Pietersz Tolck, Direkteur van Curaçao" (1638), in Schiltkamp and Smidt, comps., *West Indisch Plakaatboek*, 1:6.

142. Resolution by Peter Stuyvesant et al. (19 May 1643), in Gehring and Schiltkamp, comps., *New Netherland Documents*, no. 5b, 23; AGI SD 215, "Declarasion de un soldado yrlandes" (14 December 1642), cited in Heywood and Thornton, *Central Africans, Atlantic Creoles, and the Foundation of the Americas*, 259n96.

143. Resolution by Peter Stuyvesant et al. (14 April 1643), in Gehring and Schiltkamp, comps., *New Netherland Documents*, no. 5a, 22–23; Resolution by Peter Stuyvesant et al. (19 May 1643), in Gehring and Schiltkamp, comps., *New Netherland Documents*, no. 5b, 23–24; Resolution by Peter Stuyvesant et al. (18 July 1644), in Gehring and Schiltkamp, comps., *New Netherland Documents*, no. 9a, 42; Resolution by Peter Stuyvesant et al. (22 July 1644), in Gehring and Schiltkamp, comps., *New Netherland Documents*, no. 9b, 43. The quote is from no. 9a, 42.

144. Resolution by Peter Stuyvesant et al. (14 April 1643), in Gehring and Schiltkamp, comps., *New Netherland Documents*, no. 5a, 23 (source of quote); Resolution by Peter Stuyvesant et al. (19 May 1643), in Gehring and Schiltkamp, comps., *New Netherland Documents*, no. 5b, 24.

145. Resolution by Peter Stuyvesant et al. (19 May 1643), in Gehring and Schiltkamp, comps., *New Netherland Documents*, no. 5b, 23.

146. Resolution by Peter Stuyvesant et al. (22 July 1644), in Gehring and Schiltkamp, comps., *New Netherland Documents*, no. 9b, 43.

147. Cited in Goslinga, *Dutch in the Caribbean and on the Wild Coast*, 343.

148. Ibid.

149. Emmanuel and Emmanuel, *History of the Jews of the Netherlands Antilles*, 49.

150. Goslinga, *Dutch in the Caribbean and in the Guianas*, 530.

151. "Instructie voor Jacob Pietersz Tolck, Direkteur van Curaçao" (1638), in Schiltkamp and Smidt, comps., *West Indisch Plakaatboek*, 1:3–8. The translation is from a later copy dated 15 August 1640, and published in Gehring and Schiltkamp, comps., *New Netherland Documents*, no. 1, 3–7. The quotes are from page 5.

152. Resolution (26 February 1643), in Gehring and Schiltkamp, comps., *New Netherland Documents*, no. 2d, 11; "Freedoms and Exemptions granted to the Company's Servants . . ." (10 March 1643), in Gehring and Schiltkamp, comps., *New Netherland Documents*, no. 3, 12.

153. Instructions left by Director General Petrus Stuyvesant to Vice-Director Matthias Beck (8 June 1655), in Gehring and Schiltkamp, comps., *New Netherland Documents*, no. 19, 73.

154. See, among many others, the resolution by Director Petrus Stuyvesant and his council (13 March 1643), in Gehring and Schiltkamp, comps., *New Netherland Documents*, no. 3b, 18, and the letter from Matthias Beck to Amsterdam Directors (16 April 1665), in Gehring and Schiltkamp, comps., *New Netherland Documents*, no. 104, 211.

155. Heywood and Thornton, *Central Africans, Atlantic Creoles, and the Foundation of the Americas*, 290–91.

156. Ibid., 291.

3 / "Cruising to the Most Advantageous Places"

1. "Instructie voor Jacob Pietersz Tolck, Direkteur van Curaçao" (1638), in Schiltkamp and Smidt, comps., *West Indisch Plakaatboek*, 1:7. A version of the document dated 15 August 1640, is reproduced in English in Gehring and Schiltkamp, comps., *New Netherland Documents*, no. 1, 6.

2. Among others, Resolution (13 March 1643), in Gehring and Schiltkamp, comps., *New Netherland Documents*, no. 3b, 18; Resolution (January 1644), in Gehring and Schiltkamp, comps., *New Netherland Documents*, no. 7c, 32–33.

3. Resolution (16 June 1644), in Gehring and Schiltkamp, comps., *New Netherland Documents*, no. 8e, 41.

4. The full Spanish-language versions of all three documents, including the wordy text of the official ratifications, is produced as Appendices 1 and 2 in Felice, *Curazao hispánico*, 469–507. All translations of the text are mine.

5. Treaty text ibid., Appendix 1, 472–77.

6. Ibid., Appendix 1, 474.

7. Ibid., Appendix 1, 476.

8. Ibid., Appendix 1, 477.

9. Ibid., Appendix 1, 495–96.

10. Ibid., 501. The entire treaty is reproduced as Appendix 2, 500–507, followed by the text of the Spanish ambassador's lengthy recommendation for ratification. All translations are mine.

11. Treaty text in Felice, *Curazao hispánico*, Appendix 2, 502–3.

12. Benjamin Schmidt calls this period "the exemplary Dutch Atlantic"; see Schmidt, "Dutch Atlantic," 171–75.

13. Vice-director Matthias Beck to Petrus Stuyvesant (23 August 1659), in Gehring and Schiltkamp, comps., *New Netherland Documents*, no. 41, 126.

14. Matthias Beck to Petrus Stuyvesant (15 November 1664), in Gehring and Schiltkamp, comps., *New Netherland Documents*, no. 96, 196.

15. Vice-director Matthias Beck to Amsterdam directors (11 June 1657), in Gehring and Schiltkamp, comps., *New Netherland Documents*, no. 27, 95, 98.

16. Vice-director Matthias Beck to Amsterdam directors (11 June 1657), Gehring and Schiltkamp, comps., *New Netherland Documents*, no. 27, 95.

17. Vice-director Matthias Beck to Amsterdam directors (11 June 1657), in Gehring and Schiltkamp, comps., *New Netherland Documents*, no. 27, 96; Matthias Beck to Amsterdam directors (28 July 1657), in Gehring and Schiltkamp, comps., *New Netherland Documents*, no. 28, 103.

18. Vice-director Matthias Beck to Amsterdam Directors (28 July 1657), in Donnan, comp., *Documents Illustrative of the History of the Slave Trade to America*, vol. 1, no. 30, 138–39.

19. Governor Lucas Rodenburch to Amsterdam Directors (2 April 1654), in Gehring and Schiltkamp, comps., *New Netherland Documents*, no. 14, 57–58; Amsterdam Directors to Governor Lucas Rodenburch, (7 July 1654), in Gehring and Schiltkamp, comps., *New Netherland Documents*, no. 15, 61–63; Emanuel and Emanuel, *History of*

the Jews of the Netherlands Antilles, 68–69; "Extraordinary session held in the residence of the honorable vice-director M. Beck" (21 February 1656), in Gehring and Schiltkamp, comps., *New Netherland Documents*, no. 25a, 87–88; and "Session held in residence of the honorable vice-director M. Beck" (23 February 1656), in Gehring and Schiltkamp, comps., *New Netherland Documents*, no. 25b, 88–89. The quote is from the latter, 89.

20. Vice-director Matthias Beck to Company directors in Amsterdam (11 June 1657), in Gehring and Schiltkamp, comps., *New Netherland Documents*, no. 27, 93–95; Matthias Beck to Amsterdam directors (28 July 1657), in Gehring and Schiltkamp, comps., *New Netherland Documents*, no. 28, 104–5.

21. Curaçao Governor Matthias Beck to Directors of the West India Company (11 June 1657), in Gehring and Schiltkamp, comps., *New Netherland Documents*, no. 27, 93–95; Curaçao Governor Matthias Beck to Directors of the West India Company (28 June 1657), in Gehring and Schiltkamp, comps., *New Netherland Documents*, no. 28, 103–5.

22. Curaçao Governor Matthias Beck to Directors of the West India Company (28 June 1657), in Gehring and Schiltkamp, comps., *New Netherland Documents*, no. 28, 5.

23. Vice-director Matthias Beck to Company directors in Amsterdam (4 February 1660), in Gehring and Schiltkamp, comps., *New Netherland Documents*, no. 57, 161.

24. Swetschinski, "Conflict and Opportunity in Europe's 'Other Sea,'" 226.

25. Spanish King to Governor of Mérida (1656), in Troconis, comp., *Documentos*, no. 43, 209–10.

26. Col. Richard Nicolls, New York, to Lord Arlington (9 April 1666), in Brodhead, comp., *Documents Relative to the Colonial History of the State of New York*, 3:115.

27. For North America: Amsterdam directors to vice-director Matthias Beck (7 July 1654), in Gehring and Schiltkamp, comps., *New Netherland Documents*, no. 15, 63; Matthias Beck to Petrus Stuyvesant (16 May 1659), in Gehring and Schiltkamp, comps., *New Netherland Documents*, no. 40, 122; "Memorandum of Necessities for Curaçao" (26 April 1664), in Gehring and Schiltkamp, comps., *New Netherland Documents*, no. 83, 184.

28. Klooster, "Overview of Dutch Trade with the Americas," 372.

29. "Petition of merchants, planters, and others concerned in the good government of St. Christopher's to the Council of State" (25 January 1659), in Sainsbury, ed., *Calendar of State Papers, Colonial Series*, 1574–1660, no. 63, 473; Gov. William Byam of Antigua to William Lord Willoughby, Governor of Barbados (1670), in Sainsbury, ed., *Calendar of State Papers*, 1669–74, no. 508, 205.

30. Lt. Col. Thomas Lynch of Jamaica to Lord Arlington (25 May 1664), in Sainsbury, ed., *Calendar of State Papers, Colonial Series*, 1661–68, no. 744, 211.

31. Peter Stuyvesant, "Resolution" (16 July 1643), in Gehring and Schiltkamp, comps., *New Netherland Documents*, no. 5d, 25.

32. For discussion of the wider context of these and other mercantile policies in the seventeenth-century Atlantic world, see Davies, *North Atlantic World in the Seventeenth Century*.

33. For the circumstances that led to the disbanding of the first WIC and the creation of the second, see, among others, Heijer, "Dutch West India Company"; Goslinga, *Dutch in the Caribbean and on the Wild Coast*, chaps. 12, 13; and Goslinga, *Dutch in the Caribbean and in the Guianas*, chap. 1.

34. Goslinga, *Dutch in the Caribbean and in the Guianas*, 81.

35. Therefore the description of this trade as contraband, smuggling, or illicit refers to its characterization by other European powers, not to its role within the Dutch system.

36. Robert Quarry, Philadelphia, to Council of Trade and Plantations (30 August 1698), in Headlam, ed., *Calendar of State Papers,* vol. 16, no. 786, 480.

37. For example, Colonel Stapleton, governor of Leeward Islands (22 November 1676), in Sainsbury, ed., *Calendar of State Papers, 1675–76,* no. 1152, 499.

38. Resolution (18 July 1644), in Gehring and Schiltkamp, comps., *New Netherland Documents,* no. 9a, 42; Goslinga, *Dutch in the Caribbean and in the Guianas,* 81.

39. Klooster, *Illicit Riches,* 175, 202.

40. Ibid., 91.

41. Goslinga, *Dutch in the Caribbean and on the Wild Coast,* 263, 336; Hamelberg, *Documenten.*

42. Goslinga, *Dutch in the Caribbean and in the Guianas,* 129, 131.

43. Goslinga, *Dutch in the Caribbean and on the Wild Coast,* 263, 336, 389.

44. Goslinga, *Dutch in the Caribbean and in the Guianas,* 131.

45. Cited ibid., 7.

46. Goslinga, *Dutch in the Caribbean and on the Wild Coast,* 262, 335; Goslinga, *Dutch in the Caribbean and in the Guianas,* 31, 128

47. For more information see Goslinga, *Dutch in the Caribbean and on the Wild Coast,* 336, 389–90, 395–401, 467–72, and Goslinga, *Dutch in the Caribbean and in the Guianas* 93, 130.

48. Klooster, *Illicit Riches,* 41–42.

49. Emmer, "Jesus Christ Was Good, but Trade Was Better," 102.

50. Welie, "Slave Trading and Slavery in the Dutch Colonial Empire," 55, 61.

51. Calculated from Welie, "Slave Trading and Slavery in the Dutch Colonial Empire," table 3, 56; also see table 6, 63.

52. Ibid., table 6, 63.

53. Postma, *Dutch in the Atlantic Slave Trade,* 27.

54. Ibid.

55. Ibid.

56. Goslinga, *Dutch in the Caribbean and the Wild Coast,* 353.

57. "Sobre contraband de negros efectuado por los holandeses" (20 December 1656), in Troconis, comp., *Documentos,* no. 43, 209–10.

58. "Copia enviado al Rey por Gaspar del Hoyo" (1693), in Troconis, comp., *Documentos,* no. 51, 226–27.

59. Information in this and the following paragraph is from Goslinga, *Dutch in the Caribbean and on the Wild Coast,* 360; Goslinga, *Dutch in the Caribbean and in the Guianas,* 156–79.

60. Goslinga, *Dutch in the Caribbean and on the Wild Coast,* 360; Goslinga, *Dutch in the Caribbean and in the Guianas.* For a detailed account of the convoluted politics and intrigues of the Coymans asiento see Wright, "Coymans Asiento."

61. Jordaan, "Curaçao Slave Market," 223.

62. See Haviser and Simmons-Brito, "Excavations at the Zuurzak Site."

63. Goslinga, *Dutch in the Caribbean and in the Guianas,* 166.

64. Goslinga, *Dutch in the Caribbean and on the Wild Coast,* 362–63.

65. Goslinga, *Dutch in the Caribbean and in the Guianas,* 166.

66. Rev. Philippus Speght to Classis of Amsterdam (26 April 1673), cited in Emmanuel and Emmanuel, *History of the Jews of the Netherlands Antilles*, 55.

67. LUSC COLLBN 001–11–082.

68. For example, Governor M. Beck (15 November 1664), in Gehring and Schiltkamp, comps., *New Netherland Documents*, no. 94, 192.

69. "Acta del Cabildo de Caracas" (30 January 1680), in Troconis, comp., *Documentos*, no. 47, 219.

70. Postma, *Dutch in the Atlantic Slave Trade*, 27, 33.

71. Calculated from the transatlantic slave trade database (TSTD), http://www.slavevoyages.org.

72. TSTD, http://www.slavevoyages.org.

73. Matthias Beck to Peter Stuyvesant (2 August 1659), in Gehring and Schiltkamp, comps., *New Netherland Documents*, no. 41, 125.

74. Postma, *Dutch in the Atlantic Slave Trade*, 27, 33; Jordaan, "Curaçao Slave Market," 223.

75. Among others, Spanish King to Governor of Mérida (1656), in Troconis, comp., *Documentos*, no. 43, 209–10; "Acta del Cabildo de Caracas" (30 January 1680), in Troconis, comp., *Documentos*, no. 47, 219–20.

76. Calculated from TSTD, http://www.slavevoyages.org.

77. Vice-director Matthias Beck to Amsterdam directors (28 July 1657), in Gehring and Schiltkamp, comps., *New Netherland Documents*, no. 28, 104–5; Matthias Beck to company directors in Amsterdam (4 February 1660), in Gehring and Schiltkamp, comps., *New Netherland Documents*, no. 57, 161; Governor van Beek to Amsterdam Chamber (18 September 1700), NAN NWIC 1146:21.

78. Matthias Beck to Peter Stuyvesant (23 August 1659), in Gehring and Schiltkamp, comps., *New Netherland Documents*, no. 41, 125.

79. Postma, *Dutch in the Atlantic Slave Trade*, 25.

80. TSTD, http://www.slavevoyages.org; Sijmen Cornelissen Gilde (21 July 1664), in Gehring and Schiltkamp, comps., *New Netherland Documents*, no. 86, 187; Governor M. Beck (15 November 1664), in Gehring and Schiltkamp, comps., *New Netherland Documents*, no. 94, 192. The use of the term "Loangos" was not necessarily geographically or ethnically precise.

81. See, for example, NAN NWIC 1157:101–3 (22 August 1740).

82. Postma, *Dutch in the Atlantic Slave Trade*, 37. The spelling of the term "*macqueron*" varies in the primary documents. Today the term in Curaçao's creole language, Papiamentu, refers to a handicapped person.

83. Postma, *Dutch in the Atlantic Slave Trade*, 38.

84. Calculated from NAN NWI 1148 (4 August 1707).

85. These are reproduced in Marley, comp., *Reales asientos y licencias*, documents 3 and 5 (no pagination).

86. *Real cédula* (30 January 1690), reproduced in "Banda sobre negros 'de mala entrada'" (24 March 1692), in Marley, comp., *Reales asientos y licencias*, document V, no pagination.

87. Hernando Costilla and Lazaro de Vallejo Aldrete to the Spanish Crown (8 January 1568 and 26? September 1568), in Wright, comp., *Spanish Documents concerning English Voyages to the Caribbean*, no. 22, 118; and no. 19, 109–10. See Chapter 1 of this book.

88. "Bando sobre negros 'de mala entrada'" (24 March 1692), document 5 in Marley, comp., *Reales asientos y licencias*, no pagination. In this document the king also reproduces his decrees of 1685 and 1690. All translations are mine.

89. *Real cédula* (25 October 1705), in Troconis, comp., *Documentos*, no. 57, 240–43.

90. "Licencia para comprar esclavos negros en Curazao" (10 February 1680), in Marley, comp., *Reales asientos y licencias*, document 2, no pagination.

91. Drescher, "Jews and New Christians in the Atlantic Slave Trade," 447; Scott, "Common Wind," 75–81.

92. Jordaan, "Curaçao Slave Market," 230. For a listing of WIC rural holdings in 1700 with their corresponding slaves see NAN NWIC 200:9, 11, 13, 15.

93. "Reglement voor de West-Indische Compagnie" (26 April 1634), cited in Schunk, "Lost Catholic Houses of Prayer in Curaçao," 129.

94. Brada, *Bisdom Coro.*

95. For example, Matthias Beck to Amsterdam directors (28 July 1657), in Gehring and Schiltkamp, comps., *New Netherland Documents*, no. 28, 103; Gonzalez, *Antillas y Tierra Firme*, 41.

96. For example, see Felice, *Curazao hispánico*, 392n9.

97. Brada, *Prefect Caysedo*, 40.

98. Schunk, "Lost Catholic Houses of Prayer in Curaçao," 129.

99. Felice, *Curazao hispánico*, 392.

100. Bishop of Caracas (8 January 1779), AANH Caracas, Sección Manuscritos, cited in Felice, *Curazao hispánico*, 393–95; Schunk, "Lost Catholic Houses of Prayer in Curaçao," 129.

101. Bishop of Caracas (8 January 1779), AANH Caracas, Sección Manuscritos cited in Felice, *Curazao hispánico*, 394.

102. Nooijen, *De slavenparochie van Curaçao*, 21, 68–69.

103. Ibid.; Gonzalez, *Antillas y Tierra Firme*, 34. Lampe speculates that local Caquetíos may have baptized people of African descent during these decades, but he gives no evidence for this assertion, which does not seem as likely as the other possibilities (Lampe, "Christianity and Slavery in the Dutch Caribbean," 131).

104. Brada, *Kerkgeschiedenis Curaçao 1680–1707*, 1, refers to a detailed list Father Caicedo sent to Rome in 1730; Nooijen, *Historia de Kòrsou Católiko*, 58–59. Felice lists all the priests who visited Curaçao from Venezuela in this period (*Curazao hispánico*, 394–96n13).

105. Bishop of Caracas (8 January 1779), AANH Caracas, Sección Manuscritos, cited in Felice, *Curazao hispánico*, 393; Schunk, "Lost Catholic Houses of Prayer in Curaçao," 129.

106. Felice, *Curazao hispánico*, 412.

107. Alvarez Abreu, *Instrucción* (17 June 1715), 145–46.

108. Schunk, "Lost Catholic Houses of Prayer in Curaçao," 130–32.

109. Brada, *Pater Schabel*, 61, and Brada, *Kerkgeschiedenis Curaçao 1680–1707*, 9.

110. Brada, *Paters Jezuieten*, 7; Felice, *Curazao Hispánico*, 397, 392–93; Schunk, "Lost Catholic Houses of Prayer in Curaçao," 129.

111. Loon and Lucasius, "From Priest to Architect," 54.

112. Gonzalez, *Antillas y Tierra Firme*, 33.

113. See Felice, *Curazao Hispánico*, 394n13.

114. Bishop of Caracas (8 January 1779), AANH Caracas, Sección Manuscritos, cited in Felice, *Curazao hispánico*, 393.

115. Matthias Beck to Amsterdam directors (28 July 1657), in Gehring and Schilt-kamp, comps., *New Netherland Documents*, no. 28, 103.

116. Gonzalez, *Antillas y Tierra Firme*, 41, citing Archivo Arquidiocesano de Caracas, Sección Episcopales.

117. "Relación de los objetos que Don Bartolomé de Capocelato . . . entregó a Don José Renjifo Pimentel" (1702), AGI SD, reproduced in Borges, *La casa de Austria*, 132–33. Also see Borges, *La casa de Austria,* 81, and Hartog, "José Díaz Pimienta."

118. Schabel, "Dagboek-Fragment van Pater Michael Alexius Schabel Societatis Jesu Missionaris op het eiland Curaçao loopend van 21 October 1707 tot 4 Februari 1708" (NANA); Schunk, "Michael Johannes Schabel, S.J.," 96, 100.

119. Quoted in Gonzalez, *Antillas y Tierra Firme*, 36. Also see Brada, *Prefect Caysedo*, 7–8; Goslinga, *Dutch in the Caribbean and in the Guianas*, 259. The spelling of the priest's name varies. Spanish sources tend to use Caicedo, as do I. Brada's spelling is the creolized Papiamentu version, which apparently was adopted later.

120. Goslinga, *Dutch in the Caribbean and in the Guianas, 258.*

121. *Real cédula* (29 April 1703), reproduced in Borges, *La casa de Austria*, 102.

122. For detailed analysis of this point, and of how the Catholic clergy participated in the contraband trade, see Arauz, *El contrabando holandés en el Caribe*, 1:135–39. Also see Schunk, "Michael Johannes Schabel, S.J.," 97–98. Much of the analysis here is drawn from Borges, *La casa de Austria.*

123. "'t Eijland Curaçao ende de Afbeeldinghe van 't Fort Amsterdam." Buddingh', *Van Punt en Snoa*, reproduces the entire map (18) and an enlargement of the town insert (50); for more about its publishing history and authorship see 17–20.

124. For detailed analysis see ibid., 46–59.

125. See LUSC COLLBN 002–09–029.

126. Buddingh', *Van Punt en Snoa.*

127. The town clearly was named in honor of one of the various Williams of Orange who governed the Netherlands, although there is debate as to which one. For discussion of this point see ibid., 46–47.

128. NWIC 617: 63–64 (29 October 1680); also cited in Buddingh', *Van Punt en Snoa*, 46.

129. NAN NWIC 617 passim, Schiltkamp and Smidt, comps., *West Indisch Plakaatboek, 1638–1782*, passim.

130. "Notificatie Algemene heffing ten behoeve van de vestingweren" (17 August 1705), in Schiltkamp and Smidt, comps., *West Indisch Plakaatboek*, vol. 1, no. 58, 90–91.

131. NAN NWIC 617, various; NAN NWIC 569:500 (20 August 1707).

132. NAN NWIC 206:35r. Buddingh', *Van Punt en Snoa*, 46–47. Changing usage can be traced in the compendium of island laws transcribed in Schiltkamp and Smidt, comps., *West Indisch Plakaatboek, 1638–1782*, passim.

133. For example, NA VEL 590–B; LUSC COLLBN 001–11–082; LUSC MB Portef 63 no. 21.

134. Sir Thomas Modyford's Proposition (February 1665), in Sainsbury, ed., *Calendar of State Papers*, 1661–68 no. 944, 281; Governor Stapleton of Nevis to the Council for Trade and Foreign Plantations (17 July 1672), in Sainsbury, ed., *Calendar of State Papers*, 1669–74, no. 896, 392.

274 / NOTES TO CHAPTER 3

135. Nooijen, *De slavenparochie van Curaçao*, 21, 68–69; Gonzalez, *Antillas y Tierra Firme*, 33.

136. For the Dutch transatlantic trade, see, among others, Klooster, *Illicit Riches*; Emmer, *Dutch in the Atlantic Economy*, and Postma and Enthoven, eds., *Riches from Atlantic Commerce*.

137. Edward Randolph, New York, to Council of Trade and Plantations (25 August 1698), in Headlam, ed., *Calendar of State Papers*, vol. 16 no. 769 ii, 403. Unfortunately detailed trade statistics for the late seventeenth century against which to measure this claim are not available.

138. Unfortunately trade statistics for the seventeenth century are incomplete, especially from the first WIC, most of whose records were destroyed or severely damaged. The most complete records are for the slave trade.

139. NAN NWIC 569:146v.

140. NAN NWIC 201 (May–June 2702):137–143.

141. The changing ownership of these estates can be traced in Lee, comp., *Plantages op Curaçao*.

142. Emmanuel and Emmanuel, *History of the Jews of the Netherlands Antilles*, 681.

143. The area is clearly depicted on an undated Dutch map from the period; see LUSC COLLBN 002–09–029. Also see Emmanuel, *Precious Stones of the Jews of Curaçao*, 34–35, and Emmanuel and Emmanuel, *History of the Jews of the Netherlands Antilles*, 49, 62–63, 653.

144. Emmanuel and Emmanuel, *History of the Jews of the Netherlands Antilles*, 62–64.

145. Ibid., 64.

146. See ibid., vol. 2, Appendix 1, 542–46, and summarized in 1:56–58, for the 1671 regulations.

147. Ibid., 7.

148. Ibid., 52, 88.

149. Ibid., 93.

150. NAN NWIC 201: 93–100.

151. Emmanuel and Emmanuel, *History of the Jews of the Netherlands Antilles*, 93.

152. "Instructie voor Jacob Pietersz Tolck, Direkteur van Curaçao" (1638), in Schiltkamp and Smidt, comps., *West Indisch Plakaatboek*, 1, 6.

153. Aizpurua, "En busca de la libertad," 75.

154. Resolution of island directors of Curaçao (26 May 1644), in Gehring and Schiltkamp, comps., *New Netherland Documents*, no. 8c, 39.

155. L. Rodenburch to Amsterdam Directors (2 April 1654), in Gehring and Schiltkamp, comps., *New Netherland Documents*, no. 14, 59.

156. Letter from governor of Curaçao to directors of the West India Company (11 June 1657), in Gehring and Schiltkamp, comps., *New Netherland Documents*, no. 27, 98.

157. AF CC no. 914 (9 September 1688). Or they may have been enslaved companions of the Sephardic woman. See Rupert, "Waters of Faith, Currents of Freedom."

158. Peter Stuyvesant et al., Resolution (26 May 1644), in Gehring and Schiltkamp, comps., *New Netherland Documents*, no. 8c, 39.

159. See, among others, vice-director Matthias Beck to Amsterdam directors (28 July 1657), in Gehring and Schiltkamp, comps., *New Netherland Documents*, no. 28, 104.

160. "Sobre negros esclavos complicados en comercio ilícito" (27 November 1687), in Troconis, comp., *Documentos*, no. 49, 223.

161. Spanish King to Governor Marqués de Casal (1690), cited in Castillo, comp., *Apuntes para la historia colonial de Barlovento*, 343. Also see Castillo, comp., *Apuntes para la historia colonial de Barlovento*, 345–46.

162. Aizpurua, "En busca de la libertad," 76.

163. "Representación de D. Luis Perez sobre la libertad de esclavos" (1704), in Gonzalez, comp., *Documentos*, Causas Civiles, no. 8, 120–21; Castillo, comp., *Apuntes para la historia colonial de Barlovento*, 345.

164. Klooster, "Inter-Imperial Smuggling in the Americas," 165.

165. NAN NWIC 569:146 (28 January 1707).

166. NAN NWIC 201:85 (Governor of Jamaica, 3 February 1702).

167. NAN NWIC 201:258r–259r (26 October 1703).

168. NAN NWIC 569:505–6 (20 August 1707).

169. Goslinga, *Dutch in the Caribbean and in the Guianas*, 176; Klooster, "Inter-Imperial Smuggling in the Americas," 163–65.

170. Goslinga, "Curaçao as a Slave Trading Center," 12–13.

171. Ibid., 17.

172. Schmidt, "Dutch Atlantic," 180; Enthoven, "Early Dutch Expansion," 17–47; Seed, *Ceremonies of Possession*, 154–60; Benton, *Search for Sovereignty*, 2.

173. Benton, *Search for Sovereignty*, 2.

4 / A Caribbean Port City

1. NAN OAC 185:73; also see Lee, comp., *Curaçaose Vrijbrieven*, 86.

2. Emmanuel and Emmanuel, *History of the Jews of the Netherlands Antilles*, 577–78, 788, 220, 696–98, 828.

3. There is a photograph of the tombstone on the plate facing page 352 in Emmanuel, *Precious Stones of the Jews of Curaçao*. The marker has since been all but destroyed by the fumes from a nearby oil refinery.

4. NAN OAC 179:110; also see Lee, comp., *Curaçaose Vrijbrieven*, 60. Typically, spelling of the names varies in the different documents.

5. NAN OAC 192:149; Emmanuel and Emmanuel, *History of the Jews of the Netherlands Antilles*, 1036; Lee, comp., *Curaçaose Vrijbrieven*, 117.

6. Emmanuel, *Precious Stones of the Jews of Curaçao*, 382–83. Emmanuel and Emmanuel, *History of the Jews of the Netherlands Antilles*, 687–710. An alternate spelling of his second last name is Morao.

7. Emmanuel, *Precious Stones of the Jews of Curaçao*, 383; Emmanuel and Emmanuel, *History of the Jews of the Netherlands Antilles*, 787, 788, 814.

8. Emmanuel and Emmanuel, *History of the Jews of the Netherlands Antilles*, 220, 218.

9. Emmanuel, *Precious Stones of the Jews of Curaçao*, 383; Emmanuel and Emmanuel, *History of the Jews of the Netherlands Antilles*, 219, 704.

10. Calculated from Lee, comp.,*Curaçaose vrijbrieven*, 28–170. For more analysis of this point see Rupert, "Marronage, Manumission, and Maritime Trade," 361–82.

11. Welch, *Slave Society in the City*; Hart, "Building Charleston," 202–20.

12. For more details about the trade in each of these commodities, with statistics, see Klooster, *Illicit Riches*, 173–98.

13. Calculated from Klooster, *Illicit Riches*, table 5, 174. Klooster has estimated average values for each decade because complete trade statistics are not available for every year.

14. Emmer, "Jesus Christ Was Good, but Trade Was Better," 102.

15. Klooster, *Illicit Riches*, 174. For detailed discussion of the relative value of the major transatlantic commodities—cacao, tobacco, sugar, coffee, logwood, and hides, see 182–97.

16. Calculated from Klooster, *Illicit Riches*, Appendix 3. Because statistics are missing for several years I have factored in each decade's average annual value (omitting the highest and lowest years) for each missing year. Apparently trade statistics are spotty for the second half of the century (Klooster, *Illicit Riches*, 175).

17. Calculated from Klooster, *Illicit Riches*, table 5, 174.

18. Klooster, "Curaçao and the Caribbean Transit Trade," 216.

19. Ibid., 215. Numbers have been rounded off. Aizpurua arrives at somewhat different numbers for cacao, tobacco, and hides, using the same Dutch sources (*Curazao y la costa de Caracas*, 311, 315, 319, respectively; for detailed analysis of how he arrived at these amounts see 305–21).

20. Aizpurua, *Curazao y la costa de Caracas*, 76.

21. Klooster, *Illicit Riches*, 196. Aizpurua comes up with somewhat different numbers, using the same sources but measured in fanegas (equivalent to about one and a half bushels), in *Curaçao y la costa de Caracas*, table 14, 319.

22. For discussion of the limitations of Venezuela's local textile production see Arcila, *Economía colonial de Venezuela*, 114–16.

23. Klooster, "Curaçao and the Caribbean Transit Trade," 211–13.

24. Ibid., 206; data for 1734 are missing. Aizpurua calculated a total of only 704 vessels for the same period (*Curazao y la costa de Caracas*, 303). Goslinga has slightly different numbers, noting that as many as thirty-seven vessels sailed from Curaçao to the Netherlands in 1748 (*Dutch in the Caribbean and in the Guianas*, 207). All three historians used the data in the *Dagregisters* of Willemstad in the NAN, which are only complete for the period 1700–1755.

25. Klooster, "Curaçao and the Caribbean Transit Trade," 207.

26. Goslinga, *Dutch in the Caribbean and in the Guianas*, 218–20.

27. Klooster, *Illicit Riches*, 173.

28. Emmer, "Jesus Christ Was Good, but Trade Was Better," 102.

29. Klooster, *Illicit Riches*, 200; Goslinga, *Dutch in the Caribbean and in the Guianas: 1680–1791*, 120.

30. Klooster, *Illicit Riches*, 200.

31. Lt. Governor Hope of Bermuda to the duke of Newcastle (30 September 1725), in Headlam, ed., *Calendar of State Papers*, no. 742, 443.

32. Report of the British Council of Trade and Plantations in the Americas, in Headlam, ed., *Calendar of State Papers*, vol. 16, no. 47, 13–16.

33. Smith, *Inquiry into the Nature and Causes of the Wealth of Nations*, 537–38.

34. Klooster, *Illicit Riches*, 89. For more on Statia's demographics see Goslinga, *Dutch in the Caribbean and in the Guianas*, 131, 138, 152.

35. Goslinga, *Dutch in the Caribbean and in the Guianas*, 203.

36. Michael Jarvis has suggested that the frequent changing of hands stimulated Statia's trade, as merchants could adapt more easily than planters, especially since

plantations were damaged during several of the takeovers (Jarvis, *In the Eye of All Trade*, 165). This was not a factor in the rise of other Caribbean trade centers such as Curaçao and St. Thomas, however.

37. Klooster, *Illicit Riches*, 95–96; Jarvis, *In the Eye of All Trade*, 162–67.

38. Klooster, "Overview of Dutch Trade with the Americas," 377.

39. Klooster, *Illicit Riches*, 176. The only exception was the 1760s, when Suriname's trade averaged 52.6 percent of the total.

40. Klooster, "Overview of Dutch Trade with the Americas," 378.

41. Calculated from Klooster, *Illicit Riches*, Appendixes 3, 4, 224–25. Total trade statistics are missing for both islands for 1749.

42. Ibid., 95.

43. Goslinga, *Dutch in the Caribbean and in the Guianas*, 228; tobacco figures from the 1740s calculated from Klooster, *Illicit Riches*, Appendix 5, 226, and Klooster, "Curaçao and the Caribbean Transit Trade," table 8.3, 215.

44. Goslinga, *Dutch in the Caribbean and in the Guianas*, 140.

45. Ibid., 142.

46. Ibid., 127.

47. Jarvis, *In the Eye of All Trade*, 354–55. According to Klooster, however, Statia's commerce with British colonies has been exaggerated and remained second to that with the French islands (Klooster, *Illicit Riches*, 95).

48. Goslinga, *Dutch in the Caribbean and in the Guianas*, 127.

49. Klooster, *Illicit Riches*, 41–42.

50. Sensbach, *Rebecca's Revival*, 14, 21, 36, 144–46.

51. Goslinga, *Dutch in the Caribbean and in the Guianas*, 128, 196.

52. Klooster, "Overview of Dutch Trade with the Americas," 129.

53. AGI Caracas 784, reproduced in Aizpurua, *Curazao y la costa de Caracas*, 366.

54. This has been richly documented in, among others, Klooster, *Illicit Riches*; Arauz, *El contrabando holandés en el Caribe*; Aizpurua, *Curazao y la costa de Caracas*.

55. NAN NWIC 1149, "Leijste der familien" (10 July 1709).

56. Welch, *Slave Society in the City*, 97; Jarvis, *In the Eye of All Trade*, 262–63.

57. These records include a new income tax the governor began charging island residents in 1702 (for 1702: NAN NWIC 201: 93–100; for 1707: Emmanuel and Emmanuel, *History of the Jews of the Netherlands Antilles*, vol. 2, Appendix 8, 763–68); a household census of the walled town, conducted in 1709, which included a breakdown by name, age, category, and gender of all the residents of each registered dwelling (NAN NWIC 1149: "Leijste den familien," 10 July 1709); and another census in 1715 that listed the names of both the owners and the heads of household for each privately owned dwelling within the town walls but not information about the occupants (NAN NWIC 206: 35–42, 12 March 1715). None of these provided information about the buildings or residents within the fort complex.

58. NAN NWIC 201: 93–100; Emmanuel and Emmanuel, *History of the Jews of the Netherlands Antilles*, vol. 2, Appendix 8, 763–68.

59. Buddingh', *Van Punt en Snoa*, 70, citing 1707 tax list.

60. NAN NWIC 1149.

61. Calculated from Emanuel and Emanuel, *History of the Jews of the Netherlands Antilles*, vol. 2, Appendix 8, 763–68.

62. Calculated from NAN NWIC 1149.

63. NAN NWIC 1149.

64. Calculated from NAN NWIC 206:35–42.

65. NAN NWIC 201:93–100.

66. NAN NWIC 1149.

67. Calculated from NAN NWIC 1149.

68. NAN NWIC 206:35–42.

69. NAN NWIC 201:93–100. There are also several other people whose names suggest they may have been free blacks although they are not explicitly identified as such.

70. NAN NWIC 201:135v (4 May 1703).

71. NAN NWIC 201:136r.

72. NAN NWIC 206:350–53.

73. NAN NWIC 206:35.

74. For example, NAN VEL 595 and NAN VEL 590–B.

75. For example, LUSC COLLBN 002–09–020 (1742).

76. NAN NWIC 206: 41; Ozinga, *De monumenten van Curaçao*, 139.

77. NAN NWIC 1149 (10 July 1709); NAN NWIC 206: 35–42 (12 March 1715).

78. LUSC COLLBN 001–11–082.

79. Goslinga, *Dutch in the Caribbean and in the Guianas*, 501.

80. NAN NWIC 201:89; NAN NWIC 210:53, 214; NAN NWIC 217 (10 June 1737).

81. NAN VEL 1439, 1440, 1456; for analysis see Ozinga, *De Monumenten van Curaçao*, 25, and Goslinga, *Dutch in the Caribbean and in the Guianas*, 497–99. Also see NAN NWIC 1161 (1 March 1754).

82. I use the names The Point, Punda, and the walled town interchangeably to refer to this area.

83. I use the terms the Other Side, *Oversijde*, Otrobanda (the contemporary Papiamentu name), and "across the bay" interchangeably to refer to this area.

84. NAN NWIC 569: 500–501 (20 August 1707); also see Woude, "'Plezierhuis' in Otrobanda," 137, and Goslinga, *Dutch in the Caribbean and in the Guianas*, 499–500.

85. "'t Eijland Curaçao ende de Afbeeldinghe van 't Fort Amsterdam," reproduced in Buddingh', *Van Punt en Snoa*, 18, 50.

86. For example, "Kaart van het Eiland Curaçao," published in Hering, *Beschryving van het Eiland Curaçao*, in 1779 (LUSC MB P 63 no. 25); Goslinga, *Dutch in the Caribbean and in the Guianas*, 502; Emmanuel and Emmanuel, *History of the Jews of the Netherlands Antilles*, 772.

87. Emmanuel and Emmanuel, *History of the Jews of the Netherlands Antilles*, 772.

88. NAN NWIC 206:40r–41v.

89. For more on this see Buddingh', *Otrobanda*.

90. Goslinga, *Dutch in the Caribbean and in the Guianas*, 503.

91. LUSC COLLBN 002–09–020.

92. Newton, "Fo'i Porta, 19.

93. For a depiction of Pietermaai at the end of the century see NMM PAI0334 (1786).

94. LUSC COLLBN 002–09–020 (1742); NAN VEL 1452: "Plan van de Willemstad en het Fort Amsterdam," Generaal van Burmania, 14 November 1751.

95. NAN VEL 600: "Plan van de Haaven van Curaçao," 18 April 1768.

96. NAN VEL 1454: "Aanmerkinge Weegens de Situatie der Willemstad," S. Geertz, 1754.

97. 1753 report by Governor Faesch, cited in Goslinga, *Dutch in the Caribbean and in the Guianas*, 503.

98. Report by Governor Rodier, cited in Woude, "'Plezierhuis' in Otrobanda," 138.

99. See, for example, NMM PAI0334 (1786).

100. NAN VEL 1454; "Aanmerkinge Weegens de Situatie der Willemstad," S. Geertz, 1754.

101. LUSC COLLBN 002–09–020 (1742); NA VEL 1452 (1751).

102. Although many of the buildings were abandoned and in a state of total decay by the mid-twentieth century, an aggressive restoration/renovation of the area was undertaken beginning in the late 1980s, which was given a boost by UNESCO's decision to declare Willemstad a World Heritage Site in 1997.

103. NMM PAI0334 (1786).

104. 1753 report by Governor Faesch, cited in Goslinga, *Dutch in the Caribbean and in the Guianas*, 503.

105. For detailed depictions of the fort complex at midcentury, including comprehensive descriptions in the legends, see especially NAN VEL 1444 (1742), NAN VEL 1452 (1751), NAN VEL 1454 (1754).

106. Goslinga, *Dutch in the Caribbean and in the Guianas*, 506–7; Ozinga, *De Monumenten van Curaçao*, 87–94.

107. "Aanmerkinge Weegens de Situatie der Willemstad," S. Geertz, 1754 (NAN VEL 1454). Also see NAN VEL 1444 (1742).

108. Among others, NAN VEL 1444, NAN VEL 1456. Ozinga reproduces several more in *De Monumenten van Curaçao*, plates 22–28.

109. NMM PAI0334 (1786).

110. LUSC MB P 63 no. 26 (1795); LUSC COLLBN 002–12–017 (January 1751).

111. NAN VEL 1454, "Aanmerkinge Weegens de Situatie der Willemstad" (S. Geertz, 1754); NMM PAI0334 (1786).

112. NA NWIC 206:40 (12 March 1715). The document uses the Dutch spelling for the town.

113. For example, LUSC COLLBN 002–09–020 (1742), LUSC COLLBN 002–09–004, LUSC COLLBN 002–12–017 (1754).

114. The exact dateline was frequently *Curaçao in 't Ft. Amsterdam* ("Curaçao in Ft. Amsterdam") or *In 't Ft. Amsterdam op Curaçao* ("In Ft. Amsterdam on Curaçao"); see, among many others, Nicolás van Liebergen to company directors in Amsterdam, NAN NWIC 617: 7–10 (10 January 1681), NAN NWIC 201:218 (23 January 1750).

115. The laws are reproduced in Schiltkamp and Smidt, comps., *West Indisch Plakaatboek*, vols. 1, 2 passim. Inclusion of Willemstad in the dateline seems to have peaked at the mid-eighteenth century and declined thereafter. However, in many cases Schiltkamp and Smidt's transcriptions of the laws omit the place of issuance; it is unclear whether or not this reflects the original archival document. The name Willemstad seems to have appeared more frequently in the text of the laws than in the dateline.

116. For example, NAN NWIC 569:510 (20 January 1706); NAN NWIC 210:301 (23 December 1754).

117. NAN NWIC 202 (16 January 1708): 312.

118. NAN VEL 598, NAN VEL 599, NAN NWIC 210:212; NAN OAC 188:4 (1756); NMM PAI0334 (1786).

119. NAN NWIC 1176.

120. NAN NWIC 1176: 415.

121. NAN NWIC 223 no. 1, 24. See Chapter 6. There is no clearly accepted etymology or meaning for either Punta or its full creole rendition, Punda.

122. NAN NWIC 210:212; NAN NWIC 1176:415; LUSC COLLBN 002-12-017; Hering, *Beschryving van het Eiland Curaçao*, 39, 47. Occasionally the area is rendered as *Overseij* (NMM PAI0334).

123. For example, NAN OAC 188:4 (1756).

124. "Sobre el canje de escalvos" (5 April–24 May 1751), in Gonzalez, comp., *Documentos*, 127.

125. Among others, LUSC MB Portef 63 no. 32 and LUSC MB Portef 63 no. 33. Note, however, that both use the Spanish version of the name, with its concordance between adjective and noun (Otrabanda, literally also meaning "the other side"). Such concordance does not exist in full-fledged Papiamentu, which renders the word "Otrobanda."

126. NAN NWIC 1176 (9 August 1790).

127. Price, "Summation," 263.

128. NAN NWIC 1176 (9 August 1790). All demographic material in this paragraph is from this document, which was the first comprehensive census to be taken of the port since the beginning of the century, and the first of the entire island population.

129. For example, LU COLLBN 002-09-020 (February 1742); MNN PAI0334 (1786).

130. For a detailed description of Willemstad in 1779 see Hering, *Beschrijving van het Eiland Curaçao*, chap. 5, 38–50; for a visual depiction see NMM PAI0334 (1786).

131. MNN PAI0334 (1786).

132. Hering, *Beschryving van het Eiland Curaçao*.

133. Ozinga, *De monumenten van Curaçao*, 139.

134. Ibid.

135. The development of Curaçao's Dutch colonial buildings has been studied in great detail by architects and urban planners. See, among others, Ozinga, *De Monumenten van Curaçao*, the essays in *Building Up the Future from the Past*, ed. Coomans, Newton, and Coomans-Eustatia, and the detailed work by Buddingh', *Van Punt en Snoa* and *Otrobanda*. For discussion of architectural creolization in another Caribbean entrepôt see Jarvis, *In the Eye of All Trade*, 93–94, 117, 307–14.

136. NAN NWIC 200:9, 11, 13, 15; NAN NWIC 201:137–43, 216–17. For a full catalogue of the changing ownership of rural estates, see Lee, *Plantages op Curaçao*.

137. Jordaan, "Curaçao Slave Market," 230.

138. This was common in the port cities of the colonial Atlantic world. See Herndon, "Domestic Cost of Seafaring," and for a slightly later period, Norling, "Ahab's Wife."

139. Martinus, "Victory of the Concubines and the Nannies"; Martinus, *Kiss of a Slave*, 128–30.

140. Hoetink, *Het patroon van de oude Curaçaose samenleving*. For an English summary, see 164–68.

141. Felice, *Curazao hispánico*, 401–2, 404, 412–13.

142. Klooster, "Subordinate but Proud," 284.

143. For more information about the middling white sectors, see Goslinga, *Dutch in the Caribbean and in the Guianas*, 231–34.

144. *Prince Frederick v. Ufro Sarah*, in Towle, ed., *Records of the Vice-Admiralty Court of Rhode Island*, 239, 241, 243.

145. *Polly v. Pearl*, in Towle, ed., *Records of the Vice-Admiralty Court of Rhode Island*, 349.

146. Henriques, *Ta Asina? O ta Asana?*, 181.

147. Martinus, "Value of Guene for Folklore and Culture," 181–93; Martinus, *Kiss of a Slave*, 17–19.

148. See Chapter 6 for elaboration of this process.

149. NAN NWIC 1149, "Leijste der familien," 10 July 1709; NAN NWIC 1176: 430–47, 9 August 1790; Emmanuel and Emmanuel, *History of the Jews of the Netherlands Antilles*, 222; Abraham-van der Mark, "Marriage and Concubinage among the Sephardic Merchant Elite of Curaçao," 40–41; Soest, *Trustee of the Netherlands Antilles*, 3.

150. NAN NWIC 215 (14 April 1722); NAN NWIC 217 (14 May 1737).

151. NAN NWIC 224 (5 July 1774).

152. Emmanuel and Emmanuel, *History of the Jews of the Netherlands Antilles*, 214, citing NAN OAC 803 (8 August 1734).

153. Herndon, "Domestic Cost of Seafaring," 57; Jarvis, *In the Eye of All Trade*, 262–63, Welch, *Slave Society in the City*, 97–98.

154. Klooster, "Contraband Trade by Curaçao's Jews with Countries of Idolatry," 68.

155. Ibid., 61.

156. Emmanuel and Emmanuel, *History of the Jews of the Netherlands Antilles*, 83. Appendix 3 (681–746) provides a comprehensive list of Sephardic ship owners and captains beginning in the 1680s.

157. NAN OAC 803 (8 August 1734), cited in Emmanuel and Emmanuel, *History of the Jews of the Netherlands Antilles*, 213; Klooster, *Illicit Riches*, 66.

158. Emmanuel and Emmanuel, *History of the Jews of the Netherlands Antilles*. Volume 1 contains photos of five Sephardic tombstones in Curaçao from the seventeenth and eighteenth centuries that were decorated with maritime vessels. Fumes from the nearby oil refinery have since virtually destroyed most of them.

159. Calculated from Emmanuel and Emmanuel, *History of the Jews of the Netherlands Antilles*, Appendix 3, 681–738.

160. See ibid., 213–14.

161. For the regional trade ties of Curaçao's Sephardim, see Emmanuel and Emmanuel, *History of the Jews of the Netherlands Antilles*, Appendix 16, 822–40; Emmanuel, *Precious Stones of the Jews of Curaçao*, 261–339; Klooster, "Contraband Trade by Curaçao's Jews with Countries of Idolatry."

162. See Emmanuel, *Precious Stones of the Jews of Curaçao*, 261–339.

163. Klooster, "Contraband Trade by Curaçao's Jews with Countries of Idolatry," 70.

164. For a detailed listing, see Emmanuel and Emmanuel, *History of the Jews of the Netherlands Antilles*, Appendix 16, 822–40.

165. For example, NAN NWIC 216 (29 April 1727).

166. AGI SD 764 cited in Borges, *Alvarez Abreu*, 55; Emmanuel, *Jews of Coro*, 6; Arbell, "Rediscovering Tucacas."

167. Rowland, "New Christian, Marrano, Jew," 145.

168. *Polly v. Pearl*, in Towle, ed., *Records of the Vice-Admiralty Court of Rhode Island*, 343, 348.

169. NAN NWIC 1166:83, "Leijste van de familien" (2 June 1775). Also see Emmanuel and Emmanuel, *History of the Jews of the Netherlands Antilles*, Appendix 8, 763–68.

170. Emmanuel and Emmanuel, *History of the Jews of the Netherlands Antilles*, 214.

171. Israel, Introduction to *Dutch Jewry*, ed. Israel and Salverda, 14.

172. Emmanuel and Emmanuel, *History of the Jews of the Netherlands Antilles*, 335.

173. Emmanuel and Emmanuel, *History of the Jews of the Netherlands Antilles*, 62–63. For a detailed list of all Jewish landholdings throughout the eighteenth century see Appendix 2, 618–80, and also Lee, *Plantages op Curaçao*.

174. For example, NAN NWIC 569:510 (20 January 1706); NAN NWIC 216 (28 January 1727); NAN OAC 179:110 (27 June 1747); NAN OAC 188:3 (1756). Such terminology was employed throughout the Sephardic diaspora. See Bodian, *Hebrews of the Portuguese Nation*.

175. Many of the records were destroyed in the 1969 riots, when the main Catholic Church was burned.

176. Quoted in Goslinga, *Dutch in the Caribbean and in the Guianas*, 247.

177. Quoted in Felice, *Curazao hispánico*, 404.

178. Cited ibid., 406.

179. Among others, Teniente Justicia Mayor de Coro (1 June 1795), in *Documentos de la Insurrección de José Leonardo Chirinos* 1:83; Bishop Mariano Martí (1773), cited in Aizpurua, "En busca de la libertad," 74.

180. Manuel de Carrera (26 September 1796), in *Documentos de la Insurrección de José Leonardo Chirinos* 1:160.

181. Klooster, "Subordinate but Proud," 291–93, 295.

182. Lampe, *Descubrir a Dios en el Caribe*, 39.

183. Cited in Aizpurua, "En busca de la libertad," 74.

184. Lampe, "Chrisitianity and Slavery in the Dutch Caribbean," 132n15.

185. For analysis of the development of the island's legal codes as they related to both slaves and freemen and women see Jordaan, "Free Blacks and Coloreds," 63–86.

186. Hering, *Beschryving van het Eiland Curaçao* (1779), 30, 59; NMM PAI0334 (1786).

187. Goslinga, *Dutch in the Caribbean and in the Guianas*, 508.

188. *Defiance v. Catharina* and *Defiance v. Young Johannes*, in Towle, ed., *Records of the Vice-Admiralty Court of Rhode Island*, 386, 422, respectively.

189. Klooster, *Illicit Riches*, 68; NAN NWIC 232; NAN NWIC 233.

190. NAN NWIC 232 (1768).

191. *Polly v. Pearl*, in Towle, ed., *Records of the Vice-Admiralty Court of Rhode Island*, 343.

192. See, for example, *Reprisal v. Hope, 1745*, in Towle, ed., *Records of the Vice-Admiralty Court of Rhode Island*, 329.

193. Goslinga, *Dutch in the Caribbean and in the Guianas*, 542.

194. NAN NWIC 1161: 43 (1 March 1754); NAN NWIC 1176:430–47 (9 August 1790).

195. NAN NWIC 210: 205.

196. NAN NWIC 210: 200–203 (23 January 1750)

197. "Verbod op het gooien van stenen door negers en mulatten," 26 June 1737, in Schiltkamp and Smidt, comps., *West Indisch Plakaatboek*, vol. 1, no. 116, 164.

198. Calculated from Lee, comp., *Curaçaose Vrijbrieven*. Exact numbers are impossible to obtain, as the records for several years are either missing or incomplete, and manumission petitions that include children rarely specify how many.

199. Goslinga, *Dutch in the Caribbean and in the Guianas*, 535.

200. Emmanuel and Emmanuel, *History of the Jews of the Netherlands Antilles*, 1036; Jordaan, "Curaçao Slave Market," 221–22; Goslinga, *Dutch in the Caribbean and in the Guianas*, 535–56.

201. Emmanuel and Emmanuel, *History of the Jews of the Netherlands Antilles*, 1036; Jordaan, "Curaçao Slave Market," 222.

202. Goslinga, *Dutch in the Caribbean and in the Guianas*, 535. Goslinga says this fee reduction took place in 1767; the Emmanuels say it happened four years earlier (Emmanuel and Emmanuel, *History of the Jews of the Netherlands Antilles*, 1036).

203. Jordaan, "Curaçao Slave Market," 222.

204. NAN NWIC 1176, 430–47 (4 August 1790).

205. The Emmanuels suggest that the list of 1764 is the most accurate one, because it was the first one after the tax was reduced, and so compliance was especially high. See Emmanuel and Emmanuel, *History of the Jews of the Netherlands Antilles*, 1036.

206. Jarvis, *In the Eye of All Trade*, 267.

207. Jordaan, "Curaçao Slave Market," 249.

208. Average prices calculated from documents in Gonzalez, comp., *Documentos para la historia de las antillas neerlandesas*, Instruments Públicos/Colonia, vols. 1–4, 35–52.

209. NAN NWIC 202:487.

210. Hoetink, *Het patroon van de oude Curaçaose samenleving*, 71.

211. Gil, Dovale, and Lusmila, *La insurrección de los negros de la serranía coriana*, 69–71.

212. Among many others: "Declaraciones de Josef Leonardo Chirinos, Juan Felipe Guillermo, Francisco Castro, y Juan Domingo Corriel" (Coro, 14 September 1795), ANH Caracas A16–e54–D11182, 29r and 30r.

213. Such was the case of Jacobus Elisa Joannes Capitein. See Capitein, *Agony of Asar*.

214. Klooster "Manumission in an Entrepôt," 168.

215. NAN NWIC 1176: 430–47 (9 August 1790).

216. Calculated from the petitions reproduced in Lee, comp., *Curaçaose Vrijbrieven*. Records from the first half of the century are spotty, at best. For the second half of the century records are missing for 1763, 1784, and 1788, and those of several other years are incomplete.

217. Klooster, "Subordinate but Proud," 286.

218. Klooster "Manumission in an Entrepôt," 166–67.

219. OAC 820:17–30 (Captain Gaspar Antonio de Quirigazo, 11 January 1749).

284 / NOTES TO CHAPTER 4

220. NAN NWIC 217, various.

221. NMM PAI0334 (1786).

222. NAN NWIC 217 (22 June 1737 and various).

223. NAN OAC 806:296 (1737); NAN OAC 188 various (1756).

224. NAN NWIC 1176 (9 August 1790).

225. NAN OAC 829:370 (29 August 1753); NAN OAC 829:371 (28 August 1751).

226. NAN NWIC 217 (22 May 1737); NAN OAC 829:328 and others (1753). Lee, *Plantages op Curaçao*, documents ownership of several rural estates by several free blacks throughout the eighteenth century.

227. Klooster, "Subordinate but Proud," 287–88.

228. Jordaan, "Free Blacks and Coloreds," 63, 66.

229. Ibid., 77.

230. Goslinga, *Dutch in the Caribbean and in the Guianas*, 541.

231. Ibid., 123.

232. Klooster, "Subordinate but Proud," 289.

233. Ibid.

234. Jordaan, "Free Blacks and Coloreds," 81.

235. Goslinga, *Dutch in the Caribbean and in the Guianas*, 111.

236. Ibid., 113.

237. Ibid., 542.

238. Jordaan, "Free Blacks and Coloreds," 83; Klooster "Manumission in an Entrepôt," 169; Goslinga, *Dutch in the Caribbean and in the Guianas*, 547.

239. "Alle Engelse, Fraanse, en Spaanse vrije negers en mulatten . . ." (4 March 1754), in Schiltkamp and Smidt, comps., *West Indisch Plakaatboek*, vol. 1, no. 236, 290.

240. OAC 820:17–30, Captain Gaspar Antonio de Quirigazo (11 January 1749). The spelling of his last name varies in the different documents.

241. "Sobre la propiedad de una esclava curazoleña" (October 1748), in Gonzalez, comp., *Documentos*, 126.

242. Gaspar Antonio de Quirijazo (29 November 1748), in Gonzalez, comp., *Documentos*, 80–81.

243. "Sobre negros fugitivos de Curazao" (22 April 1751–1 February 1752), in Gonzalez, *Documentos*, 130.

244. Capitán D. Antonio de Lugo (7 July 1763), in Gonzalez, comp., *Documentos*, 84.

245. Lee, comp., *Plantages op Curaçao*, 9, 33, 44.

246. Klooster, "Subordinate but Proud," 287.

247. Testimony of Antonio Beltrán (7 March 1746), AANH 1740 G no. 283 Arch. 1, f 12r.

248. Jordaan, "Free Blacks and Coloreds," 81.

249. Klooster, "Subordinate but Proud," 294–95; Jordaan, "Free Blacks and Coloreds," 81.

250. For discussion of how different socioeconomic circumstances were mirrored in church architecture throughout the colonial Americas see Nelson, "Diversity of Countries."

251. Lampe, "Christianity and Slavery in the Dutch Caribbean," 132.

252. NAN VEL 1452 (1751).

253. NAN NWIC 1176: 430–47 (9 August 1790).

254. Portions of the letter are reproduced in bishop of Caracas (8 January 1779), Coro (AANH Caracas, Sección Manuscritos) cited in Felice, *Curazao hispánico*, 392–93.

255. See the various publications by Brada in the bibliography.

256. For analysis of the complexity of such layers of jurisdiction within the Society of Jesus in the eighteenth century see Martínez-Serna, "Procuradores and the Making of the Jesuits' Atlantic Networks."

257. Borges, *La casa de Austria*, 78.

258. Information about Schabel is from Brada, *Pater Schabel*, and Brada, *Paters Jezuieten op Curaçao*. For an English summary of some of this material see Schunk, "Lost Catholic Houses of Prayer in Curaçao," 130–32.

259. Felice, *Curazao hispánico*, 395–97.

260. NAN NWIC 206:36v.

261. Information in this paragraph is from Brada, *Prefect Caysedo*, and Felice, *Curazao hispánico*, 397–404. For an English summary see Schunk, "Lost Catholic Houses of Prayer in Curaçao," 132–33.

262. NAN NWIC 206:36r.

263. Brada, *Paters Jezuieten op Curaçao*, 32.

264. Felice, *Curazao hispánico*, 401.

265. See Brada, *Kerkgeschiedenis Curaçao (1742–1776)*, 11–12, 18–20, and Nooijen, *Historia di Kòrsou Katóliko*, 86–89. For a list of the itinerant priests who visited in this period see Nooijen, *De slavenparochie van Curaçao*, 4–5.

266. Father Brada, the premier historian of Curaçao's Catholic Church, termed this the era of "stray priests."

267. Nooijen, *De slavenparochie van Curaçao*, 7.

268. For information about white Catholic families in Curaçao at midcentury, including several lists by nationality, see ibid., 85–110.

269. Ibid., 7.

270. NAN OAC 188:71 (20 September 1756). The law is also reproduced in Brada, *Kerkgeschiedenis Curaçao (1742–1776)*, 25–27.

271. See, for example, Nooijen, *De slavenparochie van Curaçao*, 100–101.

272. For example, see ibid., 85.

273. "Relación de P. Navarro" (19 May 1759), Archivo Archidiocesano de Caracas Censos, cited in Gonzalez, *Antillas y Tierra Firme*, 108.

274. Letter from Father Grimón (8 August 1753), Archivo Arquedicesano de Caracas, Censos no. 122, quoted in Gonzalez, *Antillas y Tierra Firme*, 103.

275. Quoted in Gonzalez, *Antillas y Tierra Firme*, 103.

276. Brada, *Prefect Caysedo*, 43; NAN VEL 1454: "Aanmerkinge Weegens de Situatie der Willemstad," S. Geertz (1754). For detailed information about the construction of the church see Gonzalez, *Antillas y Tierra Firme*, 102–8.

277. Archivo Arquedicesano de Caracas, Censos no. 122 (1765), quoted in Gonzalez, *Antillas y Tierra Firme*, 104; details about the construction, 103–4.

278. The architectural decisions involved in the construction of permanent church buildings in the colonial Americas often drove the specifics of the creolization of material culture as it played out in specific local settings. See, for example, Nelson, "Diversity of Countries."

279. Felice, *Curazao hispánico*; Gonzalez, *Antillas y Tierra Firme*.

280. Letter from Dutch Protestants (2 August 1753), Archivo Archdiocesano de Carracas, Censos no. 22, cited in Gonzalez, *Antillas y Tierra Firme*, 103.

281. Buddingh', "Hendrik Schielach, Builder or Bungler?," 115–16, 118–20.

282. Goslinga, *Dutch in the Caribbean and in the Guianas*, 507–8.

283. Woude, "'Plezierhuis' in Otrobanda," 137–38; NAN VEL 1454, "Aanmerkinge Weegens de Situatie der Willemstad," S. Geertz (1754).

284. Hering, *Beschryving van het Eiland Curaçao*, 40–47; Goslinga, *Dutch in the Caribbean and in the Guianas*, 256; Woude, "'Plezierhuis' in Otrobanda," 138.

285. Goslinga, *Dutch in the Caribbean and in the Guianas*, 506–7.

286. Hartog, "Building the Fortchurch."

287. Most of the material in this section is reproduced and adapted from pages 367–74 of Rupert, "Marronage, Manumission, and Maritime Trade." Used with permission. For more discussion of slave laws in eighteenth-century Curaçao see Goslinga, *Dutch in the Caribbean and in the Guianas,* especially Chapter 5. For discussion of the impact of this system on free blacks see Jordaan, "Free Blacks and Coloreds."

288. For discussion of this point in the wider Caribbean and Atlantic contexts, see, among others, Scott, "Common Wind," and Bolster, *Black Jacks.*

289. Klooster, "Manumission in an Entrepôt," 20. I suspect his estimate may be low.

290. For example, *Robert Flowers et al. v. Sloop Three Brothers* (1742); *Polly v. Pearl* (1746); testimony of Leonard Lockman (24 January 1744/5), all in Towle, ed., *Records of the Vice-Admiralty Court of Rhode Island,* 188, 302, 350–51, respectively.

291. *Prince Frederick v. Postilion* (1746), in Towle, ed., *Records of the Vice-Admiralty Court of Rhode Island,* 397–98.

292. For example, *Prince Frederick v. Ufro Sarah* (1743), in Towle, ed., *Records of the Vice-Admiralty Court of Rhode Island,* 243.

293. Testimony of Cosme Q. Zegarain (13 April, 1735), in Towle, ed., *Records of the Vice-Admiralty Court of Rhode Island,* 305.

294. Equiano, "Interesting Narrative"; Linebaugh and Rediker, *Many-Headed Hydra*; Bolster, *Black Jacks.*

295. "Schippers moeten alvorens te vertrekken hun scheppen laten visiteren en een lijst inleveren van bemanning en passagiers" (30 December 1710), in Schiltkamp and Smidt, comps., *West Indische Plakaatboek,* vol. 1, no. 69, 105–8.

296. "Verbod om zonder voorkennis van de Gouverneur slaven van het eiland te vervoeren; verstekelingen moeten bij de eerste gelegenheid worden teruggestuurd" (5 June 1714), in Schiltkamp and Smidt, comps., *West Indische Plakaatboek,* vol. 1, no. 88, 127–29.

297. AGN D XVII: 1734–1748. The activities of the Caracas Company are covered in more detail in Chapter 5.

298. The original 1741 law has not been found in the archives, but it is mentioned in the 1742 law. See Schiltkamp and Smidt, comps., *West Indische Plakaatboek,* vol. 1, no. 162, 223–24.

299. "Negers en mulatten moeten bij aanmonstering aantonen dat zij vrij zijn" (7 May 1742), in Schiltkamp and Smidt, comps., *West Indische Plakaatboek,* vol. 1, no. 162, 223–24. Authorities republished this law in 1743 and again in 1744; see Schiltkamp and Smidt, comps., *West Indische Plakaatboek,*vol. 1, no. 162, 223.

300. "Publicatie uitvaren en vastleggen van visserboten" (31 August 1754) in Schiltkamp and Smidt, comps., *West Indische Plakaatboek,* vol. 1, no. 239, 291–92; "Slaven mogen alleen uitvaren als zij voorzien zijn van paspoort en na verlof van hun meester . . ." (16 Nov. 1755), in Schiltkamp and Smidt, comps., *West Indische Plakaatboek,* vol. 1, no. 245, 295; "Verbod aan vissers om zonder paspoort uit te varen . . . " (18 November 1761), in Schiltkamp and Smidt, comps., *West Indische Plakaatboek,* vol. 1, no. 274, 327; "Regeling voor de aanmonstering van slaven, vrije negers en mulatten" (29 July–4 August 1761), in Schiltkamp and Smidt, comps., *West Indische Plakaatboek,* vol. 1, no. 271, 324–26 (this law was republished in 1780, perhaps indicating either that it was not being regularly enforced, or that changing circumstances required renewed vigilance); "Regeling voor de aanmonstering van slaven, vrije negers en mulatten" (10–11 July 1766) in Schiltkamp and Smidt, comps., *West Indische Plakaatboek,* vol. 1, no. 286, 336–37.

301. These cases are scattered throughout Lee, comp., *Curaçaose Vrijbrieven,* a compendium of all known manumissions on the island between 1722 and 1863. Most relevant documents before 1722 are missing; 1863 was the year of emancipation in the Dutch colonies.

302. NAN OAC 172:43, transcribed in Lee, comp., *Curaçaose Vrijbrieven,* 28; NAN OAC 173:21, transcribed in Lee, comp., *Curaçaose Vrijbrieven,* 29. Jordaan has found references to two pro forma manumissions that occurred earlier, in 1709 and 1712 (OAC 804:366 f 798).

303. NAN OAC 1.05.12.01 no. 204, transcribed in Lee, comp., *Curaçaose Vrij-brieven,* 166.

304. For example, black seafarers who worked on British privateering vessels in the 1720s were eligible for prisoner exchange rather than enslavement if they produced proof of manumission (Kinkor, "Black Men under the Black Flag," 203). Similarly, ship masters in mid-eighteenth-century Bermuda issued certificates of freedom to their enslaved crew members so they would be taken prisoner rather than sold if they were captured by French or Spanish privateers (Jarvis, "Maritime Masters and Seafaring Slaves in Bermuda," n. 43).

5 / Curaçao and Tierra Firme

1. "Ana María Motete, morena libre, contra oficiales de Real Hacienda," AGN ARDF-T 1767-M-1. The case is also discussed in Castillo, comp., *Apuntes para la historia colonial de Barlovento,* 325–26, 378–79, 577. He incorrectly transcribes her last name as Mohele, an error I repeated in previous writings, before I located the original document.

2. See Bushnell and Greene, "Peripheries, Centers, and the Construction of Early Modern American Empires," 3–6.

3. Olavarriaga, *Instrucción,* 301.

4. Ibid.

5. Cisneros, *Descripción exacta,* 150, 152, 154, 173, 182.

6. Ibid., 146, 150.

7. Klooster, *Illicit Riches,* 175.

8. Aizpurua, *Curazao y la costa de Caracas,* 293.

9. TePaske, "Integral to Empire," 30–36.

10. Kamen, *Empire,* 315.

11. Ibid., 84, 118, 134.

12. For extensive treatment of the role of geography in trade between the two areas see Olavarriaga, *Instrucción*, 221–48, and Arauz, *El contrabando holandés en el Caribe*, 71–129. For detailed description of the geography of the coast, see Humboldt, *Viaje*, vol. 3, especially chaps. 14–16. Physical and human geography played a role in the development of other major smuggling centers around the globe. See, for example, Smith, *Borderland Smuggling*, 13.

13. Castillo, comp., *Apuntes para la historia colonial de Barlovento*, 353.

14. Olavarriaga, *Instrucción*, 248.

15. Francisco Nuñez Melian to Spanish Crown, Valencia (11 February 1635); Francisco Nuñez Melián to Spanish Crown, Valencia (15 July 1635), both in Wright, comp., *Nederlandsche Zeevaarders*, no. 60, 199, and no. 62, 211, respectively. For a detailed description of the exact route a small vessel would sail, see Domingo Antonio Francisco to Caracas (12–13 July 1635), in Wright, comp., *Nederlandsche Zeevaarders*, no. 62 Annex, 215.

16. NAN NWIC 1161:3 (13 June 1753).

17. *Dolphin v. Sloop Amity* (1745), in Towle, ed., *Records of the Vice-Admiralty Court of Rhode Island*, 522, 524; Klooster, *Illicit Riches*, 124.

18. *Reprisal v. Hope; Polly v. Pearl; Defiance v. Catharina; Dolphin v. Sloop Amity*, all in Towle, ed., *Records of the Vice-Admiralty Court of Rhode Island*, 329, 331; 343, 345; 386; 522, 524, respectively.

19. Hussey, *Caracas Company*, 5–7.

20. Kamen, *Empire*, 472.

21. Olavarriaga, *Instrucción*, 294.

22. Alvarez Abreu, *Instrucción* (17 June 1715), 98.

23. Olavarriaga, *Instrucción*, 294.

24. NAN NWIC 569:505v (20 Aug 1707); NAN OAC 188:45 (19 July 1756); Hering, *Beschryving van het Eiland Curaçao*, 17, 50.

25. NAN OAC 188:50v (28 July 1756).

26. Cisneros, *Descripción exacta*, 166.

27. Among others, Vice-director Matthias Beck to Amsterdam directors (28 July 1657), in Gehring and Schiltkamp, comps., *New Netherland Documents*, no. 28, 104.

28. Cisneros, *Descripción exacta*, 167.

29. For the development of cacao production and export in the seventeenth century see Arcila, *Economía colonial de Venezuela*, 141–58.

30. Aizpurua, *Curazao y la costa de Caracas*, 64–65.

31. Ibid., 72–23.

32. Piñero, *Town of San Felipe and Colonial Cacao Economies*, 146.

33. Aizpurua, *Curazao y la costa de Caracas*, 72; Piñero, *Town of San Felipe and Colonial Cacao Economies*, 142.

34. Aizpurua, *Curazao y la costa de Caracas*, table 2, 74. A fanega was a dryweight measure usually equal to just over one and a half bushels.The exact measure varied according to time, place, and crop. In the cacao trade it typically ranged between forty-four and fifty kilograms of dry weight.

35. Aizpurua, *Curazao y la costa de Caracas*, graph 15a, 323.

36. Brito, *La estructura económica de Venezuela colonial*, 248.

37. For the early tobacco trade in the sixteenth and seventeenth centuries see Arcila, *Economía colonial de Venezuela*, 128–39.

38. Aizpurua, *Curazao y la costa de Caracas*, 76, 83–84.

39. Cisneros, *Descripción exacta*, 70.

40. Olavarriaga, *Instrucción*, 295; Aizpurua, *Curazao y la costa de Caracas*, 77.

41. Calculated from Aizpurua, *Curazao y la costa de Caracas*, table 17, 327. For analysis of how he arrived at these numbers see 77–83.

42. Arcila, *Economía colonial de Venezuela*, 1:121–24.

43. Humboldt, *Viaje*, 237.

44. Cisneros, *Descripción exacta*, 73–75.

45. Arcila, *Economía colonial de Venezuela*, 1:124.

46. Olavarriaga, *Instrucción*, 295, 297.

47. Klooster, *Illicit Riches*, 196.

48. Humboldt, *Viaje*, 237.

49. Brito, *La estructura económica de Venezuela colonial*, 231.

50. Aizpurua, *Curazao y la costa de Caracas*, 321.

51. Humboldt, *Viaje*, 237–38.

52. Cisneros, *Descripción exacta*, 74, 175.

53. Ferry, *Colonial Elite of Early Caracas*, 124; Piñero, *Town of San Felipe and Colonial Cacao Economies*, 105–8.

54. Piñero, *Town of San Felipe and Colonial Cacao Economies*, 144.

55. Aizpurua, "Las mulas venezolanas," 128; *Documentos de la Insurrección de José Leonardo Chirinos*, 2:186; Brito, *El problema tierra y esclavos*, 225–26; Alvarez Abreu, *Instrucción* (17 June 1715), 99.

56. AGI Caracas 784, reproduced in Aizpurua, *Curazao y la costa de Caracas*, Appendix 5, 365; Aizpurua, "Las mulas venezolanas," 130, 133; Humboldt, *Viaje*, 238.

57. Cisneros, *Descripción exacta*, 124–25; Brito, *La estructura económica de Venezuela colonial*, 231, 247; AGI Caracas 784, reproduced in Aizpurua, *Curazao y la costa de Caracas*, Appendix 5, 365; Aizpurua, "Las mulas venezolanas," 128; *Defiance v. Catharina*, in Towle, ed., *Records of the Vice-Admiralty Court of Rhode Island*, 395.

58. Arcila, *Economía Colonial de Venezuela*, 2:167.

59. Report of Josef de Tellería (12 May 1794), AF.

60. Testamento de D. Juan Antonio de la Peña (28 May 1796), in Gonzalez, comp., *Documentos*, 92–93; Cisneros, *Descripción exacta*, 168; Aizpurua, "Las mulas venezolanas," 132–33.

61. Report of Manuel de Carrera (26 September 1796), in *Documentos de la Insurrección de José Leonardo Chirinos*, 1:159; Alvarez Abreu, *Instrucción* (17 June 1715), 99.

62. AGI Caracas 784, reproduced in Aizpurua, *Curazao y la costa de Caracas*, Appendix 5, 366; Cisneros, *Descripción exacta*, 149, 169.

63. *Defiance v. Catharina*, in Towle, ed., *Records of the Vice-Admiralty Court of Rhode Island*, 394.

64. "Declaración de José Leonardo Chirino" (1796), in *Documentos de la Insurrección de José Leonardo Chirinos*, 2:186.

65. *Defiance v. Catharina*, in Towle, ed., *Records of the Vice-Admiralty Court of Rhode Island*, 394.

66. Humboldt, *Viaje*, 155–56.

67. Arauz, *El contraband holandés en el Caribe*, vol. 1, table 8, 234; Aizpurua, "Las mulas venezolanas," 130–33; *Defiance v. Catharina*, in Towle, ed., *Records of the Vice-Admiralty Court of Rhode Island*, 394.

68. Humboldt, *Viaje*, 156.

69. "D. José de Tellería en la cobranza de cantidad de pesos a D. Bernardo Flores" (7 May 1782), in Gonzalez, comp., *Documentos, Causas Civiles*, no. 40, 136.

70. Olavarriaga, *Instrucción*, 288.

71. Brito, *El problema tierra y esclavos*, 182.

72. Cited in Arcila, *Economía colonial de Venezuela*, 2:103.

73. Humboldt, *Viaje*, 155; Aizpurua, "Las mulas venezolanas," 133–34.

74. Brito, *La estructura económica de Venezuela colonial*, 220–21.

75. Olavarriaga, *Instrucción*, 294–95; Aizpurua, *Curazao y la costa de Caracas*, 102–3; Klooster, *Illicit Riches*, 178–79.

76. Olavarriaga, *Instrucción*, 300–301; Alvarez Abreu, *Instrucción* (17 June 1715), 84–85; Cisneros, *Descripción exacta*, 147; Klooster, *Illicit Riches*, 178–79, Borges, "El inicio del comercio," 36–37.

77. Alvarez Abreu, *Instrucción* (17 June 1715), 85.

78. Aizpurua, *Curazao y la costa de Caracas*, 105–6; Cisneros, *Descripción exacta*, 125.

79. AGI Caracas 784, reproduced in Aizpurua, *Curazao y la costa de Caracas*, 366; Borges, "El inicio del comercio," 37.

80. Alvarez Abreu, *Instrucción* (17 June 1715), 73.

81. Olavarriaga, *Instrucción*, 296.

82. "Relación de los objetos que Don Bartolomé de Capocelato . . . entregó a Don José Renjifo Pimentel" (1702), AGI SD, reproduced in Borges, *La casa de Austria*, 132–33.

83. Alvarez Abreu, *Instrucción* (17 June 1715), 98.

84. Ibid., 110.

85. Ibid.

86. "Visita a la balandra *Abigael*" (23–30 April 1717), in Gonzalez, comp., *Documentos, Causas Civiles*, no. 11, 122.

87. Arcila, *Economía colonial de Venezuela*, 2:15–17, 44.

88. Aizpurua, *Curazao y la costa de Caracas*, 337–38; Aizpurua, "El comercio holandés en el Caribe," 128, cited in Cohen, "Informal Commerical Networks, Social Control, and Political Power in the Province of Venezuela," 43–44.

89. Klooster, *Illicit Riches*, 197–98.

90. For discussion of the impact of this jurisdictional change, see Briceño, "Estudio Preliminar," in Olavarriaga, *Instrucción*, 41–51.

91. Grahn, *Political Economy of Smuggling*, 8–9.

92. Gil, Dovale, and Lusmila, *La insurrección de los negros de la serranía coriana*, 69.

93. LUSC Portef 189 no. 78a (1705); LUSC Portef 189 no. 79 (1725); LUSC Portef 188 no. 22 (1765).

94. Castillo, comp., *Apuntes para la historia colonial de Barlovento*, 113; Ferry, *Colonial Elite of Early Caracas*, 114–17.

95. Brada, *Kerkgeschiedenis Curaçao 1680–1707*.

96. Brada, *Prefect Caysedo*; Felice, *Curazao hispánico*, 397. For detailed description of the stream of priests who visited the island throughout the eighteenth century see

Brada, especially *Kerkgeschiedenis Curaçao (1742–1776), Paters Jezuieten op Curaçao,* and *Paters Franciscanen.* A similar, if more ad hoc, situation apparently existed in St. Thomas, which occasionally hosted Roman Catholic priests from Puerto Rico to minister to white and black Catholics (Sensbach, *Rebecca's Revival,* 39).

97. For analysis of this point as it applied to the Jesuits in the eighteenth century see Martínez-Serna, "Procuradores and the Making of the Jesuits' Atlantic Network."

98. Information about Schabel is from Brada, *Pater Schabel, S.J.*

99. Felice, *Curazao hispánico,* 397–404; Schunk, "Lost Catholic Houses of Prayer in Curaçao," 132–33.

100. Brada, *Paters Jezuieten op Curaçao.*

101. For a list of the itinerant priests who visited in this period see Nooijen, *De slavenparochie van Curaçao,* 4–5.

102. Felice, *Curazao hispánico,* 397–401.

103. Archivo Arquediocesano de Caracas Censos no. 122, 14 April 1746, cited in Gonzalez, *Antillas y Tierra Firme,* 38–39; the quote is from 39. For more about Slijk see Nooijen, *De slavenparochie van Curaçao,* 13, 86.

104. Brada, *Kerkgeschiedenis Curaçao (1742–1776).*

105. AGI SD 886, cited in Felice, *Curazao hispánico,* 404; Gonzalez, *Antillas y Tierra Firme,* 38.

106. Nooijen, *De slavenparochie van Curaçao,* 5; Felice, *Curaçao hispánico.*

107. Nooijen, *Historia di Kòrsou Katóliko,* 85.

108. Extensive documentation for this is in AGI Caracas 207; for a good overview and extensive citations from the archival documents, see Felice, *Curazao hispánico,* 405–11. The quote is from 408. Felice hispanicizes the priest's name to Teodoro Ten de Oven.

109. Felice, *Curazao hispánico,* 410.

110. Cited in Gonzalez, *Antillas y Tierra Firme,* 39.

111. AGI Caracas 12, cited in Felice, *Curazao hispánico,* 410; Lampe, "Christianity and Slavery in the Dutch Caribbean," 131.

112. "Cuaderno en que se inscriben los hermanos y Cofrades del Carmen," Archivo Histórico de Coro Testamentarias 1765, cited in Gonzalez, *Antillas y Tierra Firme,* 38.

113. For more on this topic see Rupert, "Marronage, Manumission, and Maritime Trade."

114. AGN RC Sección 1a, vol. 10; Torres, comp., *Indice sobre esclavos y esclavitud,* 49–55; Castillo, *Apuntes para la historia colonial de Barlovento,* 350, 600; Ferry, *Colonial Elite of Early Caracas,* 112.

115. Manuel de Carrera (26 September 1796), in *Documentos de la Insurrección de José Leonardo Chirinos,* 1:160.

116. For example: AANH SC-E T 1742 CGPRSUZ Exp. no. 9.

117. See in Gonzalez, comp., *Documentos,* petition of Juan Hilario Bueno, 27 February 1726 or 1727 (Causas Civiles, no. 13, 122–23); Juan Lorenzo Rodriguez, 1–15 September 1746 (Causas Civiles, no. 21, 125–26); "Bando de buen gobierno sobre expulsión de vagos," 9–10 February 1756 (Causas Civiles, no. 29, 132); in Torres, comp., *Indice sobre esclavos y esclavitud:* "Autos seguidos por María Francisca de Nieto," July 1738–October 1743 (1743–BSWS, Exp. 3, 85); "Autos formados por Juan Joseph," January–July 1753 (1753–JP, Exp. 1, 92).

118. ANH Vol. 1740 G no. 283 Arch. 1.

119. Torres, *Indice sobre esclavos y esclavitud*, 49–50. For more on this see Rupert, "Seeking the Waters of Baptism."

120. Landers, "Maroon Women in Colonial Spanish America," 13–14; Wood, *Black Majority*; Hall, "Maritime Maroons," 483–84; Ferry, *Colonial Elite of Early Caracas*, 111–12; Torres, comp., *Indice sobre esclavos y esclavitud*, 84, 85, 92, 126.

121. Hall, "Maritime Maroons," 484.

122. Aizpurua, "En busca de la libertad," 80.

123. Aizpurua, *Curazao y la costa de Caracas*; Klooster, *Illicit Riches*; Arauz, *El contrabando holandés en el Caribe*.

124. Alvarez Abreu, *Instrucción* (17 June 1715), 79, 85.

125. Olavarriaga, *Instrucción*, 327.

126. See, among others, Kamen, *Empire*, 349–54.

127. Klooster, "Inter-Imperial Smuggling in the Americas," 162.

128. Ibid., 167–76.

129. In the case of British colonies see, for example, "Circular Letter from the Council of Trade and Plantations to the Governors and Proprietors of Plantations" (19 January 1710), in Headlam, ed., *Calendar of State Papers*, 1710–11 no. 47, 13–17; Governor Worsley of Barbados to Council of Trade and Plantations (26 March 1723), in Headlam, ed., *Calendar of State Papers*, 1722–23, no. 486, 234–36; Lt. Governor Hope of Bermuda to Board of Trade (14 January 1724), in Headlam, ed., *Calendar of State Papers*, 1724–25 no. 13, esp. 12–15; Governor Hart of St. Christopher to Board of Trade (12 July 1724), in Headlam, ed., *Calendar of State Papers*, 1725–26, no. 260, viii, 148–56; Governor Hart of St. Christopher to the Council of Trade and Plantations (10 April 1727), in Headlam, ed., *Calendar of State Papers*, 1726–1727, no. 503, 244–51; Lt. Governor, Council, and assembly of Antigua to Council of Trade and Plantations (17 November 1731), in Headlam, ed., *Calendar of State Papers*, 1731, no. 494, 348–50.

130. For a full treatment of rising consumerism in Venezuela and its impact on the contraband trade see Aizpurua, *Curazao y la costa de Caracas*, 96–109.

131. Governor Worsley of Barbados to Council of Trade and Plantations (16 July 1723), in Headlam, ed., *Calendar of State Papers*, 1722–23, no. 648, 306–9.

132. Grahn, *Political Economy of Smuggling*, 193.

133. Arauz, *El contrabando holandés en el Caribe*, 1:74, 102–3, 107, 178–80; Hussey, *Caracas Company*, 56; Aizpurua, *Curazao y la costa de Caracas*, chap. 3, 18; Ferry, *Colonial Elite of Early Caracas*, 141.

134. Arauz, *El contrabando holandés en el Caribe*, 1:110.

135. Olavarriaga, *Instrucción*, 289.

136. Ferry, *Colonial Elite of Early Caracas*, 121–22.

137. Computed by Piñero, *Town of San Felipe and Colonial Cacao Economies*, table 13, 74.

138. Calculated from table in Castillo, comp., *Apuntes para la historia colonial de Barlovento*, 575–77. Apparently the numbers have been rounded off.

139. Piñero, *Town of San Felipe and Colonial Cacao Economies*, 59, 136–37.

140. Ibid., 82.

141. Piñero, "Cacao Economy of the Eighteenth-Century Province of Caracas," 90.

142. Ferry, *Colonial Elite of Early Caracas*, chaps. 4, 6.

143. Ibid., part 2, and Brito, *Las insurrecciones de los esclavos negros*, 220–25.

144. For a detailed analysis of the growth of cacao plantations in Tierra Firme in the seventeenth and eighteenth centuries see Piñero, "Cacao Economy of the Eighteenth-Century Province of Caracas."

145. Ferry, *Colonial Elite of Early Caracas.*

146. See Kamen, *Empire*, 449–50.

147. For discussion of the impact of the Bourbon reforms in Tierra Firme see Ferry, *Colonial Elite of Early Caracas*, chap. 8.

148. Arauz, *El contrabando holandés en el Caribe*, 100. Also see Castillo, *Curiepe.*

149. Olavarriaga, *Instrucción.*

150. Briceño, "Estudio Preliminar," 187–88.

151. Ibid.

152. The classic study is Hussey, *Caracas Company*; also see Aresti, *Hombres de la Compañía Guipuzcoana* and, for a more recent take, Vivas, *La Aventura Naval de la Compañía Guipuzcoana.*

153. Governor du Faij to Amsterdam Chamber (7 September 1726), NAN NWIC 1154:62; Governor du Faij to Amsterdam Chamber (12 March 1727), NAN NWIC 1154:67; Governor du Faij to Amsterdam Chamber (1 September 1727), NAN NWIC 1154:74.

154. Among others: "Andrés de Cotes et al. sell captured Dutch vessel to José Campuzano Polanco of Coro" (18 September 1721), in Gonzalez, comp., *Documentos*, Instrumentos Públicos/Colonia, vol. 8, no. 7, 62; "José Campuzano Polanco sells captured Dutch vessel to Lt. Col. Juan de Inciarte of Maracaibo" (19 September 1721), in Gonzalez, comp., *Documentos*, Instrumentos Públicos/Colonia, vol. 8, no. 8, 62; "Captain Juan José Perozo in the sale of a captured Dutch vessel" (23 July 1734), in Gonzalez, comp., *Documentos*, Instrumentos Públicos/Colonia, vol. 14, no. 1, 77; "José Geraldino sells captured Dutch vessel to Miguel Paéz of Coro" (17 July 1752), in Gonzalez, comp., *Documentos*, Instrumentos Públicos/Colonia, vol. 25, no. 1, 82.

155. AHN D 30:12:1:120 (30 May 1734); AGS E Legajo 6361 (28 May 1739).

156. AGS MPD 05–177.

157. AGI Indiferente General 1596: 25 (28 May 1739).

158. Castillo, comp., *Apuntes para la historia colonial de Barlovento*, 501–2, 505–7.

159. Among many others: NAN NWIC 1154:101, Governor du Faij to Amsterdam chamber (31 July 1729); NAN NWIC 1154:106, Governor du Faij to Amsterdam chamber, (21 October 1729); NAN NWIC 1160: 74, Gov. Faesch to Amsterdam chamber (18 October 1750); NAN NWIC 1160: 89, Gov. Faesch to Amsterdam chamber (27 February 1751).

160. NAN OAC 806:296 (22 June 1737).

161. NAN OAC 807:133–5 (12 August 1737); NAN OAC 874:85–6 (20 March 1759); Klooster, *Illicit Riches*, 150.

162. Among others, NAN NWIC 216 (5 April 1729).

163. Compiled from NAN OAC records in Emmanuel and Emmanuel, *History of the Jews of the Netherlands Antilles*, 217–20.

164. NAN OAC 813:11–13 (5 September 1742).

165. Among others, NAN NWIC 216 (28 May 1728).

166. NAN OAC 188:58 (29 September 1756); NAN OAC 824:296–8 (16 August 1750), cited in Klooster, *Illicit Riches*, 127.

167. NAN NWIC 1153, Governor du Faij to Amsterdam Chamber (27 February 1723); Governor Worsley of Barbados to Council of Trade and Plantations (26 March 1723), in Headlam, ed., *Calendar of State Papers*, 722–73, no. 486, 234–35.

168. NAN OAC 813:11–13 (5 September 1742).

169. Arauz, *El contrabando holandés en el Caribe*, 1:71.

170. Lewin, *La inquisición en Hispanoamérica*, 211–12; detailed inquisitional instructions, 212–14.

171. Alvarez Abreu, *Instrucción* (17 June 1715), 85.

172. Ibid., 71–72.

173. NAN OAC 804B: 902 (7 November 1735).

174. AGI Caracas 784, reproduced in Aizpurua, *Curazao y la costa de Caracas*, 366; NAN WIC 596, fol. 275–80, J. C. van Laar (25 December 1747), reproduced in Aizpurua, *Curazao y la costa de Caracas*, 375.

175. See, for example, NAN NWIC 1158:49, Governor Faesch to Amsterdam chamber (30 April 1743).

176. Alvarez Abreu, *Instrucción* (17 June 1715), 73–74.

177. Ibid., 86, 106.

178. Ibid., 128.

179. Goslinga, *Dutch in the Caribbean and in the Guianas*, 198.

180. NAN OAC 893: 239–40, 245–47, 247–48, 268, report re pilfering on *Philadelphia* (28 February 1765); Klooster, *Illicit Riches*, 68.

181. NAN OAC 804B:900, 901 (4 November 1735).

182. NAN OAC 796:508–11 (16 September 1721); NAN OAC 808:220–1 (3 March 1738); NAN OAC 813:278–9 (7 November 1742); NAN OAC 821:354 (22 September 1749); Klooster, *Illicit Riches*, 133, 152.

183. NAN OAC 807:558–9 (4 December 1737); NAN OAC 814:567–8 (5 August 1743); Klooster, *Illicit Riches*, 150.

184. NAN OAC 812:395 (27 April 1742); Klooster, *Illicit Riches*, 150.

185. NAN OAC 812:477–9 (30 June 1742).

186. See, for example, Grahn, *Political Economy of Smuggling*, 4–5.

187. For more on the role of these different groups in interimperial trade, see Klooster, *Illicit Riches*; Aizpurua, *Curazao y la costa de Caracas*; Arauz, *El contrabando holandés en el Caribe*; Cohen, "Cultural and Commercial Intermediaries in an Extra-Legal System of Exchange."

188. Arauz, *El contrabando holandés en el Caribe*, 1:189; Olavarriaga, *Instrucción*, 325.

189. Cohen, "Cultural and Commercial Intermediaries in an Extra-Legal System of Exchange," 116.

190. Calculated from table in Castillo, comp., *Apuntes para la historia colonial de Barlovento*, 575–77.

191. See Ferry, *Colonial Elite of Early Caracas*, esp. chap. 7.

192. Calculated from Emmanuel and Emmanuel, *History of the Jews of the Netherlands Antilles*, Appendix 3, 681–738.

193. For example, NAN NWIC 1155:116 (30 April 1734); NAN NWIC 1161 (12 June 1753).

194. NAN OAC 806: 622–24, "Lijste van de Negros en Moulatte Slaven" (22 June 1737).

195. Calculated from Lee, comp., *Curaçaose Vrijbrieven*, 28–170.

196. Jordaan, "Curaçao Slave Market," 244.

197. Castillo, comp., *Apuntes para la historia colonial de Barlovento*, 358–59.

198. Ibid., 97.

199. Alvarez Abreu, *Instrucción* (17 June 1715) treats this topic at length; see especially 77, 81, 83, 86–87, 91–94.

200. Ibid., 84.

201. Ibid., 87.

202. Ibid., 127–28.

203. Ibid., 128.

204. Castillo, comp., *Apuntes para la historia colonial de Barlovento*, 112, 114–15.

205. Arauz, *El contrabando holandés en el Caribe*, 1:98, 100.

206. Cisneros, *Descripción exacta*, 168, 169.

207. Ibid., 183–84.

208. Klooster, "Curaçao and the Caribbean Transit Trade," 213; Kamen, *Empire*, 361.

209. Arauz, *El contrabando holandés en el Caribe*, 1:100–101.

210. Grahn, *Political Economy of Smuggling*, 6.

211. Arauz, *El contrabando holandés en el Caribe*, 1:71.

212. Bill of sale by Father D. José Pérez Volcán (1737), in Gonzalez, comp., *Documentos*, Instrumentos Públicos Colonia, vol. 16, no. 4, 78; Carlos de Acosta et al. in the case of forty-nine slaves from Curaçao sold by the Royal Guinea Company and then declared free (4 February 1721), in Gonzalez, comp., *Documentos*, Instrumentos Públicos/Colonia, vol. 8, no. 10, 63.

213. Arauz, *El contrabando holandés en el Caribe*, 1:100, 135–39. For more on this colorful character, see Hartog, "José Díaz Pimienta."

214. Arauz, *El contrabando holandés en el Caribe*, 1:99. His last name sometimes appears as Pimienta.

215. Piñero, *Town of San Felipe and Colonial Cacao Economies*, 104–10.

216. Alvarez Abreu, *Instrucción* (17 June 1715), 144.

217. Arauz, *El contrabando holandés en el Caribe*, 1:135–36.

218. Olavarriaga, *Instrucción*, 302.

219. NAN OAC 820:11 (6 January 1749); Governor Hart of St. Christopher to Mr. Popple (30 November 1726), in Headlam, ed., *Calendar of State Papers*, 1726–27, no. 306, 180; Emmanuel and Emmanuel, *History of the Jews of the Netherlands Antilles*, 69–70, 81–83, 222–26; Emmanuel, *Jews of Coro*, 6; Klooster, "Contraband Trade by Curaçao's Jews with Countries of Idolatry," 72–73.

220. For a legal case involving a probable *converso* merchant in Tierra Firme in the late seventeenth century see "Expediente sobre la herencia del comerciante portugués Juan Correa de Silva quien dejó por heredera a la virgen de la soledad, en la Iglesia de San Francisco de Caracas," AGI Santo Domingo leg. 197–B, in Gomez, comp., *La Provincia Franciscana de Santa Cruz de Caracas*, no. 42, 436–66. Also see Klooster, "Jews in Suriname and Curaçao," 367n58.

221. AGI SD 764, cited in Borges, *Alvarez Abreu*, 55; Emmanuel, *Jews of Coro*; Arbell, "Rediscovering Tucacas"; Borges, "El inicio del comercio internacional venezolano," 33–34.

222. Emmanuel and Emmanuel, *History of the Jews of the Netherlands Antilles*, 6; Klooster, "Contraband Trade by Curaçao's Jews with Countries of Idolatry," 72–73.

223. Borges, "El inicio del comercio internacional venezolano," 33.

224. Ibid., 34.

225. Olavarriaga, *Instrucción*, 247.

226. Ibid., 247–48.

227. NAN OAC 809:176 (October 1740); NAN OAC 809:181–82 (12 October 1740); NAN OAC 809:182 (12 October 1740); Klooster, "Jews in Suriname and Curaçao," 358–59; Klooster, *Illicit Riches*, 135–37.

228. Cisneros, *Descripción exacta*, 153.

229. Ibid., 152.

230. Buenaventura, *Misión de los Capuchinos*, 142.

231. NAN OAC 820:11 (6 January 1749); Governor Hart of St. Christopher to Mr. Popple (30 November 1726), in Headlam, ed., *Calendar of State Papers Colonial Series, America and the West Indies, 1726–1727*, no. 360, 180. For detailed treatment of this topic see Emmanuel and Emmanuel, *History of the Jews of the Netherlands Antilles*, 222–26.

232. Arbell, "Rediscovering Tucacas," 1.

233. Governor Hart of St. Christopher to Mr. Popple (30 November 1726), in Headlam, ed., *Calendar of State Papers Colonial Series, America and the West Indies, 1726–1727*, no. 360, 180.

234. For example: José Jacinto Pedrosa gives power of attorney to Nicolás Henríquez of Curaçao (11 March 1746), in Gonzalez, comp., *Documentos*, Instrumentos Públicos/Colonia, vol. 21, no. 1, 80.

235. Their extensive commercial dealings are detailed in NAN SG no. 9489.

236. See, among others, Postma, *Dutch in the Atlantic Slave Trade*, chap. 2.

237. Brito, *Las insurrecciones de los esclavos negros*, 11–12, 17–18.

238. Olavarriaga, *Instrucción*, 215.

239. For slightly different numbers but similar percentages see Brito, *Las insurrecciones de los esclavos negros*, 60, 63.

240. Gil, Dovale, and Lusmila , *La insurrección de los negros de la serranía coriana*, 99.

241. Ibid., 99–101.

242. Brito, *Las insurrecciones de los esclavos negros*, 20; Gil, Dovale, and Lusmila, *La insurrección de los negros de la serranía coriana*, 107.

243. Alvarez Abreu, *Instrucción* (17 June 1715), 138.

244. Ibid.

245. Sir Thomas Modyford's Proposition, February 1665, in Sainsbury, ed., *Calendar of State Papers, 1661–68*, no. 944, 281; Governor Stapleton of Nevis to the Council for Trade and Foreign Plantations (17 July 1672), in Sainsbury, ed., *Calendar of State Papers, 1669–74*, no. 896, 392.

246. NAN NWIC 1176: 439–47 (9 August 1790).

247. Cited in Klooster, "Subordinate but Proud," 287.

248. NAN OAC 813:11–13 (5 September, 1742).

249. NAN OAC 806 no. 622–24 (22 June 1737).

250. Capture of Curaçaoan fugitives in Casicure by Francisco de Echeverría (17 June 1742), in Gonzalez, comp., *Documentos*, Causas Civiles, no. 18, 124.

251. Rupert, "Marronage, Manumission, and Maritime Trade," 362–67.

252. Castillo, comp., *Apuntes para la historia colonial de Barlovento*, 337–56; Aizpurua, *Curazao y la costa de Caracas*, chap. 3, 13, 16.

253. Briceño, "Estudio Preliminar," 188.

254. NAN OAC 806 no. 622–24 (22 June 1737); Francisco de Echeverría re the capture of Curaçaoan fugitives (17 June 1742), in Gonzalez, comp., *Documentos*, Causas Civiles, no. 18, 124; and twenty petitions regarding smuggling filed in Coro, 1738–41, in Gonzalez, comp., *Documentos*, Causas Civiles, no. 19, 124.

255. AGN D XLII no. 12.

256. Report of Teniente de Justicia de Coro, cited in Castillo, comp., *Apuntes para la historia colonial de Barlovento,* 610; Gonzalez, *Antillas y Tierra Firme,* 96.

257. AGI, AGN; Gonzalez, *Antillas y Tierra Firme,* 50.

258. Rafael Diego Merida (1 February 1797), in *Documentos de la Insurrección de José Leonardo Chirinos,* 1:207, Plaza, "El motín de José Leonardo Chirinos," 25.

259. Gonzalez, *Antillas y Tierra Firme,* 50. Also see Aizpurua, "En busca de la libertad."

260. NAN NWIC 1166:124, "Lijste der Slaven" (7 July 1775).

261. For example, see petition by the free black Juan Hilario Bueno for freedom of Curaçao runaways (26 February 1726 or 27), in Gonzalez, comp., *Documentos*, Causas Civiles, no. 13, 122–23; Juan Casalonga on behalf of Governor of Curaçao for return of runaway slaves (7 January 1734), in Gonzalez, comp., *Documentos*, Causas Civiles, no. 17, 123–24; Pablo Ignacio de Arcaya on behalf of the Council of Curaçao regarding the return of fugitive slaves (26 September 1793), in Gonzalez, comp., *Documentos*, Causas Civiles no. 59, 140–41; report by Captain Gaspar Antonio de Quirigazo (11 January 1749), NAN OAC 820: 17–30.

262. In addition to the founders of Curiepe, Francisco Curasao is co-petitioner on documents dealing with the loss of a sloop in Coro (3–12 February 1730), in Gonzalez, comp., *Documentos*, Causas Civiles, no. 15, 123; three men with the last name Curazao appear on the list of people implicated in the 1795 slave uprising in Coro, Rafael Diego Mérida report (25 June 1795), in Troconis, comp., *Documentos*, no. 84, 311; there are sixteen people with the last name Curazao or Curazado in the onomastic index of Castillo's *Apuntes para la Historia Colonial de Barlovento,* 684.

263. Castillo, comp., *Apuntes para la historia colonial de Barlovento,* 605.

264. Gonzalez, *Antillas y Tierra Firme,* 50; Archivo Arquediocesano de Caracas, Pedrones, Coro (1767), cited in Gonzalez, *Antillas y Tierra Firme,* 52.

265. Gonzalez, *Antillas y Tierra Firme,* 52, citing documents from the AAC and Coro archives.

266. Gonzalez, comp., *Documentos,* 23.

267. See Castillo, comp., *Apuntes para la historia colonial de Barlovento,* 343–44.

268. For a detailed description of the process and mechanisms of marronage see the long account of one group of twenty-six Curaçaoan runaways who fled to Coro (1 February 1752), in Gonzalez, comp., *Documentos*, Causas Civiles, no. 26, 127–30. Also see Aizpurua, "En busca de la libertad."

269. Klooster, *Illicit Riches,* 68–69.

270. AANH vol. 1740 G no. 283 Arch. 1.

271. For example, NAN OAC 318, Jean Rodier et al. (14 April 1766).

272. Carlos de Acosta et al. (4 February 1721), in Gonzalez, comp., *Documentos*, Instrumentos Públicos/Colonia, vol. 8, no. 10, 63.

273. For example, "Capitan Juan Marcos Marin, Moreno Libre, Contra Jose Miguel de Soto, Moreno Libre," Registro Principal del Distrito Federal Tierras 1749–L.M. M-No.1, in Castillo, comp., *Apuntes para la historia colonial de Barlovento,* 312–15.

274. Castillo, comp., *Apuntes para la historia colonial de Barlovento*, 376–77, and chap. 18.

275. AGN D VXIII no. 10, 1736; Castillo, comp., *Apuntes para la historia colonial de Barlovento*, 508.

276. *Asiento* sale of three slaves to Sergeant Major D. Juan de la Colina (4 March 1723), in Gonzalez, comp., *Documentos*, Instrumentos Públicos/Colonia, vol. 9 no. 5, 64.

277. *Asiento* representative Thomas Lidderdaill empowers Sergeant Major D. Juan Pedro Borjes (18 March 1726), in Gonzalez, comp., *Documentos*, Instrumentos Públicos/Colonia, vol. 11, no. 7, 72.

278. Mosseh Henríquez (25 January 1749), in Gonzalez, comp., *Documentos*, "Instrumentos Públicos/Colonia," vol. 23, no. 1, 81; Francisco de la Colina (12 June 1749), in Gonzalez, comp., *Documentos*, Instrumentos Públicos/ Colonia, vol. 23, no. 3, 81–82; "Sobre la propiedad de una esclava curazoleña" (1–2 October 1748), in Gonzalez, comp., *Documentos*, Causas Civiles, no. 23, 126. It is highly probable that this is the same Mosseh Henriquez mentioned at the beginning of Chapter 4.

279. See, among others, NAN OAC 820:17–30.

280. "De op het eiland aanwezige spaanse negers zullen worden gerekruteerd om aan de forten te werken" (2 April 1731), in Schiltkamp and Smidt, comps., *West Indisch Plakaatboek*, vol. 1, no. 109, 156–57.

281. Goslinga, *Dutch in the Caribbean and in the Guianas*, 542.

282. "Uitwisseling met Venezuela van Weggelopen Slaven" (1 October 1748), in Schiltkamp and Smidt, comps., *West Indisch Plakaatboek*, vol. 1, no. 204, 261–62.

283. Gaspar Antonio Quirijaso (29 November 1748), in Gonzalez, comp., *Documentos*, 80–81.

284. "Sobre el canje de esclavos" (5 April–24 May 1751), in Gonzalez, comp., *Documentos*, 126–27.

285. "Sobre la fuga de un esclavo del Lic. D. Andrés Perozo a Curazao" (21 May 1745), in Gonzalez, comp., *Documentos*, 125.

286. Gonzalez, *Antillas y Tierra Firme*, 101–2; also author's reconnaissance of the coast of Venezuelan coast west of Caracas in multiple visits 2006–8.

287. Gonzalez, *Antillas y Tierra Firme*, 109.

288. Ibid., 102–8.

289. Ibid., 102.

290. For a brief treatment of each of these, see Felice, *Rebeliones, motines y movimientos de masas*, 39–92; Brito, *El problema tierra y esclavos*, 209–36; Brito, *Las insurrecciones de los esclavos negros*; and Morales, *Rebelión contra la compañía de Caracas*. For León's rebellion see Ferry, *Colonial Elite of Early Caracas*, chap. 5.

291. Felice, *Rebeliones, motines y movimientos de masas*, 28–31.

292. Brito, *El problema tierra y esclavos*, 209; Brito, *Las insurrecciones de los esclavos negros*, 47–49; Felice, *La rebelión de Andresote*; Hussey, *Caracas Company*, 66–69; Felice, *Rebeliones, motines y movimientos de masas*, 33–38.

293. Olavarriaga, *Instrucción*, 332–33.

294. Brito, *El problema tierra y esclavos*, 209; Buenaventura, *Misión de los Capuchinos*, 138.

295. OAC 1548:60 (14 January 1739); AGI Santo Domingo 782 ("Rebelión del zambo Andrés Bota," 1732–33). The primary sources mention that the vessel was Dutch,

which is how most vessels from Curaçao were identified, but it probably was owned by a Sephardic merchant.

296. "Autos sobre el levantamiento del zambo Andresote" (1732), and "Carta relacionada con el levantamiento del zambo Andresote" (18 June 1733), in Troconis, comp., *Documentos*, no. 60, 247, and no. 61, 249, respectively.

297. The trial transcripts are in AGI Santo Domingo 270, 781, 782, "Rebelión del zambo Andrés Bota" (1732–33). Also see testimony regarding Andresote's uprising (16 January 1732), in Troconis, comp., *Documentos*, no. 60, 246–48; letter from Martín de Lardizábal to the king regarding the Andresote uprising (18 June 1733), in Troconis, comp., *Documentos*, no. 61, 248–50.

298. Felice, *Rebeliones, motines y movimientos de masas*, 72.

299. Testimony of Don Manuel de Carreta (2 June 1795), in *Documentos de la Insurrección de José Leonardo Chirinos*, 1:44–45.

300. Brito, *Las insurrecciones de los esclavos negros*, 219.

301. Ibid., 60, 63.

302. Archivo Historica de Coro, Diversos (1771), quoted in Gonzalez, *Antillas y Tierra Firme*, 52.

303. Cited in Acosta, *La trata de esclavos en Venezuela*, 39.

304. "Convención entre el Rey nuestro Señor y los Estados generales de las Provincias Unidas, para la recíproca restitución de desertores y fugitivos entre las colonias de América" (23 June 1791), AGI Estado 62:20, reproduced in Aizpurua, "En busca de la libertad," 100–102.

305. Torres, *Indice sobre esclavos y esclavitud*, 50.

306. "Real Cédula de su Magestad Concediendo Libertad para el Comercio de Negros con las Islas de Cuba, Santo Domingo, Puerto Rico, y Provincia de Caracas" (28 February 1789), reproduced in Marley, comp., *Reales asientos y licencias,* Document X, no pagination.

307. Acosta, *La trata de esclavos en Venezuela*, 39.

308. The basic narrative of the rebellion has been assembled from Don Manuel de Carreta report on Coro uprising (2 June 1795), in *Documentos de la Insurrección de José Leonardo Chirinos*, 1:43–54; Troconis, comp., *Documentos*, no. 83–88, 305–19; Castillo, comp., *Apuntes para la historia colonial de Barlovento*, 602–14; Brito, *El problem tierra y esclavos*, 226–31.

309. His last name appears in the records and in the Venezuelan historiography variously as Chirino and Chirinos.

310. Mariano Ramirez Valderrain (8 June 1795) in *Documentos de la Insurrección de José Leonardo Chirinos,* 1:66–67; "Carta de Pedro Carbonell" (12 June 1795), in Troconis, comp., *Documentos*, no. 83, 308.

311. Jordán, "Acercamiento a la rebelión encabezada por José Leonardo Chirinos," 22; Plaza, "El motín de José Leonardo Chirinos," 28. The term also was used by WIC officials earlier in the century to refer to slaves brought from the area around Angola. See, for example, NAN NWIC 569:144 (28 January 1707).

312. D. José de Tellería en la cobranza de cantidad de pesos a D. Bernardo Flores" (7 May 1782), in Gonzalez, comp., *Documentos*, Causas Civiles, no. 40, 136; *Documentos de la Insurrección de José Leonardo Chirinos*, 1:22, 2:186; Brito, *El problema tierra y esclavos*, 225–26.

313. Bill of sale from Lic. D. José Pérez Volcán to D. José de Tellería (1737), in Gonzalez, comp., *Documentos*, 78.

314. Information about Gonzalez is from the following: Don Manuel de Carreta report on Coro uprising (2 June 1795), in *Documentos de la Insurrección de José Leonardo Chirinos*, 1:44–46; "Carta de Pedro Carbonell" (12 June 1795), in Troconis, comp., *Documentos*, no. 83, 307; Brito, *El problema tierra y esclavos*, 225–26; Castillo, comp., *Apuntes para la historia colonial de Barlovento*, 603–4.

315. NAN NWIC 1166:124, "Lijste der Slaven" (7 July 1775).

316. Regente de la Real Audiencia (13 May 1796), in *Documentos de la Insurrección de José Leonardo Chirinos*, 1:140.

317. Juan Guillermi (12 May 1792), in *Documentos de la Insurrección de José Leonardo Chirinos*, 2:188–89; Pedro Carbonell (12 June 1795), in *Documentos de la Insurrección de José Leonardo Chirinos*, 1:72.

318. Isidoro Gonzalez (30 October 1795), in *Documentos de la Insurrección de José Leonardo Chirinos*, 1:122.

319. Declaration of Josefa Leonarda de Piña (23 May 1795), in *Documentos de la Insurrección de José Leonardo Chirinos*, 1:115.

320. Don Manuel de Carreta report on Coro uprising (2 June 1795), in *Documentos de la Insurrección de José Leonardo Chirinos*, 1:45.

321. Full reports of the uprising and the subsequent trials are in NAN OAC 105 (1795). Transcriptions of many key documents are in Paula, comp., *1795: De Slaven Opstand van Curaçao*. For overviews see Goslinga, *Dutch in the Caribbean and in the Guianas*, 1–20; Hartog, *Curaçao: From Colonial Dependence to Autonomy*, 125–28; Do Rego, *Sklabitut i rebelion*; Hoog, *Van Rebellie tot Revolutie*, chap. 3. A compilation of the existing oral archive in Curaçao related to the uprising, published on its 200th anniversary, is Palm, comp., *E lantamentu de 1795*.

322. Rafael Diego Mérida report on Coro uprising (25 June 1795), in Troconis, comp., *Documentos*, no. 84, 310–12; instructions from the Captain General of Coro (28 June 1795), in Troconis, comp., *Documentos*, no. 85, 312–14; Brito, *El problema tierra y esclavos*, 225–36.

323. Don Manuel de Carrera (2 June 1795), in *Documentos de la Insurrección de José Leonardo Chirinos*, 1:48–49; Pedro Carbonell (22 September 1795), AANH A16-e54–D11182; "Carta de Pedro Carbonell" (12 June 1795); Rafael Diego Mérida report on Coro uprising (25 June 1795); "Carta del Capitán General al Teniente Justicia Mayor de Coro" (1795) in Troconis, comp., *Documentos*, no. 83, 308; no. 84, 310–11; no. 85, 312, respectively.

324. Isidoro Gonzalez (30 October 1795), in *Documentos de la Insurrección de José Leonardo Chirinos*, 1:120.

325. For example, Lopez Quintana and others (23 June 1795), Pedro Carbonell (30 June 1795), and Regente de la Real Audiencia (23 September 1795), ibid., 1:76, 77, and 133–34, respectively.

326. Report of Teniente Justicia Mayor de Coro (1 June 1795), ibid., 1:83.

327. Juan Luis Roxas and Juan Domingo Roxas (7 July 1795), ibid., 1:88.

328. Antonio Guillelmi (23 March 1796), ibid., 1:125.

329. List of captives (7 July 1795), ibid., 1:96.

330. "Sentencia de la Real Audiencia" (10 December 1796), ibid., 2:204

331. Manuel de Carrera (26 September 1796), ibid., 1:160.

332. Among others, Do Rego, *Sklabitut i rebelion*, 24.

333. Relaas van Pater Jacobus Schink (7 September 1795), in Paula, comp., *1795: De Slaven Opstand van Curaçao*, 268–71.

334. Goslinga, *Dutch in the Caribbean and in the Guianas*, 10.

335. Don Manuel de Carreta (2 June 1795), and Pedro Carbonell (30 June 1795), in *Documentos de la Insurrección de José Leonardo Chirinos*, 1:46–47, 50–51; and 78, respectively.

336. Gil, Dovale, and Lusmila, *La insurrección de los negros de la serranía coriana*. For another interpretation of the uprising in Coro see Arcaya, *Insurrección de los negros de la Serranía de Coro*.

337. Gil, Dovale, and Lusmila, *La insurrección de los negros de la serranía coriana*. For discussion of a somewhat similar situation in mid-eighteenth century Antigua see Gaspar, *Bondmen and Rebels*.

338. NAN NWIC 1166:124, "Lijste der Slaven" (7 July 1775).

339. Regente de la Real Audiencia (22 September 1795), in *Documentos de la Insurrección de José Leonardo Chirinos*, 1:133.

340. Rupert, "Inter-colonial Networks and Revolutionary Ferment."

341. Don Manuel de Carreta report on Coro uprising (2 June 1795), in *Documentos de la Insurrección de José Leonardo Chirinos*,1:45.

342. Archivo Historica de Coro, Diversos (1771), quoted in Gonzalez, *Antillas y Tierra Firme*, 53; Archivo Arquediocesano de Caracas, Pedrones, Coro (1767), cited in Gonzalez, *Antillas y Tierra Firme*, 52; Gonzalez, *Antillas y Tierra Firme*, 50, 96; Granda, "Papiamentu en Hispanoamérica," 13n49; Castillo, comp., *Apuntes para la historia colonial de Barlovento*, 607.

343. Granda, "Papiamento en Hispanoamerica," 1, 7–13; Maduro, *Palenkero i Papiamentu* , 7–8.

6 / Language and Creolization

1. The full documentation of the case is in NAN NWIC 223. The quote in Papiamentu is from a photograph of a one-page fragment of one of Abraham's original letters which is reproduced in Emmanuel and Emmanuel, *History of the Jews of the Netherlands Antilles*, plate 78. The originals in Papiamentu subsequently disappeared from the archives. Several linguists have translated, transcribed, and analyzed the fragment. I have used the English translations in Salomon, "Earliest Known Document in Papiamentu Contextually Reconsidered," 370–71. Also see Wood, "New Light on the Origins of Papiamentu"; Eckkrammer, "Standardisation of Papiamentu"; and Martinus, *Kiss of a Slave*, 9–10. Emmanuel and Emmanuel deal with the case at length in *History of the Jews of the Netherlands Antilles*, 271–75.

2. NAN NWIC 223:1, 24. The Dutch spelling of these terms varies throughout the documents.

3. Schabel, "Dagboek-Fragment van Pater Michael Alexius Schabel Societatis Jesu Missionaris op het eiland Curaçao" (NANA); Brada, *Paters Jezuieten*, 12. It is possible that a comprehensive review of the archives would yield even earlier references than those mentioned here.

4. Caicedo to his superiors (24 April 1732). Brada reproduces a Dutch translation in *Prefect Caysedo*, 34; also see 20.

5. Caicedo to his superiors (24 April 1732), translated and reproduced in Brada, *Prefect Caysedo*, 34.

6. Cited in Brada, *Paters Franciscanen*, 4.

7. See, for example, OAC 807 f 9: 293, 23 September 1737. Further research into legal cases may well turn up additional examples, perhaps from even earlier. The developing work of Han Jordaan should be of particular interest here.

8. Cited in Brada, *Prefect Caysedo*, 20.

9. NAN NWIC 223:5 (7 August, 1776). Maduro transcribes and analyzes the conversations in Papiamentu in the appendix to *Bon Papiamentu*, 53–54, based on a photocopy he says a friend obtained for him from the Nationaal Archief in The Hague (NAN). Like Abraham and Sarah's letters, the only version extant in the archives is in Dutch, with a contemporary marginal note that it was translated from original testimony in creole. The fate of the original documents in Papiamentu remains a mystery.

10. NAN NWIC 223:1, 24.

11. NAN NWIC 223:5 (7 August, 1776).

12. NAN NWIC 223:3, 6, 7, 24.

13. NAN NWIC 223:24.

14. NAN NWIC 223:1.

15. NAN OAC 188:4 (1756).

16. Martinus, *Kiss of a Slave*, 8–9. Fortman reproduces and analyzes sections of the diary in "Een belangrijk dagboek."

17. Martinus, *Kiss of a Slave*, 3, 8–11, 146. The names of the vessels appear in a comprehensive list in Emmanuel and Emmanuel, *History of the Jews of the Netherlands Antilles*, 682–723.

18. NAN OAC 1560 f. 215.

19. Martinus, *Kiss of a Slave*, 9.

20. NAN OAC 942:249.

21. Brada, *Prefect Caysedo*, 20.

22. Cited in Brada, *Paters Franciscanen*, 4.

23. Apostolic Prefect Th. Brouwers to Prefect of Propaganda Fide, 12 March 1784, cited in Lampe, *Mission or Submission?* 122n6.

24. Lampe, "Christianity and Slavery in the Dutch Caribbean."

25. Hartog, *Curaçao: From Colonial Dependence to Autonomy*, 157.

26. Cited in Broek, "Rise of a Caribbean Island's Literature," 26.

27. *Defiance v. Young Johannes, 1747*, in Towle, ed., *Records of the Vice-Admiralty Court of Rhode Island*, 430–33. I am grateful to Wim Klooster for alerting me to this document.

28. Archivo Arzobispado de Caracas Censo no. 122, Informe dirigido por Dionisio Leal, 1768. Cited in Gonzalez, *Antillas y Tierra Firme*, 38–39.

29. AGI Estado 65:30 (Caracas, 5 November 1795), cited in Aizpurua, "En busca de la libertad," 96.

30. Cited in Jordaan, "Patriots, Privateers, and International Politics," paper presented at the seminar, The Impact of the Haitian and French Revolutions on Curaçao. KITLV Institute, Leiden University, the Netherlands. June 2010.

31. All cited in Hartog, *Curaçao: Van Colonie tot Autonomie*, 433.

32. Wood, "New Light on the Origins of Papiamentu," 22; Maduro, *Bon Papiamentu*, 53–57; Salomon, "Earliest Known Document"; Martinus, *Kiss of a Slave*.

33. Conversation with linguist Bart Jacobs, March 2010.

34. Jacobs, "Upper Guinea Origins of Papiamentu," 324.

35. Sensbach, *Rebecca's Revival*, 21, 36, 144.

36. Parkvall, *Out of Africa*, 154.

37. See, among others, Diouf, *Servants of Allah*.

38. Buurt, "Caquetío Indians on Curaçao during Colonial Times and Caquetío Words in the Papiamentu Language"; Buurt and Joubert, *Stemmen uit het Verleden*.

39. *History of the Jews of the Netherlands Antilles*, 482–83.

40. Henriques, *Ta Asina? O ta Asana?*, and *Loke a keda pa similla*.

41. Wood, "Hispanization of a Creole Language," 861; Birmingham, "Still More on Papiamentu," 301.

42. Major proponents of a Portuguese base have included Lenz, Wood, Navarro, and Wijk, and, more recently, Martinus, Maurer, and Jacobs. Fewer linguists have argued for a Spanish base, especially in recent years; they include Munteneau and Joubert. For short summaries of the various linguistic theories and critiques, with full bibliographic citations, see Martinus, *Kiss of a Slave*, 12–16. For more extensive linguistic critique of several of these theories see Martinus, *Kiss of a Slave*, chaps. 2–4.

43. Among others, Maduro, *Kaboberdiano i Papiamento*, and Gomes Casseres, "Papiamentu."

44. Lipski, "Spanish-based Creoles in the Caribbean," 547.

45. For example, see ibid.

46. DeCamp, "The Field of Creole Language Studies," 29.

47. Lipski, "Spanish-based Creoles in the Caribbean," 546.

48. See ibid., 547; Perl and Schwegler, *América negra*; Schwegler, "*Chi ma nkongo*."

49. See, among others, Fontaine, "Language, Society, and Development," 29–30. This trend is now changing; for example, see the work of Jacobs.

50. See Martinus, *Kiss of a Slave*, esp. chap. 7; Maurer, "Short Note about Papiamentu's Origin," 7; Jacobs, "Upper Guinea Origins of Papiamentu."

51. For useful summaries that are comprehensible to the nonspecialist see, among others, Bickerton, "Pidgin and Creole Studies"; Wood, "New Light on the Origins of Papiamentu," 18–20; DeCamp, "Field of Creole Language Studies," 29–34.

52. For an overview of the early development of the field of creole linguistics see DeCamp, "Field of Creole Language Studies," 40.

53. Arends, "Historical Study of Creoles and the Future of Creole Studies," 56, 58.

54. Wood, *Black Majority*, 171.

55. Mintz, "Socio-historical Background to Pidginization and Creolization," 481.

56. Such historical framing, which had been done previously by individual linguists, is now gaining wider currency in the field as a whole. See Arends, "Historical Study of Creoles and the Future of Creole Studies."

57. Price, "Miracle of Creolization," 59.

58. Eltis, Morgan, and Richardson, "Agency and Disapora in Atlantic History," 1332.

59. For extensive treatment of this topic see Brooks, *Eurafricans in Western Africa*; Mark, "The Evolution of 'Portuguese' Identity," esp. 173–83; and Mark and da Silva Horta, *Forgotten Diaspora*.

60. Thornton, *Africa and Africans in the Making of the Atlantic World*, 253–56; Berlin, "From Creole to African."

61. See Mark and da Silva Horta, "Catholics, Jews, and Muslims in Early Seventeenth-Century Guiné"; Mark and da Silva Horta, "Two Early Seventeenth-Century Sephardic Communities"; Green, "Further Considerations on the Sephardim"; and Mark, "Evolution of 'Portuguese' Identity."

62. See Chapter 2 for more extensive treatment of this point. Henceforth in this chapter I use the term Sephardim to refer to both groups.

63. Mark, "Evolution of 'Portuguese' Identity"; Martinus, *Kiss of a Slave*, 120.

64. See Lewin, *La Inquisición en México*, 21–22. For a succinct analysis of Sephardic participation in the slave trade see Drescher, "Jews and New Christians in the Atlantic Slave Trade." For more extensive analysis see Faber, *Jews, Slaves and the Slave Trade*.

65. Navarro, "Observaciones Sobre el Papiamento," 183–89; Wijk, "Orígenes y Evolución del Papiamentu," 170–71; Birmingham, "Lexical Decreolization in Papiamentu," 49.

66. Berlin, "From Creole to African," 258. I use the term, *fala de Guine*, advisedly, recognizing that it may, in fact, refer to multiple languages.

67. Martinus, *Kiss of a Slave*, 131.

68. Ibid., 91.

69. Lipski, "Spanish-based Creoles in the Caribbean," 548.

70. See, among others, Lovejoy, *Transformations in Slavery*, and Heywood and Thornton, eds., *Central Africans, Atlantic Creoles, and the Foundation of the Americas*.

71. Martinus, *Kiss of a Slave*, 15, 126.

72. See Bickerton, "Pidgin and Creole Studies"; Wood, "Hispanization of a Creole Language," 861; Wood, "New Light on the Origins of Papiamentu," 20, 29; Bickerton and Escalante, "Palenquero."

73. All of these except Euskadi are Romance languages that developed from Latin in the early Middle Ages.

74. For various interpretations of these processes see Mignolo, *Darker Side of the Renaissance*; Bouza, *Communication, Knowledge, and Memory in Early Modern Spain*; and Lüdtke, comp., *El español en América en el siglo XVI*.

75. Fontaine, "Language, Society, and Development," 29–30; Penny, *History of the Spanish Language*, 20–33. Also see Granda, *Español de América, español de Africa y hablas criollas Hispánica,* esp. essays 2, 49–92 and 16, 399–411. I am grateful to Jodi Bilinkoff for clarifying some of these points.

76. Apostolic Prefect Th. Brouwers to Prefect of Propaganda Fide, 12 March 1784, cited in Lampe, *Mission or Submission?* 122n6. Linguists have not found evidence to back up this claim, however (personal communication with linguist Bart Jacobs, March 2010).

77. Cervantes-Rodríguez and Lutz, "Coloniality of Power, Immigration, and the English-Spanish Asymmetry in the United States," 523–25, and Mignolo, *Darker Side of the Renaissance*, esp. chaps. 1, 2. For analysis of how European and Amerindian languages influenced each other throughout the Americas see Gray and Fiering, eds., *Language Encounter in the Americas*.

78. Schwarzwald, "Language Choice and Varieties before and after the Expulsion," 401–3.

79. See Harris, *Death of a Language*, chap. 4; Díaz-Mas, *Sephardim*, 72–73.

80. Teensma, "Take Florida." The proposal is undated.

81. See Harris, *Death of a Language*, 18–29; Díaz-Mas, *Sephardim*, 75–77.

82. For a useful overview see Harris, *Death of a Language*, 18–29; Díaz-Mas, *Sephardim*, 74–75.

83. Díaz-Mas, *Sephardim*, 73–74.

84. Schwarzwald, "Language Choice and Varieties," 407.

85. Rosenberg, "Adoption of the Dutch Language by Dutch Jewry," 155–57.

86. Ibid., 161.

87. Schwarzwald, "Language Choice and Varieties," 400.

88. See Jacobs, "Upper Guinea Origins of Papiamentu," 328.

89. I am grateful to Bart Jacobs for calling this to my attention.

90. Jacobs, "Upper Guinea Origins of Papiamentu," 319. Jacobs's research traces "at least five core grammatical categories" back to the single source of Upper Guinea Creole, indicating a tight "structural correspondence" between the two (325), and calls all the structural correspondence between Papiamentu and Upper Guinea Creole a "smoking gun" (349). He notes that the five categories are not the only ones in which the two languages exhibit shared characteristics; for his full presentation of the linguistic evidence and analysis, see 326–49.

91. Ibid., 361.

92. Ibid., 351.

93. Martinus, *Kiss of a Slave*, 1.

94. Ibid., 262.

95. Maurer, "Short Note about Papiamentu's Origin," 7.

96. Quoted in Jacobs, "Upper Guinea Origins of Papiamentu," 351.

97. Klooster, *Illicit Riches*, 117.

98. Jacobs, "Upper Guinea Origins of Papiamentu," 322–23.

99. Mark and da Silva Horta, "Two Early Seventeenth-Century Sephardic Communities," 256.

100. Klooster, *Illicit Riches*, 67. His name is also spelled Phelipe.

101. Ibid., 117.

102. Green, "Further Considerations on the Sephardim," 179.

103. OAC 807 f 9: 293 (23 September 1737); NAN NWIC 223, various.

104. Emmanuel and Emmanuel, *History of the Jews of the Netherlands Antilles*, 482. The Emmanuels reproduce photographs of several documents in Portuguese throughout their two-volume work.

105. NAN NWIC 223, various.

106. NAN NWIC 213:8.

107. NAN NWIC 216 (28 January 1727); Emmanuel, *Precious Stones of the Jews of Curaçao*.

108. For example, see NAN OAC 188:3 (1756).

109. See, for example, NAN NWIC 213 (14 February 1705).

110. NAN NWIC 216 (29 January 1727).

111. NAN NWIC 223: various.

112. See, for example, NAN NWIC 617:101 & 102 (1681), and NAN NWIC 213:18 (1705).

113. For example, NAN NWIC 216 (29 January 1727); NAN OAC 188:3–33 (1756); NAN OAC 188:34–36 (11 January 1756).

114. Schwarzwald, "Language Choice and Varieties," 400.

115. NAN NWIC 1176, 9 August 1790.

116. *South Carolina Gazette* 25 June–2 July 1763, cited in Bolster, *Black Jacks*, 40n62.

117. Martinus, *Kiss of a Slave*, 17–19. For extensive analysis of Guene texts and grammar, see chaps. 9, 10.

118. Martinus, *Kiss of a Slave*, 18.

119. In this respect Guene is much more like Gullah, the creole spoken on the Atlantic islands off the coast of South Carolina and Georgia. See Turner's classic study, *Africanisms in the Gullah Dialect*, and also Wood, *Black Majority*, chap. 6.

120. The Curaçaoan anthropologist Richenel Ansano has found a high percentage of words of Kongolese-Angolan origins, and also many from the Bight of Benin, and has compiled an unpublished list of the probable origins of some two hundred Guene words based on extensive analysis of the *Sambumbu* and *Zikinká* collections, and his own interviews with now-deceased elderly Afro-Curaçaoan informants. I am grateful to Ansano for sharing the tentative results of this ongoing, unpublished research with me.

121. See Martinus, *Kiss of a Slave*, chaps. 9, 10; Martinus, "Guene Kriole of the Netherlands Antilles"; Martinus, "Value of Guene for Folklore and Culture." To my knowledge Martinus is the only trained linguist who has published an analysis of Guene.

122. Personal communication, March 2010.

123. Since the 1940s, Curaçaoan researchers have conducted extensive oral histories among elderly informants, most of them now deceased. The two largest such collections, and the most extensive Guene archives in existence, are the multivolume *Sambumbu*, compiled by Father Paul Brenneker, and the *Zikinzá* audio recordings, assembled by Brenneker and Elis Juliana, between 1955 and 1969. They were based on interviews with hundreds of elderly Afro-Curaçaoans who had been raised by or grew up among former slaves, all of them now deceased. Together the two collections contain more than fourteen hundred Guene words and phrases. At least a half dozen other Curaçaoan researchers have put together smaller collections.

124. Bickerton, "Perspectives on Creole Language History," 98–99.

125. Hoetink, *Het patroon van de oude Curaçaose samenleving*, 97.

126. Hartog, *Curaçao: Van Colonie tot Autonomie*, 433–34; Martinus, "Guene Kriole of the Netherlands Antilles," 46.

127. Martinus, *Kiss of a Slave*, 9, 11.

128. Ibid., 9.

129. This was the contention of Brenneker, cited in Martinus, *Kiss of a Slave*, 17.

130. Ibid.

131. Castillo, comp., *Apuntes para la historia colonial de Barlovento*, 610; Jordán, "Acercamiento a la rebelión encabezada por José Leonardo Chirinos," 22–23; Declaration of Josefa Leonarda de Piña (23 May 1795), in *Documentos de la Insurrección de José Leonardo Chirinos*, 1:115.

132. Hoetink, *Het patroon van de oude Curaçaose samenleving*. For a summary of his argument in English, see Mintz, "Socio-historical Background to Pidginization and Creolization."

133. NAN NWIC 1166:83, "Leijste van de familien," 2 June 1775.

134. Schunk, "Lost Catholic Houses of Prayer in Curaçao," 132.

135. Felice, *Curazao hispanico*, 412.

136. Ibid., 409–10, 412.

137. Gonzalez, *Antillas y Tierra Firme,* 38–39.

138. Martinus, "Victory of the Concubines and the Nannies"; Martinus, *Kiss of a Slave*, 128–30.

139. Broek, "Rise of a Caribbean Island's Literature," 26.

140. For Papiamentu, see Martinus, "Victory of the Concubines and the Nannies"; and Bickerton, "Afro-Creole Origin for Eena Meena Mina Mo," 225–28. For the role of children in developing the creole of the Cape Verde islands see Martinus, *Kiss of a Slave*, 128–30.

141. Martinus, "Victory of the Concubines and the Nannies"; Eckkrammer, "Standardisation of Papiamentu," 61; Wijk, "Orígenes y Evolución del Papiamentu," 181.

142. Eckkrammer, "Standardisation of Papiamentu," 61; Martinus, "Victory of the Concubines and the Nannies," 114; Reinecke, "Trade Jargons and Creole Dialects as Marginal Languages," 115.

143. Martinus, *Kiss of a Slave*, 103; Henriques, *Ta Asina? O ta Asana?*

144. Quoted in Brathwaite, *Development of Creole Society in Jamaica*, 302.

145. Ibid.

146. Ibid.

147. NAN NWIC 223:5 (7 August 1776); NAN NWIC 223:24.

148. See Reinecke, "Trade Jargons and Creole Dialects as Marginal Languages," 115; Bickerton, "Afro-Creole Origin for Eena Meena Mina Mo"; and Jourdan, "Pidgins and Creoles," 195.

149. Rickford, "Ethnicity as a Sociolinguistic Boundary," 113–14.

150. St. Hilaire, "Globalization, Urbanization, and Language in Caribbean Development," 65.

151. Hartog, *Curaçao: Van Colonie tot Autonomie*, 433–34; Martinus, *Kiss of a Slave*, 17–19.

152. NAN NWIC 223:5 (7 August 1776).

153. AF CC no. 914, 9 September 1688.

154. Granda, "Papiamentu en Hispanoamerica," 9.

155. Reinecke, "Trade Jargons and Creole Dialects as Marginal Languages," 107–11.

156. *Defiance v. Young Johannes*, in Towle, ed., *Records of the Vice-Admiralty Court of Rhode Island*, 420–39.

157. For example, *Polly v. Pearl*, in Towle, ed., *Records of the Vice-Admiralty Court of Rhode Island*, 349.

158. NAN NWIC 223:3 (11 December 1775).

159. Henriquez, *Ta Asina? O ta Asana?*, and *Loke a keda pa similla*.

160. Granda, "Papiamento en Hispanoamerica," 1, 7–13; Maduro, *Palenkero i Papiamentu*, 7–8. Also see Bickerton, "Pidgin and Creole Studies"; Wood, "Hispanization of a Creole Language," 861; Wood, "New Light on the Origins of Papiamentu," 20, 29; Bickerton and Escalante, "Palenquero."

161. Reinecke, "Trade Jargons and Creole Dialects as Marginal Languages," 107–18.

162. Granda, "Papiamento en Hispanoamerica," 2–3.

163. See ibid., 1–3.

164. Lipski, "Contacto de criollos en el Caribe hispánico," 31–60.

165. Bickerton and Escalante, "Palenquero"; Granda, *Español de América, español de Africa y hablas criollas hispánica,* chap. 16.

166. Lipski, "Spanish-based Creoles in the Caribbean," 546–47.

167. Castillo, comp., *Apuntes para la historia colonial de Barlovento,* 379–83.

168. Gonzalez, *Antillas y Tierra Firme,* 96.

169. Ibid., 50; Archivo Arquediocesano de Caracas, Pedrones, Coro, 1767, cited in Gonzalez, *Antillas y Tierra Firme,* 52.

170. Archivo Historica de Coro, Diversos, 1771, quoted in Gonzalez, *Antillas y Tierra Firme,* 53; Granda, "Papiamentu en Hispanoamérica," 13n49.

171. Castillo, comp., *Apuntes para la historia colonial de Barlovento,* 684.

172. Ibid., 375.

173. Archivo Arquediocesano de Caracas, Pedrones, Coro, 1767, cited in Gonzalez, *Antillas y Tierra Firme,* 52. For Coro, among others: Francisco Curasao is co-petitioner on documents dealing with the loss of a sloop in Coro (3–12 February 1730), in Gonzalez, comp., *Documentos,* Causas Civiles, no. 15, 123.

174. Rafael Diego Mérida report, 25 June 1795, reproduced in Troconis, comp., *Documentos,* no. 84, 311.

175. NAN NWIC 617:101, 102.

176. Archivo Arquediocesano de Caracas, Pedrones, Coro, 1767, cited in Gonzalez, *Antillas y Tierra Firme,* 52.

177. Don Manuel de Carreta report on Coro uprising (2 June 1795), in *Documentos de la Insurrección de José Leonardo Chirinos,* 1:45.

178. Declaration of Josefa Leonarda de Piña (23 May 1795), in *Documentos de la Insurrección de José Leonardo Chirinos,* 1:115.

179. Cited in Castillo, comp., *Apuntes para la historia colonial de Barlovento,* 610; also see Jordán, "Acercamiento a la rebelión encabezada por José Leonardo Chirinos," 22–23.

180. "Sobre el canje de escalvos" (5 April–24 May 1751), in Gonzalez, comp., *Documentos,* 127.

181. "Sobre la lucha entre franceses e ingleses en Willemstad" (10 September 1800–12 March 1801), in Gonzalez, comp., *Documentos,* 143.

182. Granda, "Papiamento en Hispanoamérica," 9–11; Lipski, "Spanish-based Creoles in the Caribbean," 547.

183. Granda, "Papiamento en Hispanoamérica," 1, 11–12.

184. Klooster, "Rising Expectations of Free and Enslaved Blacks," 67.

185. Ibid.

186. Lipski, "Spanish-based Creoles in the Caribbean," 547.

187. Granda, "Papiamento en Hispanoamérica," 1–2, citing research by Alvarez Nazario.

188. Oostindie, "Ethnicity, Nationalism, and the Exodus"; Benjamin, *Jews of the Dutch Caribbean,* 82–86.

189. McWhorter, *Missing Spanish Creoles,* 202, cited in Lipski, "Spanish-based Creoles in the Caribbean," 544.

190. See, among others, Brathwaite, *Development of Creole Society in Jamaica.*

191. Benjamin, *Jews of the Dutch Caribbean,* 150–51; Oostindie, "Ethnicity, Nationalism, and the Exodus."

Conclusions

1. For extensive treatment of the turn of the century in Curaçao and the island's relationship to wider regional and Atlantic revolutionary currents, see the pieces in *Curaçao in the Age of Revolutions,* ed. Klooster and Oostindie.

2. For a detailed analysis of the company's financial situation throughout the eighteenth century and the circumstances that led to its demise see Goslinga, *Dutch in the Caribbean and in the Guianas,* chap. 16, 564–608.

3. As early as 1795, the Prince of Orange, exiled in England, had urged the governors of all the colonies to regard the British as allies, in an effort to keep Dutch overseas possessions out of the hands of the French invaders.

4. Soest, *Trustee of the Netherlands Antilles,* 11–14.

5. Geggus, "Caribbean in the Age of Revolution," 85–87.

6. One of the oldest known printed documents in Papiamentu is a four-page communiqué from Monsignor Niewindt to the island's Catholic population, dated 1833. (Prefecto Apostolico di Curaçao, *Na Cristian di su mision*).

7. Wood, "Hispanization of a Creole Language," 857–58; Reinecke, "Trade Jargons and Creole Dialects as Marginal Languages," 117.

8. Emmanuel and Emmanuel, *History of the Jews of the Netherlands Antilles,* 347–48.

9. Soest, *Trustee of the Netherlands Antilles,* 225–37.

10. For a comprehensive analysis of this transformation see Soest, *Olie als water.*

11. Benjamin, *Jews of the Dutch Caribbean,* 150–51; Oostindie, "Ethnicity, Nationalism, and the Exodus."

12. Eckkrammer, "Standardisation of Papiamentu"; Wijk, "Orígenes y Evolución del Papiamentu," 177–78, 180; Rutgers, "Dutch Caribbean Literature," 545–46; Wood, "Hispanization of a Creole Language," 857.

13. Karras, *Smuggling,* 131.

14. Hancock, *Oceans of Wine,* xvi.

15. See, for example, Brathwaite, *Development of Creole Society in Jamaica,* esp. chaps. 19, 20.

16. Schwartz, ed., *Tropical Babylons*; Welch, *Slave Society in the City,* 139.

17. Welch, *Slave Society in the City,* 139.

18. Benton, *Search for Sovereignty,* 2.

19. Hancock, *Oceans of Wine,* xvi.

Bibliography

Archives Consulted

Archivo de la Academia National de la Historia; Caracas, Venezuela (AANH)

Archivo del Registro del Distrito Federal, Cajas Negras (ARDF-CN)
Sección Civiles, Esclavos (SC-E)

Archivo de Falcón; Coro, Venezuela (AF; formerly Archivo Histórico de Coro)

Causas Civiles (CC)
Instrumentos Públicos Colonia (IPC)

Archivo General de Indias; Sevilla, Spain (AGI)

Caracas (C)
Indiferente General (IG)
Mapas y Planos (MP)
Patronato (P)
Santo Domingo (SD)

Archivo General de la Nación; Caracas, Venezuela (AGN)

Archivo del Registro del Distrito Federal, Tierras (ARDF-T)
Diversos (D)
Reales Cédulas (RC)

Archivo General de Simancas; Simancas, Spain (AGS)

Estado (E)
Mapas, Planos y Dibujos (MPD)

Archivo Histórico Nacional; Madrid, Spain (AHN)
Codices (C)
Diversos (D)

Leiden University Library Special Collections; Leiden, the Netherlands (LUSC)
Bodel Nijenhuis Collection (COLLBN)
Museum Bodellianum (MB)

Nationaal Archief Nederland; The Hague, the Netherlands (NAN; formerly Algemeen Rijksarchief)
Nieuwe West Indische Compagnie (NWIC)
Colonial Maps and Drawings (VEL)
Oude Archief Curaçao (OAC)
Staten-Generaal (SG)
Verspreide WI Stukken (VWIS)

National Archives of the Netherlands Antilles; Willemstad, Curaçao (NANA)

National Maritime Museum; Greenwich, UK (NMM)

Nederlands Scheepvaartmuseum; Amsterdam, the Netherlands (NSM)

Printed Documents and Edited Collections

Aguado, Pedro de. *Historia de Venezuela*. 1581. Prologue, notes, and appendices by Jerónimo Bécker. Madrid: Establecimiento Tipográfico de Jaime Ratés, 1918.

Alvarez Abreu, Antonio José. *Instrucción, 1715*. In Analola Borges, *Alvarez Abreu y su extraordinaria misión en Indias*, 68–165. Tenerife: Instituto de Estudios Hispánicas de Canaras, 1963.

Andrews, Kenneth R., ed. *English Privateering Voyages to the West Indies, 1588–1595. Documents relating to English voyages to the West Indies from the defeat of the Armada to the last voyage of Sir Francis Drake, including Spanish documents contributed by Irene A. Wright*. Cambridge: Hakluyt Society, Cambridge University Press, 1959.

Brenneker, Paul, comp. *Sambumbu: Volkskunde van Curaçao, Aruba, en Bonaire*. Multiple volumes. Curaçao: Van Dorp, 1969–75.

Brenneker, Paul, and Elis Juliana, comp. *Zikinzá*. Audio recordings. Multiple volumes. Curaçao: 1955–1969.

Brodhead, John Romeyn, comp. *Documents Relative to the Colonial History of the State of New York procured in Holland, England and France*. Vol. 3. Albany, N.Y.: Weed, Parsons, 1853.

Capitein, Jacobus Elisa Joannes. *The Agony of Asar: A Thesis on Slavery by the Former Slave Jacobus Elisa Joannes Capitein, 1717–1747*. Translated with commentary by Grant Parker. Princeton, N.J.: Markus Wiener, 2001.

Castellanos, Juan de. *Elegías de varones ilustres de Indias*. 1589. Introduction and notes by Isaac J. Pardo. Caracas: Biblioteca de la Academía Nacional de la Historia no. 57, 1962.

Castillo Lara, Lucas Guillermo, comp. *Apuntes para la historia colonial de Barlovento*. Caracas: Biblioteca de la Academia Nacional de la Historia, Fuentes para la Historia Colonial de Venezuela no. 151, 1981.

Cedularios de la Monarquía Española Relativos a la Provincia de Venezuela (1529–1552). 2 vols. Caracas: Fundación John Boulton and Fundación Eugenio Mendoza, 1959.

Cisneros, José Luis de. *Descripción exacta de la Provincia de Venezuela*. 1764. Caracas: Biblioteca de la Academia Nacional de la Historia, Fuentes para la Historia Colonial de Venezuela no. 149, 1981.

Documentos de la Insurrección de José Leonardo Chirinos. Vols. 1, 2. Caracas, Venezuela: Editorial Metrópolis, 1994, 1997.

Donnan, Elizabeth, comp. *Documents Illustrative of the History of the Slave Trade to America*. 1932. Vols. 1–4. New York: Octagon Books, 1969.

Equiano, Olaudah. "The Interesting Narrative of the Life of Olaudah Equiano or Gustavus Vassa, The African. Written by Himself." In Henry Louis Gates, ed., *The Classic Slave Narratives*, 1–182. New York, Mentor, Penguin, 1987.

Gehring, Charles T., and J. A. Schiltkamp, comps. *New Netherland Documents*. Vol. 17: *Curaçao Papers 1640–1665*. Interlaken, N.Y.: Heart of the Lakes, 1987.

Gomez Candeo, Lino, comp. *La Provincia Franciscana de Santa Cruz de Caracas. Cuerpo de documentos para su historia, consolidación, y expansion*. 3 vols. Caracas: Biblioteca de la Academia Nacional de la Historia, Fuentes para la historia colonial de Venezuela no. 121–3: 1974.

Gonzalez Batista, Carlos, comp. *Documentos para la historia de las antillas neerlandesas*. Archivo Histórico de Coro, Fondo Registro Principal I. Coro: Centro de Investigaciones Históricas Pedro Manuel Arcaya, 1987.

Hamelberg, J. H. J., comp. *Documenten behoorende bij de nederlanders op de West-Indische Eilanden*. Vol. 1: *Curaçao, Bonaire, Aruba*. Amsterdam: J. H. de Bussy, 1901.

Hawkins, John. "The voyage made by the worshipful M. John Hawkins, Esquire, now Knight Captaine of the Jesus of Lubek . . . begun in An. Dom. 1564." In *The Hawkins' Voyages*, ed. Markham, 8–64.

Headlam, ed., Cecil, ed. *Calendar of State Papers, Colonial Series. America and West Indies. Preserved in the State Paper Department of Her Majesty's Public Record Office*. Multiple volumes. London: Her Majesty's Stationery Office, 1932–36.

Hering, J. H. *Beschryving van het Eiland Curaçao en de Daar onder Hoorende Eilanden, Bon-aire, Oroba en Klein Curaçao*. 1779. Amsterdam: S. Emmering 1969.

Humboldt, Alexander von. *Viaje a las regiones equinocciales del nuevo continente hecho en 1799, 1800, 1801, 1802, 1803 y 1804.* Vol. 3. Caracas: Escuela Téchnica Industrial, Talleres de Artes Gráficas, 1941.

Juicios de Residencia en la Provincia de Venezuela. Vol. 1: *Los Welser.* Caracas: Biblioteca de la Academia Nacional de la Historia no. 130, 1977.

Kavenagh, W. Keith. *Foundations of Colonial America: A Documentary History.* New York: Chelsea House, 1973.

Laet, Johannes de. *Nieuwe Wereldt ofte beschrijvinghe van West-Indien.* Leiden, the Netherlands: Elsevier, 1625.

Lee, T. van der, comp. *Curaçaose Vrijbrieven, 1722–1863.* Den Haag: Algemeen Rijksarchief, 1998.

———. *Plantages op Curaçao en hun eigennaren (1708–1845): Namen en data voornamelijk ontleend aan transportakten.* Leiden, the Netherlands: Grafaria, 1989.

Maduro, A. J. *Documenten uit de jaren 1639 en 1640 welke zich in de 'Archivo General de Indias' te Sevilla bevinden en betrekking hebben op de door de Spanjaarden beraamde plannen om het eiland Curaçao op de Nederlanders te heroveren.* Curaçao: van Dorp, 1962.

Marcus, Jacob Rader, ed. *The Jew in the American World: A Source Book.* Detroit: Wayne State University Press, 1996.

Markham, Clements R., ed. *The Hawkins' Voyages during the Reigns of Henry VII, Queen Elizabeth, and James I.* London: the Hakluyt Society, 1878.

Marley, David, comp. *Reales asientos y licencias para la introducción de esclavos negros a la América Española (1667–1789).* Edición facsimilar. Colección documenta novae hispaniae volúmen B-9. Windsor, Ontario, and Mexico: Rolston-Bain, 1985.

Olavarriaga, Pedro José de. *Instrucción General y Particular del Estado Presente de la Provincia de Venezuela en los Años de 1720 y 1721.* Preliminary study by Mario Briceño Perozo. Caracas: Biblioteca de la Academia Nacional de la Historia no. 76, 1965.

Otte, Enrique, comp. *Cedularios de la Monarquía Española de Margarita, Nueva Andalucía y Caracas (1553–1604).* 2 vols. Caracas: Edición de la Fundación John Bolton, Fundación Eugenio Mendoza y Fundación Shell, 1967.

———. *Cédulas reales relativas a Venezuela (1500–1550).* Caracas: Edición de la Fundación John Boulton y la Fundación Eugenio Mendoza, 1963.

Pacheco, Joaquin Francisco, ed. *Colección de Documentos Inéditos Relativos al Descubrimiento, conquista, y colonización de las Posesiones Españolas en América Occeanía sacados, en su mayor parte, del Real Archivo de Indias.* Vol. 1. Madrid: M. Bernaldo de Quirós, 1864.

Palm, L. de, comp. *E lantamentu de 1795. Datos oral. 200 aña lantamentu di katibu.* Curaçao: self-published, 1995.

Paula, A. F. de, comp. *1795: De Slaven Opstand van Curaçao: Een Bronnenuit-*

gave van de originale overheidsdocumenten. Curaçao: Centraal Historisch Archief, 1974.

Prefecto Apostolico di Curaçao na Cristian di su mision: E teksto imprimí di mas bieu na Papiamentu de 1833. Curaçao: Stichting Libri Antilliani, no date.

Ramos, Demetrio, comp. *Las Capitulaciones de descubrimiento y rescate.* Valladolid, Museo de Colón y Seminario Americanista de la Universidad, 1981.

Sainsbury, W. Noel, ed. *Calendar of State Papers, Colonial Series. America and West Indies. Preserved in the State Paper Department of Her Majesty's Public Record Office.* Multiple volumes. London: Her Majesty's Stationery Office, 1860–89.

Schiltkamp, J. A., and J. T. Smidt, comps. *West Indisch Plakaatboek: Publicaties en andere Wetten alsmede de oudste Resoluties Betrekking hebbende op Curaçao, Aruba, Bonaire.* 2 vols. Amsterdam: S. Emmering, 1978.

Smith, Adam. *An Inquiry into the Nature and Causes of the Wealth of Nations.* 1776. New York: Modern Library, 1937.

Toro, Alfonso, comp. *Los judíos en la Nueva España: Documentos del siglo XVI correspondientes al ramo de Inquisición.* 1932. México: Fondo de Cultura Económica, 1993.

Torres Pantín, Cármen, comp. *Indice sobre esclavos y esclavitud (Sección Civiles-Escalvos).* Caracas: Biblioteca de la Academia Nacional de la Historia, Serie Archivos y Catálogos no. 11, 1997.

Towle, D. S., ed. *Records of the Vice-Admiralty Court of Rhode Island, 1716–1752.* Washington, D.C.: American Historican Association, 1936.

Troconis de Veracoechea, Ermila, comp. *Documentos para el estudio de los esclavos negros en Venezuela.* Caracas: Biblioteca de la Academia Nacional de la Historia, Fuentes para la Historia Colonial de Venezuela no. 103, 1969.

Vespucci, Amerigo. "Letter from Seville, 1500." In *Amerigo Vespucci: Pilot Major,* ed. Frederick J. Pohl, 76–90. New York: Columbia University Press, 1944.

———. *Vida y cartas de Americo Vespucio.* Collected and published in 1745 by Angel María Bandini. Arranged and annotated by José Miglia M. Lima, Perú: Editorial PTCM, 1948.

Wiznitzer, Arnold, comp. *Records of the Earliest Jewish Community in the New World.* New York: American Jewish Historical Society, 1954.

Wright, Irene, comp. *Nederlandsche Zeevaarders op de Eilanden in de Caribische Zee en aan de Kust van Colombia en Venezuela Gedurende de Jaren 1621–1648(9): Documenten hoofdzakelijk uit het Archivo General de Indias te Sevilla.* Vol. 1: *1621–1641.* Utrecht: Kemink en Zoon, 1935.

———. *Documents concerning English Voyages to the Spanish Main, 1569–1580.* 2nd series. Vol. 81. London: Hakluyt Society, 1932.

———. *Spanish Documents concerning English Voyages to the Caribbean, 1527–1568.* 2nd series. Vol. 62. London: Hakluyt Society, 1929.

Secondary Sources

Abraham-van der Mark, Eva. "Marriage and Concubinage among the Sephardic Merchant Elite of Curaçao." In *Women and Change in the Caribbean,* ed. Janet H. Momsen, 38–49. London: James Currey, 1993.

Acosta Saignes, Miguel. *La trata de esclavos en Venezuela.* Caracas: Centro de Estudios Históricos, Revista de Historia, 1961.

Aizpurua, Ramón. *Curazao y la costa de Caracas: Introducción al estudio del contrabando de la provincia de Venezuela en tiempos de la Compañía Guipuzcoana 1730–1788.* Caracas: Biblioteca de la Academia Nacional de la Historia, 1993.

———. "En busca de la libertad: Los esclavos fugados de Curazao a Coro en el siglo XVIII." In *Influencias Africanas en las culturas tradicionales de los países andinos. Memorias,* 69–102. Bogotá, Colombia: Dipligráficas, 2001.

———. "Las mulas venezolanas y el Caribe oriental del siglo XVIII: Datos para una historia olvidada." *Tierra Firme,* no. 26 (1989): 125–39.

Akveld, Leo, and Els M. Jacobs, eds. *The Colorful World of the VOC.* Bussem, the Netherlands: THOTH, 2002.

Allaire, Louise. "Agricultural Societies in the Caribbean: The Lesser Antilles." In *Autochthonous Societies,* ed. Sued-Badillo, 195–227.

Allen, Carolyn. "Creole: The Problem of Definition." In *Questioning Creole,* ed. Shepherd and Richards, 47–63.

Almeida Mendes, António de. "The Foundations of the System: A Reassessment of the Slave Trade to the Spanish Americas in the Sixteenth and Seventeenth Centuries." In *Extending the Frontiers,* ed. Eltis and Richardson, 63–94.

American Jewish History. Special Issue, 250th Anniversary of the Dedication of Synagogue Mikve Israel-Emmanuel, Curaçao, 1732–1982. 72, no. 2 (1982).

Arauz Monfante, Celestino Andrés. *El contrabando holandés en el Caribe durante la primera mitad del siglo XVIII.* Vols. 1, 2. Caracas: Biblioteca de la Academia Nacional de la Historia, 1984.

Arbel, Benjamin. "Shipping and Toleration: The Emergence of Jewish Shipowners in the Early Modern Period." In *Seafaring and the Jews,* ed. Kashtan, 56–71.

Arbell, Mordechai. "Jewish Settlements in the French Colonies." In *Jews and the Expansion of Europe to the West, 1450–1800,* ed. Bernardini and Fiering, 287–313.

———. "Rediscovering Tucacas." *American Jewish Archives Journal* 48, no. 1(1996), 35–43.

Arcaya, Pedro Manuel. *Insurrección de los negros de la Serranía de Coro,* Caracas: Instituto Panamericano de Geografía e Historia. Comisión de Historia. Comité de Orígenes de la Emancipación. Publicación no. 7, 1949.

Arcila Farias, Eduardo. *Economía colonial de Venezuela.* Vols. 1, 2. 2nd ed. Caracas: Italgráfica, 1973.

Arends, Jacques. "The Historical Study of Creoles and the Future of Creole Studies." In *Pidgin and Creole Linguistics in the Twenty-first Century,* ed. Glenn Gilbert, 49–68. New York: Peter Lang, 2002.

Aresti de Amezaga, Vicente. *Hombres de la Compañía Guipuzcoana*. Caracas: Banco Central de Venezuela, 1963.

Bailyn Bernard. *The New England Merchants in the Seventeenth Century*. Cambridge, Mass.: Harvard University Press, 1979.

Bailyn, Bernard, and Pat Denault, eds. *Soundings in Atlantic History: Latent Structures and Intellectual Currents, 1500–1830*. Cambridge, Mass.: Harvard University Press, 2009.

Barbour, Violet. *Capitalism in Amsterdam in the Seventeenth Century*. Johns Hopkins University Studies in the Historical and Political Science 65, no. 1 (1950).

Bastide, Roger. *The African Religions of Brazil*. Baltimore: Johns Hopkins University Press, 1978.

Bauer, Ralph, and José Antonio Mazzotti, eds. *Creole Subjects in the Colonial Americas: Empires, Texts, Identities*. Chapel Hill: University of North Carolina Press, 2009.

Bell, Herbert C. "The West India Trade before the American Revolution." *American Historical Review* 22, no. 2 (1917): 272–87.

Benjamin, Alan. *Jews of the Dutch Caribbean: Exploring Ethnic Identity on Curaçao*. London: Routledge, 2002.

Bennett, Herman. *Africans in Colonial Mexico: Absolutism, Christianity, and Afro-Creole Consciousness, 1570–1640*. Bloomington: Indiana University Press, 2003.

Bentley, Jerry H. *Old World Encounters: Cross-Cultural Contacts and Exchanges in Pre-Modern Times*. New York: Oxford University Press, 1993.

———. "Regional Histories, Global Processes, Cross-Cultural Interactions." In *Interactions*, ed. Bentley, Bridenthal, and Yang, 1–13. Honolulu: University of Hawai'i Press, 2005.

———. "Sea and Ocean Basins as Frameworks of Historical Analysis." *Geographical Review* 89, no. 2 (1999): 215–25.

Bentley, Jerry H., Renate Bridenthal, and Anand A. Yang, eds. *Interactions: Transregional Perspectives on World History*. Honolulu: University of Hawai'i Press, 2005.

Benton, Lauren. *Law and Colonial Cultures: Legal Regimes in World History, 1400–1900*. Cambridge: Cambridge University Press, 2002.

———. *A Search for Sovereignty: Law and Geography in European Empires, 1400–1900*. Cambridge: Cambridge University Press, 2010.

Berlin, Ira. "From Creole to African: Atlantic Creoles and the Origins of African-American Society in Mainland North America." *William and Mary Quarterly*, 3rd series, 53, no. 2 (1996): 251–88.

———. *Many Thousands Gone: The First Two Centuries of Slavery in North America*. Cambridge, Mass.: Harvard University Press, 1998.

Bernardini, Paolo, and Norman Fiering, eds. *The Jews and the Expansion of Europe to the West, 1450–1800*. New York: Berghahn Books, 2001.

Bernfeld, Tirtsah Levie. "Financing Poor Relief in the Spanish-Portuguese Community in Amsterdam." In *Dutch Jewry*, ed. Israel and Salverda, 63–102.

Bickerton, Derek. "An Afro-Creole Origin for Eena Meena Mina Mo." *American Speech* 57, no. 3 (1982): 225–28.

———. "Perspectives on Creole Language History." *New West Indian Guide* 73, no. 1/2 (1999): 97–102.

———. "Pidgin and Creole Studies." *Annual Review of Anthropology* 5 (1976): 169–93.

Bickterton, Derek, and Aquilas Escalante. "Palenquero: A Spanish-Based Creole of Northern Colombia." *Lingua* 24 (1970): 254–67.

Birmingham, J. C., Jr. "Lexical Decreolization in Papiamentu." *Kristòf* 4, no. 2 (1977?): 49–59.

———. "Still More on Papiamentu." *Hispania* 54, no. 2 (1971): 300–301.

Blakely, Allison. *Blacks in the Dutch World: The Evolution of Racial Imagery in a Modern Society.* Bloomington: Indiana University Press, 1993.

Bloom, Herbert I. *The Economic Activities of the Jews of Amsterdam in the Seventeenth and Eighteenth Centuries.* Williamsport, Penn.: Bayard Press, 1937.

Bodian, Miriam. *Hebrews of the Portuguese Nation: Conversos and Community in Early Modern Amsterdam.* Bloomington: Indiana University Press, 1997.

———. "'Men of the Nation': The Shaping of Converso Identity in Early Modern Europe." *Past and Present* 143 (May 1994): 48–76.

Böhm, Günter. *Los sefardíes en los dominios holandeses de América del sur y del Caribe, 1630–1750.* Frankfurt, Germany: Vervuert Verlag, 1992.

Boland, O. Nigel. "Creolisation and Creole Societies: A Cultural and Nationalist View of Caribbean Social History." In *Questioning Creole*, ed. Shepherd and Richards, 15–46.

Bolster, W. Jeffrey. *Black Jacks: African American Seamen in the Age of Sail.* Cambridge, Mass.: Harvard University Press, 1997.

Boomert, Arie. "Island Carib Archaeology." In *Wolves from the Sea*, ed. Whitehead, 23–35.

Borges, Analola. *Alvarez Abreu y su extraordinaria misión en Indias.* Tenerife: Instituto de Estudios Hispánicas de Canaras, 1963.

———. "El inicio del comercio internacional venezolano (siglo XVIII)." *Boletín de la Academia Nacional de la Historia* 46, no. 189 (1965): 27–37.

———. *La casa de Austria en Venezuela durante la guerra de la Sucesión Española (1702–1715).* Tenerife: Goya Artes Gráficas, 1963.

Bouza, Fernando. *Communication, Knowledge, and Memory in Early Modern Spain.* Translated by Sonia López and Michael Agnew. Philadelphia: University of Pennsylvania Press, 1999.

Boxer, C. R. *The Church Militant and Iberian Expansion, 1440–1770.* Baltimore: Johns Hopkins University Press, 1978.

———. *The Dutch Seaborne Empire, 1600–1800.* London: Hutchinson, 1965.

Brada, Father, O.P. *Bisdom Coro (1531–1637).* Willemstad, Curaçao, 1953.

———. *Kerkgeschiedenis Antillen*. Willemstad, Curaçao, 1963.

———. *Kerkgeschiedenis Curaçao 1680–1707*. Willemstad, Curaçao, 1961.

———. *Kerkgeschiedenis Curaçao (1742–1776)*. Willemstad, Curaçao, 1951.

———. *Pater Schabel, S.J., 1704–1713*. Willemstad, Curaçao, 1965.

———. *Paters Franciscanen op Curaçao*. Willemstad, Curaçao, 1950.

———. *Paters Jezuieten op Curaçao*. Willemstad, Curaçao, 1950.

———. *Prefect Caysedo 1715–1738*. Willemstad, Curaçao, 1956.

Brathwaite, Kamau. *The Development of Creole Society in Jamaica, 1770–1820*. 1971. Kingston: Ian Randle, 2005.

Brereton, Bridget. "Regional Histories." In *UNESCO General History of the Caribbean. Vol. 6. Methodology and Historiography of the Caribbean*, ed. B. W. Higman (New York: Palgrave Macmillan, 1999), 308–42.

Briceño Perozo, Mario. "Estudio Preliminar." In Olavarriaga, *Instrucción General y Particular del Estado Presente de la Provincia de Venezuela en los Años de 1720 y 1721*," 11–207.

Brito Figueroa, Federico. *El problema tierra y esclavos en la historia de Venezuela*. Caracas: Universidad Central de Venezuela, 1985.

———. *La estructura económica de Venezuela colonial*. Caracas: Universidad Central de Venezuela, 1963.

———. *Las insurrecciones de los esclavos negros en la sociedad colonial venezolana*. Caracas: Editorial Cantaclaro, 1961.

Broek, Aard. "The Rise of a Caribbean Island's Literature. The Case of Curaçao and Its Writing in Papiamentu." PhD diss. Free University of Amsterdam, 1990.

Brooks, George E. *Eurafricans in Western Africa: Commerce, Social Status, Gender, and Religious Observance from the Sixteenth to the Eighteenth Century*. Athens: Ohio University Press, 2003.

Buddingh', Bernard R. "Hendrik Schielach, Builder or Bungler?" In *Building Up the Future from the Past*, ed. Coomans, Newton, and Coomans-Eustatia, 115–21.

———. *Otrobanda: 'Aan de oversijde van deese haven,' de geschiedenis van Otrobanda, stadsdeel van Willemstad, Curaçao van 1696 tot 1755*. Willemstad, Curaçao, 2006.

———. *Van Punt en Snoa: Ontstaan en groi van Willemstad, Curaçao vanaf 1634, de Willemstad tussen 1700 en 1732 en de bouwgeschiedenisvan de synagoge Mikvé Israel-Emanuel 1730–1732*. 's-Hertogenbosch, the Netherlands: Aldus, 1994.

Buenaventura de Carrocera, P. *Misión de los Capuchinos en los Llanos de Caracas*. Caracas: Biblioteca de la Academia Nacional de Historia, 1972.

Buisseret, David, and Steven G. Reinhardt, eds. *Creolization in the Americas*. College Station: Texas A&M University Press, 2000.

Bushnell, Amy Turner, and Jack P. Greene. "Peripheries, Centers, and the Construction of Early Modern American Empires." In *Negotiated Empires*, ed. Daniels and Kennedy, 1–14.

Buurt, Gerard van. "Caquetío Indians on Curaçao during Colonial Times and Caquetío Words in the Papiamentu Language." In *Leeward Voices*, ed. Nicholas Faraclas et al.

Buurt, G. van, and S. M. Joubert. *Stemmen uit het Verleden: Indiaanse woorden in het Papiamentu*. Alphen aan den Rijn, the Netherlands: Van Buurt Boek Produkties, 1997.

Callalloo. Special Issue: Caribbean Literature from Suriname, the Netherlands Antilles, Aruba, and the Netherlands 21, no. 3 (1998).

Cain, Artwell, ed. *Tula: De Slavenopstand van 1795 op Curaçao*. Amsterdam: NiNsee/Amrit, 2009.

Canny, Nicholas, and Anthony Pagden, eds. *Colonial Identity in the Atlantic World, 1500–1800*. Princeton, N.J.: Princeton University Press, 1987.

Caribbean Quarterly. Special issue, Konversations in Kreole. Essays in Honour of Kamau Brathwaite 44, no. 1/2 (1998).

Carney, Judith. *Black Rice: The African Origins of Rice Cultivation in the Americas*. Cambridge, Mass.: Harvard University Press, 2001.

Castillo Lara, Lucas Guillermo. *Curiepe: Orígenes históricos*. Caracas, Venezuela: Biblioteca de la Academia Nacional de Historia, 1981.

———. *Las acciones militares del Gobernador Ruy Fernández de Fuenmayor (1637–1644)*. Caracas, Venezuela: Biblioteca de la Academia Nacional de Historia, 1978.

Cervantes-Rodríguez, Ana Margarita, and Amy Lutz. "Coloniality of Power, Immigration, and the English-Spanish Assymetry in the United States." *Nepantla: Views from the South* 4, no. 3 (2003): 532–60.

Cesarani, David, ed. *Port Jews: Jewish Communities in Cosmopolitan Maritime Trading Centres, 1550–1950*. London: Frank Cass, 2002.

Cesarani, David, and Gemma Romain, eds. *Jews and Port Cities, 1590–1990: Commerce, Community and Cosmopolitanism*. London: Vallentine Mitchell, 2006.

Cohen, Abner. "Cultural Strategies in the Organization of Trading Diasporas." In *The Development of Indigenous Trade and Markets in West Africa*, ed. Claude Meillassoux, 266–79. London: Oxford University Press, 1971.

Cohen, Jeremy David. "Cultural and Commercial Intermediaries in an Extra-Legal System of Exchange. The *Prácticos* of the Venezuelan Littoral in the Eighteenth Century." *Itinerario* 27 no. 2 (2003): 105–24.

———. "Informal Commercial Networks, Social Control, and Political Power in the Province of Venezuela, 1700–1757." PhD diss. University of Florida, 2003.

Cohen, Martin A., and Abraham J. Peck, eds. *Sephardim in the Americas: Studies in Culture and History*. Tuscaloosa: University of Alabama Press, 1993.

Coomans, Henry E., Michael A. Newton, and Maritza Coomans-Eustatia, eds. *Building Up the Future from the Past: Studies on the Architecture and Historic Monuments in the Dutch Caribbean*. Zutphen, the Netherlands: De Walburg Press, 1990.

Coomans-Eustatia, Maritza, Henry E. Coomans, and T. van der Lee, eds. *Breekbare banden: feiten en visies over Aruba, Bonaire en Curaçao na de Vrede van Munster, 1648–1998*. Bloemendaal: Stichting Libri Antilliani, 1998.

Cordingly, David. *Women Sailors and Sailors' Women: An Untold Maritime History*. New York: Random House, 2001.

Costigan, Lúcia Helena. "Self- and Collective Identity among New Christians in the Periphery of the Iberian Empires: Bento Teixeira, Ambrósio Fernandes Brandão, and Manuel Beckman." In *Creole Subjects in the Colonial Americas*, ed. Bauer and Mazzotti, 241–64.

Creighton, Margaret S., and Lisa Norling, eds. *Iron Men, Wooden Women: Gender and Seafaring in the Atlantic World, 1700–1920*. Baltimore: Johns Hopkins University Press, 1996.

Crespo Solana, Ana, and Manuel Herrero Sánchez, eds. *España y las 17 provincias de los paises bajos: una revision histiorgráfica (XVI-XVIII)*. Córdoba: Universidad de Córdoba, 2002.

Curtin, Philip D. *The Atlantic Slave Trade: A Census*. Madison: University of Wisconsin Press, 1969.

———. *Cross-Cultural Trade in World History*. Cambridge: Cambridge University Press, 1984.

Daniels, Christine, and Michael V. Kennedy, eds. *Negotiated Empires: Centers and Peripheries in the Americas, 1500–1820*. New York: Routledge, 2002.

Davies, D. W. *A Primer of Dutch Seventeenth Century Overseas Trade*. The Hague: Martinus Nijhoff, 1961.

Davies, K. G. *The North Atlantic World in the Seventeenth Century*. Vol. 4 of *Europe and the World in the Age of Expansion*. Minneapolis: University of Minnesota Press, 1974.

Davis, Ralph. *The Rise of the Atlantic Economies*. Ithaca, N.Y.: Cornell University Press, 1973.

DeCamp, David. "The Field of Creole Language Studies." *Latin American Research Review* 3, no. 3 (1968): 25–46.

Díaz-Mas, Paloma. *Sephardim: The Jews from Spain*. Translated by George K. Zucker. Chicago: University of Chicago Press, 1992.

Diouf, Sylviane A. *Servants of Allah: African Muslims Enslaved in the Americas*. New York: New York University Press, 1998.

Do Rego, Charles P. *Sklabitut i rebelion 1795*. Curaçao: Asosiashon Promoshon Konsenshi Istóriko. No date (1983?).

Drescher, Seymour. "Jews and New Christians in the Atlantic Slave Trade." In *Jews and the Expansion of Europe to the West*, ed. Bernardini and Fiering, 439–70.

Dubois, Laurent. *A Colony of Citizens: Revolution and Slave Emancipation in the French Caribbean, 1787–1804*. Chapel Hill: University of North Carolina Press, 2004.

Dunn, Richard S. *Sugar and Slaves: The Rise of the Planter Class in the Eng-*

lish West Indies, 1624–1713. Chapel Hill: University of North Carolina Press, 1972.

Ebert, Christopher. "Dutch Trade with Brazil before the Dutch West India Company, 1587–1621." In *Riches from Atlantic Commerce*, ed. Postma and Enthoven, 49–75.

Eckkrammer, Eva Martha. "The Standardisation of Papiamentu: New Trends, Problems, and Perspectives." *Bulletin suisse de linguistique appliquée* 69, no. 1 (1999): 59–74

Elliott, John. "Introduction: Colonial Identity in the Atlantic World." In *Colonial Identity in the Atlantic World*, ed. Canny and Pagden, 3–13.

Eltis, David, Philip Morgan, and David Richardson. "Agency and Disapora in Atlantic History: Reassessing the African Contribution to Rice Cultivation in the Americas." *American Historical Review* 112, no. 5 (2007): 1329–58.

Eltis, David, and David Richardson, eds. *Extending the Frontiers: Essays on the New Transatlantic Slave Trade Database*. New Haven, Conn.: Yale University Press, 2008.

Emmanuel, Isaac S. *The Jews of Coro, Venezuela*. Monographs of the American Jewish Archives no. 8. Edited by Jacob R. Marcus and Stanley F. Chyet. Cincinnati: American Jewish Archives, 1973.

———. *Precious Stones of the Jews of Curaçao*. New York: Block, 1957.

Emmanuel, Isaac S., and Suzanne Emmanuel. *History of the Jews of the Netherlands Antilles*. Vols. 1, 2. Cincinnati: American Jewish Archives, 1970.

Emmer, Pieter. "The Dutch and the Making of the Second Atlantic System." In *Dutch in the Atlantic Economy*, by Emmer, 11–32.

———. *The Dutch in the Atlantic Economy, 1580–1800*. Aldershot: Ashgate, 1998.

———. "History of the Dutch Slave Trade: A Bibliographic Survey." *Journal of Economic History* 32, no. 3 (1972): 728–47.

———. "'Jesus Christ Was Good, but Trade Was Better': An Overview of the Transit Trade of the Dutch Antilles, 1634–1795." In *Dutch in the Atlantic Economy*, by Emmer, 91–109.

———. "The West India Company, 1621–1791: Dutch or Atlantic?" In *Dutch in the Atlantic Economy*, by Emmer, 65–90.

Emmer, Pieter, and Ernst van den Boogaart. "The Dutch Participation in the Atlantic Slave Trade, 1596–1650." In *Dutch in the Atlantic Economy*, by Emmer, 33–63.

Enthoven, Victor. "An Assessment of Dutch Transatlantic Commerce, 1585–1817." In *Riches from Atlantic Commerce*, ed. Postma and Enthoven, 385–445.

———. "Early Dutch Expansion in the Atlantic Region, 1585–1621." In *Riches from Atlantic Commerce*, ed. Postma and Enthoven, 17–47.

Faber, Eli. *Jews, Slaves, and the Slave Trade: Setting the Record Straight*. New York: New York University Press, 1998.

Faraclas, Nicholas, et al., eds. *Leeward Voices: Fresh Perspectives on Papiamentu and the Literatures and Cultures of the ABC Islands*. Proceedings of the Eleventh Annual Eastern Caribbean Island Cultures Conference. Curaçao: Fundashon pa Planificashon di Idioma, 2008.

Felice Cardot, Carlos. *Curazao hispánico (Antagonismo flamenco-español)*. Caracas: Ediciones de la Presidencia de la República, 1982.

———. *La rebelión de Andresote (Valles del Yaracuy, 1730–1733)*. Caracas: Imprenta Nacional, 1952.

———. *Rebeliones, motines y movimientos de masas en el siglo XVIII venezolano (1730–1781)*. Caracas: Academia Nacional de la Historia, 1977.

Ferry, Robert J. *The Colonial Elite of Early Caracas: Formation and Crisis, 1567–1767*. Berkeley: University of California Press, 1989.

Fog Olwig, Karen, ed. *Small Islands, Large Questions: Society, Culture, and Resistance in the Post-Emancipation Caribbean*. London: Frank Cass, 1995.

Fontaine, Pierre-Michel. "Language, Society, and Development: Dialectic of French and Creole Use in Haiti." *Latin American Perspectives* 8, no. 1 (1981): 28–46.

Fortune, Stephen Alexander. *Merchants and Jews: The Struggle for British West Indian Commerce, 1650–1750*. Gainesville: University Press of Florida, 1984.

Fouse, Gary C. *The Story of Papiamentu: A Study in Slavery and Language*. Lanham, Md.: University Press of America, 2002.

Friede, Juan. *Los Welser en la conquista de Venezuela*. Caracas: Ediciones Edime, 1961.

Friedman, Saul S. *Jews and the American Slave Trade*. New Brunswick, N.J.: Transaction, 1998.

Gaastra, Femme S. *De geschiedenis van de VOC*. Zutphen, the Netherlands: Walburg Press, 2002.

Gaaij Fortman, B. de. "Een belangrijk dagboek." *De Westindies Gids* 6 (1924–25): 241–70.

Games, Alison. *The Web of Empire: English Cosmopolitans in an Age of Expansion, 1560–1660*. Oxford: Oxford University Press, 2008.

Garfield, Robert. "A Forgotten Fragment of the Diaspora: The Jews of São Tomé Island, 1492–1654." In *Expulsion of the Jews*, ed. Waddington and Williamson, 73–87.

Garrigus, John D. "Blue and Brown: Contraband Indigo and the Rise of a Free Colored Planter Class in French Saint-Domingue." *Americas* 50, no. 2 (1993): 233–63.

———. "New Christians/'New Whites': Sephardic Jews, Free People of Color, and Citizenship in French Saint-Domingue, 1760–1789." In *Jews and the Expansion of Europe to the West*, ed. Bernardini and Fiering, 314–32.

Gaspar, David Barry. *Bondmen and Rebels: A Study of Master-Slave Relations in Antigua*. Durham: Duke University Press, 1993.

Gaspar, David Barry, and Darlene Clark Hine, eds. *Beyond Bondage: Free Women of Color in the Americas*. Urbana: University of Illinois Press, 2004.

Gaspar, David Barry, and David Patrick Geggus, eds. *A Turbulent Time: The*

French Revolution and the Greater Caribbean. Bloomington: Indiana University Press, 1997.

Gedenkboek Nederland-Curaçao, 1634–1934. Amsterdam: de Bussy, 1934.

Geggus, David. "The Caribbean in the Age of Revolution." In *The Age of Revolutions in Global Context,* ed. David Armitage and Sanjay Subrah, 83–100. New York: Palgrave Macmillan, 2010.

Geographical Review. Special issue. Oceans Connect. 89, no. 2 (1999).

Geyl, Pieter. *The Netherlands in the Seventeenth Century.* Vols. 1, 2. London: Ernest Benn, 1964.

Gil Rivas, Pedro A., Luis Dovale Prado, and Lidia Lusmila Bello. *La insurrección de los negros de la sierra coriana, 10 de mayo de 1795: Notas para la discusión.* Caracas: Dirección de Cultura, Universidad Central de Venezuela, 1996.

Gómez Canedo, Lino. *Evangelización y conquista: Experiencia franciscano en Hispanoamérica.* Mexico: Editorial Porrúa, 1977.

Gomes Casseres, Charles. "Papiamentu: The Language of Curaçao and its Sephardim." Unpublished manuscript. Curaçao, 1997.

Gonzalez Batista, Carlos. "Conversiones judaicas en Coro durante la época española." *Croizatia* 1, no. 1 (2000): 15–22.

———. *Antillas y Tierra Firme: Historia de la Influencia de Curazao en la Arquitectura Antigua de Venezuela.* Caracas: Refinería Isla (Curazao) S.A., 1990.

———. "Prólogo." In *Documentos para la historia de las antillas neerlandesas* (Archivo Histórico de Coro, Fondo Registro Principal I. Coro: Centro de Investigaciones Históricas Pedro Manuel Arcaya, 1987), 7–31.

Goslinga, Cornelis C. "Curaçao as a Slave Trading Center during the War of the Spanish Succession (1702–1714)." *New West Indian Guide* 1/2, 52nd year (November 1977): 1–50.

———. *The Dutch in the Caribbean and in the Guianas, 1680–1791.* Assen/Maastricht, the Netherlands: van Gorcum, 1985.

———. *The Dutch in the Caribbean and on the Wild Coast, 1580–1680.* Assen, the Netherlands: van Gorcum, 1971.

———. *A Short History of the Netherlands Antilles and Surinam.* The Hague: Martinus Nijhoff, 1979.

Grahn, Lance. *The Political Economy of Smuggling: Regional Informal Economies in Early Bourbon New Granada.* Boulder, Colo.: Westview Press, 1997.

Granda, Germán de. "El repertorio linguistic de los sefarditas de Curaçao durante los siglos XVII y XVIII y el problema del origen del papiamentu." *Romance Philology* 28, no. 1 (1974): 1–16.

———. *Español de América, español de Africa y hablas criollas hispánicas: Cambios, contactos, y contextos.* Madrid: Gredos, 1994.

———. "On the Study of the Creole Dialects in Spanish-Speaking Areas." *Orbis* 19 (1970): 72–81.

———. "Papiamento en Hispanoamerica (Siglos XVII–XIX)." *Thesaurus: Boletín del Instituto Caro y Cuervo* 28, no. 1 (1973): 1–13.

Gray, Edward G., and Norman Fiering, eds. *The Language Encounter in the Americas, 1492–1800*. New York: Berghahn Books, 2000.

Green, Tobias. "Further Considerations on the Sephardim of the Petit Côte." *History in Africa* 32 (2005): 165–83.

Hall, N. A. T. "Maritime Maroons: *Grand Marronage* from the Danish West Indies." *William and Mary Quarterly*, 3rd series, 42 (October 1985): 476–97.

Hancock, David. *Citizens of the World: London Merchants and the Integration of the British Atlantic Community, 1735–1785*. Cambridge: Cambridge University Press, 1995.

———. *Oceans of Wine: Madeira and the Emergence of American Trade and Taste*. New Haven, Conn.: Yale University Press, 2009.

Harris, Tracy K. *Death of a Language: The History of Judeo-Spanish*. Newark: University of Delaware Press, 1994.

Hart, Emma. "Building Charleston: The Expansion of an Eighteenth-Century British Atlantic Town." In *Material Culture in Ango-America*, ed. Shields, 202–20.

Hartog, Johannes. "Building the Fortchurch." In *Building Up the Future from the Past*, ed. Coomans, Newton, and Coomans-Eustatia, 122–27.

———. *Curaçao: From Colonial Dependence to Autonomy*. Aruba: De Wit, 1968.

———. *Curaçao: Van Kolonie tot Autonomie*. Aruba: De Wit, 1961.

———. "José Díaz Pimienta: Rogue Priest." *American Jewish Archives* 34, no. 2 (1982): 153–63.

Haviser, Jay B. "Amerindian Cultural Geography on Curaçao." PhD diss. Rijksuniversiteit, 1987.

Haviser, Jay B., and Nadia Simmons-Brito. "Excavations at the Zuurzak Site: A Possible 17th Century Dutch Slave Camp on Curacao, Netherlands Antilles." In Proceedings of the 15th International Congress for Caribbean Archaeology, ed. Ricardo Alegria and Miguel Rodriquez, 71–82. San Juan, Puerto Rico: Centro de Estudios Avanzados de Puerto Rico y el Caribe, 1995,

Heijer, Henk den. *De geschiedenis van de WIC*. Zutphen, the Netherlands: Walberg Pers, 2002.

———. "The Dutch West India Company, 1621–1791." In *Riches from Atlantic Commerce*, ed. Postma and Enthoven, 77–112.

———. "The West African Trade of the Dutch West India Company, 1674–1740." In *Riches from Atlantic Commerce*, ed. Postma and Enthoven, 139–69.

Henriques, May. *Loke a keda pa similla*. Curaçao: self-published, 1991.

———. *Ta Asina? O ta Asana? Abla, uzu, i kustumber sefardí*. Curaçao: self-published; 1988.

Herndon, Ruth Wallace. "The Domestic Cost of Seafaring: Town Leaders and Seamen's Families in Eighteenth-Century Rhode Island." In *Iron Men, Wooden Women*, ed. Creighton and Norling, 55–69.

Hertzberg, Arthur. *The Jews in America: Four Centuries of an Uneasy Encounter.* New York: Columbia University Press, 1997.

Heywood, Linda, ed. *Central Africans and Cultural Transformations in the American Diaspora.* Cambridge: Cambridge University Press, 2002.

Heywood, Linda M., and John K. Thornton. *Central Africans, Atlantic Creoles, and the Foundation of the Americas, 1585–1660.* Cambridge: Cambridge University Press, 2007.

Hoetink, H. *Caribbean Race Relations: A Study of Two Variants.* London: Oxford University Press, 1967.

———. *Het patroon van de oude Curaçaose samenleving.* 1958. Amsterdam: S. Emmering, 1987.

Hoetink, H., ed. *Encyclopedie van de Nederlandse Antillen.* Amsterdam: Elsevier, 1969.

Hoog, L. de. *Van Rebellie tot Revolutie: Oorzaken en achtergronden van de Curaçaose slavenopstanden in 1750 en 1795.* Curaçao: University of the Netherlands Antilles , 1983.

Hoyer, W. M. *Papiamentoe i su Manera de Skirbié.* Curaçao: Bethencourt, 1918.

Hoyle, Brian. "Fields of Tension: Development Dynamics at the Port-City Interface." In *Port Jews,* ed. Cesarani, 12–30.

Huber, Magnus, and Mikael Parkvall, eds. *Spreading the Word: The Issue of Diffusion among the Atlantic Creoles.* London: University of Westminster Press, 1999.

Hussey, Roland Dennis. *The Caracas Company, 1728–1784: A Study in the History of Spanish Monopolistic Trade.* Cambridge, Mass.: Harvard University Press, 1934.

Huussen, Arend H. "The Legal Position of the Jews in the Dutch Republic, 1590–1796." In *Dutch Jewry,* ed. Israel and Salverda, 25–41.

Huussen, Arend H., Jr. *Historical Dictionary of the Netherlands.* Lanham, Md.: Scarecrow Press, 1998.

Hymes, D., ed. *Pidginization and Creolization of Languages.* Cambridge: Cambridge University Press, 1971.

Inikori, Joseph E., and Stanley L. Engerman, eds. *The Atlantic Slave Trade: Effects on Economies, Societies, and Peoples in Africa, the Americas, and Europe.* Durham, N.C.: Duke University Press, 1992.

Israel, Jonathan I. *Diasporas within a Diaspora: Jews, Crypto-Jews and World Maritime Empires (1540–1740).* Leiden, the Netherlands: Brill, 2002.

———. *Dutch Primacy in World Trade, 1585–1740.* Oxford: Clarendon Press, 1989.

———. *The Dutch Republic: Its Rise, Greatness, and Fall, 1477–1806.* Oxford: Clarendon Press, 1998 (corrected edition).

———. *The Dutch Republic and the Hispanic World, 1606–1661.* Oxford: Clarendon Press, 1982.

———. *Empires and Entrepôts: The Dutch, the Spanish Monarchy and the Jews, 1585–1713.* London: Hambledon Press, 1990.

———. *European Jewry in the Age of Mercantilism, 1550–1750*. Oxford: Clarendon Press, 1985.

———. Introduction to *Dutch Jewry*, ed. Israel and Salverda, 1–21.

———. "Jews and Crypto-Jews in the Atlantic World System, 1500–1800." In *Atlantic Diasporas*, ed. Kagan and Morgan, 3–17.

———. "The Jews of Dutch America." In *Jews and the Expansion of Europe*, ed. Bernardini and Fiering, 335–49.

———. "The Legal Position of the Jews in the Dutch Republic 1590–1796." In *Dutch Jewry*, ed. Israel and Salverda, 25–41.

Israel, Jonathan, and Reinier Salverda, eds. *Dutch Jewry: Its History and Secular Culture (1500–2000)*. Leiden, the Netherlands: Brill, 2002.

Jacobs, Bart. "On the Dutch Presence in 17th Century Senegambia and the Emergence of Papiamentu." Unpublished paper. 2009.

———. "The Origins of Portuguese Features in Papiamentu." In *Leeward Voices*, ed. Faraclas et al., 11–38.

———. "The Upper Guinea Origins of Papiamentu: Linguistic and Historical Evidence," *Diachronica* 26, no. 3 (2009): 319–79.

Jarvis, Michael J. *In the Eye of All Trade: Bermuda, Bermudians, and the Maritime Atlantic World, 1680–1783*. Chapel Hill: University of North Carolina Press, 2010.

———. "Maritime Masters and Seafaring Slaves in Bermuda, 1680–1783." *William and Mary Quarterly*, 3rd series, 59, no. 3 (2002): 585–622.

Jeuda, David M. "Early Newspaper Texts in Papiamentu: Internal and External Comparisons." In *Studies in Caribbean Language*, ed. Lawrence D. Carrington, 70–74. St. Augustine, Trinidad: Society for Caribbean Linguistics, 1983.

Jordaan, Han. "The Curaçao Slave Market: From *Asiento* Trade to Free Trade." In *Riches from Atlantic Commerce*, ed. Postma and Enthoven, 219–57.

———. "Free Blacks and Coloreds and the Administration of Justice in Eighteenth-Century Curaçao." *New West Indian Guide* 84, no. 1/2 (2010): 63–86.

———. "Patriots, Privateers, and International Politics: The Myth of the Conspiracy of Jean Baptiste Tierce Cadet." In *Curaçao in the Age of Revolutions*, ed. Klooster and Oostindie, 141–69.

Jordán, Josefina. "Acercamiento a la rebelión encabezada por José Leonardo Chirinos in 1795." In *Documentos de la Insurrección de José Leonardo Chirinos*, 1:10–29.

Joubert, Sidney. "Literatura Neerlandoantillana." *Kristòf* 3, no. 2 (1976): 75–95.

Jourdan, C. "Pidgins and Creoles: The Blurring of Categories." *Annual Review of Anthropology* 20 (1991): 187–209.

Kagan, Richard L. and Philip D. Morgan, eds. *Atlantic Diasporas: Jews, Conversos, and Crypto-Jews in the Age of Mercantilism, 1500–1800*. Baltimore: Johns Hopkins University Press, 2009.

Kamen, Henry. *Empire: How Spain Became a World Power, 1492–1763*. New York: HarperCollins, 2003.

———. *The Spanish Inquisition: A Historical Revision*. New Haven, Conn.: Yale University Press, 1997.

Kaplan, Yosef. "The Curaçao and Amsterdam Jewish Communities in the 17th and 18th Centuries." *American Jewish History* 72, no. 2 (1982): 193–211.

Karner, Frances P. *The Sephardics of Curaçao: A Study of Socio-cultural Patterns in Flux*. Assen, the Netherlands: van Gorcum, 1969.

Karras, Alan L. *Smuggling: Contraband and Corruption in World History*. Lanham, Md.: Rowman and Littlefield, 2010.

———. "Smuggling and Its Malcontents." In *Interactions*, ed. Bentley, Bridenthal, and Yang, 135–49.

Kashtan, Nadav, ed. *Seafaring and the Jews*. London: Frank Cass, 2001.

Kinkor, Kenneth J. "Black Men under the Black Flag." In *Bandits at Sea: A Pirates Reader*, ed. C. R. Pennell, 195–210. New York: New York University Press, 2001.

Klooster, Wim. "Between Hapsburg Neglect and Bourbon Assertiveness: Hispano-Dutch Relations in the New World, 1650–1750." In *España y las 17 provincias de los países bajos: una revision histórica*, ed. Ana Crespo Solano and Manuel Herrero Sánchez, 705–18. Córdoba, Spain: Universidad de Córdoba, 2002,

———. "Contraband Trade by Curaçao's Jews with Countries of Idolatry, 1660–1800." *Studia Rosenthaliana* 31: 1/2 (1997): 58–73.

———. "Curaçao and the Caribbean Transit Trade." In *Riches from Atlantic Commerce*, ed. Postma and Enthoven, 203–18.

———. "Curaçao ten tijde van de West-Indische Compagnie: Een Atlantische entrepôt zonder weerga." *De Archiefvriend* 5, no. 4 (1999): 2–8.

———. "Economische malaise, politieke onrust en misdaad op Curaçao in de Patriottentijd." In *Breekbare banden*, ed. Coomans-Eustatia, Coomans, and van der Lee, 101–8.

———. "Het begin van de Nederlandse slavenhandel in het Atlantisch gebied." In *Alle streken van het kompas: Maritieme geschiedenis in Nederland*, ed. Maurits Ebben, Henk Heijer, and Joost Schokkenbroek, 249–62. Zutphen: Walburg Pers, 2010.

———. *Illicit Riches: Dutch Trade in the Caribbean 1648–1795*. Leiden, the Netherlands: KITLV Press, 1998.

———. "Inter-Imperial Smuggling in the Americas, 1600–1800." In *Soundings in Atlantic History*, ed. Bailyn and Denault, 141–80.

———. "The Jews in Suriname and Curaçao." In *Jews and the Expansion of Europe to the West*, ed. Bernardini and Fiering, 350–68.

———. "Manumission in an Entrepôt: The Case of Curaçao." In *Paths to Freedom: Manumission in the Atlantic World*, ed. Rosemary Brane Shulte and Randy J. Sparks, 161–73. Columbia: University of South Carolina Press, 2009.

———. "Networks of Colonial Entrepreneurs: The Founders of the Jewish Settlements in Dutch America, 1650s and 1660s." In *Atlantic Diasporas*, ed. Kagan and Morgan, 33–49.

———. "An Overview of Dutch Trade with the Americas, 1600–1800." In *Riches from Atlantic Commerce*, ed. Postma and Enthoven, 365–83.

———. "The Rising Expectations of Free and Enslaved Blacks in the Greater Caribbean." In *Curaçao in the Age of Revolutions*, ed. Klooster and Oostindie, 57–74.

———. "Slavenvaart op Spaanse kusten: De Nederlandse met Spaans Amerika, 1648–1701." *Tijdschrift voor zeegeschiedenis* 16, no. 2 (1997): 121–40.

———. "Subordinate but Proud: Curaçao's Free Blacks and Mulattoes in the Eighteenth Century." *New West Indian Guide* 68, no. 3/4 (1994): 283–300.

———. "Winds of Change: Colonization, Commerce, and Consolidation in the Seventeenth-Century Atlantic World." *De Halve Maen* 70, no. 3 (1997): 53–58.

Klooster, Wim, and Gert Oostindie, eds. *Curaçao in the Age of Revolutions, 1795–1800*. Leiden, the Netherlands: KITLV Press, 2011.

Knight, Franklin W., ed. *The Slave Societies of the Caribbean: General History of the Caribbean*. Vol. 2. London: UNESCO, 1997.

Knight, Franklin W., and Peggy K. Liss, eds. *Atlantic Port Cities: Economy, Culture, and Society in the Atlantic World, 1650–1850*. Knoxville: University of Tennessee Press, 1991.

Koot, Christian J. *Empire at the Periphery: British Colonists, Anglo-Dutch Trade, and the Development of the British Atlantic, 1621–1713*. New York: New York University Press, 2011.

Kunst, A. J. M. *Recht, Commercie en Kolonialisme in West-Indie vanaf de Zestiende tot in de Negentiende Eeuw*. Zutphen, the Netherlands: Walburg Press, 1981.

Lampe, Armando. "Christianity and Slavery in the Dutch Caribbean." In *Christianity in the Caribbean: Essays on Church History*, ed. Armando Lampe, 126–53. Barbados: University of the West Indies Press, 2001.

———. *Mission or Submission? Moravian and Catholic Missionaries in the Dutch Caribbean during the 19th Century*. Göttingen: Vandenhoek and Ruprecht, 2001.

———. *Descubrir a Dios en el Caribe: Ensayos sobre la historia de la iglesia*. San José, Costa Rica, DEI, 1991.

———. *Yo te nombro libertad: Iglesia y Estado in la sociedad esclavista de Curazao (1816–1863)*. PhD diss. Vrije Universiteit te Amsterdam, 1988.

Lamur, Humphrey E. "Demographic Performance of Two Slave Populations of the Dutch-Speaking Caribbean." *Boletin de Estudios Latinoamericanos y del Caribe* 30 (June 1981): 87–102.

Landers, Jane. "Maroon Women in Colonial Spanish America: Case Studies in the Circum-Caribbean from the Sixteenth through the Eighteenth Centuries." In *Beyond Bondage*, ed. Gaspar and Hine, 3–18.

Lane, Kris. *Quito, 1599: City and Colony in Transition*. Albuquerque: University of New Mexico Press, 2002.

Lenz, Rodolfo. *El Papiamento, la Lengua Criolla de Curazao: La Gramática más Sencilla*. Santiago de Chile: Balcells, 1928.

Levi Bernfield, Tirtsah. "Financing Poor-Relief in the Spanish-Portuguese Community in Amsterdam." In *Dutch Jewry*, ed. Israel and Salverda, 63–102.

Levine, Allan. *Scattered among the Peoples: The Jewish Diaspora in Twelve Portraits*. New York: Overlook Duckworth, 2003.

Lewin, Boleslao. *La inquisición en Hispanoamérica: Judíos, protestantes y patriotas*. Buenos Aires: Editorial Proyección, 1962.

———. *La inquisición en México: Impresionantes relatos del siglo XVI*. Puebla, Mexico: Editorial J. M. Cajica, Jr., 1968.

Lewis, Martin W., and Kären E. Wigen. *The Myth of Continents: A Critique of Metageography*. Berkeley: University of California Press, 1997.

Linebaugh, Peter, and Marcus Rediker. *The Many-Headed Hydra: Sailors, Slaves, Commoners, and the Hidden History of the Revolutionary Atlantic*. Boston: Beacon Press, 2000.

Lipski, John M. "Contacto de criollos en el Caribe hispánico: contribuciones al español *bozal*." *América Negra*, no. 11 (1996): 31–60.

———. "Spanish-based Creoles in the Caribbean." In *The Handbook of Pidgin and Creole Studies*, ed. Silvia Kouwewnberg and John Victor Singler. Blackwell, 2008.

Lorenzino, Gerardo A. "African vs. Austronesian Substrate Influence on the Spanish-Based Creoles." In *Atlantic Meets Pacific: A Global View of Pidginization and Creolization*, ed. Francis Byrn and John Holm, 399–408. Amsterdam: Benjamins, 1993.

Loon, Anita van, and Enid A. C. Lucasius. "From Priest to Architect: An Architectural Review of the Roman Catholic Churches of Curaçao." In *Building Up the Future from the Past*, ed. Coomans, Newton, and Coomans-Eustatia, 54–63.

Lovejoy, Paul. *Transformations in Slavery: A History of Slavery in Africa*. Cambridge: Cambridge University Press, 2000.

Lüdtke, Jean, comp. *El español en América en el siglo XVI: Actas del simposio del Instituto Ibero-Americano de Berlin, 23 y 24 de abril de 1992*. Frankfurt: Vervuert, 1994.

Maduro, Antoine. *Bon Papiamentu (I un Appendix interesante)*. Curaçao: self-published, 1971.

———. *Kaboberdiano i Papiamento*. Curaçao: Maduro and Curiel's Bank, 1987.

———. *Palenkero i Papiamentu*. Curaçao: self-published, 1987.

Magallanes, Manuel Vicente. *Tucacas: Desde el umbral histórico de Venezuela*. Caracas, Venezuela: Academia Nacional de la Historia, 2001.

Marcus, Jacob Rader. *The Colonial American Jew, 1492–1776*. 3 vols. Detroit: Wayne State University Press, 1970.

———. *The Jew in the American World: A Source Book.* Detroit: Wayne State University Press, 1996.

Mark, Peter. "The Evolution of 'Portuguese' Identity: Luso-Africans on the Upper Guinea Coast from the Sixteenth to the Early Nineteenth Century." *Journal of African History* 40, no. 2 (1999): 173–91.

———. *"Portuguese" Style and Luso-African Identity: Precolonial Senegambia, Sixteenth to Nineteenth Centuries.* Bloomington: Indiana University Press, 2002.

Mark, Peter, and José da Silva Horta. "Catholics, Jews, and Muslims in Early Seventeenth-Century Guiné." In *Atlantic Diasporas,* ed. Kagan and Morgan, 170–290.

———. *The Forgotten Diaspora: Jewish Communities in West Africa and the Making of the Atlantic World.* Cambridge: Cambridge University Press, 2011.

———. "Two Early Seventeenth-Century Sephardic Communities on Senegal's Petite Côte." *History in Africa* 31 (2004): 231–56.

Martinus Arion, Efraim Frank. *Double Play: The Story of an Amazing World Record.* 1973. Translated by Paul Vincent. London: Faber, 1998.

———. "The Guene Kriole of the Netherlands Antilles: Its Theoretical and Practical Consequences for Better Understanding Papiamento and Other Portuguese-Based Creoles." *Anales del Caribe* 4–5 (1984–85): 335–50.

———. *The Kiss of a Slave: Papiamentu's West-African Connections.* Published PhD diss. University of Amsterdam, 1996.

———. "The Value of Guene for Folklore and Culture." In *Papers of the Third Seminar on Latin-American and Caribbean Folklore,* ed. Edwin N. Ayubi, 181–93. Curaçao: Archaeology-Anthropology Institute of the Netherlands Antilles, 1996.

———. "The Victory of the Concubines and the Nannies." In *Caribbean Creolization: Reflections on the Cultural Dynamics of Language, Literature, and Identity,* ed. Kathleen M. Balutansky and Marie-Agnès Sourieau, 110–17. Gainesville: University Press of Florida, 1998.

Martínez-Serna, J. Gabriel. "Procuradores and the Making of the Jesuits' Atlantic Network." In *Soundings in Atlantic History,* ed. Bailyn and Denault, 181–209.

Maurer, Philippe. "A Short Note about Papiamentu's Origin: Upper Guinea, Gulf of Guinea, or Elsewhere?" In *Leeward Voices,* ed. Faraclas et al., 39–47.

Mauro, Frédérik. "Merchant Communities, 1350–1750." In *Rise of Merchant Empires,* ed. Tracy, 255–86.

Meinig, D. W. *The Shaping of America: A Geographical Perspective on 500 Years of History.* Vol. 1: *Atlantic America, 1492–1800.* New Haven, Conn.: Yale University Press, 1986.

Menkman, W. R. *De West-Indische Compagnie.* Amsterdam: P. N. van Kampen & Zoon, 1947.

Metz, Allan. "'Those of the Hebrew Nation . . . ': The Sephardic Experience in Colonial Latin America." In *Sephardim in the Americas,* ed. Cohen and Peck, 209–33.

Mignolo, Walter D. *The Darker Side of the Renaissance: Literacy, Territoriality, and Colonization.* Ann Arbor: University of Michigan Press, 1995.

Mintz, Sidney. "The Socio-historical Background to Pidginization and Creolization." In *Pidginization and Creolization of Languages,* ed. Hymes, 481–96.

Mintz, Sidney W., and Richard Price. *The Birth of African-American Culture: An Anthropological Perspective.* Boston: Beacon, 1992.

Morales Padrón, Francisco. *Rebelión contra la compañía de Caracas.* Seville: Escuela de Estudios Hispano-Americanos de Sevilla, 1955.

Morón, Guillermo. *Los orígenes históricos de Venezuela.* Vol. 1. *Introducción al siglo XVI.* Madrid: Consejo Superior de Investigaciones Científicas, Instituto Gonzalo Fernandez de Oviedo, 1954.

Munteneau, Dan. *El Papiamentu, Lengua Criolla Hispánica.* Madrid: Gredos, 1996.

Navarro, Tomás. "Observaciones Sobre el Papiamento." *Nueva Revista de Filología Hispánica* 7, no. 1–2 (1953): 183–89.

Nelson, Louis P. "The Diversity of Countries: Anglican Churches in Virginia, South Carolina, and Jamaica." In *Material Culture in Ango-America,* ed. Shields, 74–101.

Nettleford, Rex. *Caribbean Cultural Identity: The Case of Jamaica.* Los Angeles: UCLA Latin American Center Publications, 1979.

Newton, Michael. "Fo'i Porta: The Wilhelminapark and its Surroundings." In *Building Up the Future from the Past,* ed. Coomans, Newton, and Coomans-Eustatia, 19–40.

Nieuwenhoff, W. van. *Gepriviligieerde priesters op Curaçao van 1701 tot 1741.* Vols. 1, 2. Amsterdam: C. L. Van Langenhuysen, year of publication unknown.

Nooijen, R. H. *De slavenparochie van Curaçao rond het jaar 1750: Een demografie van het katholieke volksdeel.* Curaçao: Institute of Archaeology and Anthropology of the Netherlands Antilles, Report no. 11. 1995.

———. *Historia di Kòrsou Katóliko: Un rekuento di Pader Hein Nooijen.* Amsterdam: Carib, 2008.

Norling, Lisa. "Ahab's Wife: Women and the American Whaling Industry, 1820–1870." In *Iron Men, Wooden Women,* ed. Creighton and Norling, 70–91.

Nusteling, Herbert P. H. "The Jews in the Republic of the United Provinces: Origin, Numbers, and Disperson." In *Dutch Jewry,* ed. Israel and Salverda, 43–62.

Oest, Eric van der. "The Forgotten Colonies of Essequibo and Demerara, 1700–1814." In *Riches from Atlantic Commerce,* ed. Postma and Enthoven, 323–61.

Olwig, Karen Fog, ed. *Small Islands, Large Questions: Society, Culture, and Resistance in the Post-Emancipation Caribbean.* London: Frank Cass, 1995.

Oostindie, Gert, ed. *Ethnicity in the Caribbean: Essays in Honor of Harry Hoetink.* London: Macmillan Caribbean, 1996.

———. "Ethnicity, Nationalism, and the Exodus: The Dutch Caribbean Predic-
ament." In *Ethnicity in the Caribbean*, ed. Oostindie, 206–31.

Ozinga, M. D. *De Monumenten van Curaçao in Woord en Beeld*. The Hague:
Staatsdrukkerij, 1959.

Palmié, Stephan. "The 'C-Word' Again." in *Creolization: History, Ethnography,
Theory*, ed. Stewart, 66–83.

Panhorst, Carlos. *Los Alemanes en Venezuela durante en siglo XVI: Carlos y la casa
Welser*. Colección Hispania. Vol. III. Serie A. Madrid: Editorial Voluntad, 1927.

Papiamentu: Problems and Possibilities. Papers presented at the conference "Papiamentu: Problema i Posibilidat." Zutphen, the Netherlands: de Walburg
Pers, 1981.

Parker, Geoffrey. *The Dutch Revolt*. Rev. ed. London: Penguin, 2002.

Parkvall, Mikael. *Out of Africa: African Influences in Atlantic Creoles*. London:
Battlebridge, 2000.

Penny, Ralph. *A History of the Spanish Language*. Cambridge: Cambridge University Press, 1997.

Perl, Matthias, and Armin Schwegler, eds. *América negra: Panorámica actual
de los estudios lingüísticos sobre variedades hispanas, portuguesas y criollas*.
Frankfurt, Germany: Vervuert Verlag, 1998.

Pérotin-Dumon, Anne. "Cabotage, Contraband, and Corsairs: The Port Cities
of Guadaloupe and their Inhabitants, 1650–1800." In *Atlantic Port Cities*, ed.
Knight and Liss, 58–86.

Pijning, Ernst. "New Christians as Sugar Cultivators and Traders in the Portuguese Atlantic, 1450–1800." In *Jews and the Expansion of Europe to the West*,
ed. Bernardini and Fiering, 485–500.

Piñero, Eugenio. "The Cacao Economy of the Eighteenth-Century Province of
Caracas and the Spanish Cacao Market." *Hispanic American Historical Review* 68, no. 1 (1988): 75–100.

———. *The Town of San Felipe and Colonial Cacao Economies*. Philadelphia:
American Philosophical Society, 1994.

Plaza, Elena. "El motín de José Leonardo Chirinos y el problema de la subversion del orden." In *Documentos de la Insurrección de José Leonardo Chirinos*
2:18–28.

Pomerantz, Kenneth, and Steven Topik. *The World That Trade Created: Society, Culture and the World Economy, 1400 to the Present*. Armonk, N.Y.: M.
E. Sharpe, 1999.

Ponce de Behrens, Marianela, Diana Rengifo, and Letizia Vaccari de Venturini, "Estudio Preliminar." In *Juicios de Residencia en la Provincia de Venezuela*, 15–78.

Postma, Johannes. "The Dispersal of African Slaves in the West by Dutch Slave
Traders, 1630–1803." In *Atlantic Slave Trade*, ed. Inikori and Engerman,
283–99.

———. "The Dutch and the Making of the Second Atlantic System." In *Slavery
and the Rise of the Atlantic System*, ed. Solow, 75–96.

———. *The Dutch in the Atlantic Slave Trade, 1600–1815.* Cambridge: Cambridge University Press, 1990.

———. "A Reassessment of the Dutch Atlantic Slave Trade." In *Riches from Atlantic Commerce,* ed. Postma and Enthoven, 115–38.

Postma, Johannes, and Victor Enthoven, eds. *Riches from Atlantic Commerce: Dutch Transatlantic Trade and Shipping, 1585–1817.* Leiden: Brill, 2003.

Price, Jacob. *Perry of London: A Family and a Firm on the Seaborne Frontier, 1615–1753.* Cambridge, Mass.: Harvard University Press, 1992.

———. "Summation: The American Panorama of Atlantic Port Cities." In *Atlantic Port Cities,* ed. Knight and Liss, 262–76.

Price, Richard. "The Miracle of Creolization: A Retrospective." *New West Indian Guide* 75, no. 1/2 (2001): 35–64.

Ramos Pérez, Demetrio. *La fundación de Venezuela: Ampiés y Coro, una singularidad historico.* Valladolid, 1978.

Reid, Basil A. *Archaeology and Geoinformatics: Case Studies from the Caribbean.* Tuscaloosa: University of Alabama Press, 2008.

Reinecke, John E. "Trade Jargons and Creole Dialects as Marginal Languages." *Social Forces* 17, no. 1 (1938): 107–18.

Renkema, W. E. *Het curaçaose plantagebedrijf in de negendiende eeuw.* Zutphen, the Netherlands: Walburg Press, 1981.

Rickford, John R. "Ethnicity as a Sociolinguistic Boundary." *American Speech* 60, no. 2 (1985): 99–125.

Rink, Oliver A. *Holland on the Hudson: An Economic and Social History of Dutch New York.* Ithaca, N.Y.: Cornell University Press, 1986.

Rojas, Arístides. *Estudios Históricos: Orígenes venezolanos.* 1891. Caracas: Oficina Central de Información, 1972.

Rosenberg, A. "The Adoption of the Dutch Language by Dutch Jewry." *Studia Rosenthaliana* 30, no. 1 (1996): 151–63.

Rowland, Robert. "New Christian, Marrano, Jew." In *Jews and the Expansion of Europe to the West,* ed. Bernardini and Fiering, 125–48.

Rupert, Linda M. "Contraband Trade and the Shaping of Colonial Societies." *Itinerario* 30, no. 3 (2006): 35–54.

———. "Inter-colonial Networks and Revolutionary Ferment in Eighteenth-Century Curaçao and Tierra Firme." In *Curaçao in the Age of Revolutions,* ed. Klooster and Oostindie, 75–96.

———. "Marronage, Manumission, and Maritime Trade in the Early Modern Caribbean." *Slavery and Abolition* 30, no. 3 (2009): 361–82.

———. "'Seeking the Waters of Baptism': Fugitive Slaves and Spanish Jurisdiction in the Early Modern Caribbean." In *Legal Pluralism and Empires, 1500–1850,* ed. Lauren Benton and Richard J. Ross. New York University Press, forthcoming.

———. "Trading Globally, Speaking Locally: Curaçao's Sephardim in the Making of a Caribbean Creole," *Jewish Culture and History* 7, no. 1/2 (2004): 109–22.

———. "Waters of Faith, Currents of Freedom: Gender, Religion, and Ethnicity in Inter-imperial Trade between Curaçao and Tierra Firme." In *Race, Religion, and Gender in the Colonization of the Americas,* ed. Nora Jaffary, 151–64. Aldershot, UK: Ashgate, 2007.

Rutgers, Wim. "Dutch Caribbean Literature." Translated by Scott Rollins. *Callalloo* Special Issue: 542–55.

Sachar, Howard M. *A History of the Jews in America.* New York: Alfred A Knopf, 1992.

Salomon, H. P. "The Earliest Known Document in Papiamentu Contextually Reconsidered." *Neophilologus* 66, no. 3 (1982): 367–76.

Sauer, Carl Ortwin. *The Early Spanish Main.* Berkeley: University of California Press, 1966.

Scelle, G. "The Slave-Trade in the Spanish Colonies of America: The Assiento." *American Journal of International Law* 4, no. 3 (1910): 612–61.

Schama, Simon. *The Embarrassment of Riches: An Interpretation of Dutch Culture in the Golden Age.* New York: Random House Vintage, 1987.

Schiltkamp, Jacob A. "Legislation, Government, Jurisprudence, and Law in the Dutch West Indian Colonies: The Order of Government of 1629." *Pro Memoria. Bijdragen tot de rechtsgeschiedenis der Nederlanden* 5, no. 2 (2003): 320–34.

Schmidt, Benjamin. "The Dutch Atlantic: From Provincialism to Globalism." In *Atlantic History: A Critical Appraisal,* ed. Jack P. Greene and Philip D. Morgan, 163–87. Oxford: Oxford University Press, 2009.

Schnurmann, Claudia. "'Wherever Profit Leads Us, to Every Sea and Shore . . .': The VOC, the WIC and Dutch Methods of Globalization in the Seventeenth Century." *Renaissance Studies* 17, no. 3 (2003): 474–93.

Schorsch, Jonathan. *Jews and Blacks in the Early Modern World.* Cambridge: Cambridge University Press, 2004.

———. "Portmanteau Jews: Sephardim and Race in the Early Modern Atlantic World." In *Port Jews,* ed. Cesarani, 59–74.

Schunk, Christine W. M. "The Lost Catholic Houses of Prayer in Curaçao." In *Building Up the Future from the Past,* ed. Coomans, Newton, and Coomans-Eustatia, 128–135.

———. "Michael Johannes Schabel, S.J., 'Notitia de Coraçao, Bonayre, Oruba,' 1705 and 'Diurnum (1707–1708)." *Archivum Historicum Societatis Iesu* 66, no. 131 (1997): 89–162.

Schwartz, Stuart, ed. "A Commonwealth within Itself: The Early Brazilian Sugar Industry, 1550–1670." In *Tropical Babylons,* ed. Schwartz, 158–200.

———. "The Formation of a Colonial Identity in Brazil." In *Colonial Identity in the Atlantic World,* ed. Canny and Pagden, 15–50.

———. *Tropical Babylons: Sugar and the Making of the Atlantic World, 1450–1680.* Chapel Hill: University of North Carolina Press, 2004.

Schwegler, Armin. *"Chi ma nkongo": Lengua y rito ancestrales en el Palenque de San Basilio.* Frankfurt am Main: Vervuert, 1996.

Scott, Julius S., III. "The Common Wind: Currents of Afro-American Communication in the Era of the Haitian Revolution." PhD diss. Duke University, 1986.

Schwarzwald, Ora Ridrigue. "Language Choice and Language Varieties before and after the Expusion." In *From Iberia to Diaspora*, ed. Stillman and Stillman, 399–415.

Seed, Patricia. *Ceremonies of Possession in Europe's Conquest of the New World, 1492–1640.* Cambridge: Cambridge University Press, 1995.

Sensbach, Jon F. *Rebecca's Revival: Creating Black Christianity in the Atlantic World.* Cambridge, Mass.: Harvard University Press, 2005.

Shepherd, Verene A. "Unity and Disunity, Creolization and Marronage in the Atlantic World: Conceptualizing Atlantic Studies." *Atlantic Studies* 1, no. 1 (2004): 49–65.

———, ed. *Slavery without Sugar: Diversity in Caribbean Economy and Society since the 17th Century.* Gainsville: University Press of Florida, 2002.

Shepherd, Verene A., and Glen L. Richards, eds. *Questioning Creole: Creolisation Discourses in Caribbean Culture.* Kingston: Ian Randle, 2002.

Shields, David S., ed. *Material Culture in Ango-America: Regional Identity and Urbanity in the Tidewater, Lowcountry, and Caribbean.* Columbia: University of South Carolina Press, 2009.

Shorto, Russell. *The Island at the Center of the World: The Epic Story of Dutch Manhattan and the Forgotten Colony That Shaped America.* New York: Random House Doubleday, 2004.

Silva Horta, José da. "Evidence for a Luso-African Identity in 'Portuguese' Accounts on 'Guinea of Cape Verde.'" *History in Africa* 27 (2000): 99–130.

Sintiago, Alfred. *Gramatica Corticoe de Idioma Papiamentoe.* Curaçao: Bethencourt, 1898.

Smith, Joshua M. *Borderland Smuggling: Patriots, Loyalists, and Illicit Trade in the Northeast, 1783–1820.* Gainesville: University Press of Florida, 2006.

Soest, Jaap van. *Olie als water: De Curaçaose economie en de eerste helft van de twintigste eeuw.* Curaçao: Centraal Historisch Archief Hogeschool van de Neederlandse Antillen, 1976.

———. *Trustee of the Netherlands Antilles: A History of Money, Banking, and the Economy with Special Reference to the Central Bank van de Nederlandse Antillen 1828-1978.* Zutphen, the Netherlands: Walburg, 1979.

Solow, Barbara L., ed., *Slavery and the Rise of the Atlantic System.* Cambridge: Cambridge University Press, 1991.

St. Hilaire, Aonghas. "Globalization, Urbanization, and Language in Caribbean Development: The Assimilation of St. Lucia." *New West Indian Guide* 77, no. 1/2 (2003): 65–83.

Stewart, Charles, ed. *Creolization: History, Ethnography, Theory.* Walnut Creek, Calif.: Left Coast Press, 2007.

Stillman, Yedida K. and Norman A. Stillman, eds. *From Iberia to Diaspora: Studies in Sephardic History and Culture.* Leiden: Brill, 1999.

Studnicki-Gizbert, Daviken. *A Nation upon the Ocean Sea: Portugal's Atlantic*

Diaspora and the Crisis of the Spanish Empire, 1492–1640. Oxford: Oxford University Press, 2007.

Sued-Badillo, Jalil, ed. *Autochthonous Societies: General History of the Caribbean.* Vol. 1. Paris: UNESCO, 2003.

Sutcliffe, Adam. "Jewish History in an Age of Atlanticism." In *Atlantic Diasporas,* ed. Kagan and Morgan, 18–30.

Sweet, James H. *Recreating Africa: Culture, Kinship, and Religion in the Portuguese World, 1441–1770.* Chapel Hill: University of North Carolina Press, 2003.

Swetschinski, Daniel. "Conflict and Opportunity in Europe's 'Other Sea': The Adventure of Caribbean Jewish Settlement," *American Jewish History* 72, no. 2 (1982): 212–40.

———. *Reluctant Cosmopolitans: The Portuguese Jews of Seventeenth-Century Amsterdam.* London: Littman Library of Jewish Civilization, 2000.

Taylor, Douglas. "New Languages for Old in the West Indies." *Comparative Studies in Society and History* 3, no. 3 (1961): 277–88.

Teensma, B. N. "Take Florida: Or the Unattended Project of a Dutch Sephardi Phantast." *Itinerario* 21, no. 3 (1997): 142–50, and *Itinerario* 22, no. 1 (1998): 131–42.

TePaske, John Jay. "Integral to Empire: The Vital Peripheries of Colonial Spanish America." In *Negotiated Empires,* ed. Daniels and Kennedy, 29–41.

Thornton, John. *The Kongolese Saint Anthony: Dona Beatriz Kimpa Vita and the Antonian Movement, 1684–1706.* Cambridge: Cambridge University Press, 1998.

———. *Africa and Africans in the Making of the Atlantic World, 1400–1800.* 2nd ed. Cambridge: Cambridge University Press, 1998.

Torres, Joshua M., and Reniel Rodríguez Ramos. "The Caribbean: A Continent Divided by Water." In *Archaeology and Geoinformatics,* ed. Reid, 13–29.

Tracy, James D., ed. *The Rise of Merchant Empires: Long-Distance Trade in the Early Modern World, 1350–1750.* Cambridge: Cambridge University Press, 1990.

Trivellato, Francesca. *The Familiarity of Strangers: The Sephardic Diaspora, Livorno, and Cross-Cultural Trade in the Early Modern Period.* New Haven, Conn.: Yale University Press, 2009.

Troconis de Veracoechea, Ermila. "Estudio Preliminar." In *Documentos para el estudio de los esclavos negros en Venezuela,* xi–xl. Caracas: Biblioteca de la Academia Nacional de la Historia, Fuentes para la Historia Colonial de Venezuela no. 103. 1969.

Trouillot, Michel-Rolph. *Silencing the Past: Power and the Production of History.* Boston: Beacon Press, 1995.

Turner, Lorenzo. *Africanisms in the Gullah Dialect.* Ann Arbor: University of Michigan Press, 1949.

Vink, Wieke. *Creole Jews: Negotiating Community in Colonial Suriname.* Leiden, the Netherlands: KITLV Press, 2010.

Vivas Pineda, Gerardo. *La Aventura Naval de la Compañía Guipuzcoana de Caracas.* Caracas: Editorial Exlibris, 1998.

Vos, Jelmer, David Eltis, and David Richardson. "The Dutch in the Atlantic World: New Perspectives from the Slave Trade with Particular Reference to the African Origins of the Traffic." In *Extending the Frontiers*, ed. Eltis and Richardson, 228–49.

Wachtel, Nathan. "Marrano Religiosity in Hispanic America in the Seventeenth Century. In *Jews and the Expansion of Europe to the West*, ed. Bernardini and Fiering, 149–71.

Waddington, Raymond B., and Arthur H. Williamson, eds. *The Expulsion of the Jews: 1492 and After*. New York: Garland, 1994.

Watlington, Francisco. "The Physical Environment: Biogeographical Teleconnections in Caribbean Prehistory." In *Autochthonous Societies*, ed. Sued-Badillo, 30–92.

Welch, Pedro L. V. *Slave Society in the City: Bridgetown, Barbados, 1680–1834*. Kingston, Jamaica: Ian Randle, 2003.

Welie, Rik van. "Slave Trading and Slavery in the Dutch Colonial Empire: A Global Comparison." *New West Indian Guide* 82, no. 1/2 (2008): 47–96.

Whinnom, Keith. "The Origin of the European-Based Creoles and Pidgins." *Orbis* 14 (1965): 509–27.

Whitehead, Neil L. "Introduction. The Island Carib as an Anthropological Icon." In *Wolves from the Sea*, ed. Whitehead, 9–22.

———, ed. *Wolves from the Sea: Readings in the Anthropology of the Native Caribbean*. Leiden, the Netherlands: KITLV Press, 1995.

Wijk, H. L. A. van. "Orígenes y Evolución del Papiamentu." *Neophilologus* 42 (1958): 169–82.

Wiznitzer, Arnold. *Jews in Colonial Brazil*. New York: Columbia University Press, 1960.

Wood, Peter H. *Black Majority: Negroes in Colonial South Carolina from 1670 through the Stono Rebellion*. 1974. New York: W. W. Norton, 1996.

Wood, Richard E. "The Hispanization of a Creole Language: Papiamentu." *Hispania* 55, no. 4 (1972): 857–64.

———. "New Light on the Origins of Papiamentu: An Eighteenth-Century Letter." *Neophilologus* 56, no. 1 (1972): 18–29.

Woude, Anko van der. "The 'Plezierhuis' in Otrobanda." In *Building Up the Future from the Past*, ed. Coomans, Newton, and Coomans-Eustatia, 137–47.

Wright, I. A. "The Coymans Asiento (1685–1689)." In *Bijdragen voor Vaderlandsche Geschiedenis en Oudheidkunde*, ed. P. J. Blok and N. Japikse, 23–62. The Hague: Martinus Nijhoff, 1924.

Yerushalmi, Yosef Hayim. "Between Amsterdam and New Amsterdam: The Place of Curaçao and the Caribbean in Early Modern Jewish History." *American Jewish History* 72, no. 2 (1982): 172–91.

Zahedieh, Nuala. "The Merchants of Port Royal, Jamaica, and the Spanish Contraband Trade, 1655–1692," *William and Mary Quarterly*, 3rd series, 43, no. 4 (1986): 570–93.

Zandvliet, Kees. *The Dutch Encounter with Asia, 1600–1950*. Amsterdam: Rijksmuseum, 2002.

INDEX

ABC islands, 21–25, 35, 38, 40, 85. *See also* Aruba; Bonaire

Abigail, 104, 173

Act of Abjuration, 30

Africa, 1; creolization in, 47–48, 220–25, 240; European presence in, 7, 220, 222. *See also* Dutch; Dutch West India Company; Sephardim; Slave trade

African, ethnicities in Curaçao, 144, 206

Afro-Curaçaoans, 3, 4, 9, 42, 44; collusion with Caquetios, 38; ethnicity of, 61; in militias, 146–47; religion, 136, 179; in trade, 125. *See also* Free blacks; Slaves

Age of Revolutions, 182

Agriculture, 92–94, 135

Aguado, Father Pedro de, 25

Alps, 29

Amazon River, 33, 175

Ampíes, Juan de, 21–23, 169

Ampíes, María, 23

Amsterdam, 12, 92, 95, 127, 130, 176; during Eighty Years' War, 29–32; mapmaking firms, 132; merchant houses in, 134; Reformed Church, 140; 150, 176; Sephardic synagogue, 154; Sephardim in, 44, 46–50, 52–56, 139, 212, 227, 230–31; in transatlantic trade, 40, 94, 121

Anaure. *See* Manaure

Andes, 25, 174

Andresote, 202–3

Anglo-Dutch Wars, 74, 76

Angola, 47, 48, 57, 59, 61, 64, 76, 144, 229

Anien, 1

Anthonij, 126

Antigua, 35, 75

Antwerp, 28–30, 32, 49

Aragon, 44

Araujo, Juan de, 52

Arawaks, 18

Ardra, 81

Aruba, 19, 21, 24, 70, 75, 94, 124, 171, 179, 187

Ascensión, 24, 25

Asiento de negros, 48, 59, 65, 73, 78–80, 90, 97–98, 173

Atlantic Creole, 62, 64

Audiencia of Santo Domingo, 174–75, 199

Augustinian Order, 87, 148–53

Axim, 59

Awa pasaharina, 215

Bahia, Brazil, 34

Baltic Sea, 29, 30, 31

Barbados, 35, 52, 55, 119, 125, 139, 181

Barbuda, 35

Barlovento, 167, 198, 241

Barroso and Porcio, commercial house of, 78–79, 83–84

Bastiaan, Juan, 126

Batavian Republic, 245
Beck, Balthazar, 87
Beck, Matthias, 37, 54, 66, 71–73, 81–82, 88, 95, 128
Bejarano, Lázaro, 17, 23, 24, 25, 27
Belgium, 28
Beltrán, Antonio, 147, 152
Benguela, 61
Berbice River, 33
Bermuda, 5, 121, 125, 143
Beth Haim Cemetery, 48, 103
Bight of Benin, 61, 306
Bight of Biafra, 61
Bishopric: of Caracas, 85, 149, 176, 179; of Venezuela, 10, 23–24
Black speech, 213, 215
Bogotá, 150
Bonaire, 21, 24, 36, 40, 64, 70, 75, 124, 142, 146, 160, 187
Borburata, 18
Bourbon, House of, 89, 90, 183, 293
Brazil: as a possible slave trade center, 63, 65; Dutch in, 30, 34, 36, 40–41, 59, 70, 71, 74, 77; Sephardic merchants in, 48, 51–54, 56, 65, 229; uprising of Portuguese planters, 48, 59
Brazilwood, 22, 35, 63
Breedestraat, 130
Bridgetown, Barbados, 119, 125
Brouwers, Theodorus, 216, 218, 226

Cacao, trade in, 78, 83, 93, 119, 120, 123, 141, 156, 163, 164, 167–68, 182–84, 187–88, 191–93, 196, 197, 202–6, 209, 240, 276, 288, 293
Cacheu, 229–30
Caicedo y Velasco, Agustín Beltrán, 89, 149–51, 176, 214, 272, 273
Caldera de Quiñones, D. Nicolás, 86–88, 93
Calvinism, 28
Canary Islands, 167, 169, 172, 183
Cape of Good Hope, 1, 32
Cape Verde, 229; Creole, 228, 229; Islands, 47, 223, 228, 229
Capuchin Order, 87, 88, 149, 150, 190
Caquetios, 12, 18, 20–24, 36–38, 41, 85–87, 93, 142, 166, 195, 219, 272
Caracas Company, 159, 168, 173, 184–85, 202–3
Carbonell, Pedro, 217

Caribbean: as a Spanish sea, 1; effect of wars in, 159; geography of, 19, 174; geopolitics of, 98–99; seafaring, 20, 26; slave societies of, 6; Spanish policy towards, 25, 27, 35, 184–85; trade, 7–11, 13, 17–18, 20, 28, 67–68, 75, 80, 93–94, 97, 124, 181. See also Dutch expansion; Slave trade; Venezuela
Castro, Juan Fernández de, 22
Cartagena de Colombia, 31, 133, 167
Cassard, Jacques, 128
Catharina, 141, 171
Catalan, 225–26
Caysedo, Augustin. See Caicedo y Velasco, Agustin Beltán
Changuion, Pierre J., 217
Charles I, of Spain, 28, 59. See also Charles V, Holy Roman Emperor
Charles II, of Spain, 83–84, 89
Charles V, Holy Roman Emperor, 28, 166. See also Charles I, of Spain
Charlestown, South Carolina, 119, 139, 232
Chirinos, José Leonardo, 205–6
Chocolate, 163, 181, 182
Cloth/clothing, trade in, 1, 21, 63, 84, 89, 120, 170, 172, 173, 184, 247
Coast of Caracas, 4, 131, 167. See also Tierra Firme; Venezuela
Cocofío, 204
Coffee, 75, 93, 119, 171, 276
Cofradía del Carmen, 179
Cofradías, 179
Cohen, Samuel, 52
Colina, Francisco de la, 200
Collen, Jeremias van, 193
Colombia, 4, 18, 174, 176, 190, 220, 240, 246
Colón, Diego, 21
Congo, 61, 229
Conversos, 44–47, 50–52, 73, 139, 191, 192, 227, 261
Coro, 26, 36, 38, 43, 191, 237; architecture, 202; early Spanish rule of, 22–23; fugitive slaves in, 96–97, 147, 180, 197–98, 200–201, 205, 206–7, 210–11, 233–24, 240–42; geography of, 90, 167; landholdings, 204; population of, 195; religious ties to Curaçao, 24–25, 38, 85–86, 178–79; smuggling center, 170–71, 173, 177, 178; trade with Curaçao, 53, 63,

89, 153, 167, 190, 193, 205, 211, 237;
uprising in, 205–10
Corsairs. *See* Privateering
Cosa, Juan de la, 20, 21
Costa Andrade, Abraham de David de, Jr.,
212–16, 231
Costa, Isaac de, 56, 65, 265
Cotino, Mosseh Henriques, 103–4
Cotino, Abraham Henriques, 103–4
Council of the Colonies, 245
Council of the Reformed Church, 148
Council of Trade and Plantations, English, 74
Coymans, Balthasar, 78, 79, 83
Coymans, Joseph, 78
Creole languages, 11, 12, 219; Afro-
Portuguese, 62, 224–26, 228–30, 233;
theories of development, 220–22; of
St. Thomas, 124, 218. *See also* Cape
Verdean Creole; Guene; Papiamentu;
Negerhollands; Upper Guinea Creole
Creolistics, 221
Crioolse spraake. See Black speech
Crypto-Jews, 44–46, 48, 50. *See also*
Conversos; New Christians
Cuba, 33, 120, 133, 139, 205, 242
Curazao, Juana Isabel, 163–64, 193, 207
Curiepe, 163, 167, 182, 183, 188, 198, 199,
240, 241

De Jonge Johannes, 141, 216, 238
Demerara River, 33
Dominga, 126
Domingo, Juan, 103–4, 126
Dominican Order, 152
Drago, Abraham, 53
Dugout canoes. *See piraguas*
Dutch: in Africa, 30, 32, 33, 58–60, 229,
249; in Atlantic and Caribbean, 31–35,
44, 70–71, 75–76, 98–99; in Atlantic
slave trade, 56–63, 76–79, 229; in Brazil,
30; Reformed Church, 127, 131, 140–41,
148, 153, 155, 231; States General, 1, 30,
32, 39, 49, 51, 86, 98, 148, 212. *See also*
Dutch West India Company
Dutch East India Company (VOC), 31–33
Dutch Leeward Islands, 75, 76, 123. *See
also* Saba; St. Eustatius; St. Maarten
Dutch rebellion. *See* Eighty Years' War
Dutch West India Company (DWIC),
Amsterdam Chamber, 34, 36, 40, 65,
71–73, 148, 185; dismantling of, 245;
founding, 1, 32–35, 58; governance
of Curaçao, 1, 3, 8–10, 36–42, 53,
55, 56, 67–68, 71, 72, 79, 91–93, 99,
104, 128, 131–32, 143, 144, 147–48,
156; governance of Dutch Leeward
Islands, 34, 75–76; in Africa, 1, 32,
70; in Brazil, 51, 71; in the Caribbean,
35–36, 42; in North America, 33,
51, 55, 71; ownership of slaves, 135;
policies toward religious freedom, 51,
85, 88, 141, 148–54; policies toward
slavery, 156–60, 201; reorganization
of, 3, 42, 74; role in Curaçao's trade,
71–74; role in slave trade, 56, 59–65, 68,
77–85, 88; reorganization (1674), 74,
91; rural holdings in Curacao, 93–94,
135; seizure of Curacao (1634), 36–37;
Zeeland Chamber, 33–34, 39, 62–63
Dyewood, 31, 53, 93, 119, 120

East Indies, 31, 69
Edict of Nantes, 51, 95
Eighty Years' War, 10, 28–31, 38, 41, 68
El Dorado, 22
Ellis, Johannes, 161
Elmina, 59, 65, 144, 223, 224
El Tocuyo, 203
Encomienda, 195
England, 52, 235; attacks on Curaçao,
39, 174; challenge to Iberians, 60;
control of asiento de negros, 85, 97,
173, 200; opposition to smuggling, 8;
participation in slave trade, 58, 62,
78–79; patrols in Caribbean, 98, 104;
possessions in Caribbean, 35, 41, 52,
73, 122, 235–36; rise during War of
Spanish Succession, 97; seizure of New
Netherland, 40, 54, 74, 82; war with the
Netherlands, 173. *See also* Privateering
English language, 123, 232, 235, 239
Essequibo, 52, 76
Essequibo River, 33
European expansion, 12–13, 35; role of
Sephardim in, 46–49
Euskadi, 225–26

Fala de Guine. See Creole languages;
Guinea speech
Fathers of Mercy, 87
Fonseca, Joseph Nunes de, 53, 55
Fonsekou, Isaeck de, 55, 72

Fort Amsterdam, 1, 10, 39, 40, 72, 74, 79, 90–93, 99, 124, 127–32, 148, 154, 231, 247, 250
Fort Nassau (Mori), 33, 58
France, 28; attacks on Curaçao, 39; challenge to Iberians, 60; control of asiento de negros, 85, 97–98, 173; incursions in Africa, 224, 229; invasions in Europe, 28, 174, 209, 245; patrols in Caribbean, 98, 185; possessions in Caribbean, 34, 35, 50–52, 54, 70–71, 73, 75, 119, 122–24, 133, 174, 175, 180; revocation of Edict of Nantes, 95; slave trade, 79; trade with Curaçao, 98; War of Spanish Succession, 89, 97. See also Privateering
Franciscan Order, 43, 191, 216
Francisco, Fray, 88
Francisco, Miguel, 43
Free blacks, 140, 145, 242; in Willemstad, 64, 87, 93, 126–28, 133–34, 142, 144–45, 126–27, 140–41, 144–47, 196, 246; in Otrobanda, 3, 129, 132, 145, 147; legal restrictions on, 146–47, 157–58; in militias, 146–47; nannies, 235; ownership of slaves, 126–27; population, 144–45; in Roman Catholic Church, 140–41, 151–53, 177; as seafarers, 136, 141, 145, 156, 167, 200–201, 237, 238; as slaveowners, 145; as traders, 147, 193, 196; in uprisings, 203, 205–8; in Venezuela, 163, 168, 183, 188, 194–99, 240–41
Freedom, rumors in Tierra Firme, 204
French, language, 29, 172, 207, 209, 217, 219, 232, 239; Catholics on Curaçao, 152, 176; crew on Curaçaoan vessels, 167; immigrants to Curaçao, 138, 147, 151; Revolution, 204, 209
Fugitive slaves. See Marronage

Galician, 216
Gambier, Petrus, 177
Garcia, Antonio, 78–79
Gemba, Dominga, 188
Geography, Caribbean, 18–20; between Curaçao and Tierra Firme, 96; of Tierra Firme, 166
Gideon, 82
Ghana. See Gold Coast
Gold Coast, 33, 58, 61
Golden Rock, 123. See also St. Eustatius

Gomez, Daniel, 139
Gonzalez, José Caridad, 206–8, 210–11, 234, 241
Gorée, 229
Gran Colombia, 246
Grand, Pierre le, 36–37
Grasie, 126
Grillo, Domingo, 78
Grimón, Miguel, 140, 153, 176–77
Grotius, Hugo, 34
Guadaloupe, 52, 133
Guajiros, 190
Guene, 137, 219, 229, 232–35, 237, 239
Guinea, 47, 63, 144, 197, 228, 229, 233, 234, 240, 241
Guinea speech, 224
Gulf of Guinea, 228
Gullah, 221, 236

Haiti, 209
Haitian Revolution, 174, 204, 205, 208–9
Hapsburg, House of, 28, 30, 38, 49, 183
Hato plantation, 85, 135, 146
Havana, Cuba, 133
Hawkins, John, 17–18, 26–28, 55, 63, 69
Hebreo, Samuel, 191
Heijn, Piet, 34
Henriquez, Filipe, 191, 193, 230
Henriquez, Jeosuah, 54, 72
Henriquez, Moses, 200
Henriquez, Phillip. See Henriquez, Filipe
Hides, trade in, 17, 25, 31, 36, 40, 63, 73, 83, 93, 119, 120, 123, 141, 56, 167, 169, 190, 276
Hispaniola, 21, 23, 64, 174
Holland, Province of, 28, 29, 30, 31
Honduras, 94
Hudson River, 33
Hughes, William Carlyon, 237
Hurricanes, 18, 19, 69

Iberian Peninsula, 44, 49, 50, 224
Indian Ocean, 30–33, 60, 249
Indigo, 75, 93, 119
Indonesia, 30
Inquisition, 23, 24, 45, 47, 50, 53, 172, 186, 192–93
Island Council of Curaçao, 40, 55

Jamaica, 52, 55, 73, 97, 120, 133, 139, 171, 213, 235

Japan, 30
Jesuit Order, 150–52, 176, 214
Jewish Nation, 49, 52, 54, 55, 91, 140, 231
Jews. *See* Sephardim
Jones, William, 235
Joode Quartier, 94

Karpata, 207
Kenepa plantation, 207
Kerckrinck, Clara Catharina, 193
Keulen, van, 127
Kikongo, 61–62, 239
Kimbundu, 61–62, 239
Kingston, Jamaica, 133
Klein Curacao, 171
Knip. *See* Kenepa plantation
Kongo, 47, 61, 62, 144
Koning Salomon, 81
Kopra, José, 206. *See also* Gonzalez, José
    Caridad

La Americana, 205
Ladino, 219, 226–27
Laet, Johannes de, 35–36
La Guaira, Venezuela, 173, 184–85
Lançados, 222
Landstaal, 217
Langton, James, 26
Leon, Juan Francisco de, 203
Lesser Antilles, 32, 35
Leupenius, Johannes, 90
Levy, Gabriel, 94
Levy Maduro, Aron, 94
Levy Maduro, Samuel, 215
Liebergen, Arnout van, 62
Loangos, 61, 144, 206
Lomelino, Ambrosio, 78
Logwood, 242. *See also* Dyewood
London, 52
Lopes, Torinio, 216
Louis XIV, 51, 95
Lovell, John, 27
Low Countries. *See* Belgium; Luxemburg;
    Netherlands
Luanda, 62
Luso-Africans, 223
Lutherans, 24, 154–55
Luxemburg, 28

Madrid, 191
Manaure, 18, 22, 23

Mancarones, 143–44
Manhattan, 33, 139
Manumission: of Curaçaoan slaves in
    Tierra Firme, 83–84, 179–80, 199; pro
    forma, 103–4, 160–61
Manzo, Juan Gomez, 86–88, 93
Maracaibo: Basin, 18; Gulf of, 21; Lake, 19,
    169, 247; town of, 246
Marco, 160
Margarita Island, 19, 31
Marronage, inter-colonial, 95–97, 132, 147,
    162, 163–64, 179–80, 196–201, 204–7,
    208, 246; in Colombia, 220; and creole
    language, 232, 234, 237; 240–42; within
    Venezuela, 195, 197, 204; from Tierra
    Firme to Curaçao, 200–201
Marta, 126
Martha, 126
Martin, Jan, 143
Martinique, 52, 95, 172
Matanzas, Cuba, 33
Mattheuw, 103, 104
May, Pieter de, 129
Mediterranean Sea, 30, 31
Melián, Francisco Nuñez, 36
Mérida, 77, 84, 203
Mestiço, Juan, 25
Mexico, 25, 27, 53, 133, 139, 165, 167, 168,
    192
Meyer, Willem, 160
Middle Passage, 56, 57, 224, 225
Mina, 229
Montserrat, 35, 75
Morena, Nicolaas, 126
Mori, 33
Moron, Aron Henriques, 103–4
Motete, Ana María, 163, 182, 188, 194, 207
Mouree, 59
Mulattos, 48, 64, 87, 93, 129, 136, 142, 147;
    in Amsterdam, 230; in the church,
    140–41, 151; as fugitives, 41, 95; in
    militias, 146, 147; restrictions on,
    146, 147, 157, 158–59; as seafarers, 136,
    158–59, 167; in Venezuela, 181, 194, 197,
    203, 207, 217; women, 145
Mules, trade in, 26, 124, 141, 167, 170–72,
    173, 184, 192, 203, 202

Nassau fleet, 36
Nassi, David. *See* Fonseca, Joseph Nunes
    de

Navarro, Antonio, 140, 177–78, 235
Navigation Acts, 74
Ndongo, 61
Negerhollands, 218
Negerhuisen, 131
Negers spraake. See Black speech
Nevis, 35
New Christians, 44, 46, 47, 51, 223
New Guinea, 32
New Netherland, 33, 40–41, 70, 71, 72, 74;
    Sephardim in, 51–52, 54–56; slave trade
    to, 82. *See also* Manhattan; New York
New Netherland Company, 33
New Orleans, 139
Newport, Rhode Island, 139, 216, 238
New York, 40, 52, 54, 73, 74, 93, 139. *See
    also* Manhattan; New Netherland
Nicolaas, 126
North Sea, 1, 28, 29, 30
Nueva España, 168
Nueva Granada, Viceroyalty of, 124,
    174–75
Nugent, María, 235

Oever, Theodorus ten, 178, 235
Ojeda, Alonso de, 20
Olavarriaga, Pedro José de, 167, 181,
    183–84, 192, 195, 203
Orinoco River, 23, 33, 174–75; Valley, 150
Other Side, the. *See* Otrobanda
Otrobanda, 92, 246; depiction on maps,
    128, 131–33; development, 128–30;
    gallows in, 131; houses of worship in,
    153–54; militia patrols of, 145; name, 3,
    92, 132, 215; population of, 133–34, 142,
    145; role in language development, 235;
    Roman Catholic Church in, 149–53,
    202, 214, 217, 234
Oversijde. See Otrobanda

Papiamentu, 3, 11–12, 128, 132, 137–38,
    207, 210–11, 212–43, 246–47, 249, 250
Paraguaná Peninsula, 18, 21, 22, 43, 96,
    167, 171, 195, 202
Pardo y Vaz Farro, Sarah, 212–18, 231
Pereyra, Yssac, 94
Pernambuco, Brazil, 34, 40, 51, 53, 74
Peru, 25, 27, 165, 167
Philip II of Spain, 28, 30
Philip III of Spain, 31
Pietermaai, 129–30, 13–14, 142, 152–53

Pieza de India, 82–83
Philadelphia, 74
Pinedo, Manuel Hisquiao, 215
Pinto, Juan, 64
Piraguas, 20, 37, 38, 63, 166–67
Plantations, 93–94, 135, 139–40
Point, the. *See* Punda
Polly, 137, 139, 141–42
Population: of Curaçao, 24–25, 41, 63–64,
    92–93, 142–43, 144–45; of Tierra Firme,
    194–96; of Willemstad, 8, 125–27,
    133–34
Porto de Ale, 47
Portugal, 28, 33, 44, 47, 48, 50, 53, 227;
    overseas expansion, 30–31, 47–48, 59,
    61–62, 63, 222–23; participation in slave
    trade, 58–60, 63, 65, 70, 77–78, 229–30,
    223
Portuguese: breakway from Spanish
    crown, 60; language, 21, 50, 132, 137,
    214, 215, 218, 219–20, 224–27, 231–32,
    234, 239; rebellion in Brazil, 34, 40–41,
    47, 48, 51, 59, 65
Pozo, Juan Barroso del, 84
Primero, 103–4
Privateering, 36, 64, 159–60, 174; Dutch,
    33, 39; English/British,1–2, 24–27, 39,
    69, 104, 139, 156, 167, 173–74, 185, 216,
    217, 238; French, 24, 26, 63, 98, 104,
    128, 185, 209; Spanish, 104; in slave
    trade, 58–59, 62, 63, 64; threats to black
    seafarers, 156; threats to Curaçao, 71,
    128, 131, 138; in waters off Tierra Firme,
    159, 165–66, 173–74, 185, 189, 238
Protestant Reformation, 28
Providence, RI, 139
Puerto Cabello, Venezuela, 19, 40, 98, 172,
    173, 183, 186, 202, 205
Puerto de la Vela, Venezuela, 202
Puerto Rico, 120, 139, 187, 205, 211, 242
Punda, 127, 128, 129, 130; early
    development, 39; name, 92, 127, 132,
    215; population of, 134; role in language
    development, 235; Roman Catholic
    Church in, 150–51
Punt, de. *See* Punda

Quarry, Robert, 74
Quiñones, D. Nicolás Caldera de, 86, 88
Quirigazo, Gasper Antonio, 147, 200–1
Quito, 174

Quixán, Mariana, 188

Rasvelt, Wigboldus, 140
Real Compañía Guipuzcoana de Caracas.
    See Caracas Company
Relief Fund for the Poor, 155
Religious orders, 148–49
Reyes, Diego de los, 36, 64
Ribeira Grande, 223
Rigaud, Benoit Joseph, 208
Rio de la Hacha, 17, 27, 84, 120, 190
Rodenburch, Lucas, 54, 95
Rodriguez Camejo, Francisco, 190
Roman Catholic Church: in Africa, 62;
    clergy participation in smuggling,
    73, 88–89, 153, 164, 190–91; in
    development of Papiamentu, 214,
    216, 234–35, 246; evangelization of
    black majority, 10, 86–88, 136, 140–41,
    148–51; laity, 150–53, 177; in Mexico,
    46; negotiation with slave rebels,
    208–9; in the Netherlands, 28; religious
    jurisdiction of Curaçao, 10, 11, 38,
    85–89, 148–49, 174–79, 217; religious
    orders, 148–49, 176, 188, 190–91;
    restrictions on clergy, 88; in Venezuela,
    140, 163, 179–80
Rosario, Andrés López del. See Andresote
Rotterdam, 57, 121
Roubio, Juan Nicolaas, 161
Royal decrees, Spanish, 22, 26, 32, 63,
    83–84, 184, 185, 204, 207
Royal Guinea Company, 199
Rufisque, 47
Runaway slaves. See Marronage

Saba, 70, 75–76, 123–24
Sabonet, 87
Saint Domingue, 133, 170, 174, 206, 208,
    242
Salazar, Diego, 21
Salt: pans, 22, 30–31, 34, 35, 39, 53, 64, 75,
    142, 146; trade, 30, 31, 34, 35, 64, 93
Salvador, Brazil, 34
San Felipe, 183, 190, 203
San Juan, 87
Santa Anna Church, 153
Santa Cruz, Curaçao, 87, 207
Santa María de la Chapa, 198, 240, 241
Santa María de los Negros de Curazao, 241
Santa Marta, Colombia, 46, 139, 190–91

Santiago, 228
Santo Domingo, 23, 120, 139, 187, 205, 211,
    242
São Jorge de Elmina. See Elmina
Schabel, Miguel Alexis, 89, 140, 149, 176,
    214, 218
Scharloo, 129, 130, 134, 142
Schink, Jacobus, 208–9
Schottegat, 36, 56, 79, 82, 91, 94, 140
Sea Beggars, 29
Sea Island, South Carolina, 236
Sefarad, 44
Senegal, 47
Senegambia, 17, 47, 48, 61, 63, 228, 229
Senior, Felipe. See Henriquez, Felipe
Sephardim, 44–52; in Africa, 47–48, 50,
    230; in agriculture, 94, 139–40; in the
    Caribbean, 50–52; in Curaçao, 52–56,
    93–95, 138–40, 154; in inter-colonial
    trade, 72, 93–94, 103, 138–40, 191–93;
    language use by, 212–15, 226–32,
    238–39; ownership of slaves, 65, 66,
    participation in slave trade, 46–47, 230
Seven Years' War, 119, 121, 122, 159, 173
Seville, 22
Sierra Leone, 17, 61, 63, 144
Silver, 25, 30, 32, 33, 89, 172
Simson, Nathan, 139
Slaves: baptism of, 86–88; in Curaçao, 56;
    domestic, 127, 130, 131, 137, 212, 232,
    235, 236; early presence on Curaçao,
    63–65; ethnicities of, 144; laborers in
    salt pans, 75; laws related to, 65–66,
    156–60; in maritime economy, 40,
    119, 125, 141–42, 163–64; in militias,
    146–47; ownership of, 93, 126–27,
    136, 143–44, 196, 200; population
    distribution of, 63–66, 133, 134, 142–43;
    rebellion in Curaçao, 145, 207–10,
    216, 217, 233, 245; rebellion in Tierra
    Firme, 203, 205–10, 241, 245; religion
    of, 140–41, 148, 151; rural, 137, 232,
    233; sailors, 135, 141–42, 155–62, 197,
    198–99, 237; as traders, 68, 104, 185–86,
    189, 193, 196–98; in Venezuela, 27, 75,
    183–84, 194–96, 199–200; urban, 3, 129,
    141, 232, 246. See also Manumission;
    Marronage
Slave trade, 17–18, 21, 46–48, 56–63;
    Caribbean, 76–77; between Curaçao
    and Tierra Firme, 62–63, 72–73, 76–85,

98; as a conduit for contraband, 73, 84, 97; demographic impact, 82–83; early, 223–24; impact on Curaçao, 77, 79–80, 87–88; impact on language creolization, 224–25, 228, 229; with North America, 82–83, 93; participation of clergy in, 86, 89; to Tierra Firme, 26–27, 31, 63, 71–73, 77–79, 80–85, 167–68, 172–73, 192, 205

Slijk, Antonio, 177

Snouck, Jan, 34

Soorbeek, Daniel, 216, 218

South Carolina, 119, 139, 221, 232, 236

Spain: attempts to retake Curaçao, 37–38; Caribbean colonies, 1, 3–4, 17; conquest and rule of Curaçao, 20–27; control of colonial trade, 8, 90; Venezuela exports to, 168–69, 172, 184

Spanish language, 43, 50, 137, 138, 214, 216, 217, 219, 227, 231, 232, 234, 235, 239; Spanish Catholics on Curaçao, 136; Spanish merchants on Curaçao, 137, 151

Speght, Phillip, 80

St. Anna Bay, 36, 38–41, 74, 88, 90–92, 129, 130, 132, 134, 141, 147, 149

St. Barbara Bay, 24

St. Christopher, 52, 62, 192

St. Croix, 35

St. Eustatius, 34, 35, 70, 75, 76, 122–24, 171

St. John, 76, 124

St. Kitts, 35

St. Maarten, 34, 35, 70, 75, 123–24, 143

St. Thomas, 76, 124, 213, 218, 242

St. Vincent, 34

Statia. See St. Eustatius

Stoppel, Johannes, 217

Stuyvesant, Peter, 39–40, 54–55, 62–64, 66, 74, 95–96

Sugar, 21, 30, 31, 34, 59, 63, 65, 71, 75, 93, 94, 119, 123, 135, 170, 171, 196

Suriname, 76, 122

Suriname River, 33

Swedish-African Company, 77

Talmud Torah, 48, 230

Tellería, José, 206

Textiles. See Cloth/clothing

Tierra Firme: architecture in, 201–2; geography of, 166; Papiamentu in, 242, rebellions in, 202–7, 209–11;

religious jurisdiction of Curacao, 23–24, 38, 85–89, 148–49, 175–79; Spanish jurisdiction of, 174–75; ties to Curaçao, 4, 18–20, 23, 38, 71–73, 77–79, 80–85, 119–20, 165–74, 187–93. See also Venezuela

Tobacco, trade in, 19, 31, 34, 73, 75, 89, 93, 94, 119, 120, 123, 150, 156, 165, 167–69, 172, 192, 193, 203

Tobago, 33–34, 56, 70

Tolck, Jacob Pietersz, 64–65, 67

Treaty of Tordesillas, 59

Treaty of Westphalia, 10, 41, 67, 68–70, 75, 178

Trinidad, 34, 57, 139, 242

Tropic of Cancer, 1, 32

Tucacas, 46, 139, 166, 171, 184, 191, 192, 203, 237

Tula, 207–9

Twelve Year Truce, 32–34, 49, 50, 58

Twi, 233, 239

Ufro Sarah, 137

Union of Spanish and Portuguese Crowns, 28, 33, 57, 60, 226

Upper Guinea Creole, 228

Useless islands, 21

Usselincx, Willem, 32

Utrecht, 28; Treaty of, 97, 178, 183; Union of, 30, 49

Valencia, Venezuela, 188

Venezuela: province of, 4, 190, 195; administration of Curaçao, 23; Caribbean coast of, 165–67; colonial authorities in, 182; geography of, 33, 197; governor of, 36; independence, 245–46; oil refinery on Curaçao, 246–47; political jurisdiction of, 174–75; role in contraband trade, 180–93; slave ownership in, 195–96; ties to Curaçao, 10, 89–90, 140, 147, 165–72, 182–85 219; trade with Caribbean, 169–74. See also Coast of Caracas; Slave trade; Tierra Firme

Vera Cruz, Mexico, 133

Vespucci, Amerigo, 20–21

Vivas, David Bueno, 189

Vivas, Rachel, 189

Waaigat, 91

Walbeeck, Joannes van, 36–37, 64–65

War of Jenkins's Ear, 119, 122, 123, 159, 173
War of the Spanish Succession, 10, 77, 128, 146, 149, 158, 179, 183, 214; impact on imperial relations, 97; impact on slave trade, 85, 173, 193; impact on trade, 89–90, 119, 172, 180
Waterfort, 38, 39
Welsers, 22–23, 169
West Central Africa, 61, 62, 66, 87, 206
West India Company. See Dutch West India Company
Wiapoco River, 33
Wild Coast, 33, 52, 54, 56, 70, 76, 135, 175
Willemstad, Curaçao, 104, 135–37, 201, 232, 249; architecture of, 134–35; depictions of, 1, 39, 90, 127, 128, 130; founding of, 39; growth of, 127–30; languages spoken in, 237, 239–40; name, 39, 91–92, 131–32; as a port city, 3–4, 8, 11, 13, 30, 97, 99, 104, 124–33, 160–61, 187, 193, 198, 204; religions in, 87–88, 136–37, 147–55, 214; role in development of Papiamentu, 213, 233, 235–37, 239–40, 242–43; social relations in, 80, 104, 124–27; 133–47, 246–47; as a trade center, 10, 90–93, 119–24, 196; walls of, 11, 127, 129, 130. See also Otrobanda; Pietermaai; Punda; Scharloo
William of Orange, 28, 39
Women, 43–44, 129, 163–64, 188–89, 198, 235–37; and creole languages, 235, 236; enslaved, 43–44, 163, 200, 212, 214, 215, 235, 236; as majority population, 94, 125, 136, 138
Woodgars, Jurgen, 160

Yaracuy River, 139, 166, 177, 183–84, 191–92; Valley, 202–3
Yllan, João de, 53–55, 72
Yoruba, 233, 239

Zeeland, Province of, 28–31, 57, 121
Zuider Zee, 29

EARLY AMERICAN PLACES

On Slavery's Border: Missouri's Small Slaveholding Households, 1815–1865
by Diane Mutti Burke

*Sounding America: Identity and the Music Culture of the Lower Mississippi
River Valley, 1800–1860*
by Ann Ostendorf

*The Year of the Lash: Free People of Color in Cuba and the Nineteenth-
Century Atlantic World*
by Michele Reid-Vazquez

*Ordinary Lives in the Early Caribbean: Religion, Colonial Competition,
and the Politics of Profit*
by Kristen Block

Creolization and Contraband: Curaçao in the Early Modern Atlantic World
by Linda M. Rupert

CPSIA information can be obtained
at www.ICGtesting.com
Printed in the USA
LVHW032226120722
723319LV00004B/519

9 780820 343068